Inventing DISASTER

Inventing DISASTER

THE CULTURE OF CALAMITY

from the Jamestown Colony
to the Johnstown Flood

CYNTHIA A. KIERNER

THE UNIVERSITY OF NORTH CAROLINA PRESS

Chapel Hill

Publication of this book was supported in part by a generous gift from Catherine Lawrence and Eric Papenfuse.

Designed by Jamison Cockerham
Set in Arno, Scala Sans, Klabasto, Blaisdell, Cutright, and Fell DW Pica by Tseng Information Systems, Inc.

Cover art: Claude-Joseph Vernet, *The Shipwreck*, 1772, courtesy of the National Gallery of Art.

LIBRARY OF CONGRESS CATALOGING-IN-PUBLICATION DATA
Names: Kierner, Cynthia A., 1958– author.
Title: Inventing disaster : the culture of calamity from the Jamestown colony to the Johnstown flood / Cynthia A. Kierner.
Description: First edition. | Chapel Hill : The University of North Carolina Press, [2019] | Includes bibliographical references and index.
Identifiers: LCCN 2019016542 | ISBN 9781469652511
(cloth : alk. paper) | ISBN 9781469679327 (pbk. : alk. paper) |
ISBN 9781469652528 (ebook)
Subjects: LCSH: Disasters—North Atlantic Region—History—18th century. | Disasters—North Atlantic Region—History—19th century. | Disasters—North Atlantic Region—History—17th century. | Disasters—Social aspects—History. | Disasters—Political aspects—History.
Classification: LCC D24 .K54 2019 | DDC 303.48/50903—dc23
LC record available at https://lccn.loc.gov/2019016542

FOR

ANDERS

(Now you owe me one.)

CONTENTS

ILLUSTRATIONS

Jet Star Roller Coaster, Seaside Heights, N.J. On 29 October 2012,
Superstorm Sandy pummeled the Jersey Shore, destroying the Casino Pier
in Seaside Heights and plunging its iconic roller coaster into the Atlantic
Ocean. The wrecked amusement, which work crews removed the following
May, nevertheless became an enduring symbol of the unprecedented
devastation that Sandy brought to the mid-Atlantic region.
Photo by Patsy Lynch/FEMA.

PREFACE

For most twenty-first-century Americans, Hurricane Katrina, which devastated New Orleans and much of the Gulf Coast in 2005, was an iconic moment, the incident that my students (and perhaps most people) think of when they hear the word "disaster." As a New Jersey native and a part-time Jersey Shore beach bum, however, I found Superstorm Sandy, in 2012, even more compelling. The roller coaster that plunged into the stormy ocean when the Seaside Heights boardwalk collapsed was my childhood roller coaster. Not normally a fan of TV news, I nonetheless spent much of the week after Sandy glued to CNN and online local news. As I watched the riveting coverage, I found that, though focused specifically on Sandy, it nonetheless followed a pattern that was familiar from Katrina and other disasters. Quantitative information about what happened—how many lives and dollars lost—and insights from hurricane science preceded human-interest stories with heroes and villains, uplifting news of relief and resilience, and (eventually) post-disaster investigations and recriminations. These reports and conversations, in turn, revealed and aggravated cultural and political tensions, both nationwide and in storm-ravaged coastal communities.

Although Superstorm Sandy did not change my plans for summer vacation, it did inspire a dramatic shift in my research interests—and this book is the result. As a historian, I knew that micro-histories of past events or incidents could use their specific stories—and the rich documentary and material evidence they produced—to shed light on the culture and experiences of people in the past. I myself had written a micro-history of a sex scandal in Virginia in the 1790s, which yielded telling insights into the fragility and contingency of traditional social and political relationships—between gentlemen and middling farmers, masters and slaves, husbands and wives—in the unsettled decades after the American Revolution. I now hoped to produce a case study of an early American disaster, which would tell a good story in the service of reconstructing the culture and experiences of a colonial community, just as Sandy had exposed or accentuated certain aspects of life at the Jersey Shore and, more generally, in twenty-first-century America.

As I moved forward on this project, I found plenty of bad things that happened in early America but discovered no true "disasters" in the modern sense. Especially in the seventeenth century, colonists had scant information about distant calamities; in their print-scarce and rigidly hierarchical world, there was little public accounting of lost property and lives. Only gradually did these matters become topics for public discourse. More gradual still was the emergence and widespread acceptance of the ideas that disaster was a physical process that people could sometimes understand and explain, that human initiative could control the vagaries of the natural world, and that society had both the means and the responsibility to relieve suffering and prevent future calamities. *Inventing Disaster* attempts to explain this absence of both the concept and culture of disaster in the premodern world and how over time ideas about the causes, consequences, and meanings of famines, fires, hurricanes, floods, epidemics, and other catastrophic events changed profoundly and became recognizably modern.

Inspired by Sandy and completed over the course of several years when disasters were constantly in the news, this project is a history that can be read as a timely prequel to our own disaster-ridden times. Since the 1980s, and especially since the start of the new millennium, the frequency of recorded disasters—storms, droughts, floods, wildfires, earthquakes, tsunamis—has increased exponentially. One study estimates that between 2007 and 2016 roughly 3 percent of the earth's population—210 million people—were killed, injured, or otherwise affected by disasters worldwide and that disasters accounted for an annual average of 9,503 officially reported deaths and $141 billion in property losses during that ten-year period. Weather-related disasters arising from climate change and environmental degradation have particularly become routine across the globe. In 2017 alone, there were a total of 318 such occurrences, fewer than one-third of which took place in the Americas.[1]

Most analysts expect disasters to be more frequent, more severe, and more expensive in the United States and globally in the coming decades. According to recent Government Accountability Office reports, the U.S. government spent more than $300 billion on disaster relief between 2005 and 2014, in addition to money and provisions supplied by the Red Cross and other nongovernmental sources. The cost of, and demand for, disaster relief continues to skyrocket, with no end in sight. Indeed, hurricanes Harvey, Irma, and Maria, coupled with California's wildfires and other problems, made 2017 the single most costly year to date, with the federal government assuming a total of $307 billion in disaster-related expenditures.[2] Besides an increasingly dire environmental reckoning, governments and citizens must anticipate and plan for disasters' escalating economic tolls.

In part because of these mounting costs, disasters have become politically potent, giving rise to polarizing discussions that both reveal and aggravate divisions in society, many of which were on display in Sandy's aftermath. Huge government expenditures for disaster relief are controversial, as officials and citizens in unaffected regions often balk at funding relief and rebuilding in distant disaster-ravaged areas. Some experts, pundits, and social-media-empowered citizens invoke climate science to explain devastating hurricanes and wildfires—advocating policy changes to reverse or at least lessen environmental degradation—while others describe disasters as unavoidable acts of God or nature. The abysmal performance of the Federal Emergency Management Agency (FEMA) in New Orleans after Katrina and the U.S. government's willful underreporting of deaths in Puerto Rico after Hurricane Maria have undermined faith in the efficacy of political institutions, at least in some circles. Critics decry the limits of public disaster relief and prevention and argue that such efforts typically favor the wealthy over less privileged people in the United States and elsewhere. When defenders of the status quo distinguish between more and less deserving recipients of protection and relief, they often disparage and discount people who do not conform to their own subjective standards of virtue and respectability.

Understanding the history of attitudes toward disaster causation, relief, and prevention helps to illuminate the assumptions and priorities shaping approaches to disaster in twenty-first-century America. *Inventing Disaster* locates the historical roots of our contemporary culture of disaster in three interrelated developments that historians generally associate with the Enlightenment, a forward-looking intellectual and cultural movement of the seventeenth and eighteenth centuries: access to news and information, faith in the efficacy of science and human agency, and belief in the power of heartfelt emotions to inspire virtue and benevolence—all qualities that our own culture in the twenty-first century still exhibits and values. That being said, there are some profound and significant differences between our own times and the period on which this book focuses. The expansive role of government in disaster management and relief, for instance, is a relatively recent development. Nevertheless, as the following chapters show, time travelers from the eighteenth or nineteenth century would find much that they would recognize in our contemporary understanding of and response to hurricanes, floods, and other calamities.

Inventing DISASTER

INTRODUCTION

Perhaps because disasters are so commonplace in twenty-first-century America, responses to such occurrences—whether a tornado in Missouri, wildfires in California, or a hurricane on the Gulf Coast—are predictable, even ritualized, features of our political and cultural life. When disaster strikes, the news media quickly provide basic information about the incident to people outside the affected area. Those reports gradually become more detailed and more expansive, quantifying losses of both lives and property and highlighting human-interest stories that generate sympathy for the suffering and admiration for volunteers providing assistance, either on the scene or remotely as facilitators and fund-raisers. Official and quasi-official groups—FEMA, the National Guard, the Red Cross—arrive to maintain order and provide relief, with varying degrees of effectiveness. In time, the affluent turn to insurance to recoup their losses, but for others, suffering and deprivation continue long after public sympathy wanes. Meanwhile, government and business leaders consider initiatives to prevent future disasters or limit their effects but mostly reject them as too expensive or inconvenient. Then another disaster occurs, and the entire process begins all over.

Experts struggle to provide a single concise definition for the term "disaster." All agree that disasters involve collective or community suffering and not merely individual losses. Some favor quantitative measures—typically the number of fatalities or the dollar amount of property losses—as criteria for deciding whether an event qualifies for disaster status. Others argue that certain qualitative features—geographic scope, duration, length of forewarning, speed of onset—are disasters' defining attributes. Historians and social scientists see disaster less as an event than as a process that unfolds in its particular social and cultural context, exposing social fissures and tensions that engender robust and often revealing public debates and conflicts.[1]

Scholars in the interdisciplinary field of disaster studies reject the rhetorical binary that distinguishes so-called natural disasters from those caused by human error or agency in favor of a spectrum of disaster causation. No disaster is purely the result of natural causes, they argue perceptively, because "human decisions frequently exacerbate the effects of disaster agents, as earthquakes, for example, tear through areas that either should not have been populated in the first place or should have been retrofitted once the area's vulnerability became clear." In this sense, all disasters are to some degree "man-made," no matter how much our current political discourse chooses to cast them as "acts of God." A hurricane becomes a disaster only when it intersects with humans — and that intersection becomes more likely when humans choose to live in hurricane-prone areas and when their leaders neglect to construct the levees and enforce the building codes needed to protect such vulnerable populations.[2]

At the same time, however much human agency can be responsible for any particular disaster, scholarly definitions of disaster do not embrace catastrophic events that are intentional or foreseeable. The deplorable mass shootings that have become appallingly routine in the United States are tragedies but not disasters because the resulting fatalities are both intentional and foreseeable. Nor can we categorize even the most costly or unexpected military defeat as a disaster because death and destruction are always foreseeable as possible outcomes of war.

In this book, I use the term "disaster" to describe bad things that happened that resulted in substantial and unintended losses of lives and property, measuring the significance of a particular episode primarily in terms of its larger cultural resonance. *Inventing Disaster* is less a descriptive narrative of specific incidents than a cultural history of the idea of disaster and of responses to calamities ranging from shipwrecks and fires, on the one hand, to more seemingly "natural" phenomena, such as hurricanes and earthquakes, on the other. The book is not a comprehensive account of every disaster that occurred globally, or even in North America, between 1607 (Jamestown) and 1889 (Johnstown) but rather focuses on select occurrences — some famous, many more less so — that help to explain how and why a modern culture of disaster emerged incrementally during this period.

Understanding the historical and cultural roots of our contemporary culture of calamity is a prerequisite for assessing how we approach prevention, relief, and recovery efforts in our own disaster-ridden times. For one thing, our modern approach to disaster is rooted fundamentally in an Enlightenment-inspired confidence in humanity's ability to conquer and control nature. Is that confidence sustainable now — indeed, was it ever? Should disaster prevention be a matter for government mandates, or for community voluntarism? Should disaster relief be a social priority, and, if so, which people or entities should provide aid to disaster victims and how should such assistance be funded? In a democratic society, is disaster relief first and foremost an expression of sympathy, or an effort to maintain social order? When disaster strikes, who deserves sympathy and attention? Who decides? How do disaster stories, in the media and elsewhere, shape our often-conflicted understandings of why disasters happen and how we should plan for such occurrences and react to them in times of crisis? These questions, which were first pondered during the eighteenth and nineteenth centuries, continue to drive whatever debates we have about disasters in twenty-first-century America.

§ Hurricanes, floods, fires, and other calamities have afflicted people since time immemorial, but our own contemporary response to such episodes—what one historian has called "a new code of calamity etiquette"—is a relatively recent development.[3] *Inventing Disaster* traces the gradual coalescence of this modern culture of disaster over nearly three centuries, in the British Atlantic world and then in the independent American republic. My story begins in Jamestown, England's first American colony, where settlers died in large numbers from famine, disease, and other catastrophes, though few outside Virginia knew much about their misery and fewer still sought to provide relief or help. It ends with the great flood that destroyed Johnstown, Pennsylvania, when a poorly constructed dam burst in May 1889, killing more than 2,000 people in what was the deadliest American disaster to date. Much like a twenty-first-century disaster—but very much unlike the fatalities at Jamestown—the flood brought hundreds of journalists (including illustrators) and relief workers (including the Red Cross) to Johnstown. It also generated a massive outpouring of public sympathy and charitable donations as well as post-disaster investigations and litigation. Although radio—and later television and social media—would make news of and opinions about future disasters travel even faster, public discourse about Johnstown was timely, vigorous, and varied. And like New Orleans after Hurricane Katrina in 2005, Johnstown became a tourist attraction, as curious visitors snapped photos of the devastated area and took souvenirs from the piles of wreckage that engulfed the ruined community.[4]

This response to calamity, so prominently displayed in Johnstown and in the aftermath of other contemporary disasters, grew out of three interrelated developments that scholars associate with modernity, which I define broadly as the questioning worldview that both inspired and advanced from the Enlightenment's celebration of reason and pursuit of knowledge, as well as its resulting belief in the possibility of human progress.[5] The first of these developments was the spread of information—knowledge, news, and narratives—via travel, trade, and print, initially through the missives of government officials, explorers, and merchants and later by a more widely accessible world of print that represented diverse perspectives via newspapers, magazines, broadsides, sermons, treatises, and novels. The second was the Enlightenment belief in human agency and progress, which inspired efforts to explain the causes and characteristics of hurricanes, earthquakes, and other hazards and to find ways to limit their ruinous effects. The third and final precondition for the emergence of a modern culture of disaster was a new appreciation for humans' capacity to respond to the suffering of others with genuine fellow feeling, a quality known as sensibility. By the eighteenth century, denizens of the Atlantic world read stories about hurricanes, earthquakes, and shipwrecks in the same way that they read novels. All of these narratives aimed not only to entertain but also to arouse powerful emotions that could, in turn, inspire virtue and benevolence.

Although the response to the fire that destroyed much of London in September 1666 featured some of these attributes, historians generally regard the great Lisbon earthquake of 1755—which killed tens of thousands of people and destroyed the Portuguese capital—as the first modern disaster. Letters and newspapers spread information about what happened in Lisbon quickly throughout Europe and the Americas. Although some viewed the earthquake as a sign of divine vengeance, the Lisbon disaster also led to scientific investigations of its physical causes; empirical observations and scientific findings shaped the ambitious government-funded rebuilding of the ruined city. Affecting and sometimes graphic stories from Lisbon tugged on readers' heartstrings and inspired much bad poetry, as well as the first international relief effort in world history. Above all, the Lisbon earthquake was a cultural event that elicited vigorous debates about religion and science, church and state, and the respective responsibilities of governments and citizens in times of crisis.

Although governments across Europe orchestrated and distributed most of the relief that went to Lisbon, the overwhelming majority of eighteenth- and nineteenth-century relief efforts were unofficial and ad hoc. In British North America, when colonists looked to London for aid in the aftermath of hurricanes, floods, and fires, assistance was more likely to come from philanthropic committees of merchants and clergy than from the king and Parliament. After the Revolution, when disaster struck, the affected community formed a committee to solicit donations to help injured and homeless survivors. In the United States, state and federal governments occasionally dabbled in disaster relief—and much less so in disaster prevention—before the Civil War, though federal intervention grew somewhat in the postwar era. Nevertheless, the Civil War was not a true watershed moment in the history of government involvement in disaster-related activities. No federal policies, bureaucracies, or laws specifically pertained to disasters until 1950, when the Disaster Relief Act authorized the president to declare as a major disaster "any flood, drought, fire, hurricane, earthquake, storm, or other catastrophe," which would trigger "assistance by the Federal Government to supplement the efforts and available resources of States and local governments."[6]

The 1950 law, which prioritized the preservation of property and civic order and provided no assistance to individuals, was in many ways a logical culmination of more modest earlier government interventions that aimed to manage the challenges inherent in what sociologists and culture theorists call a "risk society." Urbanization, economic growth, and especially the use of new technologies brought prosperity and comfort as well as risk, or the idea that leaving property and people vulnerable to devastation was a trade-off worth taking in pursuit of convenience, efficiency, and profits.[7]

A by-product of modernity, a risk society is one that "no longer tries to achieve security and certainty by any means . . . [but] accepts uncertainty and ignorance as an unavoidable element of modernity and tries to manage, rather than to abolish, them." In the United States, steamboats (and later railroads) were widely hailed as transformative but nonetheless dangerous technologies; exploding steamboats (and later train wrecks) raised the specter of human negligence and culpability, which, in turn, generated nineteenth-century debates about the role of government in preventing disasters and in regulating private enterprises that could occasion the loss of lives. In the twentieth century, that conversation continued and intensified in relation to the nuclear technologies of the Cold War era. The threat of nuclear attack, cultural historian Kevin Rozario has argued persuasively, "created the emotional and cultural conditions that inclined Americans to federal emergency management," which helped account for the timing of the passage of the Disaster Relief Act in 1950.[8]

An important part of this story is the normalization of disaster, or how hurricanes, fires, and other calamities—even before climate change—became almost routine and unremarkable facts of life. However much the growth of cities, factories, and improvements in transportation signaled the expanding power and prosperity of the American republic, these and

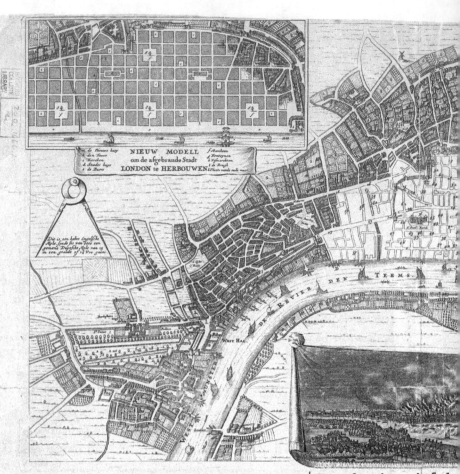

NIEUW MODELL
om de afgebrande Stadt
LONDON te HERBOUWEN

DE REVIER DEN TEEMS

WHIT HAL

Afbeelding van de
STADT LONDON.
Aenwijzende hoe verre de zelve verbrandt is, en wat
plaetzen noch overgebleven zijn.

Representation curieuse de
VILLE de LO
Avec une Demonstration exa
demeuré de reste

Aenwijsing van de Namen der verbrande Straten, Stegen, en Plaetsen in LONDON.

TOT AMSTERDAM

By *Marcus Willemsz.* Doornick, Boeckverkoo

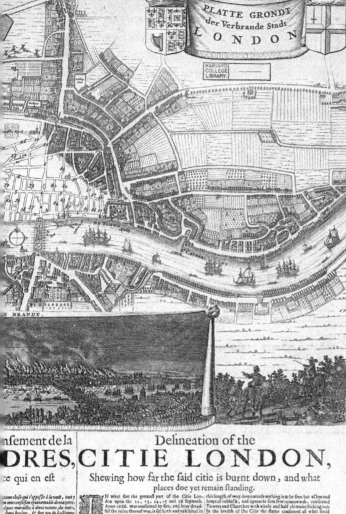

Platte Gronde der Verbrande Stadt London. London's Great Fire, in September 1666, was one of the earliest calamities to attract international attention. London was the second largest city in Europe, after Paris, and the capital of an increasingly ambitious colonial and commercial power. In this plan of London, made by Marcus Willemlz of Amsterdam shortly after the fire, huge swaths of the city the flames destroyed are shaded in black. Descriptions of the fire are in Dutch, French, and English. *Harvard Map Collection, Harvard Library.*

other contemporary developments also sowed the seeds of future calamities. Rozario writes of a "catastrophic logic of modernity" by which Americans and their leaders, who prized prosperity and economic growth and who accepted vulnerability and risk in exchange for profit and comfort, came to view disasters as agents of progress. The idea of destruction as a "blessing in disguise" and an avenue to improvement has long been a staple of post-disaster discourse, but this sort of rhetoric became especially prevalent after the mid-nineteenth century, when those who had access to insurance and credit deemed bricks and mortar expendable and readily replaceable and sometimes even stood to profit by ambitious post-disaster rebuilding efforts. In 1906, for instance, after a horrific earthquake and fire famously destroyed much of San Francisco, some cheerfully predicted that the city would be rebuilt in "brand-new splendor." After all, observed the editor of *Harper's Weekly*, Chicago, Boston, Galveston, and Baltimore were all thriving and much improved after having been "laid waste by conflagrations, earthquakes or tidal waves" in recent years.[9]

What historian Ted Steinberg calls the "demoralization" of calamity also helped government and business leaders to reconceptualize disasters as normal and inescapable consequences of modern life. When people interpreted disasters as divine vengeance, they had been able to believe that personal and collective repentance and reform might prevent future calamities. Once science explained the physical causes of disasters, however, those in power came to characterize storms, earthquakes, and other deadly phenomena as unavoidable "acts of God" or nature. As Steinberg notes, this approach typically works to preserve the status quo and to benefit the rich and powerful by promoting the belief that disasters are unpreventable and thereby justifying policies on the part of government and business that are "both environmentally unsound and socially, if not morally, bankrupt."[10]

Modern economies and technologies create conditions that put citizens at risk, but the politics of location ensures that not all people are equally vulnerable. The poor typically live in areas most susceptible to floods, fires, and other hazards, and they are less likely to have access to resources to protect their communities when disaster strikes or to rebuild when the crisis is over. Significantly, post-1950 government programs and federal flood insurance, which protect the financial interests of investors and property owners in wealthier communities that are unusually prone to hurricanes and other disasters, do not help tenants and others who own little or no property. In modern America, what scholars have variously dubbed the "federalization of risk" or "socialized disaster relief" forces all taxpayers to fund the lifestyle choices of a few, though those choices wreak environmental havoc in places like hurricane-ravaged Florida and densely populated southern California, an area that is unusually vulnerable to wildfires, mudslides, earthquakes, and other disasters. Billions of dollars spent on routine disaster relief in such regions, moreover, diminish federal funding for other programs designed to benefit less affluent Americans.[11]

While a macro-level approach to disaster history emphasizes the perspectives of governments, newspaper readers, and other outsiders, micro-histories of specific communities elucidate disaster as a process that exposes and accentuates cultural tensions and social conflicts. Disaster generates discourse—preserved in documents and other sources—that provides a window onto the values and culture of a particular society. According to its most thoughtful historian, the great Chicago fire of 1871, for example, should be read as a "case study of the interworkings of identity and power in an urban community," pitting immigrant groups against native-born reformers and relief workers and also revealing political and cultural divisions among elites at the local, state, and federal levels. More recently, the experience of New Orleans during and after Hurricane Katrina laid bare stark and troubling inequalities of race and class and exposed the callous disregard of federal authorities for the needs of poor people of color, who suffered disproportionately during and after the storm and were further stigmatized by pejorative media coverage that portrayed them as violent, hapless, or otherwise deviant others—themes that were reprised in Puerto Rico in 2017 during Hurricane Maria's sadly protracted aftermath. In these and other cases, official relief efforts aimed primarily to control or to silence the suffering survivor population. Gender, class, and race were key categories that authorities deployed to distinguish deserving relief recipients from their supposedly less worthy counterparts.[12]

This book builds on the insights of both the macro- and micro-level approaches to disaster history and is in some respects a prequel to existing cultural histories and case studies of iconic American disasters. On the one hand, I chart the evolution of larger discussions concerning the causes, meaning, and responses to bad things that happened in the English-speaking Atlantic world during a pivotal period, showing how Enlightenment ideas, the spread of literacy and print culture, and the culture of sensibility gave rise to a rudimentary culture of disaster by the middle of the eighteenth century—evidenced most prominently by the response to the Lisbon earthquake—and then explore how nation-building, economic and territorial expansion, and the increasing ubiquity of steam-driven technologies later shaped how disasters were experienced, understood, and managed (or not managed) by postrevolutionary Americans. On the other hand, case studies from the period provide the evidence that shows both change and continuity in America's culture of disaster, as well as the contested nature of most disaster-related discourse. The Philadelphia yellow fever epidemic of 1793, for instance, revealed and intensified class and racial divisions in the afflicted city while leading many non-Philadelphians to leaven sympathy for their fellow Americans with quarantines to protect themselves by barring Philadelphians from their own communities.

While episodes such as the Lisbon earthquake and the Philadelphia yellow fever epidemic are well known and amply studied, there are notably few scholarly case studies of other disasters that occurred before the late eighteenth century. Aside from the Great Fire of London of 1666, earlier disasters that have attracted the most scholarly attention are the hurricanes that habitually pummeled the Caribbean island colonies. As historians Matthew Mulcahy and Stuart Schwartz have shown, those hurricanes (and an occasional earthquake) produced treasure troves of evidence—including the correspondence of merchants and government officials, many of whom provided eyewitness accounts—that shed much light on the impact of recurrent disasters on religious beliefs, material culture, and governance in these island colonies, where capital investments in sugar, slaves, and shipping created one of the world's first wildly lucrative risk societies. Government officials, merchants, sea captains, and planters wrote so much about Caribbean hurricanes and earthquakes precisely because these colonial settlements were both strategically and militarily important and economically uniquely valuable.[13]

Discourse about the bad things that happened in England's first colony in Virginia was more muted, and the response far less purposeful, in part because the stakes may have seemed lower, at least to people across the ocean in faraway London. Chapter 1 of *Inventing Disaster* examines the discourse surrounding the trials of Virginia's early settlers and draws on first-person accounts, Virginia Company reports and apologias, and ministers' sermons to show that contemporaries viewed neither Jamestown nor the deadly things that happened there either as problems to be resolved or as disasters in the modern sense. For one thing, Jamestown's remote location and the absence of newspapers or other forms of public communications rendered the settlers' suffering virtually invisible. The only contemporary story related to the early troubles at Jamestown that circulated widely was Shakespeare's play *The Tempest*, which scholars believe was loosely based on the saga of the

Sea Venture, a ship that wrecked off the coast of Bermuda in 1609, on its way to provision the starving Jamestown colonists.

Shipwreck stories, as I argue in chapter 2, fittingly became the first genre of disaster narratives because, in an era of burgeoning overseas commerce and colonization, maritime misadventures exposed both people and property to unusual levels of vulnerability and risk on a regular basis. Early newspapers, with their heavy emphasis on commercial news, reported maritime losses, and, though some continued to interpret shipwrecks as signs of divine wrath, secular accounts increasingly featured human-interest stories that sought to elicit sympathy and benevolence more than penitence and horror.

The book's next two chapters examine the culture of disaster in the British Empire in the decades before the imperial crisis that led to the American Revolution. The focus of chapter 3 is the Lisbon earthquake as a cultural event and, more specifically, its impact in the British Atlantic world. The widely publicized generosity of Britain's King George II toward Portugal's suffering earthquake victims was a source of pride to Britons on both sides of the Atlantic, who increasingly saw themselves as a uniquely benevolent nation. After 1755, residents of British colonial America had heightened expectations for relief from London when disaster struck. Chapter 4 examines the imperial response to five colonial disasters—two fires, one flood, and two hurricanes—in the decades after Lisbon, amid deepening tensions within the empire. Benevolence and statecraft worked in tandem, but sometimes at cross-purposes, as Britons to varying degrees responded to suffering colonists' calls for help.

Americans experienced changes in both the quality and quantity of disasters in the postrevolutionary era. On the one hand, they were increasingly vulnerable to new categories of calamities, as fires and epidemics proliferated in the growing cities of the early republic. On the other hand, they inhabited a print-saturated environment in which such episodes were widely reported and sometimes assumed national significance. Focusing primarily on several disasters with national implications, chapter 5 situates the evolving American culture of disaster in its larger political context and argues that, unlike in the contemporary British Empire with its expanding program of centralized benevolence, in the American republic disaster relief was decentralized, locally orchestrated, and ad hoc. In the postrevolutionary era, disasters gave rise to new conversations about benevolence, religion, and other issues, which in turn were part of the contested process of constructing American national identity.

The idea of disaster as a recurring phenomenon that evoked sustained and meaningful public debate emerged from the virtual epidemic of steam-boat explosions that began in the 1820s. The sheer number and violence of these waterborne disasters ensured public interest in them, while print and pictures made steamboat stories both ubiquitous and sensational in the ante-bellum era. Chapter 6 explores the popular culture of steamboat explosions and argues that graphic and emotionally moving representations of steam-boat disasters, coupled with the increasing pervasiveness of steam travel, created a vast and vocal imagined community of prospective steamboat casualties in nineteenth-century America. Far more than storms and earth-quakes, or even fires, steam technology also raised the issue of human agency and culpability and therefore led to public meetings and coroners' inquests, and eventually to successful demands for federal intervention to protect the public by improving the navigability of rivers and regulating the practices and standards of steamboat corporations. A turning point in the history of American disasters, the steamboat acts of 1838 and 1852 were the first federal statutes expressly designed to protect citizens by preventing at least this one specific type of disaster-related casualty.

Although some of the disasters discussed in this book are well known, others are not. The criteria for inclusion was less the number of lives lost or the value of property destroyed than an event's resonance in the wider cul-ture — the debates it informed, the affecting narratives it generated — judged by the evidentiary trail left in newspapers, visual images, sermons, govern-ment records, and other sources. The politics of location ensured that cul-tural resonance was not always commensurate with quantifiable losses. In October 1871, for instance, the cultural impact of the Chicago fire, which took the lives of some 300 people, vastly overshadowed that of the confla-gration at Peshtigo, Wisconsin, which on the very same day killed more than 2,000, making it the deadliest fire in American history. Likewise, though the New Madrid earthquakes, which destroyed entire communities and trans-formed the topography and landscape of the Missouri River valley during the winter of 1811–12, were clearly horrific for those who experienced them, the Richmond theater fire of December 1811 inspired far more public conver-sations about faith and reason, disaster prevention and relief, and American national identity.[14] Though by some measures the events in Peshtigo and New Madrid were more significant than those in Chicago and Richmond, the latter two had a greater impact in the public discourse and popular cul-ture of their respective historical periods.

Many of the episodes discussed in this book would qualify as what scholar Mike Davis calls "ordinary disasters," or calamities in which the causes of destruction are part of the regular landscape of everyday life.[15] For Davis, whose work centers on contemporary southern California, the prime culprit is overdevelopment, which feeds a continuing cycle of ruinous droughts and wildfires. While catastrophic events related to climate change and other forms of environmental degradation have come to be the ordinary disasters of the twenty-first century, shipwrecks, urban fires, and steamboat explosions were the ordinary disasters of earlier eras.

Historicizing disaster reminds us that our own code of calamity etiquette is a cultural construction that originated—for better or worse—in the intellectual, economic, and political environments of the eighteenth and nineteenth centuries. While the advent of organized disaster relief and federal regulation might be interpreted as progress, as we shall see, the larger story is more ambiguous. Indeed, many of our twenty-first-century experiences during and after hurricanes, oil spills, and other disasters would have made sense to Americans who witnessed the urban fires of the early republic or the steamboat explosions of the antebellum era. They, too, wanted explanations and sought to assign blame; they, too, sympathetically consumed stories about people who lost their homes, their loved ones, or their lives. And perhaps most importantly, for us, as for them, understanding the causes of disasters and learning their victims' stories are often more a means of managing loss, both practically and emotionally, than a way of preventing future tragedies.

{ 1 }

DEVASTATION
WITHOUT
DISASTER

In the seventeen years following the arrival of the first Europeans in 1607, more than three-quarters of the people who came to Virginia died not long after they disembarked there. Settlers at Jamestown endured a succession of famines, fevers, and other calamities that jeopardized the physical and economic survival of England's first American colony. At least in part because of these appallingly high mortality rates, the Virginia Company of London, the joint-stock company of investors that sponsored the colony and hoped to profit from it, lost its royal charter in 1624. All in all, Jamestown's early years were defined by significant losses of both lives and property, conditions that people today see as defining hallmarks of disaster.

This chapter examines the trials of the Jamestown settlers and emphasizes the premodern orientation of contemporary discussions of and responses to the bad things that happened in the early Virginia colony. Information about the famines, fevers, and most other fatal or otherwise costly calamities that afflicted Jamestown rarely spread beyond the narrow circles of Virginia Company officials, who knew that making such information public knowledge would undermine their ability to attract the new investors and settlers needed to sustain their struggling colony. There were no sentimental narratives about Jamestown's fever and famine victims and only minimal efforts to relieve their suffering. The main form of relief for Jamestown was additional people sent by the company to replace the dead with the hope that those new settlers fared better. In most cases, they did not. Significantly absent from the Jamestown debacle was the modern notion of disaster as a process that involved conscious assessments of vulnerability and risk, cultural negotiations, and real or rhetorical efforts to relieve suffering and prevent future calamities.[1]

Yet the founding of Jamestown occurred during a forward-looking age of intellectual innovation and achievement in culture and the arts. Some of those at the forefront of these developments in early modern England moved in the same cosmopolitan circles as those who were involved in or sympathetic to the Virginia project. In 1605, one of these luminaries, the philosopher-statesman Francis Bacon, made a noteworthy and influential case for scientific inquiry and empiricism in *The Advancement of Learning*. A few years later, William Shakespeare likely based the plot of one of his plays, *The Tempest*, on the saga of the *Sea Venture*, a ship that wrecked off the coast of Bermuda in 1609 when it was carrying badly needed supplies and settlers to the struggling Jamestown colony.

Baconian science and Shakespearean secular storytelling were on the cutting edge of cultural innovation in early modern England, and both ultimately became central features of the modern culture of disaster. Neither, however, figured prominently in contemporary responses to the troubles at Jamestown. Viewed variously as the consequences of human failure or as the bitter fruit of divine providence, colonists' sufferings evoked less sympathy and rational inquiry than opprobrium and horror.

§ Failure and fatalities plagued England's initial forays into the race for American colonies. In the 1580s, efforts by Sir Walter Raleigh and others to establish a privateering base and settlement at Roanoke, in present-day North Carolina, ended with the mysterious disappearance and likely death of the ninety men, seventeen women, and eleven children who became known as the "Lost Colony." The next English attempts to establish a permanent presence in America occurred under the auspices of two joint-stock companies, the Virginia Company of London and the Virginia Company of Plymouth, both of which received their royal charters from King James I in 1606. The Plymouth group sponsored a colony located on the Sagadahoc River, in present-day Maine, but within a year all of its 120 inhabitants had either returned home or died. Meanwhile, in December 1606, the Virginia Company of London dispatched three vessels with 144 passengers to form a settlement farther south. In late April 1607, the 105 travelers who survived the voyage established Jamestown on a peninsula bounded by the Chesapeake Bay and two rivers, which they named the James and the York. The 27 percent mortality rate on the Atlantic crossing, which was high even for the time, was only the first in a series of heavy losses suffered by the fledgling colony.[2]

Over the next seventeen years, at least 6,000 people came to Virginia, but only approximately 1,200 were living there by 1624, when King Charles I revoked the company's charter and made Virginia a royal colony. In Jamestown's first year, disease and famine took the lives of all but 38 of the original 105 settlers. The company sent more people, however, raising Jamestown's population to roughly 500; unfortunately, all but 60 of these colonists perished during the famous "starving time" of 1609–10. That winter, hungry colonists ate horses, dogs, cats, rats, mice, snakes, and other "vermine," along with boots and shoe leather. Eventually, some desperate souls ate "dead corpses outt of graves" and "Licked upp the Bloode wch hathe fallen from their weake fellowes." One man murdered his pregnant wife, chopped her up, and "salted her for his foode." In the ensuing years, the company sent still more people — a total of 4,270 in 1619–22 alone — but many of these new arrivals also died. By March 1622, only 1,240 settlers were living in Virginia when an attack led by the Powhatan chief Opechancanough resulted in the death of nearly a third of its population. Famine and disease accounted for still more deaths in the coming months. Unless the situation improved, one of the company's critics opined, Virginia would "shortly get the name of a slaughterhouse, and justly become odious to ourselves and contemptible to all the world."[3]

Until relatively recently, most historians have echoed the views of Virginia Company investors and others who attributed the deadliness of Jamestown to the shortcomings of its settlers. Typical historical accounts of Virginia's early years drew on contemporary descriptions of the colony, which cast its English inhabitants as lazy and ill-suited for life in the American wilderness, unwilling to clear land, plant crops, and attend to other demanding tasks required to build and sustain their new community. As one leading historian put it, "The enterprise called for men of skill, energy, and self-sacrifice . . . [but] both leaders and followers fell far short of that mark. Virginia," he concluded, "survived not because of its settlers but in spite of them." Jamestown became a "fiasco," according to another influential historian, in large part due to its "idle" and conflict-ridden settler population.[4]

Subsequent research on Jamestown's early years reveals that the truth was more complex. The colony was settled during a period that climate historians call the Little Ice Age, a time when temperatures were colder, droughts were frequent, growing seasons were comparatively short, and crop yields were less productive. Indeed, tree-ring studies indicate that the founding of

Devastation without Disaster

Jamestown precisely coincided with "the most severe seven-year regional drought in the last 770 years" in the Chesapeake region. Although the impact of the Little Ice Age was worldwide — resulting in famines that led to social unrest and political instability across the globe — Europeans were ill-equipped either to understand or to adapt to the particularly extreme climactic conditions they found in the Americas. For one thing, they equated climate with latitude, expecting places with similar locations along the earth's north-south axis to have comparable climactic conditions. Based on that assumption, Englishmen thought that the weather in Newfoundland would be akin to that of France and that Virginia would share the mild Mediterranean climate characteristic of parts of Spain and Portugal.[5]

Jamestown's Little Ice Age climate caused or exacerbated a range of potentially fatal problems. Located on the James River but not beyond its fall line, the English settlement became especially unhealthy in the summer and during droughts when the river's level was low and colonists drank its stagnant waters, which were contaminated with salt, feces, and disease-inducing microbes. Short growing seasons and deadly winter freezes ruined crops, resulting in food shortages. Even when colonists had enough food and survived the brutal, disease-plagued summer months, their virtually all-maize diet rendered them susceptible to pellagra, a potentially fatal disease unknown in Europe. Malnutrition, in turn, exacted a profound psychological toll, resulting in what one historian has called "a fatal withdrawal from life."[6]

In Jamestown's first decade, colonists also experienced a major fire "that consumed all the buildings of the fort," along with recurring famines and plagues, any one of which would qualify as a "disaster" in modern parlance. So, too, did these episodes become occasions for strife and negotiation in the colony, much as more recent disasters — from the Chicago fire to Hurricane Katrina — have brought preexisting cultural tensions and social conflicts to the fore, often resulting in challenges to authority, institutions, and attitudes. In Jamestown, famine led to near mutiny and, in July 1608, to the ouster of President John Ratcliffe, who was succeeded in September by Captain John Smith, who established military-style discipline to force the settlers to work while he also negotiated with the Powhatans to secure the provisions needed for the colony's short-term survival. Smith's reforms did not long survive his departure for London in October 1609, however, and the resulting famine — the famous starving time of 1609–10 — exposed and exacerbated divisions in the colony. Desperate colonists expressed their pain and anger by challenging the legitimacy of their leaders. Some stole provisions from the fort at Jamestown, while others defied the authority of church and state by committing mutinous and blasphemous acts. Smith's ineffectual successor, President George Percy, reported that, on at least one occasion, he had to march out of his house "with my Sworde drawne" to disperse an angry mob. But perhaps the most subversive of all were those colonists who abandoned the English settlement and its values to join the Indians, or, as Percy disdainfully put it, to "Runn Away unto the Salvages."[7]

In London, company officials sought to restore order and discipline in Jamestown by sending new supply ships, including the ill-fated *Sea Venture*, and, more importantly, by launching a series of institutional reforms. In 1609, the Virginia Company of London obtained a second charter that reinvented the Jamestown project by giving it a compelling religious purpose — converting the Indians to Protestant Christianity — and an authoritative governor whose extensive powers included the right to rule by martial law to ensure the "most dispatch and terror . . . fittest for this governement." Implemented with the arrival of Lieutenant Governor Sir Thomas Gates in May 1610, these changes aimed more to restore order than to save lives and in fact came too late to prevent the starvation of the vast majority of the colonists — amid conflict and cannibalism — during the winter of 1609–10.[8]

Pervasive death, financial loss, conflict, and disorder nevertheless did not add up to "disaster" in early seventeenth-century English discourse. Especially in these early years, contemporaries rarely used the word "disaster" — a recent addition to the English language — to describe the sufferings of the Jamestown colonists. Derived from the French *aster*, meaning "star," the word "disaster" was initially synonymous with general misfortune or "ill lucke," and its earliest English usage often alluded to the stars or other celestial bodies as influencing the fortunes of humankind. First used by an English author in 1567, the word appeared most frequently in English publications that were translations of Latin or French originals. When early modern English writers used the word "disaster," they typically referred neither to one specific episode nor to the combination of the search for causes, relief, prevention, and sympathy that defines the term's modern usage but rather to a generally unfortunate situation. An exotic import, the word appeared in a total of only seventy-eight known English books, pamphlets, or broadsides before 1607, the year that Jamestown was founded.[9]

Shakespeare's use of the term is instructive. A linguistic innovator who knew and often employed words from other languages, Shakespeare was an early adopter of the term "disaster," but he used the word in a distinctively early modern way. For one thing, his usage was generic: for him, "disaster" meant overall bad or unfortunate circumstances rather than a specific episode, such as a famine, fire, or plague. Drawing on the original French meaning of the word, Shakespeare alluded to the stars (or the sun or the moon) as the source of general misfortune or bad luck. The playwright thus described *Romeo and Juliet* (1597) as a tragic story of "star-cross'd lovers"; in *Hamlet* (1604), he cited "Disasters in the sunne" as harbingers of defeat. In *King Lear* (1608), however, Shakespeare seemed to reject and even mock the notion of celestial bodies influencing the fortunes of humankind, instead suggesting that invoking the heavens was a stratagem that men used to elude responsibility when bad things occurred as a result of their own errors or malfeasance:

> This is the excellent foppery of the world, that,
> when we are sick in fortune, — often the surfeit
> of our own behavior, — we make guilty of our
> disasters the sun, the moon, and the stars . . .

Shakespeare's sardonic observation anticipated one of the most significant critical insights among scholars in the modern field of disaster studies: the contention that government officials, corporate leaders, and other authorities routinely evade responsibility for negligence or bad policy choices by characterizing hurricanes, earthquakes, epidemics, and other deadly calamities as unavoidable acts of God or nature. Significantly, as conditions deteriorated at Jamestown, this approach became a favorite strategy of the embattled Virginia Company.[10]

Although the use of the term "disaster" became both more common and less tied to celestial bodies by the time the Virginia Company lost its charter in 1624, most contemporary accounts of the problems at Jamestown used the word sparingly and in ways that were in keeping with the literary conventions of the era. William Strachey, a poet whose theater connections included Shakespeare, referred generically to "all these disasters and afflictions" that "descended upon our people" in the colony. Strachey was a minor investor in the Virginia Company who had been aboard the *Sea Venture* when it wrecked in 1609; he was also among those who eventually made their way from Bermuda to Jamestown, only to witness the colony's disintegration in horror as a result of the famine that spared only sixty skeletal colonists, all of whom were themselves on the verge of starvation. Captain John Smith, the military man who served briefly as Virginia's president and self-described savior and who also became its most important chronicler, did not use the term "disaster" in his earlier writings, but it appeared roughly a dozen times in his magnum opus, *The Generall Historie of Virginia, New-England, and the*

Summer Isles (1624), in which he mostly used the word as a shorthand for the cumulative effects of the years of trauma and tragedy that afflicted the Virginia colony.[11]

Like Strachey and Smith, other observers used the word "disaster" infrequently, in part because they did not see the troubles at Jamestown as the result of misaligned celestial bodies or other portents of bad luck. By contrast, those who commented on the colony's misadventures typically attributed them to purposeful human misdeeds or divine intervention, and sometimes to a combination of both. Indeed, the discourse surrounding the Jamestown colony is an apt barometer of the various ways in which early seventeenth-century English people understood the relative power of divine and human agency in causing plagues, famines, shipwrecks, and other calamities.

Captain John Smith, who wrote more about Virginia than any of his contemporaries, was also the chronicler who most unequivocally described the colony's tribulations as the result of human actions, invoking the deity relatively infrequently and mostly to explain whatever good things happened in Virginia that he either could not or would not take credit for himself. Smith penned his first brief description of Jamestown in 1608, during his thirteen-month presidency of the colony, when his strict discipline and shrewd diplomacy likely saved the fragile English settlement. Smith blamed the "famine and sicknes" at Jamestown on "the hard dealings" and "audacious command" of his rivals while attributing the colony's survival to God's benevolence and to his own prudent policies. The captain credited God with saving Jamestown from an Indian attack and convincing the Powhatans to give corn to the colonists; he also insisted that "Gods assistance" restored his own good health. Meanwhile, as a result of his own reforms, Smith claimed to have restored the settlers to "good health, all our men wel contented, free from mutinies, in love one with another, and as we hope in a continuall peace with the Indians." Unbeknownst to him, within a year famine and pestilence would once again decimate the colony.[12]

In his subsequent writings, Smith took a longer view of Virginia's history and focused more critically on the human actors whom he believed caused or aggravated various crises in the colony. An ardent champion of English colonization, Smith sought to preserve and promote Virginia, England's first significant foothold in the New World. He also hoped to prevent the abandonment of the colony by disgruntled Virginia Company investors and prospective settlers alike by defending it against the "slander" of its critics and by persuading his readers that "the defect whereof hath only beene in the managing of the business" by the company and its functionaries. In *A Map*

Devastation without Disaster

THE PORTRAICTUER OF CAPTAYNE IOHN SMITH ; ADMIRALL OF NEW ENGLAND .

Æta 37
A° 1616

These are the Lines that shew thy Face; but those
That shew thy Grace and Glory, brighter bee :-
Thy Faire-Discoueries and Fowle-Overthrowes
Of Salvages, much Civilliz'd by thee
Best shew thy Spirit; and to it Glory Wyn;
So, thou art Brasse without, but Golde within .

Captain John Smith. This portrait of Smith appeared in his *Generall Historie of Virginia, New-England, and the Summer Isles* (1624), his most extensive account of England's early colonial settlements in America. The capable but cantankerous Smith mostly blamed human incompetence or malfeasance for the famines, diseases, and other problems that afflicted Jamestown, though he sometimes interpreted good things that happened there as providential signs of divine favor and benevolence. *Library of Virginia*.

of Virginia, in which he chronicled the colony's history to 1612, Smith denounced the "pure idlenesse" of the colonists and above all the unfitness of their leaders for inciting "the worst furie of the Savages, the extremetie of sicknesse, mutinies, faction, ignorances, and want of victual" that punctuated Virginia's brief but grim history. He believed that bad behavior, not bad luck or divine wrath, caused so much suffering in the colony.[13]

In his *Generall Historie*, Smith extended his chronicle into the 1620s and included an analysis of the ruinous Indian attack of 1622—which he blamed largely on "the want of martiall discipline" among the English—that resulted in the death of hundreds of colonists and the destruction of their settlements. Smith again decried the "disgustfull" factionalism and greed of Virginia's early leaders, whom he blamed for what he pointedly characterized as the "needlesse misery" at Jamestown. He argued that the Virginia Company's practice of frequently changing governors was bad for the colony, especially because so many of the men they chose were "only ayming at their owne ends." Smith also criticized the company for investing too little in fortifications, livestock, and other "necessaries" and for not hiring the sorts of experienced workers and "mechanicall men" required to plant a stronger and more sustainable colony.[14]

Smith was the most persistent and best known of those who insisted that corrupt and incompetent men were the main source of Jamestown's problems, but others also expressed this view. One of Smith's enemies in Virginia, Gabriel Archer, unpersuasively blamed the captain and his allies for the famine and disease that devastated the settlement after Smith's departure in October 1609. At least two of Virginia's early governors, Lord De La Warr and Sir Thomas Dale, claimed that the colony, despite its rich and fertile soil, was in ruins largely because of the idleness of its inhabitants. Others blamed the Virginia Company for mismanagement and also for the absence of churches, towns, and fortifications, all of which they believed might improve conditions by enhancing order and security in the colony. These men usually were seeking to defend or to burnish their own reputations by blaming their rivals for the colony's problems.[15]

The point worth emphasizing is that, though Smith and the others were conventionally Christian adherents of the Protestant Church of England, they did not describe the famines, plagues, and other crises that ravaged Jamestown as the providential work of an omnipotent and omniscient God, despite the fact that their English contemporaries typically embraced providential explanations for these sorts of calamities when they happened closer to home. Although English Protestantism was dividing into two in-

Devastation without Disaster

creasingly hostile factions—Calvinists (including Puritans), who believed that God predestined who was saved and who was damned, and Arminians, who maintained that humans possessed the free will to accept or to reject his saving grace—both sides agreed that God was omnipotent and that everything that happened was literally an act of God. Providentialism, or the belief that God could and did intervene in earthly affairs to protect or to punish, was a central feature of English Protestantism. Unlike Catholics, who could turn to priests and saints as intermediaries between themselves and the deity, Protestants emphasized each soul's direct relationship with the Almighty and therefore strove to discern meaning in everything from storms and earthquakes to the more mundane occurrences of everyday life. Providential explanations were so central to their understanding of the world because of their complete, utter, and unmediated submission to and dependence on the mercy of God.[16]

So, it should not be surprising that, while John Smith described the colony's traumas as the result of human agency, many of his contemporaries exhibited a more expansive belief in God as the source of everything that happened in Jamestown—both good and bad—all of which they regarded as signs or messages from the Almighty. This perspective was attuned with the English cultural mainstream in an era when supernatural explanations predominated. While the clergy were the most vocal in invoking divine providence to explain ruinous fires and famines, as well as military defeats and triumphs, such interpretations were also widely embraced among the English laity.

William Strachey, the cosmopolitan poet who left Falmouth aboard the ill-fated *Sea Venture* in June 1609 is a case in point. Strachey and his shipmates survived a harrowing hurricane that wrecked their vessel and left them stranded as castaways in Bermuda, an island that they initially feared as a result of its reputation as "an inchanted den of Furies and Devils, the most dangerous, unfortunate, and forlorne place in the world." After spending ten months in what turned out to be an unexpectedly pleasant island paradise, Strachey and most of his fellow castaways boarded two boats they constructed from Bermuda cedar wood and remnants of the wrecked ship, and they arrived safely at Jamestown in late July 1610. Strachey understandably credited their seemingly miraculous survival, as well as the island's abundance, to God's beneficent providence. Unlike Smith, however, he also attributed the various crises he encountered—the shipwreck, the horrifically abysmal conditions at Jamestown—to divine providence. When Strachey chronicled his experiences aboard the *Sea Venture* and later in Bermuda and

Virginia, he interpreted both the adversity he and his companions suffered and their eventual deliverance as messages from God.[17]

Strachey called his account *A True Reportory of the wrack and redemption of Sir Thomas Gates, knight, upon and from the Islands of the Bermudas; his coming to Virginia, and the estate of that colony then, and after under the government of the Lord La Warre.* Composed in 1610 as a letter to an unidentified "Excellent Lady," Strachey's lively narrative remained unpublished until 1625, but the text circulated in manuscript form and many scholars believe that it helped to inspire Shakespeare's shipwreck play, *The Tempest*, which was first performed on a London stage in 1611. While *The Tempest* was one of Shakespeare's comedies, in which conflicts are resolved and young lovers marry and live presumably happily ever after, Strachey's *True Reportory* was a tale of suffering, redemption, and then still more suffering after the castaways' eventual arrival in Virginia.

Convinced that God was both omnipotent and ultimately benevolent, Strachey saw the shipwreck and its aftermath as divine corrections whose impact was nonetheless softened by the countervailing actions of a merciful deity. Strachey attributed the "most dreadful tempest" to divine intervention, but he also viewed the happy survival of all the ships' crew and passengers as an act of God, who inspired everyone aboard the ship to work, day and night, to bail water out of the leaky vessel. Strachey wondered "whether it were the fear of death in so great a storm or that it pleased God to be gracious unto us" that spurred on so many men who "in all their lifetimes had never done hours' work before" but who were now willing and able for four long days to "toil with the best." Strachey likewise credited God with choosing the "dangerous and dreaded" Bermuda for their refuge, even as the Almighty made "this hideous and hated place both the place of our safety and means of our deliverance" in order to "bind us to gratefulness." When treachery and blasphemy undermined the castaways' efforts to regroup and resume their voyage to Jamestown, divine providence enabled their leaders to restore peace and order. Strachey believed that God's mercy and goodness were responsible for the voyagers' relatively smooth and uneventful trip from Bermuda to Jamestown. But he also saw the hand of God in the utterly horrific conditions that he and his fellow travelers found when they finally arrived there.[18]

Like Smith and so many other observers, Strachey reported that the "disasters and afflictions [that] descended upon our people" at Jamestown were often the result of bad governance, which spawned the "sloth, riot, and vanity" that caused so much disorder and misery in the colony. At the same

Devastation without Disaster

time, however, he understood the appalling conditions at Jamestown as part of God's larger plan for Virginia and for English colonial ambitions generally. "The ground of all those miseries," he wrote, "was the permissive providence of God," who sent the hurricane that wrecked the *Sea Venture*, which delayed the arrival of the new governor, Sir Thomas Gates, and the much needed provisions, which in turn led to famine and a "tempest of dissension" among the colonists. "Having neither ruler nor preacher," Strachey surmised, the Jamestown colonists "neither feared God nor man, which provoked the Lord of Hosts, and pulled His judgments upon them." The result was that "some of our men fled, some murthered, and most by drinking of the brackish water of James Fort [were] weakened and endangered." "Famine and sickness by all these means increased," he concluded, with help from England not forthcoming.[19]

Strachey's use of providential rhetoric and explanations was inspired by a series of truly remarkable events, capped by the arrival of a new governor, Lord De La Warr, with supplies and 150 additional settlers, on the very day that the disillusioned commander of the *Sea Venture* expedition, Sir Thomas Gates, and his men had intended to evacuate the colony. Gates changed his plans, and the 140 people he brought from Bermuda, in addition to those who arrived with De La Warr, made the settlement large enough to survive another year, while the new governor reined in factional divisions and established a militarized sort of order. When Gates returned to England in 1610, he shared a version of the story of the *Sea Venture* wreck and its aftermath, which, like Strachey's, explained the storm and the castaways' ability to survive it in Bermuda, along with the subsequent suffering and redemption at Jamestown, in providential terms. On hearing Gates's story, Virginia Company officials concurred with his conclusion that "God inclineth all casual events to work the necessary help of his saints. . . . Never had any people more just cause to cast themselves at the footstool of God, and to reverence His mercy than our distressed colony!"[20]

The *Sea Venture* story became part of a larger providential discourse that increasingly framed English discussions of the Virginia project. Fierce rivalry with Catholic Spain had helped to fuel English colonization efforts since Elizabethan times, and rhetorical gestures toward the Almighty as a source of protection and beneficence were firmly rooted in the culture of the early modern era. But as circumstances in Jamestown deteriorated—with great human and financial loss—a new sense of religious purpose inspired the settlement's most ardent promoters.

In 1609, religion became an explicit priority for the newly rechartered

Virginia Company with the establishment of the London-based king's Council for Virginia, whose membership came primarily from the ranks of militant Protestants. This push to reimagine Jamestown as a Protestant mission and the English colonization of North America as an event in providential history came from two sources. Hard-pressed to attract sufficient financial support to sustain the troubled colony, company leaders hoped that their new religious fervor would inspire prospective investors who could be motivated both by piety and profits. At the same time, the men who spearheaded efforts to revamp the colony under its second charter truly believed that Protestant England was God's chosen nation. Like the Puritans who later settled in New England in the 1620s and 1630s, they saw the spread of Protestantism as a divinely ordained errand, the success of which would ensure both the greatness of England and the providential triumph of the true Protestant religion.[21]

The clergy played a key role in publicizing this notion of Virginia as a godly mission. In so doing, however, they had to explain why, if the success of Jamestown was so important to God, its settlers had experienced nothing but famine, disease, disorder, and violence. In other words, the ministers and others who shared this view of Jamestown as a holy undertaking had to persuade their audience that, in the words of the author of the suggestively titled *The New Life of Virginea*, all good and worthwhile things "are accompanied with manifold difficulties, crosses and disasters, being such as are appointed by the highest providence." Accordingly, they interpreted the circumstances that caused such suffering at Jamestown as the purposefully providential acts of an omnipotent God.[22]

The Reverend William Crashaw was the most prominent proponent of this view. A Cambridge-trained minister of a rigorously Protestant cast, Crashaw's London connections and his enthusiasm for the Virginia project made him, in the words of one scholar, "the unofficial ecclesiastical secretary of the Virginia Company." In 1609, Crashaw made the case for Virginia as a holy errand, despite its "so poore and small a beginning," in a sermon preached on the occasion of Lord De La Warr's departure to assume the governorship of colony. Crashaw acknowledged the "harsh and miserable conditions" that afflicted "them that goe and stay there," but he denounced as "lies and slander" the growing criticism of the colony, contending that the settlers' suffering was, in fact, divinely ordained. "If our men have been at any exigents," he averred, their trials "grew not from any necessitie that must needs accompanie that plantation, or that countrey; but proceeded plainly from the want of *gouvernment* . . . which was caused by the *hand of God*."

Crashaw exhorted his listeners — and then his readers, once the sermon appeared in print the following year — to heed God's message, by defeating the "Papists" and by converting "those poore Virginians," the Indians, to Protestant Christianity.[23]

The Reverend Alexander Whitaker, who sailed to Virginia with its next new governor, Sir Thomas Dale, in 1611, shared Crashaw's missionary zeal as well as his understanding of the causes of the unceasing suffering of the Jamestown colonists. "God hath heretofore plagued our countrymen with famine, death, the sword, etc., for the sins of men were intolerable," wrote this Cambridge-trained son of a late Regius professor of divinity shortly after arriving in the colony. "I marvell more that God did not sweepe them away all att once, than that he did in such a manner punishe them." Whitaker reasoned that God "in the middest of anger rememb'red mercy," ensuring the survival of Jamestown so that the English might convert the Indians and "fulfill his purpose and set up the kingdom of His Son on these parts." Two years later, in a sermon titled *Good Newes From Virginia*, Whitaker compared the colony's progress to "the growth of an Infant, which hath been afflicted from his birth with some grievous sicknes, that many times no hope of life hath remained, and yet it liveth still" as a result of God's "special providence." Whitaker, who became pastor of the church in the interior settlement of Henrico, was committed to proselytizing among the Indians — "these naked slaves of the divell" — and, citing improving conditions, including the introduction of tobacco cultivation, he concluded that the company's new religious purpose led God to shower his blessings on the still fragile colony.[24]

While there is no doubt that these clergymen and many who heard or read their sermons truly believed that Virginia's famines, diseases, and other horrors were messages from the Almighty, belief in divine providence also afforded defenders of the Virginia Company a convenient excuse for its poor performance since its initial chartering. In 1610, in the midst of its efforts to attract new investors, the Council for Virginia published *A True and Sincere Declaration of the Purpose and Ends of the Plantation begun in Virginia* to explain the "causes of some disaster and distemper" in the colony. Casting a wide net, they echoed the criticism that Captain John Smith and others had leveled against Virginia's leaders and "the Idlenesse and bestiall slouth, of the common sort," even as they maintained that it was God who ultimately controlled what transpired at Jamestown. "Who," they asked, "can avoid the hand of God, or dispute with him?" Five years later, still touting their efforts to convert the Indians and thereby reduce "that barbarous Nation, and savage people, to a quiet Christian Common-wealth," the councilors again attributed the "many disasters on Sea and Land, too long to be here recited," to the "will of Almighty God," while also claiming that recent improvements in Virginia had occurred as a result of "the favourable assistance of God." Whether or not they sincerely thought that the settlers' suffering was divinely ordained, espousing this position rendered efforts to relieve or prevent Jamestown's calamities at best pointless and at worst blasphemous.[25]

For the colony's defenders, attributing the problems at Jamestown to purposeful divine intervention also provided an alternative to the more hopelessly sinister notion that Virginia — and, indeed, the New World generally — was a place that existed, as one scholar puts it, "beyond the bounds of English norms or even English understanding," a venue in which conventional rules of cause and effect did not apply, where suffering was constant, and where horrific things inevitably happened. English writers portrayed America as both a paradisiacal land of plenty and a place of disorderly malevolence. William Bradford's description of Cape Cod in 1620 is a good example of the latter. From aboard the *Mayflower*, this leader of the Plymouth colony beheld a "hideous and desolate wilderness, full of beasts and willd men," an ocean away from "all the civill parts of the world." Bradford imagined America as lacking all the amenities of civilization. There were "no friends to wellcome them, nor inns to entertaine or refresh their weather-beaten bodys, no houses or much less townes to repair to, to seek for succoure." Settlers in both Massachusetts and Virginia also looked askance at native peoples they encountered, often viewing them — in the words of the Virginia clergyman Alexander Whitaker — as barbarous "slaves of the divell."[26]

Nearly from the start, pervasive famine and disease, violence, and disorder led some to see misery as intrinsic to Virginia. The settlers' first president, Edward Maria Wingfield, explained the failures and controversies of his lackluster five-month tenure in part by asserting that Jamestown was fundamentally different from any place in England because of the seemingly pervasive "whipping, lawing, beating, and hanging," and overall brutal conditions which he feared would "drive many well affected myndes" from supporting the colony. A decade later, John Pory, who served as the first speaker of the House of Burgesses and was overall optimistic for the future of Virginia, nonetheless worried about the dire effects of its remoteness from the civilized world. Pory felt a profound sense of isolation in this "contemptible" colonial outpost, where planters inexplicably defied the norms of English agriculture, farming without plows or cattle, and where the few ships that arrived came "fraighted more with ignorance, then with any other marchandize."[27]

Others emphasized how Virginia's depraved environment dehumanized labor in ways that would have been unconscionable in England. Colonist William Capps wrote of men "rooteinge in the earth like a hog" to survive and "ventureing our lyves for smoke" by their onerous toil in the tobacco fields. Richard Frethorne, an English indentured servant who arrived in Virginia in 1622, claimed that conditions there were so brutal that many settlers "would not care to loose anie lymbe to bee in England againe, yea though they [must] beg from doore to doore." In other words, in his view, the experience of bonded workers in Virginia was more demeaning and dehumanizing than was the abject poverty and dependence they would endure as limbless mendicants on the streets of London.[28]

George Percy, who succeeded John Smith as president of the colony and who penned an anguished account of the extreme suffering in Virginia during his brief tenure, was the most important spokesman for the notion of misery as the defining characteristic of Jamestown and its environs during the settlement's early years. Although Percy's "True Relation" is best known for its graphic descriptions of the starving time, the author constructed his entire account of life in Virginia—before, during, and after the famine—around gruesome episodes of suffering and violence, both between Indians and settlers and among the settlers themselves. Percy believed that the colonial experience transformed Englishmen (himself included) into an uncivilized other, and he argued that this perverse degeneration of Europeans in the New World was not unique to Virginia. "If we Trewley Consider the diversety of miseries mutenies and famishments wch have Attended upon discoveries and plantacyons in theis our moderne Tymes," he maintained, "we shall nott fynde our plantacyon in Virginia to have Suffered Aloane."[29]

These two otherworldly explanations for the settlers' suffering—the providential and the perverse—together justified the passivity of Virginia Company authorities in London, discouraging them from trying to understand the physical and climactic causes of famines, disease, and other fatal calamities that afflicted the Jamestown colony. At the same time, Jamestown's corporate origins likely weakened the English state's perceived responsibility for the colonists' suffering, just as removal to Virginia had fractured traditional Old World bonds of patronage and community.

By the early seventeenth century, European governments, motivated primarily by the desire to prevent riots and rebellions, intervened in famines, plagues, and other crises. Though they still understood these episodes in a providential light, authorities also increasingly adopted practical precautions aimed at minimizing social disruption and loss of life. In England, national-level strategies promoted public health as early as 1518, and regulatory codes designed to prevent the spread of plague and provide charity for its victims were in place in London and elsewhere by the early seventeenth century. Government-sponsored efforts to regulate the prices of crops in times of dearth and to distribute scarce food to those in need occurred in England as early as 1527 and became systematized with the adoption of the Book of Orders for the Relief of Dearth in 1586. In 1607, the year of Jamestown's founding, when poor people in England rioted to protest their lack of food, the king responded by punishing hoarders, prohibiting farmers from feeding peas to pigs, curtailing the use of malt for beer, and even banning the use of starch on collars and other clothing. Although these measures did not end England's food shortages, they stand in marked contrast to the inaction of the Virginia Company in response to the scarcity and disease that endangered the lives of settlers in the Jamestown colony.[30]

Captain John Smith was almost alone in trying to replicate these functions of the home government, in a limited way, by addressing the health and dietary crises that were killing so many settlers. During his time in Virginia, Smith noticed that the Indians moved inland and dispersed during the dry and disease-ridden summer months; he also observed that they survived the summer at a much higher rate than did the English, who remained clustered together at Jamestown. Smith did not know that moving away from the stagnant and microbe-infested waters of the James River at its lowest levels was what saved the Powhatans, but he intuitively followed their example, despite opposition from his rivals, who would not repeat his experiment in subsequent years — despite the fact that the settlers whom Smith moved into the freshwater zone survived the summer of 1608, while half of those who remained at Jamestown did not.[31]

Although the belief that Jamestown was inherently deadly and deviant helps to explain the inaction of the company and most of Virginia's governors, so, too, does the fact that the settlers' suffering, unlike that of starving or plague-ridden Londoners, was essentially invisible to anyone outside the Virginia colony. There were no newspapers in England before the 1630s; there was no printing press in Virginia until the 1680s, no permanent press until 1730, and no newspaper until 1736. As a result, most of what was written about conditions in Jamestown and its environs circulated only among Virginia Company officials and investors in London. The company did what it could to squelch bad publicity. William Strachey's *True Reportory*, which detailed the horrors of the starving time, remained unpublished until 1625, the year after the company lost its charter and Virginia became a royal colony.

Devastation without Disaster

George Percy's "True Relation," the most damning description of the colony, did not appear in print until 1922.[32]

Unlike the inhospitable climate and seasonal fevers and famines that took the lives of thousands but were mostly unknown outside the Virginia Company, the shocking Indian attacks on the English settlements in March 1622 received widespread attention in London and became an acknowledged turning point in the colony's relationship with God, the Virginia Company, and the English government. By 1622, many people on both sides of the Atlantic believed that Virginia was progressing, at least in terms of colonists' efforts to Christianize the Indians—with Pocahontas's well-publicized conversion and marriage to John Rolfe as a signal achievement—and to produce something profitable, the latter objective having been met by the recent adoption of tobacco as an export crop. One English clergyman went so far as to argue that God's "wonderfull works" had brought colonists "good health, every one busied in their vocations, as Bees in their Hives," and had "mollifie[d] the hearts of Salvages, . . . to make some of them voluntarily . . . remoove from their owne warme and well seated and peopled habitations," calmly ceding their lands to English settlers. From the Indians' perspective, the growth and dispersal of the English settlements, spurred by the profitability of tobacco and the Virginia Company's initiative to increase production by offering land grants, known as "headrights," to prospective planters, was alarming. The Powhatan leader Opechancanough's response to English expansion and arrogance was a massive assault on their settlements on 22 March 1622.[33]

The English called this episode a "massacre," a term that denoted not only unspeakable brutality but also something that was, for early modern English people, both extraordinary and foreign. The word "massacre" had entered the English language as recently as the 1570s, after the St. Bartholomew's Day Massacre (Massacre de la Saint-Barthélemy) of August 1572, when France's Catholic monarchy orchestrated the assassination of the country's leading Protestants and also countenanced (and likely encouraged) the violent assaults of Catholic mobs, which resulted in the murder of thousands of other French Protestants. Appalling to Protestant Elizabethans, this brutal, large-scale, and indiscriminate slaughter of innocents had no English parallel. Although 312 pious English Protestants had been publicly executed—284 burned at the stake, 28 pressed to death, and 1 hanged, drawn, and quartered—during the reign of "Bloody Mary" Tudor (1553–58), those deaths, however grisly and lamentable, were the result of orderly judicial proceedings, not the vengeance of angry mobs. At the time of Jamestown's founding in 1607, English people still typically used the term "massacre" in reference to the St. Bartholomew's Day tragedy, though they sometimes employed it to describe other scenes of disorderly and seemingly senseless violence that occurred in foreign places. In 1594, for instance, Shakespeare used the word "massacre," as both a noun and a verb, in *Titus Andronicus*, arguably his most violent play, which was set in ancient Rome.[34]

English observers saw Opechancanough's attack not as a military defeat but rather as a bloody providential message delivered by diabolical forces. Professing to see themselves as innocents benevolently spreading religion and civilization among Virginia's native peoples, colonists deemed the assault both unexpected and unwarranted. Stunned eyewitnesses reported that friendly Indians, who arrived in the English settlements that fateful day bearing gifts and mingling freely with their hosts, suddenly and inexplicably turned violent, killing families in their houses and workers in the fields. In all, 347 settlers—men, women, and children—died, their bodies left exposed and mutilated as a sign of contempt. A combined force of some 600 Powhatan and Pamunkey warriors, supported by members of other native groups, burned plantations and settlements along the James River as far inland as Henrico, destroying crops and livestock and thereby depriving survivors of much-needed food and other supplies. Famine and disease in the wake of the 1622 attacks made the ensuing twelve months, in the words of one historian, "the worst year the English had endured in Virginia," during which "at least a thousand settlers perished, leaving survivors fearful and traumatized."[35]

When Captain John Smith and some other Virginia Company critics blamed the colony's dire losses at least in part on human actions—specifically the company's mismanagement and lack of military preparedness—company spokesmen responded defensively, sponsoring the publication of a statement signed by sixteen men who had either lived in Virginia as planters or who, as mariners, had visited the colony. Charged with defending the company's record, these men flipped Smith's narrative and instead attributed the horrid conditions in Virginia to the "massacre," declaring that the settlers' problems would have been minimal "had itt not pleased God to suffer this Disaster to fall out by the Indians." Virginia Company apologists took this position again in 1625, after the company's charter had been revoked and Virginia had become a royal colony. Defenders of the "Old Company" asserted that their colony had been doing reasonably well until "it pleased God in his secret judgment to give leave to the enemies thereof, by many powerfull and most wicked meanes to bring it downe agayne to the ground." In their view, the first and most potent divinely ordained setback was the "blowdy massacre,

Devastation without Disaster

when by the Treacherous cruelty of the savages about 400 of our People were slayne," which caused such a "sodayne alteracon of the state of all things, [and] so dismaide the whole Colony, as they allmost gave themselves for gone."[36]

Those who discerned a divine message in Virginia's providential ruin declared that the massacre justified retaliation against the Indians to "make their Countrey wholly English," in the words of the Reverend Samuel Purchas. An Anglican clergyman and amateur geographer, Purchas had admired Pocahontas when he met her in London in 1616 and had hoped for good relations between her people and the English. Now, however, just six years later, Purchas concluded that the Indians' recent "butchery" proved them to be "more brutish than the beasts they hunt." Because their actions had revealed the Indians to be less than human, Purchas insisted that God would justify the English in avenging the "unnaturall, inhumane wrongs" they suffered because the Powhatans "bee not worthy of the name of a Nation, being wilde and Savage, . . . and Out-Lawes of Humanity."[37]

Like Purchas, Edward Waterhouse believed that the bloodshed of 1622 was an act of God that abrogated any previous obligation to convert the Indians and endowed the English with divine justification for conquering Virginia's native peoples and appropriating their land and other resources. Waterhouse saw both God's wrath and his mercy in the 1622 attacks. On the one hand, the Almighty clearly allowed the colonists to be "basely and barbarously murthered" by the Indians, who, "not being content with taking away life alone, . . . fell after againe upon the dead, making as well as they could, a fresh murder, defacing, dragging, and mangling the dead carkasses into many pieces, and carrying some parts away in derision, with base and bruitish triumph." On the other hand, Waterhouse believed that God also intervened to defeat the Indians before they were able to destroy the English settlements completely. "The slaughter would have been universall," he explained, had a Christian Indian not alerted some colonists in the Jamestown area to the dangers posed by the approaching warriors. "For even in the delivery of us that now survive," Waterhouse wrote, "no mans particular carefulnesse saved any one person, but the mere goodnesse of [God], freely and miraculously preserved whom it pleased him," leaving the survivors "set at liberty by the treacherous violence of the Savages" to make Virginia a prosperous, safe, expansive, and wholly English colony.[38]

With the possible exception of the wreck of the *Sea Venture*, the 1622 "massacre" received more publicity in England than any other news from Virginia since the founding of Jamestown in 1607. Besides the usual sermons and official correspondence, there were at least six representations of the episode that were accessible to wider public audiences. Based on eyewitness testimony, Waterhouse's *Declaration of the State of the Colony and Affaires in Virginia* was the most detailed account. Christopher Brooke, a lawyer and poet who, like Waterhouse, was connected to the Virginia Company, published a narrative titled *A Poem on the Late Massacre in Virginia*. There was also a massacre-themed play called *The Plantation of Virginia*, two ballads that circulated as cheaply produced broadsides, and an engraving that showed nearly naked Indian warriors ambushing the houses and dining tables of civilized English men, women, and children, whom they savagely slaughter using various sorts of swords, knives, and clubs. It is impossible to know the contents of the play and of the ballad titled "Mourning Virginia," neither of which are extant; the other ballad, "Good Newes from Virginia," written in 1623, celebrated the survival of the colony and its violent retaliation against the Indians in the wake of the attacks. Significantly, Waterhouse's pamphlet and Brooke's poem, like the engraving by Matthaeus Merian, were notable for highlighting the suffering of ordinary white Virginians.[39]

Most previous descriptions of the Virginia colony had focused on the place more than on the people, who appeared mostly as a faceless collective, with the notable exception of the colony's presidents and governors (or their most colorful or influential rivals). Even the *Sea Venture* saga, a dramatic and ultimately inspiring story of the trials and tribulations of brave and hardy Englishmen abroad, mostly lionized the expedition's leaders for their heroics on land and sea. By contrast, both Waterhouse and Brooke cast comparatively ordinary people — or at least those who were neither military men nor important colonial officials — as their most compelling characters. Although other named characters appeared in their accounts, the stories they told most vividly were those of Nathaniel Powell and George Thorpe.

According to his friend the poet Christopher Brooke, Nathaniel Powell arrived in Virginia in 1607 and worked hard to get ahead in the colony. Powell survived diseases and famines and, after years of striving, had attained both prosperity and a happy family life. The "most honest Powle" lived with his wife, who was "great with childe," at Powle-Brook, his plantation located on the south side of the James River. But he lost everything in one fell swoop when the Indians attacked in 1622. As Brooke put it,

> When all thy Joyes were full, dreadlesse of harmes,
> Then came these Hell-hounds in their ugly formes
> Which all thy Grounds, and Family o're spread,
> Thee, thy Wife, Servants, and all, strooke dead.

Devastation without Disaster

CAPVT NONVM.

De magna clade, quam Angli anno 1622.22.Martij in virginia acceperunt,

Beo tempore, quo Angli primùm in Virginiam venerũt, multas curas, moleſtias, labores & pericula exantlarunt. Nam Diabolus per ſua organa, nempe ſacerdotes, barbaros contra eos incitauit, ita, vt multos, quoties facultas fuit, obtruncarint. Tandem res eò deducta fuit, vt firma pax inter Anglos & barbaros ad aliquot annos contraheretur, & vtrinq; iureiurã-do ſanciretur. Rex quoq; Povvhatan promiſit, ſe regi Angliæ ſubiectum ac tri-butarium fore, pacemq; factam in æs incidi, & tabulam maximæ quercui ad ſuum palatium affigi curauit: quam pacem vtraq; pars magno cum gaudio amplexa eſt. Ad eam rem barbaros neceſſitas impulit, vt ſe Anglorum ope contra hoſtes tuerentur. Angli verò eò ſpe-ctabant, vt per hanc pacem res ſuas tanto melius in ea regione ſtabilirent. Hæc pax longo tempo-re inuiolata perſtitit, adeò vt Angli paſſim ſine gladiis & ſcloppetis incederent : & barbari eos crebrò inuiſere, cum iis cibum capere, ac familiariter conuerſari cæperunt. Viciſſim Angli in ſoli-tudines ad ipſos ſe contulerunt, & ſpem conceperunt, fore, vt barbari tanto citiùs ac facilius ad Chriſtianam fidem conuerterentur. Nam omnia inter ipſos tranquilla ac pacata erant.

Atq; vt pax hæc tantò firmiùs ſeruaretur, Angli Povvhatan, cum quo ipſis aliquid negotij erat, menſe Martio pacis memoriam refricarunt: quibus ille inter alia reſpondit, ſe pacem cũ ipſis optima fide culturum, futurumq;, vt cælum potius diſſoluatur, quàm illa rumpatur. Sed hæc me-ra fuit fraus, ſimulatio & hypocriſis. Nam barbari clam conſilium iniuerant, Anglos omnes truci-dandi. Biduo antequàm hoc facinus exequi decreuerat, quoſdam Anglos per periculoſas ſolitudi-nes, incolumes deduxerant, & eos, qui linguæ addiſcendæ cauſà aliquandiu apud ipſos comorati fuerant, amicè dimiſerant: præterea alios Anglos, qui cum ſuis nauibus appulerant, benignè exce-

Opechancanough's uprising. This copperplate engraving is the only known visual representation of the attack that took the lives of 347 colonists in 1622. Although most of the violence occurred on plantations along the James River, this fanciful image shows savages ruthlessly assailing innocent inhabitants of a European-style village. The work of Matthaeus Merian of Frankfort, the engraving appeared, as shown here, as an illustration in Theodor de Bry's multivolume description of the Americas.
General Collection, Beinecke Rare Book and Manuscript Library, Yale University.

Brooke reported that Nathaniel Powell was the first to die. The attackers, those "off-spring of Hells damned brood," vaunted their "victorious cruelty" by decapitating him and bringing his head as a "Trophee" to their chief.[40]

George Thorpe's story, as told by both Brooke and Waterhouse, was, if anything, even more shocking. Thorpe had arrived in Virginia in 1620. Universally esteemed as a "worthy religious Gentleman," he was especially notable for his unwavering commitment to bring Christianity to the Indians. Both authors emphasized Thorpe's kindness toward Virginia's native peoples. Waterhouse claimed that Thorpe never denied the Indians "any thing that they asked him," noting that he even killed some dogs owned by English settlers when they "complained unto him of the fiercenesse of our [mastiffs], most implacable and terrible unto them." Cultivating the Indians' goodwill, Thorpe gave them presents and built their king a "fayre house according to the English fashion." Yet, as Waterhouse reported pointedly, "all was little regarded after by this Viperous brood . . . for they not only wilfully murdered him, but cruelly and fully, out of devillish malice, did so many barbarous despights and foule scornes after to his dead corpes, as are unbefitting to be heard by any civill eare." Thorpe's story was worth knowing both because his death was brutal and undeserved and also because he died a "glorious martyr" to the Protestant English cause.[41]

The industrious man who made good (Powell) and the virtuous man who put others first (Thorpe) would eventually become important stock figures in an expanding literature of disaster narratives that aimed to generate sympathy and sadness, but in the aftermath of the 1622 Powhatan insurgency, Waterhouse and Brooke used their grisly stories to evoke outrage more than sympathy, to demonstrate that vengeance against the Indians was justified and divinely ordained, and to reassure English readers (and prospective settlers and investors) that the colony would be saved. In describing his own emotions on hearing of what he called the "disaster" in Virginia, the poet Brooke modeled the appropriate emotional response for his intended readers. "Amazement strooke me, horror ceaz'd my powres," he wrote. "Tearelesse as Tonguelesse; and for certaine howres I seemed a breathing Statue." Brooke excoriated the Indians, mourned and eulogized his lost friends, and interrogated God about his role in replacing "Uniformity and Order" with "Chaos" in the colony:

> Thou didst let in that Heart of Hells black brood,
> Wolves, Tygars, Tyrants, that have suckt the blood
> Of Christian Soules; hundreds in ruthful slaughter,

Devastation without Disaster

Those Divelish hands have layd upon thine Altar,
Made tunelesse jarrs in musique of their peace,
Fir'd, ransakt, spoyl'd, destroyed their increase.[42]

Both Brooke and Waterhouse concluded that the English should trust in God, ruthlessly extirpate the savages, and expand the Virginia colony. As Waterhouse put it, "every good Patriot" should "consider how deeply the prosecution of this noble Enterprise concerneth the honor of His *Majestie* and the whole Nation, the propagation of the Christian Religion, the enlargement, strength, and safety of His Majestie's Dominions.... Some may helpe with their purses, some with their persons, some with their favour, some with their counsell.... [L]et Ministers in their public and private prayers commend these Plantations to the blessing of Almighty God."[43]

§ The full title of Christopher Brooke's account of the Powhatan attacks was *A Poem on the Late Massacre in Virginia, With particular mention of those men of note that suffered in that disaster*. Although Brooke and some others spread the news of the horrific event by telling stories of individual suffering, even using the word "disaster" to describe what had transpired in the colony, their approach was still in other respects premodern.[44] By interpreting the violence of 1622, like other calamities, within a providential framework, Brooke and his associates elided human agency as the cause of suffering, except to the extent that they blamed the Indians (whom they deemed satanically subhuman and whose brutality they recognized as a pronouncement from Almighty God). Viewing famines and disease, hurricanes and violence, as signs from the deity, in turn, meant that such episodes evoked horror or wonder but not the more human-centered emotions that would animate later responses to calamity. Ideas about the causes of and appropriate responses to catastrophic situations would change incrementally in the coming decades as trade, travel, and print brought more people more knowledge of death and devastation beyond their own communities.

{ 2 }

NARRATING

DISASTER

In 1584, the Elizabethan writer and playwright Robert Greene became the first known English author to use the term "disaster" to describe a specific event or episode. He did so in *Gwydonius; The Carde of Fancie*, a fictional romance that chronicles the adventures of the son of a duke who leaves home to travel the world after a dispute with his tyrannical father. The young nobleman journeys long distances, mostly by sea, having various adventures along the way. In his text, Greene used the word "disaster" in reference to a hypothetical shipwreck that never happens, but his choice was nonetheless prescient.[1] Over the course of the next century, shipwrecks became the archetype for an emerging culture of disaster in the Atlantic world.

In an age of exploration, trade, and colonization, shipwrecks were for many both familiar and compelling episodes, and with the expansion of print culture, shipwreck stories became a pervasive and popular literary genre. Clergy drew lessons from shipwreck stories in oral and published sermons, as well as in their other writings, to reveal the power and mercy of God. Newspapers reported shipwrecks from across the globe as commercial or military losses and as matters of general interest to their readers, many of whom resided in shipping and trading communities. Published in newspapers and in other formats, first-person shipwreck narratives informed and entertained and sometimes aimed to elicit emotional responses from their readers. Because shipwrecks subjected people to unusual and challenging circumstances — often with transformative results — they were also a favored topic in fiction and poetry. Daniel Defoe's *Robinson Crusoe* (1719), arguably the earliest English novel of immense and enduring popularity, was a shipwreck story. William Falconer's lyrical saga *The Shipwreck: A Poem, In Three*

Cantos (1762), was published in at least twenty-seven separate editions by 1800 and remained popular throughout the nineteenth century.[2]

Focusing primarily on shipwrecks, this chapter charts the evolution of disaster stories through the middle decades of the eighteenth century. Although scholars have studied shipwreck narratives as artifacts of national identity, religious belief, attitudes toward gender and race, and imperial ambitions, the main concern here is the role of shipwreck stories in the construction of a rudimentary culture of disaster that did not exist at the dawn of the seventeenth century.[3] A century or more after the founding of Jamestown, the frequency of shipwrecks and the spread of information about them, coupled with an emerging culture of sensibility, made their victims subjects of sympathy and occasionally recipients of relief, while Enlightenment-inspired ideas about reason and human progress encouraged tentative efforts to prevent or limit maritime losses of property and lives. Although some authors and their readers continued to view shipwrecks and other calamities first and foremost as divine portents, others read them mainly as compelling stories of human perseverance, tragedy, and triumph.

§ In the seventeenth and eighteenth centuries, shipwrecks were remarkably common. Each week, newspapers regularly reported as many as fifteen to twenty wrecks; published lists of lost ships sometimes overflowed into multiple columns during hurricane season. Seafaring vessels were vulnerable to storms and also to collisions with submerged rocks and other hazards in shallow coastal waters. Scholars estimate that during this period roughly 5 percent of all ships were either wrecked or lost at sea. In terms of property losses, the costs were sufficiently high to make diving and salvaging a profitable and increasingly sophisticated industry. The using of diving bells for underwater salvage operations, first undertaken in 1531, became widespread in Europe by the second half of the seventeenth century. English divers were employed in reclaiming sunken cargoes in the hurricane-prone West Indies by the 1720s.[4]

Lost lives were unrecoverable, of course, and death tolls could be high. One concerned Englishman estimated that as many as 4,200 Britons perished each year at sea, a figure that did not include the many foreign sailors employed on British ships or those who manned the substantial merchant and fishing fleets that were based in colonial ports. The fishing community of Gloucester, Massachusetts, alone lost roughly 150 ships and many seafaring men during the eighteenth century. As one Englishman who had survived three wrecks or near-wrecks in the course of a single voyage from Bermuda to London observed ominously, "The Dangers at Sea are certainly more imminent than those on shore; even in the fairest Weather, the Space is very small between this World and the next."[5]

In Britain and its colonies, people cared about shipwrecks at least in part because the sea and waterborne transportation were often central to their lives and livelihoods. The inhabitants of Great Britain were a maritime people whose naval and mercantile exploits were important components of an emerging national identity. Residents of British colonial America, if anything, had an even closer relationship with the sea. Between 1700 and 1775 alone, hundreds of thousands of Europeans made the transatlantic journey to settle in the thirteen mainland colonies (as did nearly 300,000 enslaved Africans). Many of those who survived the onerous crossing must have shared their sometimes-harrowing shipboard stories with American-born children and grandchildren, many of whom themselves lived either on or near the seacoast or other waterways. Settled colonists depended on waterborne commerce to market what they produced and to purchase what they did not. In New England especially, many made their livings from shipbuilding, seafaring, fishing, or other maritime-related activities. For such people, shipwrecks were an ordinary, if unfortunate, part of life. Indeed, because most Atlantic shipwrecks occurred within sight of land, at the beginning or end of a voyage, many colonists would have witnessed one, even if they had never been to sea themselves.[6]

Seafaring peoples have told shipwreck tales since ancient times—Homer's *Odyssey* is in part a shipwreck story—but beginning in the sixteenth century, narratives devoted specifically to maritime disasters became a distinctive literary form, a subset of the burgeoning genre of travel writing that chronicled European adventures in an age of exploration and colonization. The Portuguese, encouraged by the ambitious Prince Henry the Navigator and his successors, pioneered European exploration, trade, and colonization on three continents, and they also invented the shipwreck narrative as a literary genre. Portuguese authors, most of whom were survivors of shipwrecks, produced at least eighteen narratives between 1550 and 1650. These were gripping stories, full of horrifying details about proud vessels violently fractured by wind and waves and castaways marooned in exotic and dangerous locales. These narratives also revealed the dire costs of Portugal's imperial ambitions, suggesting—in the words of one scholar—"that empire contains disaster at its core, that it is built on the seeds of its own undoing." As Portugal declined as an imperial and commercial power after 1660, these shipwreck stories remained popular and, in fact, were collected and republished in Lisbon in the 1730s in an important two-volume anthology, which presented the narratives together as stories of tragic heroism and envisaged shipwrecks as metaphors for ill-fated ambition and for the fragility of temporal life.[7]

As other Europeans entered the race for colonization and conquest, they, too, began to produce shipwreck stories for popular consumption. Richard Hakluyt — clergyman, amateur geographer, and vocal supporter of English colonization in North America — included accounts of several shipwrecks in his magisterial *Principal Navigations, Voyages, Traffiques and Discoveries of the English Nation* (1589–1600), though his main objective in that work was to celebrate the successful voyages of English seafarers to inspire a new generation of explorers, traders, and colonizers. Sylvester Jourdain's *A Discovery of the Bermudas, otherwise called the Ile of Devils*, which recounted the saga of the *Sea Venture*, was the first English shipwreck narrative to be printed as a stand-alone volume. Its author survived the wreck of the *Sea Venture* and returned to London, where he published his narrative in 1610. Unlike William Strachey, whose account of the same expedition included a detailed description of the horrific conditions in the English settlement at Jamestown, Jourdain focused his narrative on the shipwreck and the survivors' lives as castaways in an alien island paradise. Jourdain's short book, which stimulated English interest in colonizing Bermuda, was published nearly immediately after it was written, though the Virginia Company managed to delay publication of Strachey's far more damning version of the *Sea Venture* story until 1625.[8]

Overall, the earliest English shipwreck narratives were more thoroughly God-centered than their Portuguese counterparts. Strachey was a poet and Jourdain was a merchant, but the vast majority of seventeenth-century English shipwreck stories were penned or at least popularized by clergy, particularly those of a strong Calvinist Protestant bent. Like the Portuguese writers who credited God (or the Blessed Virgin) with their deliverance from danger on the high seas, both Jourdain and Strachey looked to divine providence as the source of their own rescue, but they wrote mostly to entertain their readers and, by publicizing the exploits of Englishmen at sea and in the New World, also to inspire national pride and to counter the notion — made more plausible by the recurring troubles at Jamestown — that God did not support English colonization efforts.[9] By contrast, clergy who preached and wrote about shipwrecks deployed their stories mainly as powerful evidence of divine omnipotence in a single-minded effort to move their audiences to repent of their sins and to open their hearts and souls to God.

The two most prolific and widely read chroniclers of shipwrecks in the seventeenth-century English-speaking world were James Janeway, a nonconformist London clergyman, and Increase Mather of Boston, the most influential minister in New England and probably in all of English America. Both men were members of the Calvinist subset of a larger transatlantic English Protestant community. Before he died in 1674, Janeway published six books or pamphlets, most of which appeared in multiple London editions, but one of his most influential works was his posthumously published *Mr. James Janeway's Legacy to his Friends, Containing Twenty Seven Famous Instances of Gods Providence in and about Sea Dangers and Deliverances* (1674). New England colonists, who imported many of their books from London, read *Mr. James Janeway's Legacy*, which Mather acknowledged as a key source for his own *Essay for the Recording of Illustrious Providences* (1684). Thomas Parkhurst, the Calvinist bookseller who distributed most of Janeway's works in London and its environs, also sold the second edition of Mather's book. In 1700, Cotton Mather, Increase's equally influential son, adapted Janeway's popular children's devotional book, *A Token for Children*, for a New England audience, though Janeway's original version was also published in Boston that year, with subsequent North American editions printed in Boston, Philadelphia, and Burlington, New Jersey, during the colonial era.[10]

Mr. James Janeway's Legacy, an anthology of "remarkable sea deliverances," went through four editions between 1674 and 1683 and was then reissued with few changes under the title *A Token for Mariners* in 1698 and 1708.[11] Janeway presented his readers with twenty-seven stories, most of which involved ships carrying crews and sometimes passengers from England or New England who ultimately survived storms, starvation, captivity, violence, or other crises. Janeway had gathered these stories, according to his editor, John Ryther, to help sinners "in getting Acquaintance with God" so they might be saved and to remind the pious that the Almighty is their "Best Friend in the Worst of Times." Ryther believed that these narratives evinced "the Power of Prayer, the Wonder-working Power of God, . . . and [the] tender Mercies of God, to poor Perishing, Sinking, Drowning, Starving, dying Men." Just in case his readers somehow missed the stories' seemingly incontrovertible message, Janeway added a sermon at the end of his book to drive the point home. His biblical text was Acts 27–30, the story of the apostle Paul's shipwreck and providential deliverance, from which Janeway drew lessons that considered the dangers of the sea both as lived experience and as a metaphor for daily life. At sea, as in life, people are alone and only God can save them, he warned his readers. "Your Dangers are Wonderful in this Re-

Mr. **James Janeway**'s

LEGACY

TO HIS

FRIENDS,

Containing Twenty Seven Famous Inſtances of Gods Providences in and about **Sea Dangers** and **Deliverances**, with the Names of Several that were Eye-witneſſes to many of them.

Whereunto is Added a Sermon on the ſame Subject.

Go up now, look towards the Sea ; and he went up and looked, and ſaid, there is nothing ; and he ſaid, Go up ſeven times : And at the ſeventh time he ſaid, behold, there ariſeth a little Cloud, &c. 1 King. 18. 44.

Come and Hear all ye that fear God, and I will declare what he hath done for my ſoul, Pſal. 66. 16.

London, Printed for *Dorman Newman*, at the *Kings Armes* in the *Poultry*, 1674.

Mr. James Janeway's Legacy. The shipwreck stories in this popular compilation, first published in 1674, told of terror-stricken people facing certain death on the high seas, only to be saved by the providential intervention of a merciful God. Janeway provided readers with the "Names of Several that were Eye-witnesses" to prove the veracity of these tales of suffering and ultimate redemption. Two Bible verses on the book's title page emphasize God's control over temporal affairs and his power to save souls. © *The British Library Board.*

spect, they are not Dangers in which your Bodies are concerned only. . . . It is not only the danger of a Ship-wrack'd Vessel, and a Shipwrack'd Estate, and a Shipwrack'd Body, but a Shipwrack'd Soul."[12]

A representative example of the pious shipwreck narrative is the tale of Major Gibbons, the opening story in Janeway's volume, which also appeared in Increase Mather's collection and later in *Magnalia Christi Americana* (1702), Cotton Mather's history of New England. Gibbons was a New Englander whose merchant ship was driven off course by "hard weather, and contrary winds," leaving the vessel and its crew lost and "much distressed." When the men's provisions ran out, they "look[ed] one up one another, as men already under a Sentence of death." Near starvation, they eventually drew lots to determine who would "dye first, to be a Sacrifice for ravenous Hunger to feed upon." Before they took the grisly and fateful step of killing the "poor Innocent," however, Gibbons led the sufferers in anguished prayer. While they prayed, a "mighty Fish" leaped into the boat, which they regarded as a "happy Omen of their deliverance, and a pledg of approaching mercy" from God. Their ordeal dragged on, however, and at length the starving castaways again drew lots to see who would be killed to feed the rest. Once again, before they "put the Knife to the throat of the Sacrifice," Gibbons led them in prayer. This time, a "great Bird" landed on the ship, within reach of one of the crew, who viewed this new source of sustenance as "a second Answer from above." Still the men remained adrift, and they began to lose hope as they drew lots for the third time. Again, they prayed, but this time no edible beast appeared, and they despaired. Then they saw a ship in the distance, but their joy turned to fear when they realized that the vessel belonged to French pirates.[13]

The story of Gibbons and his crew nevertheless ended happily and inspirationally because their fate depended not, in fact, on the kindness of the pirates but on the mercy of Almighty God. Against all earthly odds — after all, the Catholic French were enemies of the English, and pirates were known to be ruthless — Major Gibbons and his men were not harmed by the pirates, whose commander had met the New Englander years earlier in Boston, where Gibbons had shown him a "signal Kindness" that the Frenchman believed had saved his life. Janeway made it clear that God, not the pirates, had saved the castaways. "Thus the Lord appeared [as] God," he concluded, "hearing Prayers in Extremitys, which appearances are not to be forgotten in succeeding Generations." The men's long and painful ordeal, too, was part of God's plan, Janeway argued, because their extreme suffering led them to prayer and to appreciate more fully both the power and mercy of the Almighty. Janeway told the story of the suffering Gibbons and his crew, along with the others in his collection, not to generate sympathy for the castaways but rather to elicit emotions that could lead his readers to reverence for and submission to Almighty God.[14]

Like Janeway, Increase Mather wrote to impel his readers to worship an omnipotent and merciful God, but his stories, unlike Janeway's, had a message specific to Massachusetts Puritans and their descendants. In fact, Mather envisioned his collection of "Remarkable Providences" as the first installment of a potentially limitless project. He urged future generations and "our Brethren, the Elders of the Neighboring Colonies" in New England, to continue to collect and publish providential stories to stimulate piety and appreciation for the special protection that God afforded to his faithful. While ten of Janeway's twenty-seven shipwreck stories involved New Englanders, Mather drew all his narratives from the region's history to reaffirm his readers' identity as an exceptional and chosen people who providentially survived repeated ordeals on land and sea so that they might fulfill their divine errand of establishing and nurturing godly colonial communities.[15]

Perhaps in recognition of the centrality of maritime life in New England's economy and culture, Mather's first of twelve chapters covered "Remarkable Sea Deliverances," most of which he took from Janeway. Mather began with the story of Anthony Thacher and his family, which had not appeared in Janeway's collection but which had circulated in New England (by oral tradition and also in a letter that Thacher had written to his brother) for nearly half a century. In August 1635, a ship carrying Thacher, along with his wife, children, and other relations — twenty-three souls in all — sailed from England to Massachusetts. As they neared their destination, the ship encountered "so mighty a storm, as the like was never known in New England since the English came, nor in the memory of any of the Indians." Those aboard the ship prayed mightily as the vessel thrashed against the rocks near the shores of Cape Ann, but only Thacher and his wife survived. In his sorrowful account, Thacher bemoaned his inability to save his own children — "Oh, I yet see their cheeks, poor silent lambs, pleading pity and help at my hands," he wrote — despite "God's goodness" in saving him and his wife, who found food and shelter on a "desolate island" where they awaited rescue. Mather presented the Thachers as a latter-day Adam and Eve "stripped of all they have known yet equipped with a promise as they walk forth to establish a new phase of human history" in Massachusetts for the greater glory of God. He stated the essential point of their story succinctly at the head

Increase Mather.
A prominent Puritan
minister, Mather was a
prolific author whose
*Essay for the Recording
of Illustrious Providences*
(1684) included
accounts of New
Englanders suffering,
but then surviving,
lightning strikes,
hurricanes, shipwrecks,
and other calamities.
Although he sought
to understand the
physical explanations
for such phenomena,
Mather was certain
that Almighty God was
the first cause both
of these unfortunate
events and of humans'
ability to survive them.
*Library of Congress Prints
and Photographs Division.*

of his chapter: man and wife had been "marvelously preserved alive," saved by God.[16]

Mather's collection also included chapters that told of prayerful people surviving hurricanes, tornadoes, floods, and earthquakes, all of which he considered wondrous works of God, though he appreciated and sometimes tried to explain their physical causes. This Harvard-educated clergyman, who had written a book on comets, was interested in science and nature. Like most of his contemporaries, however, Mather believed that physical explanations for celestial phenomena, storms, and earthquakes were secondary causes that God set in motion to achieve his providential goals. Earlier and later generations of New England's learned elite shared this view. In 1635, William Bradford, the governor of Plymouth Colony, had pondered the hurricane that caused the wreck of several ships, including Anthony Thacher's, with a mixture of piety and empiricism, positing a relationship between the great storm and a lunar eclipse that occurred shortly thereafter. Two generations later, Cotton Mather—Harvard graduate, fellow of the prestigious Royal Society of London, and one of the first New Englanders to take the controversial position of supporting inoculation to thwart the spread of

Narrating Disaster

smallpox—was also interested in the physical causes of that famous hurricane, which he nonetheless viewed first and foremost as evidence of the inscrutability of divine providence. "The judgments of God are a great deep," he observed wistfully, reflecting on the sad fate of Thacher's shipmates, who included a godly clergyman who had journeyed to Massachusetts to minister to the faithful.[17]

These pious purveyors of early shipwreck stories wrote not to generate sympathy for those who suffered the perils of the seas but rather to engender fear of God's wrath and reverence for his mercy and power. They understood shipwrecks not as disasters that could be prevented or ameliorated but rather as providential judgments or messages from God, who orchestrated these harrowing episodes to proffer sinners opportunities for personal reflection and reformation. Mather and Janeway wanted readers to respond to their stories with prayer and introspection, so that they might tend to their souls and nurture their relationships with God. The appropriate response to shipwrecks and other "Heart-affecting Spectacles," according to Cotton Mather, was for "every Man, and especially every Unregenerate Man, [to] Look Inward upon the state of his own SOUL."[18]

When readers of pious shipwreck stories drew lessons that had applications beyond themselves, Mather and other like-minded authors directed their outward gaze neither toward humanity in general nor to individuals or families who lost loved ones in the wrecks—both perspectives that came to characterize subsequent approaches to shipwrecks and other calamities. Instead, they emphasized connections among English Protestants (or New Englanders) as a chosen people, members of a community who were bound to each other chiefly through their shared duty to God. Just as Increase Mather fashioned the Thacher family tragedy into a parable about New England's divine mission, pastor Deodat Lawson, from the town of Scituate, Massachusetts, interpreted the wreck of the *Threnodia* in December 1693—which resulted in the deaths of all five people aboard the ship—as a providential act, which, because the virtuous Captain Anthony Collamore was among the dead, inflicted "a Publick loss" on both church and town. As Lawson put it,

> But GOD hath by his Sov'raign Providence,
> Of such an Usefull Man this place bereft,
> A deep Affecting and Afflicting sense,
> Is well becoming each one that is left.
> We all in his remove a loss sustain,
> Which sure GOD onely can make up again.

Lawson called on his congregation to humbly accept God's judgment, even as they mourned the loss of a virtuous man who was valued by their church and their community. Indeed, he insisted that Collamore's death was itself a message to the people of Scituate. "God tryes by Others DEATH us to Provoke," he declared, to repent and to accept the will of God.[19]

Similarly, when Cotton Mather recounted the story of another shipwreck whose survivors nearly starved to death before resorting to cannibalism, he urged the members of his congregation to first "Look Inward" to tend to their souls but then encouraged them to look outward to see "what prevailing Iniquities threaten the Ruine" of "Our Land," despite their sacred duty to create a "Land of Uprightness" and godliness. Mather recounted the ordeal of the infamous *Nottingham Galley*, an English merchant ship that wrecked at Boon Island, off the coast of Maine, in December 1710, whose crew eventually consumed a dead shipmate to avert starvation. "What an *Affecting* Story!" he exclaimed, "And capable of being improved unto many Purposes of Piety!" Mather told the stories of the *Nottingham Galley* and of some other "miserable spectacles" to engage his readers' emotions, but the main feelings he hoped to evoke were inwardly directed anger, horror, and fear. As he put it, "If there be Sin joined with Misery in the Spectacle, there must be *Anger*. . . . The *sight of sin in Others*, must *affect* us with a *Fear of our Selves*."[20]

By the time Mather drew these lessons from the wreck of the *Nottingham Galley*, other English and colonial writers were situating shipwreck stories in alternative contexts. These other shipwreck stories appeared both as standalone narratives and as newspaper articles. Their authors were not members of the clergy but rather ship captains, shipwreck survivors, or others who shared their stories for a variety of reasons. Some detailed commercial losses, while others lauded seafaring men for saving vessels and their passengers in times of crisis. Some of these narratives also reflected and exemplified one of the most significant developments in eighteenth-century print culture: the rise of sensibility, or the belief that heartfelt emotions were both emblems of gentility or politeness and sources of benevolence and morality. These newer approaches did not necessarily remove God from the story, though the deity of the culture of sensibility was more benevolent than wrathful. While some non-clergy authors of shipwreck stories attributed their protagonists' rescue to God's merciful providence, these writers also praised the efforts of brave and skillful mariners, leaving readers to draw their own conclusions about the true causes of their seemingly miraculous survival.[21]

One of the earliest book-length English-language shipwreck narratives was the purposefully, though misleadingly, titled *God's Protecting Providence Man's Surest Help and Defence in Times of Greatest Difficulty and Most Imminent Danger*. Published in Philadelphia in 1699 and reprinted in London the following year, this narrative shows how one author—in collaboration with a series of editors and printers—juggled sentiment, piety, and high adventure to create a popular story that could be read, enjoyed, and interpreted on multiple levels. Its author was Jonathan Dickinson, a Quaker merchant who left Port Royal, Jamaica, in August 1696 aboard the ship *Reformation*, bound for Philadelphia with his wife and infant son. The Dickinsons' fellow passengers included the ship's captain, eight other mariners, and eleven slaves, four of whom belonged to Dickinson himself; also aboard was a pious Quaker named Robert Barrow, the sole passenger who ultimately did not survive the wreck and its aftermath, dying shortly before the group finally arrived in Philadelphia in April 1697.

Dickinson was a committed Quaker who admired Barrow for his godliness and his steadfast encouragement to his shipmates to trust in God "to work for our Deliverance," but Dickinson's story, as he wrote it, focused mainly on the group's harrowing experiences among the Indians they met when their ship wrecked in a hurricane, leaving them marooned on the eastern coast of Florida. Dickinson described the local Indians as a people whose "Countenance was very Furious and bloody," leading him and his companions to believe that they were "amongst a Barbarous people, such as were generally accounted *Man-Eaters*." Dickinson punctuated this familiar story of Christians forsaken among savages with particular episodes guaranteed to tug at the heartstrings of his readers. He told of his wife being beaten by barbarous natives who were on the verge of cutting her throat when the wife of their chief took pity and intervened to save her. On the same occasion, Dickinson's six-month-old son nearly suffocated because the Indians stuffed his mouth with sand. Readers must have reacted viscerally to Dickinson's account of their living quarters, which he described as "extream nasty" with an "abundance of many sorts of creeping things, as a large black hairy *Spider*, which hath two Claws like a *Crabb* [and] *Scorpions*." They must have shared his revulsion at the thought of an Indian woman suckling his child and his terror at the prospect that his own death would result in his innocent infant being "bred up as one of those people" in such an alien, barbarous, filthy, and decidedly un-English world.[22]

Yet with or without Dickinson's complicity, the small book that was published in Philadelphia in 1699 repackaged his narrative as a potent parable about the power and mercy of God. For one thing, the title was entirely fo-

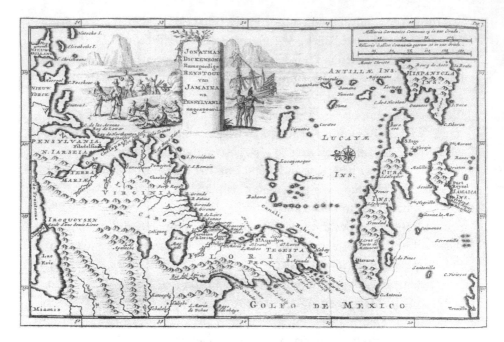

Jonathan Dickinson's journey. A thin line on this map, included in a Dutch translation of Dickinson's narrative, shows the route he and his shipmates traveled from Jamaica (far right) to Philadelphia (situated here southeast of "Nieuw Yorck"). Shipwrecked on the eastern coast of Florida, Dickinson's party eventually made their way to South Carolina (shown here as due west) and then sailed to north Philadelphia. The image surrounding the map's cartouche depicts the castaways trying to tend to their needs with near-naked natives looking on. *Courtesy of the John Carter Brown Library at Brown University.*

cused on the putative religious lesson of the story: *God's Protecting Providence Man's Surest Help and Defence in the Times of the Greatest Difficulty and Most Imminent Danger*; the more sensational "cruelly devouring jawes of the inhumane canibals of Florida," who had figured so prominently in Dickinson's story, appeared only at the end of a thirty-four-word subtitle. Moreover, someone other than Dickinson—possibly Samuel Carpenter, a leader of Philadelphia's Quaker Meeting—added a preface that dramatically differed from Dickinson's account in both tone and content. This anonymous commentator directed readers to see Dickinson's narrative specifically as a story of divine deliverance. He also pointedly emphasized that "the dangers [the castaways] were delivered from arose not only from men, but the *Elements* also God permitted to threaten them, and afflict them."[23]

Dickinson's narrative was published in fifteen separate English editions—the last of which appeared in 1868—as well as in several Dutch

Narrating Disaster

and German translations. From 1700 on, the cover page highlighted "the Remarkable Deliverance of Robert Barrow" as a central part of the story, though Barrow, the saintly Quaker, became ill and died before he and his shipmates arrived in Philadelphia, after receiving help from the Spanish governor of Florida and his English counterpart in South Carolina. One later edition changed the book's title to *The Remarkable Deliverance of Robert Barrow*; conversely, another, titled the *Narrative of a Shipwreck in the Gulph of Florida, shewing, God's Providence*, banished Barrow from the title page entirely. Some later editions omitted most of the pious preface. In sum, Dickinson's story was recast in various ways over the course of many decades. Readers could react to the story with sympathy for Dickinson's wife and child, revulsion for the Indians and their ways, admiration for Barrow, or gratitude toward (and perhaps fear of) God — or with any combination of some or all of these responses.[24]

During the eighteenth century, shipwreck narratives grew in popularity as a secular literary genre. At least twenty-two stand-alone English-language shipwreck narratives were published between 1699 and 1774, many of which were printed in multiple editions in Britain and in its colonies in America.[25] Exciting stories set in exotic locales, these narratives combined elements of two of the era's signature literary forms: travel writing and novels. Like travel writing, shipwreck narratives typically portrayed wholesome English protagonists as superior to the Indians, pirates, and others they encountered on land and sea and gave homebound readers information — however culturally skewed — about the wider world. The Library Company of Philadelphia, America's first subscription library, included at least three shipwreck narratives in its collections, catalogued under "Voyages and Travels." At the same time, like novels, shipwreck narratives featured stories that stirred readers' emotions, as Dickinson's clearly shows. Two decades later, Daniel Defoe's enormously popular *Robinson Crusoe* told the story of an Englishman who spent twenty-eight years on an island, reading his Bible and devising ingenious ways to survive and thrive, despite intermittent threats from mutineers, cannibals, and other native peoples (one of whom he makes his servant and converts to Christianity). Much like the protagonists of many shipwreck narratives, Crusoe was a resourceful Englishman who survived in a treacherous alien environment through his own efforts and with the help of divine providence. Indeed, many of Defoe's readers believed that Crusoe's epic was a true story, reading the novel as an adventure, a performance of English superiority, and vindication of the power and mercy of Almighty God.[26]

Appreciation for divine benevolence and celebrations of Christian virtue continued to shape many shipwreck narratives, as they did novels and travel writing, even as authors in all three genres deployed their literary skills to evoke emotion and sensibility. Of course, there were exceptions: perhaps in reaction to the ascendancy of sensibility, which could seem to elevate human feeling at the expense of religious devotion, the author of at least one popular narrative explicitly addressed the "Christian Reader . . . not with a View or Design to move any One's Pity or Compassion towards the Unfortunate and Distress'd" but rather to make him or her more devoutly worshipful toward the Almighty. Yet even that pious seafarer's rigorously providential account of the wreck of the New York–based *Alida and Catharine* in 1749 included an affecting portrait of the ship's "People," who were "mostly naked, without either Shoe or Stocking," and who endured seven days in "a perishing Condition" before they were saved by the mercy of God.[27]

First published in 1756, *An Authentic Narrative of the Loss of the Doddington Indiaman* is a good example of a popular shipwreck narrative that privileged the sentimental over the providential. This English vessel began its voyage to India in London, stopping first in the Cape Verde islands. Departing from the island of St. Jago on 27 May 1755, the *Doddington Indiaman* and its 270 passengers next went ashore at Cape Agulhas (on the southwestern coast of Africa) before resuming their trip on 6 July. Ten days later, however, on a "dark and stormy Night," the ship wrecked when it struck what its captain described as an "unknown rock." Only 23 people survived the wreck. They passed the next seven months marooned on an island where the ship's carpenter built a boat that would take them to Delagoa (now Maputa, in present-day Mozambique), where they met a ship captain who was willing to take them to Madagascar, from whence they sailed for India, finally arriving in Madras on 1 August 1756. Penned by William Webb, the ship's third mate, *An Authentic Narrative of the Loss of the Doddington Indiaman* was published in five separate London editions between 1756 and 1767, besides appearing in two installments in the *Gentleman's Magazine*; it was also published in New York in 1762 and included in at least two contemporary anthologies.[28]

Webb's account of the *Doddington Indiaman* included vivid descriptions of the ship's destruction, as well as of the hardships survivors suffered on an island where they were often "sunk in a foot of fowl's dung" and where wind consistently "blew away their fire." He detailed the castaways' efforts to find materials and tools that they could use to feed themselves and build their boat. He also wrote of their subsistence on fish and waterfowl, their ultimately unsuccessful efforts to manufacture salt out of copper to preserve their provisions — which proved not only poisonous but also "intolerably offensive to the taste"—and their squabbles to determine the rightful ownership of valuables that Webb and his companions had saved from the sinking ship. Religious belief played only a small and subtle role in his story. Webb briefly credited divine "providence" for affording survivors provisions sufficient to save them from starvation and for their eventual safe arrival in Madras. When he and his remaining shipmates named the boat they built to escape the island the *Happy Deliverance*, they employed what could be interpreted as providential language. Alongside his absorbing descriptions and low-key providentialism, however, Webb also engaged readers' sentimental notions about love, marriage, gender, and especially the idealized man of feeling—one who keenly feels emotions and is more virtuous and benevolent as a result—who was a staple character in the culture of sensibility.[29]

As was common in shipwrecks of the period, survivors of the wreck of the *Doddington Indiaman* included no women, but the body of Mrs. Collet, whom Webb described as a "Gentle woman" and the beloved wife of the ship's second mate, washed ashore on the island, where three men of feeling—the first and third mates and the ship's carpenter—did their best to honor the deceased and to ease the grief of their comrade, who previously had shown "remarkably tender" affection for his wife. In Webb's telling, First Mate Evan Jones "stepped aside to Mr. Collet, and found means to take him to the other side of the rock" while the others dug a grave and conducted a proper burial service for the dead woman. The men kept Collet from seeing the grave, which they believed "would most sensibly, if not fatally, have affected him." Several days later, however, the men gently revealed the truth, giving Collet the wedding ring they had taken from the finger of his beloved. "He received it with great emotion," Webb reported, "and afterwards spent many days in raising a monument over the grave . . . on top of which he fixed an elm plank, and inscribed it with her name, her age, the time of death, and some account of the fatal accident by which it was occasioned."[30]

Although he did not invent the death and burial of the unfortunate Mrs. Collet, Webb likely embellished the story to enhance its emotional impact and hence its appeal to readers who held that evoking feeling—which, in turn, was thought to inspire morality and benevolence—was a signal purpose of literature and the arts. In his own account of the shipwreck and its aftermath, which appeared in both English and colonial newspapers, First Mate Evan Jones also reported the sad fate of Mrs. Collet, but he offered a strikingly different and less sentimental version of the circumstances of her death and subsequent interment on the island. "Mr. Collet lost his Wife in the Ship; after she struck [the rock] he went down and bro't her upon Deck in his Arms, but the Ship falling down at that Time on her Broadside, and the Decks falling in, he was separated from her and never saw her afterwards," he wrote, "until some Days after they were on the Island, when [the ship's first mate] Mr. Jones and he saw her Body; but Mr. Collet did not know her Body, but Mr. Jones did, and had it buried without his Knowledge."[31]

Jones's more concise account of the *Doddington Indiaman* was widely circulated in both British and colonial newspapers, which often reported shipwrecks and other calamities. His approach—to eschew both sentiment and providentialism in favor of a succinct description of where the *Doddington Indiaman* traveled, how the storm and subsequent collision affected the ship, and how the survivors went about finding provisions and building a "large Boat, which they rigged like a Sloop" in order to leave the island—was one of several employed in journalistic accounts of shipwrecks by the 1750s. Newspapers, whose primary readership was in the port towns where they were published, initially reported shipwrecks as commercial stories because of the great financial costs of the destruction of ships and the loss of their cargoes. As they catered to an increasingly literate populace with a growing appetite for polite culture, however, newspapers also sometimes presented the stories of shipwrecks (and of other calamities) as narratives of human tragedy, reflecting the influence of the culture of sensibility. Because all three approaches—quantitative, technical, and affective—coexisted in these shipwreck stories, these narratives are significant antecedents of the modern culture of disaster.[32]

By the middle of the eighteenth century, newspapers were readily available throughout the British Atlantic world. The first English newspapers had been established in London in the mid-seventeenth century and in important provincial towns, such as Bristol and Norwich, after 1700. The earliest successful colonial newspaper was the *Boston News-Letter*, which published its premier issue in 1704. Kingston, Jamaica, and Philadelphia had their first newspapers in 1718 and 1719, respectively. By the 1730s, New York, Annapolis, Williamsburg, Newport, and Charleston each hosted local papers, and some colonial cities had more than one newspaper by the 1760s.[33]

Newspapers responded to growing demands for political, military, and commercial information in an era of frequent wars and expanding coastal and maritime trade. Colonial printers' information came mostly from London newspapers and from ship captains and others who arrived in the port towns where they published. War news from Europe dominated the front page of the first issue of the *Boston News-Letter* in April 1704, but reports about privateers and notices about ships arriving and leaving various colonial ports filled most of the remainder of its pages. The first colonial press account of a shipwreck came three months later, in July, when the *News-Letter* reprinted a brief war-related item from a London newspaper. "We hear that six *French* ships, bound with Ammunition to *Spain*, were cast away in the late Tempest," a contact in The Hague reported, "and that the new [French] Fort at *Dieppe* was ruined by it."[34]

In times of both war and peace, newspapers reported hurricanes, epidemics, and shipwrecks, all of which affected trade and, by extension, the economic concerns of many of their readers. Between 1690 and 1730, for instance, newspapers in Boston and Philadelphia noted the incidence of at least thirty-two hurricanes, most of which occurred in the West Indies, an important market for food exports from the mainland colonies and an area in which merchants and shippers in both towns conducted a significant portion of their trade.[35]

Although many early accounts simply informed readers that a hurricane had hit Bermuda or Jamaica, or that a ship had wrecked off the coast of New England, newspaper reports also increasingly enumerated deaths and property losses. For instance, in November 1723, the Philadelphia-based *American Weekly Mercury* published a list of twenty-one ships that were "lost" or damaged in the "sad Hurricanes" at Antigua, also providing their captains' names, home ports, and the status of their crews and cargoes. In the summer of 1733, the *Boston Gazette* named eleven ships that were "lost with their Loadings" at the wharves on the island of St. Christopher during a recent hurricane "notwithstanding all the care, industry and pains taken to secure them," along with a list of eight additional vessels that were damaged or destroyed at sea, in some cases with significant loss of life. That list later grew to include sixteen ships at the docks in St. Christopher along with at least nineteen in other British Caribbean ports and many more that were destroyed or lost at sea. In 1738, both Boston newspapers printed the report brought by Captain Vickery from Antigua and Montserrat, where "half the Houses were destroy'd, and 25 Wind-Mills, and . . . upwards of 50 Sails of Vessels have been lost, at least 30 of which belonged to *North America*." Year after year, such accounts informed readers of the fate of their friends and their investments and reminded them of the perils of seafaring, especially during hurricane season.[36]

Newspapers also published more descriptive accounts of shipwrecks, some of which were provided by ship captains or other knowledgeable observers who explained the specific ways in which wind, rain, lightning, and other dangerous conditions damaged their vessels. An early example of this more technically oriented style of reporting appeared in 1720 in the *American Weekly Mercury*, which published the account of a crew member from the ship *Dorothy*, who described how that vessel weathered a severe storm off the coast of Delaware for nearly a day before

> a Terrible Clap of Thunder broke on us, which carried away the Top-galant Mast, and splintered our Main Top-Mast if possible in a Thousand Peices from the Hounds to the Cap, split the Starboard Trusel-tree to peices, carried away that Check from under him, splintered the Main Mast almost half in, and for 4 foot long above, and 10 foot below the Shoulder came out from thence, and went about 8 foot above the upper Deck, and splintered down within 4 foot of the Gun Deck and about 5 inches in it, made 8 or 10 holes in our Main Sail. . . . The Top Mast did not fall by the board at that time for the Riging kept him up, but fell at daylight the next Morning hurt[ing] several of the Men, broke the Boys Legg, and bruised his Back.

In 1729, an item in the *Maryland Gazette* described the troubles of the *Carteret*, a Newfoundland-based ship that was struck by lightning near Alicante, on its way from Lisbon to Barcelona, using similarly technical language, which would have been both thrilling and informative for many readers in colonial coastal communities.[37]

Like the pious shipwreck narratives penned by Janeway and Mather, these technical newspaper accounts were detailed and descriptive. Unlike them, however, the newspaper stories taught no explicit lessons, though through them readers surely learned to appreciate the dangers of the seas and the great skill of men who safely navigated their vessels through treacherous waters. Neither the seafarers who provided printers with information about these shipwrecks nor the printers who published their accounts attempted to explain what caused the storms, collisions, or other conditions, which, in turn, caused the wrecks. They instead preferred to describe the impact of those conditions on their vessels and especially to showcase the efforts of the men who persevered to make the best of their bad situations. This approach encouraged readers to believe that human efforts could improve the ultimate outcome of shipwrecks and other unfortunate events. It also left them free to imagine hurricanes variously as phenomena that could be explained scientifically or interpreted as providential acts of God. While some continued to see hurricanes as divine portents, the spread of information about them — as well as their frequency and predictably seasonal recur-

A View from the Camp at the East End of the Naked Sand Hills, on the South East Shore of the Isle of Sable. A narrow crescent-shaped island off the coast of Nova Scotia, Sable Island has been the site of more than 350 shipwrecks, including the wreck of the *Catherine* in July 1737. This illustration from Joseph F. W. Des Barres's *Atlantic Neptune*, a four-volume nautical atlas published in the late eighteenth century for use by the British Royal Navy, shows an encampment of castaways whose beached ship can be seen in the background on the left. *Library of Congress Geography and Map Division.*

rence—made many in the Atlantic world less likely to interpret the great storms as purposeful punishments or judgments from God.[38]

Newspapers also sometimes published firsthand accounts of shipwrecks that reflected the influence of novels, secular storytelling, and the culture of sensibility. The account of the wreck of the ship *Catherine*, which appeared in newspapers in both Boston and Philadelphia in August 1737 and which also included a brief technical description of what happened to the ship when it "was drove upon a Reef of Sand" due to poor visibility, violent winds, and strong sea currents, in other respects epitomized this outward-looking and sympathetic approach to calamity. The story of the *Catherine* was recounted by "one of the Firefighters, whose Life was saved," though some members of the crew and more than half of the "Two Hundred and Two Persons, Men, Women and Children," who were aboard the ship as passengers perished in the wreck or its aftermath. The *Catherine* had left Northern Ireland for Boston in early June and wrecked in the notoriously perilous waters near Sable Island, off the coast of Nova Scotia, on 17 July. Most of its passengers were part of the vast stream of Ulster Scots who, in the middle decades of the eighteenth century, crossed the Atlantic to settle in North America. Survivors of the wreck of the *Catherine* eventually either remained in Nova Scotia or made their way to towns in northern New England.[39]

In contrast to most earlier newspaper accounts of shipwrecks, which merely informed readers what had transpired and perhaps reported the resulting human and material losses, the author of this story clearly sought to engage readers' emotions by describing the specific effects of the ship's destruction on the people aboard it, who were "left . . . to the Mercy of the Waves." As the chronicler recounted the dramatic scene,

> Very pitiful were the Crys of the poor People for Mercy. In that distressing Moment, Ninety-eight Persons perish'd in the mighty Waters. . . . The remaining Hundred and Four Persons were washed ashore by the Surff of the Sea, some being much bruis'd by the Waves and Pieces of the Vessel and others much spent by the Fatigue, Three or Four of them dyed soon after . . .
>
> After Day-light appear'd, they all got together on the Lee side of a Hill, and having took up the Main Sail, which happen'd to be cast ashore, they made a sort of Tent to shelter them from the Inclemencies of the Weather. . . . Most of the dead Bodies were wash'd on the Shore and buried by the spared Company.

Within three days, surviving crew members had repaired the ship's badly damaged longboat, which they rowed to the town of Canso, where they waited on the governor of Nova Scotia and some other "Gentlemen," to whom they told "the Circumstances of their late sad Disaster." The governor and his associates "compassionately receiv'd them, and very readily administer'd to their Relief," sending a local schooner to deliver the castaways from the "desolate island" to Canso, where they received food, lodging, and care from the town's doctor.[40]

While the compassionate response of the governor and the other townsmen certainly distinguished them as men of feeling, the firefighter-author focused his readers' attention less on the skillfulness of his fellow crew members or on the kindness of these benefactors than on the suffering of the "poor Creatures" who had been aboard the *Catherine*. "The Loss of so many Lives in such an instantaneous and awful manner," he declared pointedly, invoking the culture of sensibility without sanctimony, "must needs be very affecting to every tender hearted Christian." The author alluded to Christianity neither to suggest that the shipwreck was God's punishment to the sufferers nor to impel his readers to ponder the fate of their own eternal souls. Instead, he appealed to the sympathetic and charitable impulses of readers whose religion increasingly centered on the cultivation of human virtue and morality, as well as on the notion of a loving and benevolent God. The purpose of telling the story of the *Catherine* was not to help the sufferers but rather to generate feeling for them, and perhaps to appreciate the good works of the gentlemen of Canso who responded to their plight. The author did not seek to inspire a relief effort to benefit the shipwreck's victims, though he reported that "most, if not all, of the Estates" of the emigrants had been lost in the wreck. He did not attempt to find places to live for the survivors, who, after they recovered, were presumably left to fend for themselves.[41]

While few newspaper accounts of shipwrecks were as explicit in demanding the emotional engagement of the "tender hearted," midcentury shipwreck stories aimed to elicit a range of human-centered responses. In 1743, for instance, the *Boston Post-Boy* reprinted an item that had appeared in a Dublin newspaper in 1729. Fourteen years after it happened, this shipwreck that occurred off the coast of Ireland, which resulted in the death of 109 of 123 passengers and crew members "by Famine at Sea," was no longer news, but the accompanying letter from an eyewitness, a young gentleman, must have struck fear in the hearts of well-heeled readers, as they pondered his experiences battling both the "violent Storm" and the "Rapine of the Mobb" of starving castaways. The brief account of the wreck of the *Dolphin* off the North Carolina coast in 1731 that appeared in the *Gentleman's Magazine*, which told of seamen drinking shark's blood and their own urine to assuage their thirst, conveyed to readers a visceral sense of deprivation and horror. In 1758, widely reprinted eyewitness accounts of the "melancholy scene" of the burning of the naval ship *Prince George* enabled readers on both sides of the Atlantic to mourn the loss of 485 souls amid the "shrieking cries, lamentations, bemoanings, raving, despair, and even madness" unleashed by the deadly conflagration.[42]

Shipwreck stories that appeared in periodicals and as book-length works reflected the overall literary trends of an increasingly human-centered era. Authors across Europe reprised Daniel Defoe's successful formula from *Robinson Crusoe* in novels known collectively as "Robinsonades," a term

The Shipwreck, 1772. Claude-Joseph Vernet's stunning seascape is a sentimental shipwreck narrative in visual form. A ship thrashes in wind and rain along a rocky seacoast, while those who were aboard the sinking vessel struggle to make their way to shore. In the foreground, two men help a weak and half-naked woman who escaped the churning sea, while another man assists an anguished woman—has she lost her child?—who cries out to the heavens. A second ship, perhaps itself about to sustain a deadly lightning strike, is too far away to help. *National Gallery of Art, Washington, Gallery Archives.*

coined by a German novelist in 1731. These popular fictional stories typically featured shipwrecked protagonists who, like Crusoe, struggled to overcome various challenges and were transformed as a result of their experience.[43]

In the eighteenth-century British Atlantic world, aside from the original *Robinson Crusoe*, probably the best-known shipwreck story was the quasi-autobiographical epic poem penned by the Englishman William Falconer. A seafaring man of humble origins, Falconer was the author of the highly regarded *Universal Dictionary of the Marine* (1769), but he was also a poet, whose most popular and significant work was *The Shipwreck: A Poem, In Three Cantos*, which sported the added subtitle *A Sentimental and Descriptive Poem* in some later expanded editions. Falconer's poem featured the tearfully affecting story of the gallant seaman Palemon—who died clutching a miniature likeness of the beautiful Anna, his one true love—alongside

Narrating Disaster

detailed technical descriptions of "the rigging, sails, machinery, and movements of a ship" and crew members' heroic efforts to save the vessel, drawn from Falconer's own experiences. As one reviewer observed admiringly, "A man . . . may become a tolerable sailor" by reading this "extraordinary" poem, which also included "a great number of pathetic touches, which will not fail to interest the reader of sensibility."[44]

True or fictional, shipwreck narratives were popular, but they were not the only sentimental disaster stories available to readers in newspapers and elsewhere. Although plagues were less common than shipwrecks, both in daily life and as subjects of either factual or fictional narratives, the bubonic plague that ravaged Marseilles and its environs in the early 1720s, killing some 100,000 people, was the subject of detailed and emotion-laden reports both in Britain and its colonies. A story that appeared in Philadelphia's newspaper, based on British sources, in August 1721 was typical. The *American Weekly Mercury* reported that Marseilles was "in very bad Circumstances," with so many corpses awaiting burial and so many sufferers on the verge of death. Throughout the city, one heard "dying Groans" and "Ravings of Delirium," along with "Relations and Friends bewailing both their own Loss, and the dismal Prospect of their own sudden Departure. . . . Who would not burst to Grief, to see . . . a future Generation hang on the Breasts of their dead Mothers?" the author asked, invoking the compassion of his readers. "Or the Marriage Bed changed the first Night into a Sepulcher," he added melodramatically, "and the unhappy Pair meet with Death in their Embraces?"[45]

The Great Plague of Marseilles was also a significant milepost in the development of an Anglo-American culture of disaster because it prompted Daniel Defoe to write *A Journal of the Plague Year* (1722), which might reasonably be considered the archetypal English disaster narrative. Defoe's account of a historical event—the Great London Plague, which took as many as 100,000 lives in 1665—was a commentary on the current situation in France. His prescient book featured three elements that would characterize the modern culture of calamity: empirical observation, engaging and emotion-inducing human stories, and a real or rhetorical commitment to relieving suffering and preventing future tragedies.

Defoe was a merchant, a political activist, and a remarkably versatile writer. In this amply researched account, he employed Baconian empiricism, seeking to discern the laws of nature through observation, just as he had done years earlier when he compiled *The Storm* (1704), an anthology of eyewitness accounts of a tempest that hit London in 1703. In *A Journal of the Plague Year*, through his fictional narrator, Defoe told affecting personal stories of plague victims, crafting inspiring and sometimes appalling vignettes of both the sufferers and those who sought to help (or harm) them. As a man of commerce, Defoe also considered the economic impact of disaster, maintaining that though the plague in 1665, followed by the Great Fire in 1666, had brought trade to a temporary standstill, the dual disasters actually benefited the city's long-term commercial interests. Finally, the politically engaged Defoe also used his stories to promote an agenda of relief and social improvement by benevolence and especially by decisive government action. Through his fictional narrator, H. F., Defoe declared that government secrecy and passivity exacerbated the crisis in 1665 and urged his readers to consider *A Journal of the Plague Year* as a cautionary tale for future generations.[46]

Defoe shrewdly recognized the importance of the press in raising both popular and official awareness of—and eliciting constructive responses to—plagues and other calamities. In the 1660s, H. F. observed, "we had no such thing as printed newspapers . . . to spread rumours and reports of things, and to improve them by the invention of men, as I have lived to see practised since." Information came instead "from the letters of merchants and others who corresponded abroad, and from them was handed about by word of mouth only; so that things did not spread instantly over the whole nation, as they do now." For the most part, however, officials kept the bad news "very private . . . and people began to forget it as a thing we were very little concerned in, and that we hoped was not true," until it was too late for either government or citizens to implement effective relief and reform initiatives.[47]

By the 1720s, when Defoe wrote his *Journal of the Plague Year*, more people did, in fact, have more information about plagues, hurricanes, and shipwrecks, which they now understood in a range of overlapping contexts. Shipwrecks, in particular, were widely known to be frequent and costly, in terms of both property and lives. Although many still attributed shipwrecks and other calamites to divine providence, human agency also frequently played an important role in contemporary shipwreck narratives. Affecting stories of suffering victims inspired sympathy and benevolence. Admirable lifesaving efforts of able seamen suggested the improving possibilities of human expertise and actions.

Marine insurance was one early purposeful human intervention to mitigate the material consequences of maritime misadventures. Originating in the Italian city-states in the middle of the fourteenth century, marine insurance was a modern remedy for commercial losses born of the perils of the seas, derived from merchants' acceptance of the risk required to profit from an expansive global trade and their resulting effort to lessen the potential costs of their vulnerability to storms, gales, and other dangers of the natural world. Marine insurance was the first insurance, created by merchants who acknowledged the fact that transporting commercial goods over treacherous seas for long distances was literally risky business and who agreed to pay premiums in exchange for protection from financial ruin in the event of calamity. While some condemned marine insurance as an impious stratagem to circumvent the will of God by softening the pain of his judgment, insuring cargoes became the norm among merchants in the thriving commercial centers of Europe and North America. Although most colonial merchants purchased their insurance from London brokers or syndicates, insurance brokers also operated in Philadelphia, Boston, New York, Charleston, and Norfolk during the colonial era.[48]

While private merchants and investors arranged insurance to mitigate financial losses in the event of catastrophe, the erection of lighthouses aimed to prevent shipwrecks and thereby save both property and lives. Although there had been coastal lights in Rome and other major European ports in ancient times, they had fallen into disuse by the time Italian traders began to install guiding lights in their main ports after 1100. The timeline for the construction of lighthouses across Europe paralleled the spread of maritime trade. While England had only one lighthouse in 1600, thirteen more were erected in the ensuing century, and another ten were added by 1760. On the eve of American independence, there were twenty-four lighthouses in England and four in Scotland.[49]

While the central governments of some European countries assumed complete responsibility for building and overseeing lighthouses, in England the construction and administration of most lighthouses, beacons, and buoys before the nineteenth century were accomplished by public-private partnerships. In the early sixteenth-century England, the Royal Navy's Lord High Admiral was charged with funding and managing any apparatus pertaining to maritime safety, but in 1566 Queen Elizabeth I transferred these duties by royal charter to Trinity House, a London-based charitable organization that had once functioned as a medieval guild for mariners. As a crown corporation, Trinity House was a government-supported public entity that performed official functions — building, overseeing, and levying fees for lighthouses — which otherwise would have fallen within the purview of royal functionaries. Although Trinity House did not enjoy a monopoly over lighthouse construction and operation, it was by far the most important public institution involved in promoting maritime safety in England.[50]

In the colonies as in England, lighthouses were important early public works aimed at what we today would call disaster prevention. Lacking
preexisting institutions such as Trinity House with which they might build
public-private partnerships, colonial governments shouldered the responsibility of building and overseeing lighthouses themselves. Eleven lighthouses were erected in colonial British North America before 1776, most of
which were funded by taxes on incoming vessels (known as tonnage duties)
or by government-sanctioned public lotteries. The first colonial lighthouse
began operation near Boston Harbor in 1716; six others were built along
the busy New England coast in the succeeding half century. Tybee Island
in Georgia, Sandy Hook in New Jersey, Cape Henlopen in Pennsylvania
(now Delaware), and Charleston, South Carolina, were also sites of colonial
lighthouses, as was Louisbourg, Nova Scotia, where the French colonial government erected an excellent facility that was captured by the British during
the French and Indian War.[51]

Most advocates for lighthouses emphasized their commercial and military value, but some also promoted these projects as more broadly humane
and civic-minded. The preamble of the Massachusetts statute that authorized the Boston lighthouse project justified this undertaking on the grounds
that "the Want of a Light-House at the Entrance of the Harbour of Boston,
hath been a great Discouragement to Navigation by the Loss of the Lives
and Estates of Several of His Majesty's Subjects." Decades later, when New
York and Philadelphia — both major colonial ports — still had no lighthouses
to protect incoming vessels, one New Yorker appealed to local civic pride
when he proposed the construction of a lighthouse at nearby Sandy Hook as
"an Ornament to this Metropolis and our neighbouring Government [of the
colony of New Jersey]." Conversely, slaveholding planters and merchants in
South Carolina cited the dilapidation of Georgia's Tybee Island lighthouse
as part of their larger indictment of Georgia's colonial trustees, who out-
lawed slavery, prevented the southward expansion of the plantation system,
and (according to irate white Carolinians) may have aided and abetted a recent slave rebellion. South Carolinians believed that the Tybee light was a
"fine Piece of Workmanship, so beneficial to all," which had rotted and "is
fallen to the Ground" because the Georgia trustees neglected to maintain it.
"What better can be expected," they opined, "from Those who Regard their
own Passions and private Interest more than the Good of their Country and
Fellow Subjects?"[52]

Although the expansion of shipping and trade clearly spurred appreciation for lighthouses, this new era of lighthouse building was also an out-

growth of the Enlightenment's confidence in enlisting human reason in the service of social progress. Seamarks and coastal lights had existed since ancient times, but the eighteenth century brought major improvements in their size and durability, as well as innovations—such as the use of oil lamps, parabolic reflectors, and oscillators—to enhance their brightness and dependability.[53]

Scientists and engineers also proposed changes in shipbuilding methods to make vessels less likely to sink even after they sustained significant damage. One plan, published in 1759 in the optimistically titled *Universal Magazine of Knowledge and Pleasure*, proposed that a ship should "have its cavity beneath the lower-deck divided into three (or four) nearly equal parts, by bulk-heads, or partitions, rising from the bottom to a lower deck," with each part caulked to seal it off completely from the others. If the ship sprung a leak, incoming water would be confined to a single watertight section of the hull and its weight would be insufficient to sink the ship, "if properly lightened in other parts, by throwing heavy things, such as guns, &c., overboard." The inventor correctly predicted that this innovation, which eventually became standard practice, would improve the durability of both military and commercial vessels.[54]

The desire to save lives was the primary objective of other inventors, who experimented with various types of personal flotation devices to diminish the frequency of deaths at sea, which became both more numerous and more widely publicized as a result of the naval battles and raids in this century of frequent and ongoing Anglo-French wars. One of the earliest of these inventions was the "hydraspis," or water shield, the work of a German scholar named Johann Christoph Wagenseil, who died in 1705. Wagenseil described his invention in a Latin text, which appeared in translation in the popular London-based *Gentleman's Magazine* in 1747. A true Enlightenment polymath, Wagenseil was a noted historian and philologist who, like many of his learned contemporaries, pursued knowledge in many fields to benefit humankind. Wagenseil's "observations on the swimming of geese and ducks" led him to ponder how people might mimic their buoyancy; after experimenting with other options, he built a hollow wooden structure shaped like a squared-off donut, as thick as the space between a man's chest and groin, with a hole in the center to accommodate his torso. Equipped with hinges— so that the user could insert himself into the ring and then securely reclose it—Wagenseil's invention was to be used with "water-sandals" that approximated the webbed feet of waterfowl. His design also included two covered compartments on the device's top surface in which a shipwreck victim could

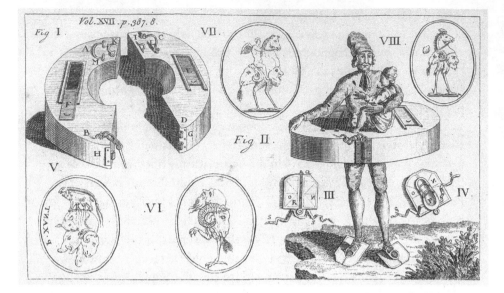

Hydraspis, or water shield. Illustrations from a 1747 issue of the *Gentleman's Magazine* show the floatation device invented decades earlier by Johann Christoph Wagenseil. Figure I illustrates how the hydraspis was constructed; in Figure II, a man wears the device, along with shoes that simulated a duck's webbed feet, also depicted separately in III and IV. A small child sits safely on the surface of the wooden structure. Interior compartments accommodate food and water to sustain castaways while they await rescue. (Figures V–VIII are illustrations for a different article.) *American Antiquarian Society*.

stow "a quantity of food sufficient for a long time, or . . . money, writings, or other valuable things" while awaiting rescue.[55]

Interest in Wagenseil's hydraspis, which had been successfully tested in Vienna and Zurich, increased in the years following the publication of the *Gentleman's Magazine* article. In 1750, the same periodical reported that a "mechanic in Yorkshire" had constructed his own version based on the illustration that had accompanied the 1747 description of Wagenseil's flotation device and also that a Frenchman had presented a plan for a similar invention to the Royal Academy of Sciences in Paris. By 1752, word had spread to the colonies that the Lords of the Admiralty would soon consider "a Proposal . . . relating to a Machine design'd for keeping Persons floating after a Shipwreck" by keeping them "buoyant as long as they can live above Water, in spite of Surffs or Breakers." Wagenseil himself had believed that his invention would "be of signal service in a shipwreck, putting a person in as much safety, amidst vast and raging waters, as a goose or a duck." He rejected critics' suggestions that he might improve his utilitarian design by making it

Narrating Disaster

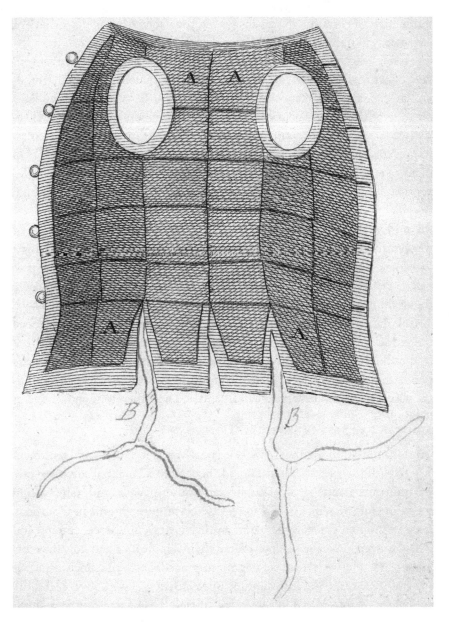

Cork-jacket. Dr. John Wilkinson invented this fabric-covered cork life jacket, which he featured as an illustration in a book he wrote in part to advocate for its adoption by the British Royal Navy. His effort was unsuccessful. Wilkinson received a patent for his invention, and he sold his life jackets to individual sailors and mariners. Though not widely accepted during his lifetime, jackets or belts made of cork were commonly used as life preservers on seafaring vessels during the nineteenth century, replaced by stronger kapok-fiber life jackets only after 1900.
© *The British Library Board.*

more attractive, cautioning against being too "sollicitous about beauty or elegance, when the case concerns a man's life."[56]

A few years later, John Wilkinson, an English physician, initiated a seven-year effort that ultimately led to his obtaining a patent for the first modern life jacket, made of cork, in 1765. In January 1758, Wilkinson attended a meeting of the Royal Society to persuade its members that as the intellectual leaders of such "a commercial and naval people," they should take steps to prevent "those very frequent disasters" at sea by which the nation lost so many people and vessels. In the two books he published to promote his invention, Wilkinson invoked Enlightenment rationalism to demonstrate both the efficiency of the "cork-jacket" and the importance of saving lives. "It was the misfortune of the Ancients," he wrote, "to have so high an opinion of their own knowledge, as to charge upon Nature, or the conduct of Divine Providence, those defects which after ages have proved to be with more propriety, ascribed to their own self-sufficiency," rather than trying to change things for the better. Wilkinson numbered among his heroes pioneers such as Columbus, Galileo, Bacon, and the anonymous tinkerer "who first placed the rudder at the stern of a ship." He offered readers an extended explanation of the "contrivance" he invented "for preserving the lives of seafaring people in the shipwreck," arguing forcefully for innovation based on empirical observation and experimentation and against "the plodding drudge of habitude."[57]

§ Like the authors of the shipwreck narratives — both pious and sentimental — the inventor Wilkinson and those who advocated the construction and maintenance of public lighthouses played important roles in spreading information about shipwrecks and proposing remedies for them. Because shipwrecks were pervasive in this age of commerce, empire, and global warfare, how people interpreted their significance and how they formulated responses to them set important precedents for dealing with other sorts of calamities. Because all three approaches — quantitative, technical, and affective — coexisted in shipwreck stories, these narratives were influential antecedents of the modern culture of disaster. Providential interpretations of shipwrecks and other events persisted, but the appeal of sentimental and scientific disaster stories, as well as efforts to prevent or limit misery and loss and to provide sympathy and relief for the sufferers, increasingly dominated both the political and cultural agendas of Britons at home and in the colonies in America.

{ 3 }

CATASTROPHE
IN AN AGE OF
ENLIGHTENMENT

On the morning of 1 November 1755, an earthquake rocked Lisbon, the Portuguese capital and a bustling port city of roughly 275,000 people. As buildings collapsed, flames from hearths and candles ignited a massive fire that burned for a week, devouring much of what the quake itself had spared. Meanwhile, not long after the last tremors ended, a tsunami—the largest in history, reaching speeds of up to fifty miles per hour—engulfed the ruined city. When it was all over, as many as 40,000 people had perished in Lisbon and its environs, though some contemporary estimates of the death toll were much higher. Thousands more died in nearby Spain and northern Africa. Rumbles from the earthquake and its aftershocks were felt throughout Europe, as far north as Scandinavia. Many believed that the tremors that shook Massachusetts, which made the house of John Adams's family "rock and reel and crack as if it would fall in ruins about us" seventeen days later, were somehow related to the earthquake in Portugal. The range of the tsunami from the Lisbon earthquake was similarly impressive, affecting tides in the Americas and causing floods on several Caribbean islands.[1]

The cultural impact of the Lisbon earthquake was nearly as extraordinary as the physical wreckage it caused. Often called the first modern disaster, the great Lisbon earthquake gave rise to vigorous investigations of its causes, with empirical observations and scientific knowledge informing the ambitious rebuilding of the ruined city that was undertaken and financed by Portugal's royal government. The horrific and widely publicized Lisbon disaster also led to the first international relief effort in world history. It elicited robust commentary from luminaries as diverse as the French philosopher Voltaire and the famed English evangelical leader George Whitefield. More than any previous disaster, the Lisbon earthquake also became the subject of sermons, songs, poems, visual representations, and eyewitness accounts that circulated throughout Europe and its colonies in America. Yet when people imagined, interpreted, and responded to the Lisbon earthquake, they also drew on preexisting understandings of the causes and meanings of hurricanes, shipwrecks, and other calamities.[2]

This chapter examines the Lisbon earthquake in an Atlantic context, focusing primarily on the response to the Portuguese disaster in Great Britain and its American colonies. Portugal was England's longtime ally, and a community of English merchants lived in its capital. These close diplomatic, military, and commercial ties influenced Britons' words and actions, but the cultural resonance of the earthquake, in Britain and elsewhere, was nevertheless unprecedented. The Lisbon earthquake was a crucial turning point in the formation of a modern culture of disaster. After Lisbon, catastrophe became a newsworthy staple of popular culture that not only inspired sympathy but also led to tentative but significant discussions concerning the responsibilities of people and governments to provide relief to help alleviate the distress of sufferers.

§ By the time Lisbon was reduced to a pile of smoldering rubble in November 1755, learned men had been accumulating information about earthquakes for roughly two millennia. The ancient sages Aristotle and Seneca had written about earthquakes, as did medieval monks, who included accounts of them in their chronicles. In 1580, shortly after tremors occurred in southern England, resulting in the closing of theaters and other pious efforts to eradicate sinfulness, the Reverend Abraham Fleming appended the first published catalog of English earthquakes — he knew of seventeen in all — to a treatise that he wrote to encourage repentance. By 1750, when a series of unusually powerful earthquakes shook London, descriptions of seismic events were so plentiful that another English clergyman, Zachary Grey, was able to produce *A Chronological and Historical Account of the Most Memorable Earthquakes: That have happened in the World, from the Beginning of the Christian period to the present Year* and its sequel, *A Farther Account of Memorable Earthquakes*, published six years later. In all, Grey, who unequivocally characterized earthquakes as divine portents, enumerated and described a total of 167 earthquakes and tremors that had occurred on four continents.[3]

By the middle of the eighteenth century, often drawing on empirical

Catastrophe in an Age of Enlightenment

information gathered in the Americas and elsewhere, erudite members of England's Royal Society theorized about the physical causes of seismic activity. The physician Hans Sloane and others in Jamaica presented accounts of the unusually severe earthquake that utterly destroyed the prosperous town of Port Royal in June 1692. In 1746, when a major quake killed thousands in Peru, the official detailed Spanish-language account of the disaster was translated into English and published first in London and then in Philadelphia by the printer (and future Royal Society fellow) Benjamin Franklin. This account of the Peruvian earthquake also appeared in French, German, and Portuguese translations.[4]

Interest in earthquakes and their physical causes was part of a more general effort to understand all sorts of natural phenomena that, for better or worse, affected human life. While the Enlightenment faith in using empirical observation and the knowledge that resulted from it to improve the human condition was one important impetus for studying climate and weather, colonization of the Americas was another. Some English farmers, such as the seventeenth-century clergyman Ralph Josselin, kept records of routine local weather patterns and acted on what they learned by trying new crops and other strategies to make their land more productive during the cold, wet summers and dry winters of the Little Ice Age. On a grander scale, after a hurricane destroyed an English naval fleet in the West Indies in 1666, the Royal Society sent barometers to Barbados to see if they could be used to predict hurricanes, which threatened both military and commercial vessels, as well as the increasingly profitable agriculture of the sugar-producing West Indies. By the 1720s, the Royal Society was promoting weather reporting by soliciting, receiving, and publishing data from weather journals kept by observers throughout Europe and North America.[5]

While the main objective of such observation and journal keeping was to gain insight into ordinary seasonal weather patterns, a parallel effort focused on understanding hurricanes, earthquakes, and other extraordinary phenomena. Because earthquakes were sudden, impossible to predict, and comparatively rare—at least in Europe—they especially elicited discussions about the relationship between God and the physical world. For example, the popular *General History of Earthquakes*, first published in two London editions in 1694 and reissued as late as 1734, combined science with providentialism, but leaned strongly toward the latter. The author began his book by briefly reviewing the possible physical or "Natural" causes of earthquakes before devoting the remainder of his 177-page treatise to recounting stories of specific earthquakes and speculating as to what provoked the wrath of the Almighty in each of these instances. The author concluded his book by denouncing ancient "Heathen Philosophers" who had believed that earthquakes were inescapable and thus meaningless while praising Christian writers who interpreted earthquakes as "punishments of [human] sins and enormities inflicted . . . by Divine Justice." Why would God cause earthquakes if not to punish sinful people? "Let us then conclude," he declared emphatically, "that Earthquakes are the Effects of Sin."[6]

By the early eighteenth century, however, many educated people tried harder to reconcile natural philosophy (or science) with Christian theology. In the English-speaking world, the earthquake that devastated the island colony of Jamaica in 1692 was an important moment in the evolution of public discussions about the causes of earthquakes and practical responses to them. Earthquakes were nearly annual occurrences in Jamaica, where their frequency led colonists eventually to take them mostly in stride. Minor earthquakes, which were occasions for stern sermons and moralizing in England and its mainland colonies, evoked no such response in earthquake-prone Jamaica. When an unusually severe earthquake struck the island in 1692, however, colonists did not doubt that this extraordinary event, which killed at least one-third of the 6,500 inhabitants of the town of Port Royal, was an act of God. Yet some observers also concluded that the town's location, its sandy topography, and its tall brick buildings were physical conditions that increased the town's vulnerability to the severe winds and rain. This more empirical interpretation of the impact of the Port Royal earthquake, in turn, made its way to England in communications from Jamaica and also in several eighteenth-century histories of the island, contributing to the overall understanding of earthquakes and their material consequences.[7]

In locales in which earthquakes were less commonplace, educated clergy likewise increasingly sought to reconcile their belief in God's omnipotence with their own understanding of the natural world. When an earthquake shook the land and everything on it from Maine to Philadelphia for two minutes in October 1727, terrified New Englanders flocked to hear their Harvard-educated ministers declare the quake an act of divine providence, even as they insisted that God worked through secondary physical causes, which they attempted to explain to their congregants. Whatever laypeople made of their ministers' scientific insights, the earthquake sparked a religious revival across northern New England and an impressive growth in church memberships.[8]

In 1750, when Londoners experienced several "Shocks of an Earthquake," the Reverend Samuel Chandler took a similar position, envisioning

A True and Perfect Relation of that most Sad and Terrible Earthquake, at Port-Royal in Jamaica. Published in London several months after the deadly Port Royal earthquake of June 1692, this broadside featured an image of the ruined town, an eyewitness account of the wreckage, and a partial list of casualties. This news from Jamaica was especially timely because northern Europe experienced its own far milder quake that September. The broadside's author characterized both earthquakes as "God's heavy Judgments . . . on a Sinful People."
Kozak Collection, NISEE Library, Berkeley.

science as a tool of the Almighty, though he stated it more contentiously. A strong opponent of deism, Chandler mocked as irrational those "Philosophers" who denied the tremors' divine origins. He insisted that he could "not conceive, how the Operation of . . . natural Causes is inconsistent with a religious Acknowledgment of God in such Events" and indignantly asked if "any Man of sober Reason" could ever accept the "Scheme of Atheism."[9]

As Chandler's strident denunciation of philosophers and atheism suggests, the London earthquakes of 1750 evoked a wide spectrum of responses, signifying the extent to which contemporary culture was both divided and in a state of flux. While these episodes stimulated renewed scientific study of earthquakes in Britain, they also inspired many providential sermons and quake-themed hymns by the Methodist Charles Wesley. One issue of the fashionable *Gentleman's Magazine* reflected this bifurcated understanding of the 1750 earthquakes and their significance by positioning a brief item affirming the providential nature of earthquakes immediately before a lengthy scientific essay on electrical currents as possible causes of seismic activity. The anonymous author of a pamphlet called *Advice to England* took still another completely different tack, following the optimist philosophers, the most famous of whom were Gottfried Wilhelm Leibniz and the English poet Alexander Pope, who believed that God created the best of all possible worlds, that universal laws of physics governed the physical universe, and that things would always turn out for the best. This author urged his readers to remain calm and passively wait for the crisis to pass:

> Think and be resolute, what's bad avoid.
> Take Prudence for your Tutor and your guide.
> Away, away with vain Experiment,
> Remedies much worse than the Event.
> If that you change your Climate, for what End
> Alter your Scheme? What Good do you intend? . . .
> If Storms and Tempests, Hurricanes arise,
> Blue Lightnings flash, and rend the vaulted Skies,
> Firm and secure you'll stand the coming Day;
> Prudence will all thy Ills and Cares repay.

Here was a God-centered approach to disaster that imagined the Creator after the Creation as wholly benevolent and inactive.[10]

The London earthquakes of 1750, like New England's quake in 1727, were of mainly local interest, in part because of the lack of casualties. The earthquake in Peru in 1746, which claimed more than 10,000 lives—a smaller number but a higher proportion of the total population compared with the death toll in Lisbon nine years later—generated more discussion, but interest in the crisis in Lima and nearby Callao still paled by comparison to discussions of the subsequent Portuguese disaster. A few pamphlets, some of which were translated from Spanish into other languages, chronicled Peru's earthquake; the most widely circulated of these, *A True and Particular Relation of the Dreadful Earthquake Which Happen'd at Lima*, combined the scientific and providential approaches, as was typical of the era. After describing Lima and its environs before the earthquake and informing readers of the area's documented susceptibility to seismic events, the author embarked on a twenty-eight-page discourse summarizing current scientific thinking on the nature of earthquakes and their causes before abruptly shifting to a God-centered interpretation. "Of all the Judgments, proceeding from natural Causes, which the Deity often inflicts on Offenders, in order to satisfy Divine Justice and manifest his almighty Power," he surmised, "the unexpected Stroke of sudden Earthquakes hath ever been the most tremendous."[11]

Although writings about the Lisbon earthquake shared many of these attributes, their quantity was unprecedented. One historian estimates that the Lisbon disaster was the subject of "hundreds of tracts"—in addition to countless poems and newspaper items—in seven languages, as well as an extraordinary number of visual representations. Within six weeks of the Portuguese disaster, more than twenty accounts of it appeared in print in London alone. The earthquake in Peru was just as spectacularly destructive as its Portuguese counterpart, and many who wrote about Lisbon knew about Lima and referred to it in their writings. But the politics of location made Lisbon, not Lima, a pivotal cultural event both because Europeans deemed a massive earthquake in a nearby city more remarkable than a seismic event in a hemisphere known for exotic climactic conditions and because so many foreign diplomats and merchants who resided in Lisbon spread their observations about the earthquake throughout the Atlantic world.[12]

Although the disruption of the quake and subsequent government censorship deterred Lisbon's sole newspaper from reporting the crisis as it unfolded, handwritten letters describing the earthquake and its aftermath made their way first to Spain, where on 11 November, ten days after the earthquake occurred, the *Gaceta de Madrid* published an account of the situation in Portugal, which included the sad news that the Spanish ambassador, along with some members of his family, was among the casualties. A week later, the story had made its way to Paris, and by late November news from Lis-

An Authentic View of Lisbon, just as the Dreadful Earthquake began and as it ended.
This print, dated 1755, was sold for one shilling in a London printshop in Covent
Garden within eight weeks of the disaster, which occurred on 1 November.
Advertised as the work of "one of the best Artists for those Things" in Portugal,
the finely detailed pre-earthquake view of Lisbon was likely made earlier, while the
cruder vista of the city after the earthquake, fire, and tsunami was "drawn from
the other Side of the Tagus [River]" either during the crisis or soon thereafter.
Royal Collection Trust / © Her Majesty Queen Elizabeth II 2018.

bon—some of which was accurate, some of which was not—that had arrived
in England via "private Letters by the Way of France" was reported in the
newspapers in London, where illustrated broadsides appeared soon after. In
the ensuing weeks, letters, newspapers, and travelers carried the story southward to Italy and eastward to Russia. The news was so extraordinary that it
was sometimes received skeptically, especially when estimated damage and
death tolls seemed exaggerated or contradictory.[13]

Ship captains first brought news of the earthquake straight from Lisbon,
across the Atlantic, to the British colonies in America. Captain Collins, who
had witnessed the debacle in Portugal before sailing for Massachusetts, was

Catastrophe in an Age of Enlightenment

the first to arrive, and his account of what happened in Lisbon appeared in two Boston newspapers on 22 December. The Boston press reported that Collins estimated the death toll from the earthquake and its aftermath at 110,000. Collins's story was reprinted in New York a week later and in Philadelphia in early January, though news from Lisbon had also reached Pennsylvania's governor via another ship captain who had arrived in Philadelphia about a week after Collins docked in Boston (and whose estimate of the death toll was significantly lower, and more accurate, at 30,000). In mid-January, the letter from Captain Collins was featured on the front page of the *Maryland Gazette*, alongside yet another ship captain's account of the disaster and reports from the Spanish coastal city of Cádiz, which also suffered serious damage. Finally, on 29 January 1756, nearly three months after the destruction of Lisbon, Collins's account appeared in the *South Carolina Gazette*, the southernmost newspaper in the mainland colonies of British America.[14]

Newspaper coverage of the earthquake and its aftermath continued for months after these first stories were published. In British America, the weekly *New-York Mercury* was typical in receiving more substantive reports from Lisbon and other affected areas beginning in early February 1756 and in publishing updated information about death tolls, relief efforts, and government attempts to restore order in and around Lisbon, where outraged observers reported that "ruffians" preyed on innocents and that the powerful and privileged Catholic clergy connived to "extort, squeeze, and force all the Money they can from the poor deluded Laity." Nearly every week, the *Mercury* included news from Lisbon, much of which came from ship captains who also reported the gradual recovery of the city's trade. In May, readers learned of the Portuguese king's plan to rebuild his capital "on the same Spot" and of rumors that he intended to abolish the Inquisition, the tribunal that ruthlessly persecuted real and suspected Jews and heretics, including Protestants. By October, however, the *Mercury* reported that the Inquisition had resumed its executions, though the power of the church was later curtailed by the "Political Earthquake" orchestrated by the king's chief minister, the draconian and increasingly dictatorial Marquis of Pombal, who was also the Enlightenment-inspired mastermind behind Lisbon's rebuilding effort.[15]

By contemporary standards, writings about Lisbon were voluminous and varied, and authors represented an array of nations and ideological perspectives. The Portuguese press produced mostly government-sanctioned reports that emphasized the employment of scientists, engineers, and other exemplars of secular rationalism in the rebuilding of the ruined city, which, in turn, Pombal and his associates interpreted as inaugurating a new era of national glory and progress. A French government agent in Lisbon crafted a version of the earthquake story to insinuate that Portugal had suffered by its dependence on greedy British allies and to present the disaster as a unique opportunity for Portuguese leaders to reassess their diplomatic and economic priorities. Commentators from the Protestant Netherlands, still embittered by more than a century of Iberian rule and religious persecution, interpreted the earthquake as divine judgment against a ruthless Catholic regime and as evidence of the utter backwardness of a corrupt and priest-ridden kingdom. The philosophe Voltaire used the earthquake and its aftermath as the backdrop for *Candide*, his celebrated satirical critique of philosophical optimism. Lisbon also represented a turning point in the intellectual development of the German philosopher Immanuel Kant, who abandoned providentialism in favor of empiricism as he struggled to understand the earthquake's physical causes.[16]

Also noteworthy was the fact that the earthquake, fire, and floods in Lisbon became the subject of so many visual representations. By 1755, artistic depictions of disaster scenes were not unprecedented, but they were not especially common. The Great Fire of London, which destroyed much of the English capital in 1666, was exceptional in that it was depicted in several contemporary prints — some of which circulated throughout western Europe — as well as in at least four paintings produced in the 1670s. The 1746 earthquake in Lima yielded no contemporary pictorial representations. By contrast, artists and engravers from across Europe soon depicted the Lisbon quake in at least forty-nine images of varying levels of refinement and accuracy. A crude generic woodcut of toppling buildings and fleeing people spread the news from Lisbon to distant Bohemia. Detailed copper engravings, mostly by German artists, illustrated the chaotic terror of the earthquake, fire, and flood, while others portrayed the Portuguese rebuilding effort at various stages. Several artistic representations conveyed a sense of the power of the earthquake by juxtaposing images of Lisbon before and after it struck. A series of French engravings, made in 1757 and available both in black-and-white and color versions, showed the ruins of churches, towers, and the city's new opera house, which had once graced one of the most opulent cities in Europe. While these sorts of images informed the public of what had transpired in Lisbon, they also appealed to a growing aesthetic taste for the sublime, or the idea that power and grandeur of nature could inspire awe and veneration.[17]

British commentators approached the Lisbon disaster from three main perspectives. The first, which included both the sermons of the clergy and

Lisbon earthquake woodcut. Although the scene depicted in this generic woodcut bore no resemblance to Lisbon, it effectively conveyed the sense of devastation and despair that afflicted the Portuguese capital. This woodcut was an illustration for a broadside, now lost, that was published in Litomyšl, Bohemia, in the months after the earthquake, when words and images describing what transpired in Lisbon spread across Europe and the Americas. *Kozak Collection, NISEE Library, Berkeley.*

contributions from the scientific community, sought to explain the causes and meaning of the quake in providential or physical terms — sometimes both — similar to their response to London's earthquakes five years earlier. A second narrative approach described people's experiences during and after the earthquake, as well as the physical devastation it caused, to evoke readers' emotions, in keeping with the ideals of the culture of sensibility. Both of these approaches drew on contemporary discourses about shipwrecks and other calamities. In the case of the Lisbon earthquake, however, some commentators chose a third option, focusing on disaster relief and benevolence toward sufferers in times of crisis, which some were coming to see as a defining characteristic of British national identity.

These three perspectives were not mutually exclusive, as the case of Thomas Hunter's *Historical Account of Earthquakes* clearly shows. Hunter gathered various sorts of earthquake writing into a single volume, which was sold both in England and America. He devoted the book's opening section to scientific theories about the physical causes of earthquakes; the next included tales of human suffering from Lisbon and earlier quakes. Other parts of the volume engaged the inextricably connected issues of religious and national identities. Hunter included material that made the case for the superiority of Protestantism over Roman Catholicism by graphically describing the burning of a supposed heretic by the Inquisition in Lisbon, which the author claimed occurred at the precise moment the earthquake struck in divine retribution, killing thousands of Portuguese Catholics who attended Mass on All Saints' Day while sparing resident English Protestants, whose losses were by comparison "inconsiderable." Hunter also chose texts that emphasized the benevolence of Britain's king and Parliament, which sent relief to Lisbon, and the generosity of British merchants who resided in the earthquake-ravaged city and who "acted with Wisdom and Honour worthy of their Country" by their "Humane Disposition" to aid the Portuguese sufferers.[18]

In the months following the earthquake, government-sponsored religious institutions and customs mediated public awareness of the Lisbon crisis in the English-speaking world. Many would have known about the earthquake chiefly through formal government pronouncements establishing days of public prayer for divine mercy and reaffirmation of religious commitment, a centuries-old practice that survived well into the modern era.

King George II set the tone by issuing a proclamation commanding "all our loving Subjects" to observe a day of prayer and fasting to seek forgiveness for their "manifold Sins and Wickedness" and to thank God for his mercy in having "protected and preserved us from imminent Destruction, especially at this Time, when some neighbouring Countries, in Alliance and Friendship with us, have been visited with a most dreadful and Extensive Earthquake, which hath also in some Degree, been felt in several Parts of our Dominions." Massachusetts leaders followed suit, urging citizens to ponder the meaning not only of Lisbon but also of their more modest local tremors by observing "a Day of Solemn Humiliation and Prayer . . . on Account of the late awful Dispensation of Providence both in Europe and in America." The governors of Pennsylvania and Maryland set aside a day for public fasting and prayer, with the latter prescribing a special liturgy—featured on the front page of the *Maryland Gazette*—to beg God's mercy and favor in light

Catastrophe in an Age of Enlightenment

of both the earthquakes and the escalating war on the colonial frontier. In Hanover, Virginia, the Presbyterian minister Samuel Davies preached a sermon in which he characterized earthquakes — along with famine, war, and pestilence — as the four "extraordinary executioners" of divine vengeance.[19]

In so doing, Davies took his place alongside the giants of transatlantic Protestant evangelicalism who drew various providential meanings from the Lisbon crisis. Charles Wesley, who composed hymns in the aftermath of the London earthquakes in 1750, revised and expanded his earthquake-related lyrics after Lisbon for use during the royally mandated day of prayer and fasting; the apocalyptic urgency of the newer version intimated that the end of the world was at hand. The views of John Wesley, Charles's brother and the acknowledged leader of the Methodist movement, were less apocalyptic, though he, too, interpreted the earthquake as a divine portent, sternly correcting those who asserted that the quake arose from "natural Causes" by avowing that all earthquakes, storms, whirlwinds, fires, and other phenomena were "under the Direction of the Lord of Nature." The renowned Anglican revivalist George Whitefield agreed. In a tract that went through four London editions, he argued, on the one hand, that the unique cruelty and wickedness of Portugal's Catholic Inquisition made Lisbon a prime target for God's wrath and, on the other, that the Almighty intended the quake's message for all sinners, including those in England who had crowded their churches after the "two alarming shocks" of 1750 but who now, five years later, had reverted to their impious and sinful ways. "May the Calamities of our Brethren of *Portugal* be a warning," Whitefield exclaimed, "not only to us, but to every City in the World!"[20]

Clergy on both sides of the Atlantic echoed these arguments as they strove to inspire their flocks to repent and be saved. While some, like Whitefield, noted the peculiar noxiousness of Portuguese Catholicism, nearly all agreed that the lessons of the earthquake were equally compelling for Protestant Britons. "Let us not give ourselves to censure the lives of other men," cautioned the Reverend Thomas Ashton, "but to reform our own." Similar sentiments were evident in a poem appended to the published version of a sermon preached by the Reverend James Hervey: "O England! England! Sleep not in your sin, / But rise and view the state you're in." The Reverend Thomas Hunter, who delivered a fast day sermon in Cheshire unambiguously titled *National Wickedness the Cause of National Misery*, likewise rejected the conceit that "this Nation and Kingdom, from our present State of Immorality and Impiety, has any Reason to presume upon it's [*sic*] Security from . . . Misery and Ruin." Noting God's beneficence in sparing his own countrymen the sad fate of so many Portuguese, another clergyman urged his audience to avoid divine wrath by repenting and thereby not *"abuse* so much Goodness, and make *Returns of Ingratitude* for such distinguishing Mercy." [21]

New England's clergy struck a similar tone, treating their own recent tremors, in the words of one historian, as "a didactic disaster for the soul." New Englanders, who experienced the "violent shock of an earthquake" on 18 November, more than a month before the news from Lisbon arrived in Boston, initially interpreted their local quake and its aftershocks as divine punishment. As the anonymous author of one popular broadside put it,

> In seventeen hundred fifty-five,
> When vice its empire did revive,
> Confirming fire, a jealous GOD
> Call'd on New-England with his rod.

The arrival of the news from Lisbon, however, complicated New Englanders' understanding of their own recent earthquake experience, as the twenty-second stanza of the lengthy poem quoted above amply shows:

> While hapless [Cádiz] and Lisbon shake,
> From God their judgments did partake,
> His mercy sav'd his grace adore
> Which spar'd New-England's happy shore.

Like the English clergy who urged the faithful to repent in appreciation of God's mercy in having spared them, New Englanders came to see their far milder earthquake, in which no one died, as a sign of divine beneficence. Still, after the earthquake, as one observer reported, sinners repented and New England's "pulpits have generally rung with terror." [22]

Seeing the hand of God in earthquakes and other calamities was nothing new, but what was new and notable in the aftermath of Lisbon was the clergy's near-universal acknowledgment of the earthquake's "natural" or "secondary" causes, along with their unequivocal and sometimes combative attribution of those causes to divine power. As early as 1684, as we have seen, Increase Mather had taken a similar position, confidently assimilating the new science into his orthodox Calvinist worldview, which emphasized God's omnipotence and humanity's helplessness and depravity. By contrast, after Lisbon, clergy who discussed the natural or physical causes of earthquake were sometimes on the defensive, reacting to the scientific pronouncements of deists like John Freke, who believed that earthquakes were caused by elec-

Catastrophe in an Age of Enlightenment

LINES MADE AFTER

The Great Earthquake,

In 1755, which shook North and South America, with great destruction
in Cales, in Lisbon, and most of the adjacent kingdoms.

I.

AWAKE New-England now and view—
Thy God is just—his words are true ;—
His out-stretch'd arm will rule us by,
That power which sinner's deeds defy.

II.

In seventeen hundred fifty-five,
When vice its empire did revive,
Consuming fire, a jealous God
Call'd on New-England with his rod.

III.

The rod God's voice bid earth to shake,
Tremors which caus'd our hearts to ache,
Did cause confusion in our minds
As may be seen in following lines.

IV.

The moon arose all fair and bright
And shed forth silver rays that night
We in our beds had found repose,
But soon from them we trembling rose.

V.

Hark New-England—loud the thunder,
Awake ye sinners from your slumber
By deeds no longer do defy,
That power descending from the sky.

VI.

We through our habitations past,
Fearing our souls in hell be cast
While shattering building's loudly cry'd,
Your deeds have God's great power defy'd.

VII.

Conscience awake, still cry'd arise,
God's grace you have too long despis'd,
His honour sends to let you know,
He is not to be mocked so.

VIII.

These judgments he has sent to you—
Know he is just—his ways are true :
If you will not with him comply,
With fiercer judgments he will try.

IX.

Here some all in amaze did stand,
And saw with dread the shaking land,
While others wep't and mourn'd their fate
And cry'd and call'd but fear'd too late.

X.

To the wise virgins they repair'd,
A midnight cry was quickly heard,
Of foolish virgins to the wise,
Which pierc'd the clouds and rent the skies.

XI.

Sinners return'd to saints for grace,
Whom they had call'd the hated race ;
Asking for grace that they might live,
Who said we've none to sell or give.

XII.

The Lord made known his power so great,
They cry'd we have now come to late,
'Gainst his grace we did rebel,
power can send us quick to hell.

XIII.

They cry'd aloud, now spare us Lord,
And thee we'll serve with one accord :
Great God thou hast our follies borne,
To thee we'll turn for sin we'll mourn.

XIV.

God heard their cries, was pleas'd to spare,
Their vows were then recorded where,
They must appear henceforth shall rise
In distant worlds beyond the skies.

XV.

They who then left their sinful ways
And in Gods service spent their days,
Or life on earth were only wise
And rose to mansions in the skies.

XVI.

Yet some alas, who knew their God
By judgments and this awful rod,
Presum'd to sin, they passed on
We saw their end they were undone.

XVII.

Hear what excuse they then shall make,
When heaven and earth again shall shake ;
When Gabriel's trump aloud shall sound :
Awake ye dead, beneath the ground.

XVIII.

For God the judge to them shall say—
Did you not know this dreadful day ;
So loud I call'd to bring you home ;
But still you did refuse to come.

XIX.

My justice will not be controul'd,
My mercy it will not be sold,
By mocking God you made delay,
Despis'd my grace you lost your day.

XX.

Like Admah you in hell must burn,
Zeboim waits for your return,
My justice must now have its right.
And you must burn in endless night.

XXI.

America I loudly call,
Return to God as one and all,
'Tis mocking God to make delay,
Come seek for mercy, never stay.

XXII.

While hapless Cales and Lisbon shake,
From God their judgments did partake,
His mercy sav'd his grace adore,
Which spar'd New-England's happy shore.

XXIII.

While Lisbon sands roll as the waves,
And thousands cast into their graves ;
While Korah and his sons are lost,
His power secures and guards our coast.

XXIV.

In Lisbon God had some who knew
His name, declar'd him just and true ;
A Temple built they fear'd his name,
His praise they spake declar'd his fame.

XXV.

When mighty power shook buildings down,
Thousands receiv'd into the ground ;
Sinners and saints did here repair,
And cry'd to God in humble prayer.

XXVI.

God heard their cries, their lives he sav'd,
And others plung'd into the grave,
Egyptians fearing Moses rod,
Escape the judgments of their God.

XXVII.

But if ye still his warning hate,
Mercy despise until too late ;
To think of God your lives to mend,
To Hell your souls 'tis fear'd he'll send.

XXVIII.

He says to day come hear my voice,
Make me your portion and your choice ;
Riches I give which shall endure
When time on earth shall be no more.

XIX.

When ye seek me with all your heart,
My grace to you I will impart,
Your feet on Pisgas top shall view,
More glories than the rich Peruc.

XXX.

When death shall close your eyes from light,
And soul from earth shall take its flight,
A seat on high I have prepar'd,
There is your kingdom and reward.

XXXI.

Now since his mercies are so great
Turn to your God strive sin to hate ;
The Day's-man is at his right hand :
Attend the call at his command.

XXXII.

See many ways and manners too,
What his Almighty power can do,
Some thousands by his sword have fell,
And doom'd for e'er to burn in hell.

XXXIII.

Gods Chariot wheels roll on apace,
And call on Adam's sinful race,
He with long-suffering waits to see,
Sinners to him for refuge flee.

XXXIV.

Warned in time to him repair,
His mercies still abounding are,
Then you shall know the grace and bliss
Of Jesus and his righteousness.

XXXV.

Thus thence in heaven you'll rest from care,
From sin, from woes, from sorrows, where
In fields of endless light, you'll rise
In mansions far beyond the skies.

XXXVI.

In mansions there in bliss unknown,
High in salvation near the throne
Where saints and angels all shall join
In songs and anthems all divine.

***Lines Made after The Great Earthquake, In 1755, which shook North and
South America, with great destruction in Cales, in Lisbon, and most of the
adjacent kingdoms.*** Published in Boston, this pious poem warned New
Englanders to repent in the aftermath of their own recent earthquake and
also to show their gratitude for the protection and mercy of the Almighty,
who had unleashed his full fury on the "hapless" sinners of Portugal.
Library of Congress Printed Ephemera Collection.

trical currents that were part of a natural world that was created, but not immediately controlled, by a passive clockmaker God. Indeed, even some clergy were now prone to minimizing God's role in directly causing earthquakes and other calamities. As the Reverend Thomas Alcock put it, "Many of the Disasters and Calamities . . . that happen to Men in this World, arise, you see, from the present Constitution of Things, and not from any Anger of the Deity." [23]

In response, many orthodox clergy vigorously defended their belief in an omniscient and omnipotent deity. The Reverend John Pennington's forceful articulation of this view was typical. The Anglican rector of All Saints Parish in Cheshire, Pennington made his case succinctly in his fast day sermon, which he later published in hopes that "every Family" would read it and be reclaimed from "Evil" as a result. Taking issue with those who argued that earthquakes had "natural" causes and wars had "moral" ones, Pennington categorically stated that God, in fact, controlled both and was the "first Cause of all Things." [24]

Others agreed. As the Reverend John Burt of Rhode Island, explained, "If we consider Earthquakes as the Product of natural Causes, yet we must ultimately resolve them into the powerful Agency of God, the great Governor of the Universe." Only God, he argued, could have "planted that Artillery in the Bowels of the Earth, and discharges it in so terrible a Manner." The Reverend Jonathan Mayhew, one of the leading liberal Congregationalist ministers in Massachusetts, likewise reminded his audience, "All things and events, whether natural or preternatural, are under one, supreme, uniform DIRECTION, unless there is either no God, or more than One. The consequence of which is, that even natural effects and events, are to be traced up to this supreme, original cause of all things, whose counsel and providence govern the world; and His hand, to be acknowledged in them." Charles Chauncy, Mayhew's friend and fellow Bostonian, concurred. "Much has been said, upon the origins of earthquakes, by men of learning, but, after all that yet has been said, and by the greatest Philosophers too, perhaps this work of God may justly be ranked among those marvellous ones, which cannot be comprehended," he observed, adding, "*Second Causes* may, while working in a natural way, produce this effect; but still God is more a great deal the cause of them than they." An Englishman named John Biddulph reiterated that point in verse: "All things created God's Designs fulfill, / And nat'ral Causes work his destin'd Will." [25]

Pious men availed themselves of the opportunity the earthquake presented to discredit deists and atheists, both of whom they deemed grow-

Catastrophe in an Age of Enlightenment

ing threats to Protestant orthodoxy. "These Men would do well to consider, that as the *Elements*, of which the World is composed, are God's *Ministers* for furnishing Mankind with all the Comforts and Conveniencies, as well as the Necessaries of Life; so are they sometimes also made the *Messengers* of his Vengeance," declared the London clergyman James Halifax. Another London Anglican, the Reverend Charles Moss, mocked "the Language now in fashion" that denied divine power and providence by attributing "such Events . . . altogether to *natural Causes*; by which doubtless you would intimate, that Providence has no hand in them." Those "who are fond of this Language would do well to examine themselves, whether they understand rightly, what *natural Causes* mean," Moss warned, asserting unequivocally that "as they exist in Matter, [natural causes] . . . are nothing more than the Impressions on it by the Hand of the Creator; and are continued and maintained by his constant Agency." The Reverend Thomas Foxcroft of Boston also decried those who did not acknowledge God as the author of earthquakes and other natural phenomena. "It would be Atheism to ascribe these events to meer Casualty, or Chance," he believed, "and it would be vain *Philosophy*, to terminate all our Inquiry in meer natural Causes." The anonymous author of a tract titled *Reflections Physical and Moral* likewise inveighed against "philosophers" who attempt to discern the causes of earthquakes and other mysteries of the physical world without acknowledging God as "the Supreme Being, the Great First Cause."[26]

Although deists and atheists constituted only a minute portion of the population of Britain and its colonies, much of the non-sermon discourse in the aftermath of Lisbon assumed a more decidedly secular tone. This ruinous earthquake caused a flurry of empirical activity, beginning with the circulation of detailed questionnaires—by the government in Spain and by the church in Portugal—to gather information about its timing and impact. It also dramatically intensified scientific inquiry into the causes of earthquakes, as scientists across Europe posited theories and Professor John Winthrop of Harvard College produced his *Lecture on Earthquakes*. Public interest also increased in the aftermath of the Lisbon debacle. Scientific theories about the causes of earthquakes appeared not only in the journal of the Royal Society but also in the popular press. Scientific treatises and empirical descriptions of what happened in Lisbon dominated the pages of the *Gentleman's Magazine*, where they far outnumbered essays that approached the earthquake from theological or moral perspectives.[27]

Serious scientific inquiry into the causes of earthquakes did not necessarily signal a decline in religious belief but rather the increasingly standardized use of a language of empiricism and observation to communicate scientific knowledge and discovery. The Englishman John Michell, whom some regard as the father of modern seismology, is a case in point. Michell was the first to argue that the earth was composed of strata or layers, which amounted to an initial step in understanding plate tectonics, the way of understanding earthquake causation that became prevalent only in the mid-twentieth century. Taking issue with those who believed that electrical currents caused earthquakes, Michell argued instead that subterraneous fire, water, and vapor caused the earth's strata to shift, which, in turn, caused seismic activity. Michell never mentioned God or providence in his writings, but he, like roughly one in ten members of the Royal Society, was an ordained minister of the Protestant Church of England. John Winthrop of Harvard was not a clergyman, but he featured a quotation from another Anglican minister, William Derham, author of *Physico-Theology*, on the title page of his *Lecture on Earthquakes*. "Subterraneous caverns and volcanos, if well considered," wrote Derham, "will be found to be wise contrivances of the Creator, serving to great uses of the Globe, and ends of GOD's government."[28]

In important ways, both scientists and clergy focused on the future, not the past, parsing the physical and providential causes of the earthquakes and their significance for survivors. Scientifically minded observers like Michell and Winthrop hoped to understand the causes of earthquakes either to render them more predictable or to enhance the ability of humans to limit the physical wreckage that future quakes might cause. Clergy of various theological stripes sought to draw moral and religious lessons from the death and devastation to inspire the living to repent, reform, and thereby attain salvation in their eternal lives.

By contrast, another group of voices in the aftermath of the Lisbon earthquake focused on the present by privileging the victims, describing their pain and suffering in ways that both replicated and expanded affecting portrayals of victims of shipwrecks and other more pedestrian calamities. Voltaire, who was profoundly shocked by the Lisbon disaster, was the most self-conscious advocate of this distinctly modern perspective that emphasized the human costs of calamity, insisting that the only ethical response to Lisbon was to mourn the dead, ease the pain of the wounded, and help the sufferers to rebuild their city and their lives. While Voltaire's most famous work, *Candide*, used humor and satire to inspire both sympathy and outrage, his earlier *Poem upon the Lisbon Disaster* was a more angry and mournful rumination on the human costs of the earthquake and a forceful rejection of the view that "God, in His bounty, urged by a just cause," by the earthquake "exhibits His eternal laws." Voltaire's verses vividly described the excruciating fate of Lisbon's innocents:

> Women and children heaped up mountain high,
> Limbs crushed which under ponderous marble lie;
> Wretches unnumbered in the pangs of death,
> Who mangled, torn, and panting for their breath,
> Buried beneath their sinking roofs expire,
> And end their wretched lives in torments dire.[29]

Compared with an earlier generation of narrative accounts of shipwrecks and other calamities, eyewitness stories from the Lisbon earthquake showed a notable increase in the use of vivid portrayals of human bodies in pain in an effort to forge emotional bonds between victims and their potential benefactors among the reading public. This rhetorical strategy involved using detailed descriptions to generate a sense of authenticity to arouse powerful emotions that, in turn, might inspire a moral imperative to benevolence. What one historian has called "humanitarian narratives" emerged from the moralism of liberal Christianity and the Scottish Enlightenment—which counted an innate moral sense among humanity's defining attributes—and, more generally, from the culture of sensibility. By the mid-eighteenth century, novels were the most well known and popular examples of such narratives, but the same humanitarian agenda also increasingly informed medical case histories and, eventually, government inquiries into the dire conditions of the poor and factory and mining fatalities.[30]

The earliest news from Lisbon had conveyed first- or secondhand reports of what transpired without much elaboration. In late November, for instance, the editors of the *Whitehall Evening Post or London Intelligencer* simply informed their readers that they had learned via "Letters from France" that a "dreadful Earthquake" and a "terrible Fire" had killed some 60,000 people and destroyed the Portuguese capital, though "the King and Queen have happily escaped; and . . . the Palace had been preserved." The first published news from Lisbon that appeared in American colonial newspapers was equally succinct and unemotional. Drawing on the eyewitness account of the recently arrived Captain Collins, the Boston newspapers reported that the quake and the fire "shook down all the Buildings in [Lisbon], save two Churches and the Mint-House," while also destroying many ships and resulting in "the Loss of many Thousand Lives."[31]

In the coming months, as newspapers updated readers' knowledge of the situation in Lisbon, they sometimes added detailed descriptions of human suffering. In January 1756, one Captain Inches carried a letter from an English merchant to Boston, where it was published and then reprinted in newspapers in New York, Philadelphia, and Charleston. Beginning with a riveting description of how he personally experienced the movement and the sights, sounds, and smells of the disaster, the unnamed merchant then focused on the spectacle of human bodies in distress. As he and his family attempted to flee Lisbon, he wrote, they "pass[ed] every where dead bodies, others maimed, others with an arm lost, and some with their heads only free [from the rubble] but yet alive." After the merchant and his family found refuge aboard an English ship, he again reflected on the carnage they left behind. "Thousands of men, women, and children are destroyed and buried in the ruins; the Portuguese that escaped, lay in the open fields without any cover, and I fear multitudes will perish for the want of provisions," he wrote, adding, "The dead lay exposed, no thought of burying them, all desolation!"[32]

These interrelated themes of bodily misery, dismemberment, and vulnerability appeared frequently in longer eyewitness accounts that were published in popular magazines and as pamphlets in the months that followed. For instance, Antonio Pereira de Figueiredo, a Portuguese theologian and Latin scholar who witnessed the earthquake and who wrote his account in part to praise "the particular care and generosity" of the Portuguese king in its aftermath, penned a gripping description of the horror that engulfed his home city, perhaps in the hopes of eliciting sympathy from potential foreign benefactors. Figueiredo told affecting stories of individual suffering, such as the case of Dionysia Rose Maria, who clutched her St. Anthony statue for nine days while she was buried in the ruins, without food or water, before she was finally rescued. He also presented vivid tableaux of human misery that came to typify the genre. Figueiredo reported that after the earthquake, Lisbon's "streets and alleys were strewn with dead bodies." He informed his readers that many people "had their brains dashed out . . . others were crushed by the tumbling walls, most of them overpowered with the weight of rubbish." After the fire destroyed what was left of the city, survivors, including many of the "principal ladies of the kingdom"—barefoot, nearly naked, and with "ghastly countenances"—trod on "heaps of ruins and on dead carcasses."[33]

By the time Figueiredo's account was published in London, with English and Latin texts on alternating pages, the *Gentleman's Magazine* had already circulated some similarly visceral reports from English eyewitnesses. Indeed, that popular periodical devoted most of its December 1755 issue to

Catastrophe in an Age of Enlightenment

coverage of the Lisbon disaster, publishing scientific essays on the causes of earthquakes, a dispassionate report from the British envoy in Lisbon, and several first-person accounts that included unusually lurid descriptions of the carnage that pervaded the ruined city. Englishmen attested to stepping over the bodies of the dead and dying, which littered the streets, and they described the "dead bodies, legs, arms, &c." floating in waterways and flooded areas. One eyewitness reported having seen "8 or 9000 dead bodies, some upon the rubbish, others half way up their bodies in the rubbish, standing like statues," and hearing "the groans, shrieks, and cries of great numbers, who were buried in and under the rubbish." The exposed and mutilated bodies betokened not only the physical pain of individuals but also the collapse of civilized society.[34]

Escape was difficult, with people being crushed and suffocated in the disorder. Many "being blinded by the smoke, lost their way, and so ran headlong into the midst of the flames," while some "women and children, and ancient people, died of the fright." One Englishman who was in Lisbon at the time of the earthquake recalled thousands of people "having their brains knocked out" by falling buildings and other debris as they sought to escape the narrow streets of the burning city. Yet even those survivors who managed to escape and take refuge in the fields of Belem, outside the city, remained both miserable and vulnerable. Many of the refugees were "half naked" and lacked both food and shelter. As one eyewitness put it, "The scene of misery and destruction is so horrible, that one's blood grows cold at giving you a description of it." Others agreed that the horror continued even after the worst was over. "It is not to be expressed by human Tongue how dreadful and how awful it was to enter the City after the Fire was abated," another Englishman reported, declaring that he was "struck with Horror in beholding dead Bodies by six or seven in a Heap, crushed to Death, half buried and half burnt."[35]

Many of the more substantive accounts from Lisbon combined explicit descriptions of bodily suffering with a compelling personal narrative. One of the most important and widely read of these was *An Account of the late Dreadful Earthquake and Fire, which destroyed the City of Lisbon . . . In a Letter from a Merchant Resident there, to his Friend in England,* a pamphlet of more than twenty pages that was published in London in 1755 and reprinted in Boston the following year. The author described his work as an eyewitness account that he composed and published to gratify the "curiosity" of his "friends." By inserting an advertisement for two recently published captivity narratives — which chronicled the shocking experiences of white colonists who had been captured by Indians and for a time had lived among the "savages"—inside his edition of the pamphlet, however, its Boston publisher hinted at what he believed to be the additional appeal of this particular work. Like a captivity narrative, this version of the Lisbon story both highlighted the unique horrors of an exotic locale and served as a vehicle for the performance of a presumed English superiority.[36]

Much of the anonymous author's story is in keeping with other eyewitness accounts of the earthquake and its aftermath. Lisbon, the author maintained, was "such a Spectacle of Terror and Amazement, as well as of Desolation . . . as perhaps has not been equaled from the Foundation of the World!" The disaster, he believed, inflicted "numberless Miseries, and terrible Distresses of all Kinds," including "the shocking Effects that it had on the Minds of all People," whose faces exhibited "Signs of Terror and Distress." Like other authors, this one included explicit descriptions of "Persons almost naked," dismemberment, and excruciating physical anguish. The numbers of "broken-limbed Persons," he reported, were "infinite"; thousands were either "buried in the Ruins of the falling Buildings" or "left to the miserable Torture of being burnt alive." Women "big with Child were delivered in the open Fields and Places, amidst the Groans and Cries of the trembling Multitudes."[37]

While the author clearly sympathized with the sufferers, he also contrasted what he believed to be the slavish ignorance of Portuguese Catholics with the stoic hardiness of the English Protestants who lived among them. Perhaps not surprisingly, the narrator himself is the closest thing to a hero in this otherwise horrific story: after saving his housekeeper from near-certain death amid the rubble, he accompanied a group of refugees to safety in "an English Gentleman's Country-house" and then returned to the city (although it is not clear what he did once he arrived there). This eyewitness believed that Catholic superstitions prevented the people of Lisbon from responding more effectively to the crisis. As the flood engulfed Lisbon, he found that "there was nothing to be seen but Gatherings of Crowds about Priests and Friars, all falling on their Knees, kissing the Earth, beating their Breasts, slapping their Cheeks, and crying out for Absolution, which was granted in general Terms to Hundreds of them at once." While this Englishman seemed to pity the benighted Portuguese laity—those "poor ignorant Creatures" who seemed unwilling and unable to help themselves—he condemned Lisbon's Catholic clergy as manipulative and self-aggrandizing. Like some other English eyewitnesses, he also took great satisfaction in reporting that his own compatriots and those other "Protestants of many Nations who resided in that Metropolis" were far more likely to survive the disaster, leaving the reader to judge whether this fortuitous outcome was due to their own resilience or the protection of the Almighty.[38]

Spurred by religion, science, sensibility, and a general curiosity about the wider world, writers and readers thus created a discourse in the aftermath of Lisbon that was by any measure unparalleled. Some contemporaries questioned the accuracy of much of what they read or heard: one Englishman decried "the plentiful stock of fiction, falsehood, nonsense and bombast, which our greedy journalists and venal pamphleteers have drain'd from the disasters of *Portugal*." But the sheer volume of tracts, sermons, essays, poems, and images devoted to the earthquake and its consequences was unrivaled. At the same time, a combination of commercial and geopolitical interests—the Portuguese king was connected by blood and marriage to Spain and Austria, and his country was diplomatically aligned with Britain—and well-publicized accounts of the suffering in Portugal made the Lisbon earthquake a pivotal moment in the history of Western humanitarianism. The earthquake gave rise to an outpouring of sympathy and a robust humanitarian discourse, along with an unprecedented international relief effort, in which Britons were prominent participants.[39]

In addition to the stories of Protestant Englishmen who responded capably to the crisis, other reports highlighted the benevolence of British residents of Lisbon, both individually and collectively. One English merchant recounted his own efforts to save his Portuguese servant from the rubble and his willingness to risk further danger by searching for a surgeon to treat her injuries. Another praised the efforts of Joseph Morley, an English tavern keeper in Lisbon, who "generously gave such relief and succour to every one as their circumstances required." Noting the competence and generosity of his countrymen, an English ship captain reported that "Every Body's Hopes [were] fixed on *England*" in the aftermath of the "dismal Catastrophe" that wrecked the Portuguese capital.[40]

Articles in the British and colonial press publicized the good deeds of their countrymen. They especially praised the British merchants who lived and worked in Lisbon for their "Sympathy, Condolence, and Compassion" in relieving the suffering of the "Widows and the Fatherless," as well as for their generosity in furnishing the Portuguese king with corn, flour, rice, and other supplies needed to avert famine as the city and its people struggled for survival. The merchants, "upon this melancholy Occasion," one eyewitness observed, "have acted with Wisdom and Honour worthy of their Country." As more than one commentator noted, a combination of benevolence and "Prudence" motivated the merchants "for amidst an unhoused and distracted People, there was no Security for Property of that Kind, especially if the Owners of [provisions] had pretended to stand upon Terms."[41]

This third approach to the Lisbon story, which focused on relief and emphasized the humanitarian contributions of the British people, drew on the widely shared belief that benevolence was a distinctive and defining characteristic of the British nation. By the 1750s, cities in both Britain and its American colonies had private societies to assist the poor and the sick, and the Church of England sponsored or was connected to various philanthropic groups, many of which received donations from the king and others in the highest ranks of British society. Like the English merchants who helped survivors of the Lisbon earthquake, these groups espoused benevolence both to aid the suffering and to maintain social order. The earthquake in Lisbon, which occasioned both extreme suffering and extreme disorder, elicited much sympathy from Britons, who also valued Portugal as a longtime military ally and important commercial partner. This blend of benevolence and self-interested practicality impelled King George II to send £100,000 in funds and provisions to Lisbon as post-disaster relief.[42]

In some ways, the king's determination to help the Portuguese was reminiscent of London's effort to aid the residents of South Carolina's capital in 1740, when a "great fire" destroyed some £250,000 in property and left a substantial portion of Charleston's population homeless and destitute. In response to the Charleston fire, Parliament sent £20,000 in aid, the first and only time that the London-based government provided such sizable disaster relief to any of its colonies before the American Revolution. This seemingly generous support for South Carolinians, however, was more a concerted effort to protect the valuable rice-producing colony, already vulnerable to both slave insurrections and Spanish depredations, than an act of conscious benevolence.[43]

There were important differences in both the quantity and perceived quality of aid sent to Lisbon and Charleston after their respective disasters. Disaster relief for Portugal not only was five times the sum sent to the South Carolina capital but also was explicitly and very publicly a performance of British benevolence by a monarch who purposefully represented the putative virtues of his people. In 1755, whatever compelling strategic considerations figured into his decision to send aid to Lisbon, George II was a model of kingly benevolence when he took the lead in orchestrating his nation's prompt, sympathetic, and highly publicized response to the Portuguese crisis. Within days of the arrival of the news from Lisbon in late November, the king drafted an address to both houses of Parliament in which he expressed his "greatest concern for so good and faithful an ally as the King of Portugal, and . . . the utmost compassion" for the people of Lisbon. The monarch recommended that Parliament authorize and send "such speedy and effectual relief as may be suitable to so afflicting and pressing an exigency." In response to the king's message, his ministers immediately organized the dispatch of four ships laden with specie, provisions, and other supplies: £50,000 in gold and silver, along with large quantities of beef, butter, flour, wheat, biscuits, rice, tools and hardware, and shoes. Parliament voted to fund the effort a few days later.[44]

Although £100,000 was only a tiny fraction of the British government's annual expenditures — which averaged roughly £7,000,000 in peacetime and much more in times of war — the gift to Portugal was an important and well-publicized demonstration of royal largesse, though, constitutionally speaking, the money actually came from Parliament. Indeed, while George II was not a particularly popular or charismatic monarch, the German-born septuagenarian received accolades for his generosity and compassion in the aftermath of the earthquake. The crisis in Lisbon inspired a remarkable amount of commemorative poetry, and some of these overly saccharine verses rhapsodized the British king. One poet described George II as the only hope of a suffering people:

> Amidst the Ruins his benev'lent Voice,
> The mournful Suff'rers ravish'd Ears rejoice;
> His Word protects them with Parental Care;
> Thrice envy'd all who GEORGE's Bounties share;
> Who tastes the Blessing that a lib'ral Hand;
> A tender Heart bequeath's [sic] a Foreign Land.[45]

Members of the British clergy likewise applauded the king's benevolence. In a sermon preached on 30 November — the first Sunday after the arrival of the alarming news from Portugal and only two days after George II sent his request for aid to Parliament — the Reverend Thomas Gibbons preached a sermon at Haberdashers Hall in London. Like many of his ecclesiastical colleagues, Gibbons believed that the earthquake was a sign from God and that Londoners should not be complacent because their own wickedness could have just as easily led the Almighty to choose their own city as its target. Before the earthquake, he argued, the main difference between Catholic Lisbon and Protestant London was that the latter enjoyed the benefits of true religion, liberty, and good government. After urging his audience to repent and show sympathy toward the suffering Portuguese, Gibbons turned to consider the "tender Benevolence of the best of Kings . . . the Father of his Country, and indeed Mankind, . . . towards these unhappy Sufferers."[46]

Well aware that Britain was once again on the brink of war with France in Europe—in fact, hostilities already had begun in America—Gibbons emphasized that the king's benevolence could have wide-ranging consequences. On the one hand, George's royal line, the House of Hanover, had survived a challenge from Catholic Stuart pretenders as recently as 1745; like most other patriotic Britons, Gibbons was a staunch Hanoverian who happily celebrated the durability of the Protestant monarchy. The benevolence of George II, he declared, "sheds more Glories upon him and the Crown he wears, and . . . will convey his Name down through the present and future Ages. . . . Let this Instance of royal Generosity silence every malignant Tongue . . . let it shew Princes what they ought to be." On the other hand, Gibbons also opined that the benevolence of George II might win him more allies—or at least fewer enemies—across Europe in the impending war, as news of his goodness could "melt down *Popish* Rancour and Malice" and "scatter every Suspicion or Surmise, that may be raised and propagated by *French* Artifice and Falshood" by showing others that "our King wants Tenderness for the Lives and Felicities of Mankind." In sum, by aiding the Portuguese, Gibbons believed that George II had acted as both a compassionate and humane Christian and a perceptive statesman.[47]

The Reverend Thomas Anguish also praised George II for his benevolent leadership. Anguish was a strong Hanoverian who had preached a sermon to celebrate the defeat of the pro-Stuart rebels who had sought to depose George II in 1745. In the sermon he delivered on the fast day appointed by royal proclamation in February 1756, Anguish criticized the sinfulness of Britons and Portuguese alike, decried the cruel intolerance of Portuguese Catholicism, and praised the Protestant monarchy of George II for its virtue and benevolence. "To the eternal honour of our most gracious Sovereign," he declared, "and the grand council of these nations assembled in Parliament, a certain intelligence of the terrible catastrophy at *Lisbon* was no sooner communicated than bewailed" by the leaders of the British nation. "No sooner was there, by the ROYAL LETTER, a speedy, generous, and effectual relief recommended, but granted with an unison of mind and voice, without hesitation, without delay!" How much more becoming of Christians, Anguish observed, to "pour out the tears of yielding humanity" and to aid the Portuguese instead of callously passing judgment on them.[48]

Because the king and Parliament represented the nation, commentators who shared little else in terms of a common perspective nonetheless agreed that the benevolence of George II was emblematic of the values and identity of the British nation generally. Shortly after Britons learned of the king's decision to aid the Portuguese, the Reverend Samuel Clark called on his subjects to emulate their sovereign by exhibiting "the most tender Sentiments of *Humanity* and Compassion" toward the suffering Portuguese. In his fast day sermon, the Reverend William Nowell agreed that "our Hearts must melt in Sympathy" and rejoiced that Britons had "a King who . . . with a Speed and Generosity equal to the extreme Necessity of the surviving Sufferers, extended that beneficent and hospitable Relief to the Distressed, for which the *English* Nation had ever been . . . renowned in the Earth!" The author of a poem written to praise the king's benevolence likewise celebrated the unrivaled humanity of his subjects. An anonymous author who identified himself only as "A Man of Business" argued that Britons should take special pride in the benevolence exhibited by George II, Parliament, and the British merchants in Lisbon, whose actions signified "the same spirit of generosity (so natural to every true born *Briton*)." Any of his countrymen who did not share and applaud this benevolent spirit, he believed, "would deserve to be deem'd a traitor to his country, for daring to tarnish its glory, by bringing upon us a scandal, which we no way deserve, and rendering us suspected of a meanness from which we are utterly averse."[49]

Across the Atlantic, where colonists were increasingly preoccupied with the war against the French and their Indian allies, the benevolence of the king nonetheless received ample coverage in the local press. In February 1756, colonial newspapers informed their readers that ships laden with "Pickaxes, Shovels, Flour, and all other Necessities" left England, bound for Portugal, along with "his Majesty's Letters of Condolance," to relieve the "unhappy destitute Inhabitants of Lisbon." In March, the *Boston Evening-Post* reported the story in a way that made it clear that, although Parliament had allocated the necessary funds, the king was chiefly responsible for aiding the victims of the quake. "In consequence of a most gracious message from His Majesty to the legislature," the *Evening-Post* reported, "both houses, we hear, have unanimously voted 100,000£ towards the relief of the unhappy sufferers of the dreadful calamity at Lisbon." Colonial newspapers also printed the text of the king's message to the House of Lords, in which he described the earthquake as a "dreadful and extensive calamity, which cannot fail to affect the hearts of all persons who have any sense of religion or humanity." In April, they reported the king of Portugal's "Return of Thanks to our Most Gracious Sovereign, and the whole Nation, for the kind benevolent Presents voted by Parliament for the Relief of his unhappy distressed Subjects." When the governor of Pennsylvania followed the king's example by proclaiming a day of fasting and prayer for his province, he noted that George II had been "touched with a deep Sense" of the suffering of the victims of the quake.[50]

This outpouring of affection and esteem among colonists was both cause and consequence of the ongoing celebration of the Protestant Hanoverians that had reached a crescendo in America, though not in Britain, by the eighteenth century's middle decades. While Britons at home viewed the actions of the king and Parliament as markers of a collective national benevolence, colonists interpreted the provision of disaster relief for Lisbon primarily as evidence of the personal beneficence of their monarch. While the nationalism that emerged in Great Britain after the defeat of the pro-Stuart rebellion in 1745 was strongly Protestant, commercial, and anti-French, it was comparatively apathetic toward the specific person who occupied the British throne. Colonists, by contrast, admired and celebrated the king for his virtue and benevolence even as the cult of monarchy declined in the mother country. Colonial newspapers and almanacs conveyed flattering accounts of the king to eager readers, many of whom likely owned mass-produced portraits of the Hanoverian monarchs, which by the 1730s were widely available in British colonial America. In 1755, when news of the king's efforts to help the Portuguese reached America, it confirmed the good feelings that many colonists already had about their king—and, by extension, about their membership in the British Empire.[51]

While the death of the seventy-six-year-old George II in October 1760, after a thirty-three-year reign, elicited elaborate but mostly emotionally subdued mourning among the British general public, members of the clergy praised the late king's generosity, and at least one specifically cited his speedy and "tender" response to the crisis in Lisbon five years earlier. Colonists, too, mourned the loss of the old king, whom their clergy eulogized as a man of benevolence and virtue and as a father to his people. In New Hampshire, the Reverend Samuel Haven averred that "as a man," the king had "display'd that kindness, that condescention, that tender pity towards the miserable . . . so that thro' the whole of his happy reign, he hath exhibited the most undoubted proof of his sincere affection, and tender conscience for his people." The pastor of Boston's Brattle Street Church called George II "the Friend of human Kind."[52]

The Reverend Samuel Davies delivered the most widely circulated posthumous colonial commemoration of George II at Princeton's Nassau Hall on 14 January 1761. The Presbyterian Davies had delivered a powerful sermon in Virginia in the aftermath of the Lisbon and New England earthquakes. A few years later, in 1759, he became the president of the College of New Jersey. A staunch supporter of the French and Indian War, Davies appreciated the old king's qualities as a leader in both war and peace, celebrating him as "GEORGE, the Mighty, the just, the Gentle, and the Wise; GEORGE, the Father of *Britain* and her Colonies, the Guardian of Laws and Liberty, the Protector of the Oppressed, the Arbiter of *Europe*, the Terror of Tyrants and *France*; GEORGE, the Friend of Man, the Benefactor of Millions." Although he did not mention the Lisbon disaster explicitly, Davies lauded the king's generosity overall. "If Majesty has any Charms, to a Mind truly noble; if Dominion has any attractive Influence upon a benevolent Spirit," he asserted, "it must be, as it affords a more extensive Sphere of Beneficence, and yields the generous disinterested God-like Pleasure of making Multitudes happy. And in this Respect, how happy and illustrious was our late King!"[53]

Like the ideal of kingly benevolence, the earthquake itself retained its hold on the popular imagination years after it was over. British magazines and colonial almanacs reprinted earthquake-related items throughout the 1760s. In 1777, the London-based *Moral & Entertaining Magazine* republished the story of the woman who clung to her St. Anthony statue for nine days while she awaited rescue amid the rubble. In 1800, a London printer published and advertised a brief account of the earthquake as a complement to a traveling show that featured a painting that "exhibits the awful and sublime effects of the Earthquake, which destroyed Lisbon, on the 1st of November, 1755." More curiously, the Lisbon disaster made a cameo appearance in the postrevolutionary debate in the United States over the ratification of the proposed federal constitution, when one New Yorker who supported ratification likened the document's allegedly lawless anti-federalist critics to the "wretches that were seen plundering the city of Lisbon during the convulsions of the earthquake." Perhaps not coincidentally, in 1848, while revolutions convulsed Europe, a "cyclorama" depicting the famous Portuguese earthquake was on display in London.[54]

Compelling images and written accounts together also helped make the city of Lisbon a magnet for visitors, an early destination for what is now called disaster tourism. Affluent Britons on the Grand Tour traditionally favored France and Italy, but after the earthquake many added Lisbon to their itinerary so that they could view the city's ruins. Some visitors recorded their impressions in travel journals, which they later published. For instance, in 1760, Joseph Baretti left London and began his European tour in Portugal before moving on to Spain, France, and Italy. "I have now visited the ruins of Lisbon," he wrote that September, "and a dreadful indelible image is now imprinted on my mind." For Baretti, the emotional impact of his visit was profound. Even five years after the "ever-memorable earthquake," so much of the city remained "leveled to the ground" and so much "rubbish" remained. "Such a scene of horrible desolation no words are equal to," he reported sadly, adding, "It is ocular inspection only that can give an adequate idea of the calamity which this city has suffer'd."[55]

§ The Lisbon earthquake was an unusually powerful cultural event that profoundly shaped understandings of and responses to disaster in Europe and America. The Portuguese crisis pushed to the forefront old questions about the relative roles of God and nature in causing earthquakes and other calamities while inspiring new scientific efforts to resolve the mysteries of the physical world. Robust discourse surrounding the earthquake and its aftermath raised both old and new questions in a variety of formats—newspapers, sermons, poems, broadsides, visual images—that were accessible to sizable audiences, while stories from Lisbon engaged their readers' sensibilities. Finally and perhaps most important, unprecedented relief efforts and the aggressive rebuilding of the Portuguese capital illuminated the potential role of the state in disaster planning and relief. After Lisbon, disasters large and small became newsworthy episodes that inspired the usual combination of piety, curiosity, and sympathy. They also increasingly led to new discussions concerning the collective responsibilities of people and governments to relieve the distress of sufferers.

{ 4 }

BENEVOLENT

EMPIRE

The Lisbon earthquake was more a turning point than a starting point in the history of British benevolence. In addition to local philanthropy to aid the poor and the sick at home, eighteenth-century Britons sometimes sent charitable gifts to the king's American subjects. The most impressive case of British aid to colonists came in response to the Charleston fire of 1740, when the relief efforts of colonial governors, London merchants, and others were supplemented by a sizable contribution from the king and Parliament. Government relief for Charleston, which was not widely publicized, was an act of statecraft designed primarily to preserve order in a valuable colony that seemed vulnerable to slave insurrections and also to Spanish attacks from nearby Florida. In 1755, by contrast, disaster relief for Lisbon, whatever its other purposes, was presented and perceived as state-sponsored humanitarianism first and foremost.[1]

Despite the outpouring of support for Charleston in 1740, colonists' routine and explicit expectation of relief from Britain in the aftermath of disasters was a post-Lisbon development. The king's gift to Portugal was a grand gesture that resonated profoundly among subjects who cherished the ideal of a benevolent monarch. Fortified by the lessons of Lisbon, colonists sought help from the mother country in the wake of calamity. More often than not, Britons assisted colonial disaster victims but—like the £20,000 dispatched to Charleston, a city that had suffered some £250,000 in fire-related losses—the sums provided were less a practical remedy for a dire situation than a performance of benevolence. Moreover, in the decades after Lisbon, only twice did the king (either on his own or together with Parliament) offer direct aid to his suffering colonial subjects. In 1765, in the midst of the Stamp Act controversy, which began the imperial crisis that eventually led to the American Revolution, George III "was pleased to give" £500 in relief to victims of a fire that had ravaged Montreal, an important commercial center in Britain's newly acquired Canadian territory. In 1781, during the American War of Independence, Parliament allocated the extraordinary sum of £120,000 to the loyal sugar-producing island colonies of Jamaica and Barbados for relief in the aftermath of the ruinous hurricanes of October 1780.[2]

Focusing primarily on five episodes between 1760 and 1780, this chapter examines the rhetoric and realities of imperial disaster relief, from Canada to the West Indies, in an increasingly tumultuous era. After fires, floods, and hurricanes, colonists invoked sensibility, benevolence, and the bonds of empire, exploiting dense networks of transatlantic, intercolonial, and local connections in hopes of obtaining assistance from government officials, merchants, and others, whose benevolence was tempered by their own interests and the shifting circumstances of imperial politics. In the decades after Lisbon, Britons on both sides of the Atlantic commonly construed disaster relief as benevolence provided to sufferers in a far-flung imperial community, though the performance of benevolence was also a tool of statecraft, a political tactic deployed to mitigate colonial discontent, strengthen the imperial bond, and solidify a shared sense of British national identity.

§ Among the most significant colonial disasters of the post-Lisbon decades were the fires in Boston and Montreal—in 1760 and 1765, respectively—the flooding of Virginia's James River Basin in 1771, and the unusually severe hurricanes that devastated the British West Indies in 1772 and 1780. Only in Boston, where the city and its residents suffered more than £50,000 sterling in property losses—some estimates were much higher—were there no deaths. At the other end of the spectrum, the hurricanes in Barbados and Jamaica in 1780 were the deadliest in Caribbean history, resulting in as many as 22,000 fatalities and financial losses in excess of £2,000,000 sterling. Local newspapers reported these calamities, and accounts of them arrived in other colonies in as little as a few days or as much as six weeks later. It typically took two months or more for news of colonial disasters to appear in London newspapers.[3]

Although newspapers were critical in spreading disaster stories and mobilizing donors for post-disaster relief efforts, the most effective requests for aid and responses to such appeals flowed through a dense combination of governmental, commercial, and personal networks. Colonial governors, who were required to report regularly to imperial authorities in London, could apply to the home government for assistance, but many also had closer contacts among officials in other colonies. For their part, colonial assemblies employed agents, most of whom were well-connected English merchants or lawyers, to represent their interests to the king, Parliament, and imperial officials in London. Colonial merchants had long-standing business and personal relationships with merchants in other provinces, as well as in London and other British ports. Some wealthy colonists forged face-to-face connections in Britain by visiting or by sending their sons abroad to be educated. Religious and philanthropic groups cultivated transatlantic ties, as did the learned men (and a few women) whose correspondence on science and other topics created an Enlightenment-inspired transatlantic intellectual community. To varying degrees, these official, commercial, and personal networks shaped responses to disasters in the post-Lisbon era.[4]

The first of these incidents was the conflagration in Boston on Thursday, 20 March 1760, which local newspapers described as "the most terrible fire that has happened to this town or perhaps in any other part of North-America." In truth, no one died as a result of the fire that began at two o'clock on that morning and raged for nearly seven hours before being extinguished by people from Boston, including some of the city's "greatest personages," and from neighboring communities. Although the fire destroyed some 400 buildings—houses, workshops, warehouses—as well as several ships laden with valuable cargoes, the estimated financial losses totaled only slightly more than one-fifth of those suffered in Charleston in 1740.[5]

But in March 1760, Bostonians assessed the severity of the fire in light of their own experiences. An omnipresent threat in densely populated areas crowded with wooden structures, fire was common in colonial Boston. At least nine major fires had occurred there previously, making conflagration a part the community's shared history and civic identity. Founded in 1630, Boston's town meeting implemented fire regulations, purchased its first fire engine, and became home to the first colonial fire company in the 1670s. By 1760, Boston had nine fire companies, each made up of twenty men who could operate fire engines that pumped water to supplement the efforts of local bucket brigades. When the creator of *A New Plan of ye Great Town of Boston in New England in America* sought to embellish his work with key information from the city's history, he chose three categories to list, with dates, at the bottom of his map: important buildings erected in the city, smallpox epidemics, and "Great Fires." The fire of 1760 was listed as Boston's "Tenth Terrible Fire," the added adjective affirming that it displaced the fire of 1711 as its most ruinous conflagration. Boston newspapers began their coverage of the 1760 fire by contrasting it with two lesser fires that had occurred the preceding year, both of which had been readily contained by the "dexterity" and "vigilance" of the "People in general of all Ranks."[6]

Telling the story of the fire was the first step in seeking relief for its victims, those left homeless and in some cases penniless as a result of the crisis. In the days immediately after the fire, three authoritative voices provided complementary narratives. Governor, clergy, and the press agreed that, though the apparently accidental fire was at least indirectly an act of God, aiding its victims—both during and after the conflagration—would depend on human agency.

The first newspaper account of the incident, published the day after the fire, set the tone by noting the "distressed Condition of those who inhabited the buildings which were consumed, scarce knowing where to take Shelter" from "the spreading Destruction," while praising the efforts of those who fought the flames and those who took special care to assist young children, the sick, and the elderly. A few days later, the *Boston Evening-Post* reminded readers in the afflicted city and beyond that "without the compassionate assistance of our Christian friends ... distress and ruin may quite overwhelm" the fire's suffering victims. At the same time, however much they recognized the real and potential impact of humans in causing, extinguishing, or preventing fires, commentators also saw the hand of God in the unfortunate event and its consequences. "Notwithstanding the long Continuance of the Fire, the Explosion of the South Battery, and the falling of the Walls and Chimnies," intoned the *Boston News-Letter*, "Divine Providence appeared mercifully in that not one Person's Life was lost: & only a few wounded."[7]

After the fire, things moved quickly in Boston, a densely populated, highly literate, and civic-minded community that was also the capital of the Massachusetts colony. Governor Thomas Pownall, a popular royal appointee who likely numbered among those esteemed personages who helped to extinguish the flames, quickly convened the colonial legislature, expressing sympathy for the fire's victims and urging the province's lawmakers to act on their behalf. Pownall emphasized the devastation caused by the fire, as a result of which some 220 families had lost their homes, three-quarters of whom were consequently "incapable of subsisting themselves, and ... reduced to extream poverty and require immediate relief." The governor urged the legislators to appoint a committee to work with Boston's local authorities to implement some "effectual measures," such as the widening of streets and new prohibitions on building with wood, to limit the damage from future fires. The legislators, in turn, voted to give £3,000 from the public treasury to Boston for humanitarian purposes; a few days later, they ordered that no taxes were to be collected from Bostonians who lost their houses to the flames, and they also agreed to work with the town of Boston on new fire regulations, as Pownall had suggested. Finally, the assembly also called on the governor to embark on a fund-raising effort throughout Massachusetts by "strongly recommending the unhappy case of the sufferers to the inhabitants, and calling upon them for a general contribution" for their relief.[8]

Pownall immediately complied with the legislators' request, issuing "a brief" as a broadside to be circulated throughout the province. Public officials had circulated charity briefs to solicit aid for victims of calamities in England since at least the sixteenth century; by the eighteenth century the practice had made its way to the colonies in America. Pownall's brief, which was also reprinted in the *Boston Evening-Post*, reiterated the logic of early press reports, nodding to divine providence while at the same time depending on human efforts to relieve the suffering of Bostonians in crisis. "It having pleased Almighty GOD to permit a Fire to break out in the Town of *Boston*," the governor began, prefacing his call for the people of Massachusetts to "express their Christian Benevolence on this Occasion, by contributing in Proportion to the Means with which GOD has blessed them" to ease the distress of "these worthy Objects of their Charity." Pownall ordered all Massachusetts clergy to "read or cause to be read" his appeal to their respective congregations.[9]

The Reverend Jonathan Mayhew, a prominent Boston minister, shared the governor's views and even anticipated his call for benevolence. Mayhew, who had affirmed the divine origins of earthquakes a few years earlier, now reiterated God's omnipotence as "the author of all those calamities and sufferings, which at any time befall a city, or community," including the recent fire. In a sermon delivered only three days after the fire, Mayhew emphasized God's purposeful providence, both in making the fire more severe than its predecessors and in preventing fatalities. Declaring that all humans were to some degree sinful, Mayhew urged people to repent and reform, but—unlike those clergy who prescribed only introspection and Bible study to

OVERLEAF *A New Plan of ye Great Town of Boston in New England in America.*
William Price made this map during the governorship of Jonathan Belcher (acknowledged in the cartouche) in the early 1730s. He later produced and sold updated versions, as Bostonians built "Additionall Buildings & New Streets" in their growing community. Price's original map listed eight "Great Fires," the earliest of which was in 1653 and the latest in 1711. This 1769 map, the last in the series, includes two more: the "Ninth Fire" in 1759 and the "Tenth Terrible Fire" in 1760.
Library of Congress Geography and Map Division.

A New Plan ... of ȳ Great Town of BOSTON in New E

With the many ... Additionall Buildings, ȳ New Streets, to the Ye

BOSTON the Metropolis of New England, is the largest, most populous and flourishing Town in the British North, and 71 Day West from London. It stands at the Botom of a large Bay, Which (by being defended by diverse delightful Islands) May be reckon'd among the safest and most Commodious Harbours in the World. At the E... and about 2 Leagues towards the Town, a Strong Castle Mounted with about 120 Cannon, The Country round ... with all Sorts of good Provisions, And all other Necessaries of Life; Thether is exceeding clear & Pleasant, Pleasant Constitutions, This Town hath been Settled ... Years, Its Number of Houses about 4000 and Inhabitants abo... 10 Congregational Meeting Houses, a French, 1 Anabaptist, 3 Irish & 2 Quakers Meeting Houses, And a very handsom... Town House where the Cours are held, The Town and Country daily increasing, In the Year 172... were built in New England above 100 Sail of Ships and other Vessels, Most of which ... are said at Boston, There are in one Year clear'd out of this Port at the Custo... House, above 200 Sail of Vessels, which may in some Measure shew the gener... Trade of this flourishing Town and Country in the Year.

1735 this Town was Divided into 12 Wards, by a Vote of the Inhabitants & bounded by the Wards are the prit Lines from ... 1720, in each Ward is a Military Company of Foot & a Captain & Also one ... Overseers of ȳ Poor Chosen Yearly in March ...

To His Excellency Jonathan Belcher Esq
Capt General and Governour in Chief
of His Majesties Provinces of ...
the Massachusets Bay New
Hampshire in New England ...
and Vice Admiral of the same,
in ȳ Plan of the great Town
LONDON is humbly
dedicated by His Excellencies
most obedient & humble ...
William Price

Printed for & Sold by W. Price at ȳ Kings Head, & Looking Glass, in Cornhill, Near the Town House in Boston, Where is Sold a Large New South East Prospect of Boston Neatly done & A Prospect of the Colledge's in Cambridge New England And Great Variety of Mapps & Prints of all Sorts in Frames & Glass or without Also Pictures Painted in Oyle in Carvd Gilt Frams, Likewise Sells and frames all Sorts & Sizes of ȳ Newest fashion'd Looking Glasses, Tea Tabl's, China Ware, English & Dutch Toys for Children, by Wholesale or Retail at Reasonable Rates
Note this hand Points to the Kings Head & Looking Glass in Cornhill Also Flutes, Hautboys & Violins, Strings, Musical Books, Songs, Spectacles, & Prospect Glasses &c.

The Names of the 12 Wards:
1. Quarter Street Ward
2. North Street Ditto
3. Fleet Street Ditto
4. Pond Ward
5. Alms St Wd
6. Hanover Ditto
7. Cambridge D.
8. Kings St D.
9. Cornhill D.
10. Malbrough D.
11. Summer St D.
12. Orange St D.

Scale of ½ a Mile.

COMMON

Powder House
Watch House

Hills Wharf

Wind Mill Point

BOSTON N E
Planted An. Dom. 1630

EXPLANATION.

A. The Old Meeting	1630
B. Old North M.	1650
C. Old South M.	1660
D. Annabaptist M.	1680
E. Kings Chappel & Foun.	1688
F. Bralile S. M.	1699
G. Quakers M.	1710
H. New North M.	1714
I. New South M.	1716
K. French M.	1716
L. New N. Brick M.	1721

a. Town House.	
b. Governours House.	
c. South Graman School.	
d. North Graman School.	
e. Writing School.	
f. Writing School.	
g. Alms House.	
h. Bridewell.	
i. Town Granary.	

The Wards Military Companies Distinguisht by the Pricke Line thus From N° 1 to 12.

Great Fires.
First	1653
Second	1676
Third	1679
Fourth	1683
Fifth	1690
Sixth	1691
Seventh	1702
Eigth	1711

Ninth Fire 1759. Tenth Terrible Fire 1760.

Small Pox.
First	1640
Second	1666
Third	1677
Fourth	1689
Fifth	1702
Sixth	1721
Seventh	1730

M. Christ Church Foun...	
N. Irish Meeting Hous...	
O. Wallis Street Meetin...	
P. Trinity Church Founded...	
Q. Lynds Street Meeting...	
R. Work House built 1738	
T. Faneuil Hall & M...	

rous Founder Peter F...
Market Days Tuesd...

Note the first letter of the name of the Street is to be the bounds of Each Street.

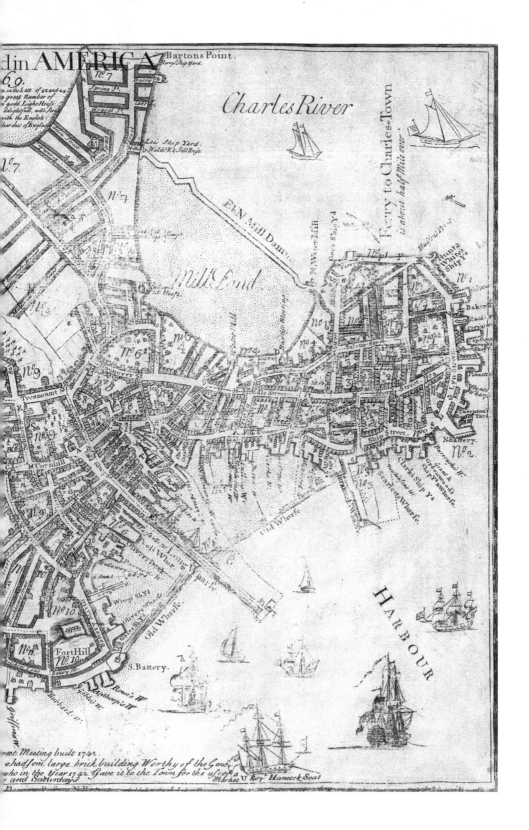

Bartons Point.

Charles River

Ferry to Charles=Town is about half Mile over

Mill Pond.

HARBOUR

FortHill

S.Battery.

N.Battery.

reet Meeting built 1742.
a hadfom large brick building Worthy of the Gen
who in the Year 1742 Gave it to the Town for the ufe of a
and Saturday)
Market U Esqr. Hancock Seat

By His EXCELLENCY

THOMAS POWNALL, Esq;

Captain-General and Governor in Chief, in and over His Majesty's Province of the *Massachusetts-Bay* in *New England*, and Vice-Admiral of the same.

A BRIEF.

IT having pleased Almighty GOD to permit a Fire to break out in the Town of *Boston*, on the 20th Instant, and to rage in such manner as to elude all Means for suppressing the same, until it had in a few Hours destroyed (according to the best Information that can be obtained in the present Confusion) One Hundred and seventy-four Dwelling-Houses, and as many Warehouses, Shops and other Buildings ; the Loss whereof, with the Furniture and Goods therein, amount, at a moderate Computation, to *One Hundred Thousand-Pounds* Sterling ; and Two Hundred and Twenty Families are turned out of Doors, the greatest Part of whom are by this Misfortune so reduced as to be rendered incapable of subsisting themselves, and stand in need of immediate Relief :

THE two Houses having, upon my Recommendation, taken these calamitous Circumstances into Consideration, and judging the Distress to be so great and extensive as to require the Charity of all well disposed Persons to mitigate and relieve the same, have desired me to send BRIEFS throughout the Province, strongly recommending the unhappy Case of these poor People to the Inhabitants, and calling upon them for a general Contribution for their Relief :

I DO hereby therefore most earnestly recommend it to all, to express their Christian Benevolence on this Occasion, by contributing in Proportion to the Means with which GOD has blessed them, and to the Distresses of these worthy Objects of their Charity ; and do further desire, That what may be collected on this Occasion may be remitted to the Select-Men and Overseers of the Poor of the Town of *Boston*, to be by them distributed among the Sufferers, as they in their Discretion shall judge proper.

AND I do require the Ministers of the several Churches and Parishes within this Province to read or cause to be read this Brief to their respective Congregations, on the First LORD'S-DAY after they receive the same, or on the Day appointed for a General FAST the Third of *April* next, as they shall judge most convenient.

GIVEN at the Council-Chamber in Boston *the Twenty-fourth Day of* March, 1760, *in the Thirty-third Year of the Reign of our Sovereign Lord* GEORGE *the Second, by the Grace of* GOD, *of* Great-Britain, France *and* Ireland, KING, *Defender of the Faith,* &c.

By His Excellency's Command,

A. OLIVER, Secr'y.

T. Pownall.

BOSTON : Printed by *John Draper*, Printer to His Excellency the Governor and the Honorable His Majesty's Council, 1760.

Charity brief. Thomas Pownall, the royal governor of Massachusetts, solicited donations to assist Bostonians left homeless by the fire and who were "incapable of subsisting themselves." The governor's call, issued under the king's seal, circulated as a broadside throughout the province. To maximize its impact, Pownall wisely ordered ministers to read his charity brief from their pulpits. Churches accounted for more than one-third of all the money collected to relieve Boston's "Sufferers." *Library of Congress Printed Ephemera Collection.*

bolster the faith of sinners—Mayhew deemed benevolence toward others the precondition for sinners' remediation. "Will it not particularly become us to shew our gratitude to God for his distinguishing mercy to us by chearfully imparting of our substance for the relief of our indigent brethren?" he asked. Indeed, Mayhew argued that God saved people from the flames precisely so that they could help those who had suffered from them. "It is partly for their sakes, not wholly for our own," he concluded, "that our substance has been preserved."[10]

To be sure, not all Bostonians who inclined toward providential thinking interpreted the fire primarily as God's call to act benevolently toward one's neighbors. Many Bostonians must have also read the sermons published by printers Zachariah Fowle and Samuel Draper, whose post-fire offerings included new editions of works by English clergy who railed against the sinfulness of Londoners after their own great fire in 1666. One of these republished sermons was the work of James Janeway, the popular author of pious shipwreck narratives, who preached the necessity of worshipful submission to the "Great & Dreadful God" who could "plague yet seven times more for our Sins" if the reprobate did not repent and seek salvation. Some fire and brimstone came from closer to home. Andrew Johonnot, a Boston distiller, composed a poem that circulated as a broadside bearing a woodcut illustration of the burning town. Johonnot described the fire as "the Rebuke of GOD's Hand" to a people "Who sin without Remorse, and cast off Shame / and pay no Reverence to his holy Name." For him, the lesson of the fire was not the need to help one's neighbors but rather to tend to one's own soul to prepare for divine judgment.[11]

Notwithstanding such pronouncements, Pownall's charity brief, which circulated in print and was read by clergy from their pulpits, helped raise a significant amount of money. Churches in Massachusetts collected more than £5,200, with £1,815 coming from Boston's congregations. Private donations arrived, too, the largest from Christopher Kilby, a Boston merchant who had made a fortune provisioning British and colonial forces during the ongoing French and Indian War. Kilby donated £200 sterling to the relief effort, while Charles W. Apthorp, a New York merchant, "upon hearing of the Calamity which had befallen this town," instructed his agent in Boston to contribute £100 "for the Relief of the Sufferers."[12]

Kilby's and Apthorp's donations stand out because they were mentioned by name in the Boston town records and reported in several colonial newspapers. Their public performances of benevolence mirrored those of contemporary British merchants who, having attained great wealth by their commercial activities, engaged in philanthropy and other nonbusiness pursuits to enhance their reputations and social status. By the mid-eighteenth century, merchants were prominent as donors in London's philanthropic community, and because so many maintained close (and profitable) ties to colonial trading partners, they also contributed money to assist suffering colonial communities. In 1760, London merchants sent £1,000 sterling to Boston even before news of the fire appeared in British newspapers. Two merchants from Bristol, England's second-largest port, also authorized their Boston correspondent, Thomas Greene, to donate £100 sterling in their names "for the Relief of the Sufferers" in the coming months. Such donations attested to both the influence of the benevolent ideal and the vitality of personal business networks.[13]

Other networks derived from imperial political relationships, some of which were wholly centered in North America. Colonial governors and other officials often knew each other, having shared military or administrative backgrounds and common patrons or acquaintances back in London. Governor Thomas Pownall drew on a remarkable network of acquaintances among his fellow governors, many of whom he met during his years in America before he received his governorship. Pownall had come to America in 1753 as the private secretary of New York's new royal governor, Sir Danvers Osborn. When Osborn committed suicide a few days after his arrival in New York, the suddenly jobless Pownall decided to tour the colonies. He visited Philadelphia, Alexandria, Annapolis, New Haven, and Providence, meeting leading men in these communities, including most colonial governors. By 1754, he was back in New York, attending the Albany Congress as the guest of Lieutenant Governor James Delancey, who became his friend and ally. Such intercolonial conferences became routine in wartime, and Pownall, who received his appointment as governor of Massachusetts in 1757, held a conference of his own for New Englanders in Boston the following year. He also collaborated with Governor Charles Lawrence of Nova Scotia to send supplies and troops to Louisbourg, where victorious British and colonial forces won a decisive victory that ended French control of eastern Canada in June 1758.[14]

In the spring of 1760, Pownall drew on these connections to obtain relief for Boston. Although some of the governor's friends and colleagues in other provinces may have learned about the fire from their local newspapers, Pownall also directly solicited aid from his fellow governors and obtained donations from colonies where he had established personal relationships. Lieutenant Governor James Delancey sent £1,875 from New York. Pennsylvania governor James Hamilton, whom Pownall first met in Philadelphia in 1753, sent £1,212. Governor Horatio Sharpe of Maryland, who had hosted Pownall at his elegant Annapolis residence, circulated a charity brief of his own, which raised £1,120 for Boston. Smaller sums arrived from the governors of Connecticut, New Hampshire, Virginia, and Nova Scotia.[15]

When Boston's town meeting convened in mid-May, town officials reported having received donations totaling more than £13,000 sterling from various donors, a substantial amount that was roughly equivalent to one-fourth of the community's losses in both real and personal property. Bostonians believed that the next logical step was to solicit help from the king and Parliament. To that end, a petition was drafted, describing the fire and the suffering it caused and noting the "care and kindness" of those who had already given aid but who were now "unable to bear any considerable addition to the heavy load of taxes which for many years past has fallen on them," mostly to help fight the long and costly war. The petitioners, 439 in all, made their case for relief from London by invoking both the "compassionate consideration" of the home government and Boston's own supposedly unique value as "the chief strength of the English interest [against the French and their Indian allies] on the continent of America, without being in the least burthensome to the mother country." Included with the petition were affidavits attesting to property losses ranging from those of the merchants Jacob Wendell and Son (who sought compensation for £5,180 in real and personal property) to the claims of poor women such as Sarah Ayers (£1 10s.) and Martha Barnes (16s.). Town officials voted to send the petition and its supporting documents to the colony's agents in London "in order to make Application . . . in such a way and manner as they may think proper for obtaining Relief for the poor distress'd Sufferers."[16]

The Bostonians' "humble Petition" was rejected in London not least because of their success in obtaining relief from other sources. Massachusetts' colonial agents, merchants William Bollan and John Thomlinson, submitted the petition, which in July 1761 was read by either the Board of Trade or the Lords of the Treasury, who deemed it "not proper to consent" to the petitioners' request. Although the men who considered the petition did not record their reasons for rejecting it, the back of the document includes some telling notations:

£53354 [sterling] Loss
13317 Charity collected
40,037

The final number represented the funds Bostonians claimed that they still needed to recoup in fire-related costs, which amounted to roughly three-quarters of their original total losses. These notations imply, first, that imperial officials believed that disaster victims should not expect full compensation for their losses and, second, that because Bostonians had already received substantial "Charity" from other sources, their situation was not sufficiently dire to warrant imperial largesse. In other words, officials in London concluded that Bostonians and their governor were primarily responsible for managing the fire and its consequences because they had, in fact, fulfilled that function so effectively.[17]

But the larger imperial context in which officials considered the Boston petition was also significant, as was the mounting expense of a war that had lasted many years and was being waged on five continents. Although the British won decisive victories that effectively ended French rule in both North America and India, the war nearly doubled the national debt and placed huge financial burdens on residents of the British Isles, who paid more than twenty times the taxes levied on colonists in America. Boston's request for aid at a time when the British government was struggling to meet its financial obligations was likely to fail, especially given the New Englanders' reputation as smugglers and tax evaders. Ultimately, no additional aid was forthcoming from the seat of empire, though the news from Boston may have inspired George Whitefield, the famed revivalist, to donate the proceeds of one of his sermons to Boston's relief effort in early 1761.[18]

Transatlantic sources of imperial relief figured more prominently in the aftermath of the Montreal fire of 18 May 1765, which led to robust debates over the appropriate uses of philanthropy and the responsibilities of affluent Britons toward the king's new subjects in formerly French Canada. Destruction from the Montreal fire was roughly comparable to that in Boston, with an estimated £87,580 in property losses and 215 families left homeless, though in Montreal "8 or 9 sick Persons in the Grey Sisters Nunnery were burnt to death" and another man "was burnt in his own House." Montreal, like Boston, had a history of frequent fires, the most serious of which occurred in 1695, 1721, and 1734. Otherwise, Boston and Montreal were very different places. Whereas Bostonians were relatively homogeneous and civic-minded, residents of recently conquered Montreal included a small number of British newcomers—mostly merchants and soldiers, groups that were mutually antagonistic—and the French majority. Montreal also lacked local institutions that could mobilize to aid fire victims because after the British takeover, local government was in a state of flux and the role of the Catholic

Church, so powerful under the French regime, was uncertain. Montreal had no fire company, no fire engine, and no printing press. The province's first and only newspaper, the bilingual *Quebec Gazette*, began publishing in the capital, distant Quebec City, less than a year earlier, around the time that the entire province, which had been under military rule since 1760, acquired a new civilian government that consisted of only a royal governor and an appointed council, with no representative assembly.[19]

The fact that the fire began in the house of merchant John Livingston and then spread rapidly "where the greatest Part of the British Merchants collected together" made the situation especially problematic for would-be local benefactors. The Montreal French had few incentives to help these newcomers, who were virulently anti-Catholic and anti-French and who had seized control of the city's valuable fur trade immediately after the British conquest. Governor James Murray, who might have been the merchants' natural ally, generally despised them as "the most cruel, Ignorant, rapacious Fanatics" and struck a conciliatory note toward the French Canadians, whom he envisioned becoming "the most faithful & useful Set of Men in this American Empire." For their part, the merchants resented Murray's tolerance toward Catholicism and French law (which he allowed Canadians to use among themselves in the lower courts), his refusal to convene an elected assembly (which the small Protestant population would inevitably control because Catholics could not vote in either Britain or its colonies), and his enforcement of trade laws and Indian treaties. Like their counterparts in New York and Boston, Montreal's British merchants also protested the quartering of troops in private houses, which led to three soldiers assaulting the merchant Thomas Walker in his home in December 1764. Although they allegedly had planned to murder Walker, the soldiers only cut off his ear instead. "In consequence of this outrage," according to one early historian of Quebec, the people of Montreal "went armed in the streets." Tensions were high, then, when flames engulfed the merchants' neighborhood the following May.[20]

Quebec's attenuated political institutions responded conscientiously, if ineffectually, to news of the conflagration. On 22 May, four days after the fire, the governor and council met to consider a recently arrived report from the magistrates in Montreal, who used the occasion both to insist that soldiers be barred from living in the town's remaining houses—which could be used instead for those rendered homeless by the fire—and to request relief for fire victims. Murray dispatched two members of his council, Benjamin Price and Adam Mabane, to survey the situation and determine "what best could be done for the distressed inhabitants." Price and Mabane left Quebec on 25 May and arrived in Montreal the next day, bringing £300 that the council had allocated for humanitarian aid for "the people most necessitous." The governor later contributed an additional £100 as his personal donation.[21]

Price and Mabane found much cause for concern when they arrived in the troubled town. Looting was rampant, the councilors reported, because local justices of the peace (most of whom were British merchants or lawyers) so distrusted the soldiers that they refused to ask them to restore order. Meanwhile, many of the homeless who had survived the fire "from Fright and Despair had fallen sick & dyed." Price and Mabane used the money from the governor and council to provide food and clothing to fire victims; they also adopted several measures to secure order and property. Troops guarded houses, workshops, and warehouses; the councilors offered monetary rewards (guaranteed in handwritten notices, in both English and French) to anyone who returned stolen merchandise. Price and Mabane summoned masons and carpenters to survey the damage and consulted local "Entrepreneurs" about the sorts of workmen they might bring in from Quebec and elsewhere to expedite the rebuilding effort. They summoned "sufferers of the late fire" to come to the courthouse to declare their losses, which they promised to report to the governor and council.[22]

Around the same time that Governor Murray dispatched Price and Mabane to Montreal, he also began calling on other colonial governors for help. Francis Bernard, who had succeeded Pownall as governor of Massachusetts, received Murray's letter by 29 May, when he asked his colony's legislators to authorize "a charitable Contribution towards alleviating the Distresses, which so immense a Loss must necessarily bring upon these unhappy People, who by all Accounts are very unable to Support themselves under it." Bernard hoped that the recent experience of the fire in Boston would generate sympathy for Montreal's fire victims and that "the Hearts of the People [of Massachusetts] will be open, and their Hands ready to relieve their Fellow Subjects labouring under the like Distress." Outraged by the recent Stamp Act—which soon led to riots in the streets of Boston—and still hostile toward their French Catholic neighbors to the north, however, the legislators did not act on the governor's request.[23]

In his letters to Bernard and to the other colonial governors, Murray maintained that the performance of imperial benevolence was both morally and politically imperative, making his case for assistance on the basis of "Motives of good Policy, as well as of Religion and Humanity." He appealed to the governors to seek money from their legislatures because, in his view, pri-

Benevolent Empire

vate contributions alone would not suffice in the wake of "so general a Calamity." Murray used the language of sensibility and emotion when he described the "miserable Sufferers, who have lost almost everything," first by
the "Ravages of War" and now by the recent fire, which served to "compleat
their Wretchedness." But he also invoked contemporary issues in imperial
governance, reminding his fellow governors that helping poor Canadians
would "rivet their Affections to the *British* Government, and silence those
among them who would insinuate, that the Professors of our [Protestant]
Religion do not possess Christian Virtues to an eminent Degree."[24]

As imperial functionaries, the other governors likely shared Murray's
perspective, but the fund-raising effort nonetheless failed, mostly due to bad
timing. Colonial legislators had vigorously opposed the Stamp Act, most
notably in Virginia, where on 29 May 1765 Patrick Henry introduced a series
of resolutions disavowing Parliament's authority to tax the colonists, which
some considered treasonous. In retaliation, Governor Francis Fauquier dis-
missed the assembly, which did not reconvene until December. Similar,
though less dramatic, scenarios unfolded in other provinces, nine of which
sent delegates to the Stamp Act Congress in New York in October. The result
was that the governors, at best, presented Murray's appeal to hostile assemblies months after its arrival. In most cases, the legislators simply ignored the
governor's request. In Pennsylvania, the assembly unctuously professed the
"tenderest Sentiments of Humanity" for their "Fellow Subjects at *Montreal*"
but tartly declared that "the low state of our Commerce and the Poverty of
the People we represent" precluded their assisting distressed fire victims in
Canada.[25]

Ultimately, only Virginia sent relief to Montreal, but even that modest
offering did not come from the provincial assembly. After the legislators' ex-
plosive reaction to the Stamp Act, Governor Fauquier delayed reconvening
the House of Burgesses until November 1766. In the intervening months,
however, he presented Murray's letter to his council, who advised him to
publish a notice informing Virginians about the fire, recommending that
"Ministers preach proper sermons" about it, and urging local churchwar-
dens to collect funds to aid Montreal's suffering inhabitants. By August 1766,
the *Virginia Gazette* reported that clergy collected a total of only £131 15s. 2d.
from ten Virginia parishes.[26]

By then, more fruitful relief efforts were well under way in London.
From the start, both Montrealers and their governor envisioned a transatlantic search for assistance. To that end, Price and Mabane returned to Quebec City in late June armed both with a detailed report of the city's needs

and losses and with petitions from representatives of Montreal's British and French communities. One petition, signed by twenty-three men, all but two bearing English or Scottish surnames, displayed their understanding of imperial networks and relationships when they pointedly asked the governor and council to recommend their case "to the Kings most excellent Majesty and the British parliament as well as to the British governments . . . on this continent." Like their English-speaking counterparts, the thirty-nine signers of the French petition hoped for relief from their "august monarch," to whom they pledged their submission, loyalty, and love, but they also appealed to the governor's sense of personal duty and benevolence, emphasizing the losses their community had endured even before the fire as a result of the war and the British government's subsequent ban on trade with France and its few remaining colonies. The governor and council sent Benjamin Price to London to present the petitions and their supporting documents to the appropriate imperial administrators "and to any other persons that he in his prudence shall think proper in order to procure Relief." In mid-July, the Board of Trade reviewed the Montreal petitions, which it neither granted nor rejected. Price soon became involved in an extra-governmental fund-raising effort.[27]

While the Boston fire and its aftermath received scant coverage in the British press, newspapers in London and elsewhere in Britain carefully followed the news from Montreal. Because fires were common in eighteenth-century towns and cities, the appeal of the Montreal story derived mostly from readers' curiosity about conditions in Britain's new Canadian territory. The first press reports more or less coincided with Price's arrival in London. Newspapers outside the capital, including some in Scotland, reprinted stories from the London press. Coverage continued throughout the summer and even, in some cases, into September and October, occasionally noting the fire's adverse effects on Canadian trade.[28]

The focus of the newspapers' coverage soon shifted from events in Montreal to the efforts of benevolent Britons to aid that city's fire victims. By the end of July, notices appeared regularly in London newspapers announcing a fund-raising campaign "for the Relief of the Unfortunate Sufferers by the Fire at Montreal in America." The fund's twenty-two trustees included councilor Benjamin Price of Quebec, as well as British government officials and merchants, including John Thornton, a devout Anglican and avid philanthropist who himself donated £50. These trustees and other volunteer "bankers" collected money from donors, known as subscribers, and then convened at the New York Coffee House in London in mid-October to assess their progress. Hoping to garner more donations, they continued to

seek subscribers through the end of the year, ultimately collecting £8,415—
or roughly one-tenth of the town's losses—from a combination of small-
and large-scale donors.[29]

Although Thornton, as treasurer, was the nominal leader of this effort,
Jonas Hanway was its most energetic and articulate advocate. Like Thornton, Hanway was a pious Anglican who had made his fortune in the Rus-
sian trade before turning his attention to philanthropy. An avid imperialist,
Hanway had worked tirelessly on behalf of organizations such as London's
Foundling Hospital and the Marine Society, which he cofounded as a charitable organization that could support poor boys while simultaneously chan-
neling them into service in the Royal Navy. In 1765–66, Hanway's cause was
disaster relief for Montreal. He published two pamphlets to promote the
fund-raising effort, which he envisioned as a golden opportunity to use benevolence to strengthen the bonds between Britain and its colonial depen-
dents. In an era when the female image of Britannia typically exuded martial
strength and ardor, the title page of one of Hanway's pamphlets featured a
more maternal representation in which a gracious Britannia extends a helpful hand to colonists in need, represented by a kneeling female supplicant.[30]

Hanway invoked sensibility to argue eloquently in favor of disaster relief
for Canada. Seeking to evoke the sympathy and compassion of his readers,
he movingly described the horrific human cost of urban conflagrations. "Behold amidst the flames, the *sick* or *maimed*, the *infirm old* woman, or the more
decrepit man, dropping under the resistless strokes of mortality, yet eagerly
flying from the *fiery darts* of death: the *tender husband* anxious to preserve his
wife, and the *more tender mother* seeking for her *children*, dearer to her than
the blood that animates her frame!" he wrote, adding, "Yet this is but the *beginning of the sorrow* that many experience on these occasions . . . [because]
many escape from fire who have no food to satisfy their hunger; no raiment
to cover their nakedness; no house to guard them from the inclemency of the
sky. Many were thus exposed on this sad occasion, and must have perished
but for the mercy of their fellow-creatures."[31]

Hanway sought to arouse the emotions of his readers, but he also appealed strongly to their moral values and religious sensibilities. Christian
charity was a recurring theme in his writing, but so, too, was the notion
that Protestant Britons had a special responsibility to aid French Canadian
Catholics—to help the suffering in Montreal not in spite of their foreignness
but, indeed, because of it. "We are now invited to give an active demonstra-
tive proof to the *Canadians*, that the essence of *Liberty* consists in a tender
regard to support each other," he declared, because the "civil and religious

MOTIVES
FOR A
SUBSCRIPTION
towards the relief of the sufferers at
MONTREAL IN CANADA,

*by a dreadful fire on the 18th of May 1765, in which 108 houses,
(containing 215 families, chiefly* CANADIANS,*) were
destroyed; and the greatest part of their inhabitants
exposed to all the miseries attending such misfortunes. The whole loss in buildings, merchandize, furniture, and apparel,
amounted to £.87580 8s. 10d.
sterling; no part of which
was, or could be insured.*

AT MONTREAL
MAY MDCCLXV.

Motives for a Subscription towards the relief of the Sufferers at Montreal in Canada.
This striking image on the title page of Jonas Hanway's fund-raising pamphlet
was emblematic of his belief in the efficacy of imperial benevolence. A strong but
maternal Britannia offers a helping hand to a distraught female supplicant, who
gestures toward her burning town and looks to Britannia for aid and comfort.
The nearby beaver indicates that the kneeling figure represents Montreal, a major
fur-trading center in the province of Quebec, which became part of the British
Empire after the defeat of France in the Seven Years' (or French and Indian) War.
Rare Books and Special Collections, McGill University Library.

rights" of Protestant Britons were uniquely "founded in reason, or a true discernment of what is just and fit to be done, *voluntarily*, and upon the principles of obedience to divine laws, and the *good of society*." Hanway embraced the ideal of Britain as the most benevolent of nations, and he warned that failure to live up to that high standard "may deprive us of the advantages which Providence hath put in our hands." Equally important, he insisted that British benevolence could show leery French Canadians the "social virtues" that "*our protestantism* inspires," which could help to "reconcile their minds" to British governance of their recently conquered province.[32]

Hanway saw disaster relief first and foremost as a tool of empire that could and should be deployed to foster loyalty among the king's newly conquered subjects. He cast the people of Montreal as "fellow-subjects" who, for both commercial and political reasons, would be integrated peacefully and profitably into the British Empire. Sending disaster relief to Montreal, he argued, would be a performance of benevolence for the benefit of both those French Canadians who were suspicious of British rule and the king's subjects in other colonies whose relationship with the mother country had been strained by the recent Stamp Act. Relief was "good policy," he maintained, "if we consider these *Canadians* as fellow-subjects, whose allegiance to the crown of these realms we would wish to preserve inviolate. . . . Or if we make an estimate of their intrinsic worth, as a comely, laborious, intrepid, obedient people." Disaster relief for Montreal would also be "substantial proof, not to *them* only, but also to our *American fellow-subjects* in general," of "mutual interest and mutual affection" among all members of the great "bulwark of liberty" that was the British Empire.[33]

Because enthusiasm for the empire and optimism about assimilating longtime French enemies into it was not universal, fund-raising efforts for Montreal spurred public debates about benevolence and its proper recipients. Some commentators blamed French Montrealers for their own woes, noting their lack of fire engines and fire insurance. (The first English fire insurance company was established in 1706; fire insurance made its debut in the British colonies in 1730, though it was not widely purchased until the postrevolutionary era.) Others argued that fund-raisers should instead dispense their benevolence closer to home, most notably among the victims of recent fires in the English communities of Honiton, Cornhill, Heytesbury, and Rotherhithe. Still others proposed dividing the proceeds from the committee's fund-raising efforts among the needy in Montreal and all these other fire-afflicted communities. But newspapers also carried letters and essays supporting Hanway's views. One essayist, writing under the name "Benevolus," reminded readers of their nation's "truly noble generosity" toward the Palatine Germans who became refugees in London during the Seven Years' War and argued that the people of Montreal—and particularly the town's newly settled English-speaking inhabitants—deserved similar consideration because they had "with great expense, credit, and industry, endeavoured to support the interest of their country in the most northern parts of our conquests" and, in so doing, advanced "the honour and advantage of their mother country."[34]

Commentators generally frowned on direct government contributions to this disaster relief effort. In the summer of 1765, there were rumors that Parliament would send aid to "the unfortunate sufferers by the late dreadful fire at Montreal." That Parliament, in fact, never considered a bill to aid the fire victims may have been due to the vocal disapproval of an already highly taxed populace. As one London newspaper put it, "Montreal is ruined by fire, and a petition preferred to a private charity for the relief of the sufferers, towards which, it is said, the Ministry has contributed most generously. But, according to the rule of one of the greatest men that ever presided over the laws of England, *men should be just before they are generous*." The secretary of state for the Southern Department—the top official for colonial affairs—personally contributed £50 to Hanway's fund, a detail that was reported in both British and colonial newspapers. The king received Thornton and Hanway "most graciously" and likewise gave them a personal donation of £500 "towards the relief of those who are in real distress."[35]

These gifts were at best celebrated and at worst uncontroversial in part because there was much historical precedent for the monarch and other powerful people offering personal charity to the poor, the sick, and the suffering. As the structure of British charitable giving changed during the eighteenth century, it became less personal, with philanthropic institutions and fund-raising subscription efforts complementing and eventually overshadowing face-to-face offerings of alms or (at least through the reign of Queen Anne) putative cures by the royal touch. In 1737, for instance, Princess Augusta of Wales, mother of the future king George III, made personal donations to poor women and men she encountered in Windsor, Kew, and Kensington—all sites of royal residences—and also to the Westminster Infirmary, the first of many charitable institutions to which she would eventually be a benefactor; along with the infirmary, three charity schools, a missionary society, and a society for the benefit of "Decayed Musicians" became annual recipients of her support over the course of the next decade. In the 1760s, King George III and Queen Charlotte were thoroughly enmeshed in

Britain's burgeoning culture of philanthropy. One historian, who estimated the annual charitable donations of George III at £14,000, concludes that "no British monarch since has given away a greater proportion of his or her private income." Among the recipients of the king's largesse were schools, hospitals, missionary groups, and benevolence societies.[36]

But George III also understood kingly benevolence, even in the form of personal donations, as a form of statecraft. The young monarch had written essays about kingly power and duty that occasionally addressed the relationship between benevolence—defined as assistance given by the mighty to the subservient—and power. Government, he wrote, "should be rever'd as well as obey'd; and belov'd as well as rever'd." In order to attain these desired results, however, "Authority should dignify Power, and Benevolence Sweeten Authority." George III saw himself as a benevolent monarch who strove to "preserve the freedom, happiness, & glory of all my Dominions, & all their Inhabitants," and whose occasional failures to fulfill that charge came "from the head not the Heart." This devout Protestant king also professed to disdain the sort of bigotry and dogmatism that might have automatically excluded Catholics from his benevolence. Such narrow-mindedness, he maintained, distorted "the true effects of . . . Religion, which are Benevolence, Charity, Justice, and Peace."[37]

So, perhaps not surprisingly, Hanway and Thornton found the king amenable to their request that he contribute to the Montreal fund. For proponents of empire, including the king himself, George's gift of £500 was an exemplary act of benevolence sweetening authority, a statement of compassion and power to Montreal's conquered French inhabitants and also to the town's small but unruly English community. To make that statement strong and unequivocal, Hanway's fund-raising group sent three items, along with the money they collected, to Canada. Two were fire engines, which showcased not only the benevolence of Britons but also their superior civic-mindedness and technological prowess, which identified membership in the British Empire with improvement and social progress. The final item included in the shipment to Montreal was a marble bust of George III, the earliest known representation of him as king, which was to be erected in Montreal's central square, the Place d'Armes. Its inscription emphasized the king's paternal protection of his subjects and, by extension, the benevolence of the imperial bond:

Temporal and eternal happiness
to the sovereign of the British Empire

GEORGE III
who relieved the distresses of the Inhabitants of his City
of Montreal Occasioned by Fire
MDCCLXV[38]

Relief efforts following a fire in Bridgetown, Barbados, in May 1766, demonstrate that the king's subjects on both sides of the Atlantic understood the political utility of such post-disaster benevolence. In that case, relief came from a committee of philanthropic Britons, neighboring islands, and also leading men in South Carolina, who remembered the Barbadians' generosity in the wake of the Charleston fire in 1740. Both Britons and colonists were likely motivated at least in part by their lucrative commercial connections with the sugar-producing island, and Jonas Hanway and other British philanthropists who solicited support for Bridgetown were surely heartened by the island's comparative calm during the recent Stamp Act crisis. Conversely, at least one Philadelphian believed that sending relief to Bridgetown might repair the mainlanders' political rift with Barbadians who refused to join the Stamp Act protests. Citing the "unrival'd Glory" that Britain had garnered by its generosity to earthquake-ravaged Lisbon, he maintained that the Bridgetown fire presented a comparable opportunity to cultivate the goodwill of Barbadians by showing a "noble Forgetfulness of their Offence" by offering them benevolence. "Is it not prudent, as well as generous," he queried, "for all the British Colonists to consider themselves as Children of the same Parents, united by Blood, but also by Interest, and by all possible Means to keep up a kind, affectionate, hearty and truly fraternal Correspondence between them, and a tender Concern for the Welfare and Prosperity of each other?"[39]

The Boston and Montreal fires occupied the extremities of a post-Lisbon imperial relief spectrum. Each fire resulted in significant and somewhat successful initiatives to assist its victims, and British merchants figured prominently in both relief efforts. Other aid, however, came from markedly different sources. Relief for Boston came primarily from North America, with the people of Boston and its environs, along with the intercolonial contacts of Governor Thomas Pownall, supplying meaningful and timely assistance. Lacking a cohesive community and established North American networks, Montrealers relied almost entirely on help from London, including a personal donation from the king who, along with enthusiasts like Jonas Hanway, saw the fire as an opportunity to deploy benevolence in the service of addressing the growing challenges of imperial politics.

In 1771, imperial and local responses to Virginia's Great Fresh unfolded

George III. This bust by Joseph Wilton was intended to symbolize the benevolence of the king and his empire. Arriving in Montreal along with two fire engines and more than £8,400 in aid for fire victims, the sculpture was erected as a monument in the town's main square. It was later defaced by British Montrealers, who opposed the Quebec Act of 1774, which secured the religious and legal rights of French Canadians without acceding to their own demands for representative government. *McCord Museum.*

within this continually evolving context. On the one hand, Virginia, like Massachusetts, was a long-established colony whose leaders were among the most intractable opponents of recent imperial policies. In 1768, three years after Patrick Henry's famous Virginia Resolves, Lord Hillsborough informed the king that Virginia's situation was "still more alarming" than even that of Massachusetts, as angry colonists there mobilized nonimportation efforts to protest the Townshend Duties. On the other hand, Virginia tobacco was valuable to British merchants, and leading Virginia planters, unlike their Boston counterparts, were perceived as gentlemen who effusively admired British culture and relied on their metropolitan connections for credit and commerce. In the aftermath of the Great Fresh, official policy — devised in Williamsburg and approved in London — seemed designed both to serve imperial economic interests and to cultivate the gratitude and loyalty of Virginia's planter elite.[40]

In late May 1771, the James River rose some forty feet above its banks, resulting in a "most dreadful Inundation" that swept away houses and livestock for more than a hundred miles upriver and destroyed tobacco warehouses in Richmond and elsewhere. The Rappahannock and Roanoke rivers were also affected. In much of Virginia, "Impetuous Torrents rushed from the mountains with such astonishing Rapidity that nothing could withstand the mighty Force," one eyewitness reported. "Promiscuous Heaps of Houses, Trees, men, Horses, Cattle, Sheep, Hogs, Merchandize, Corn, Tobacco & every other Thing that was unfortunately, within the dreadful Swamp, were seen Floating upon the Waters, without a possibility of their being saved, The finest Low-Grounds were ruined; and many of the best Lands totally destroyed." After the waters receded somewhat, the *Virginia Gazette* reported, "In some Places, Trees, Carcasses, &c., are matted together, from twelve to twenty Feet in Height; and, from the horrid Stench, there is no coming near enough to separate them." This "greatest Fresh . . . ever known" resulted in at least £50,000 in property losses, though some estimates were much higher. According to the inscription on a stone obelisk that planter Ryland Randolph placed at the high-water mark later that year, more than 150 people died as a result of the great deluge.[41]

Planters and tobacco merchants in flood-ravaged areas wrote to their commercial correspondents in London and supplied information to Williamsburg's two newspapers. These accounts, in turn, made their way into newspapers from Boston to Charleston, and then on to England and Scotland, both centers of the re-export trade in Virginia tobacco. By July, an item from the *Virginia Gazette* appeared in the London-based *Gentleman's Maga-*

Great Fresh obelisk. Located on land near the James River owned by Ryland Randolph in southeastern Henrico County, Virginia, this obelisk, erected to commemorate the Great Fresh of 1771, was perhaps the first recorded memorialization of an American disaster. The inscription on the base of the obelisk states that more than 150 people died in the unprecedented floods, "which changed the face of nature, and left traces of their violence that will remain for ages." *Library of Virginia.*

zine. Some press coverage recounted the experiences of flood victims, but many more stories focused on the physical destruction the flood caused, particularly emphasizing the loss of thousands of export-ready hogsheads of tobacco.[42]

In Virginia, the appropriate official response to the flood became a matter of public debate. Because flooding along the James River was a routine seasonal phenomenon, Virginians expended little effort pondering the causes of the deluge. Like longtime denizens of the West Indies whose familiarity with hurricanes and earthquakes led them to see such events as more mundane than meaningful, Virginians did not publicly interpret the flood, despite its severity, as a message from an angry God; nor did their leaders call for a day of fasting and prayer, though in recent decades they had done so after the Lisbon and New England earthquakes and also to seek divine protection in times of war, famine, and raging "flux." Instead, Virginia planters and merchants expected government officials to respond to this situation with tangible relief for earthly losses. They requested assistance from Virginia's acting governor, council president William Nelson, who sought the advice of his council and then forwarded the "Memorial of Merchants and Others" to imperial authorities in London.[43]

Nelson was comparatively ill-equipped to handle the situation. For one thing, he did not solicit help from other provinces because, as a Virginia native, he lacked the sorts of intercolonial and imperial connections that Massachusetts governor Thomas Pownall had used to such good effect. In 1771, Virginia had no agent in London on whom Nelson could rely. As acting governor—the most recent royal governor, Lord Botetourt, had died in Williamsburg in October 1770—Nelson also lacked the formal power to convene the colonial legislature unless doing so was necessary to preserve the "peace and welfare of the colony." Although the councilors eventually persuaded Nelson that the current circumstances met that criterion, he still felt obliged to justify his decision to convene the House of Burgesses when he wrote to his superiors in London. When the legislature met on 11 July, Nelson reported defensively, its members would deal only with the "single Object" of relief for those who suffered as a result of what was universally deemed "by far the most dredful Catastrophe that hath happened to Virginia since its first Settlement by the English" in 1607.[44]

Once they arrived in Williamsburg, the legislators spent eleven days hammering out the details of the aptly titled "Act for the relief of the Sufferers by the loss of tobacco damaged or burnt in several warehouses." The interests of wealthy tobacco planters who controlled the House of Burgesses ensured that those "Sufferers" would be defined narrowly, to benefit only tobacco producers and their British trading partners. There would be no official compensation for wheat, corn, livestock, houses, or even slaves lost in the flood, though the provincial government would reimburse planters who lost large quantities of tobacco for 20 percent of their costs and also pay for the rebuilding of two ruined Richmond tobacco warehouses (owned and operated by wealthy Virginians) on higher ground. The statute authorized the provincial government to issue £30,000 in treasury notes for payment of these expenses, with new taxes on "wheeled carriages," tavern licenses, and the processing of legal documents to fund the eventual redemption of this paper money.[45]

In fact, the Great Fresh provided the House of Burgesses with a unique opportunity to press its case for emitting local currency, a project that Virginians cherished but London strongly opposed. Beginning in 1755, the House of Burgesses had financed Virginia's military expenditures by printing paper money. Merchants, however, rejected colonial currency when its value declined relative to the British pound sterling. In 1764, in response to merchant pressure, Parliament passed the Currency Act, which prohibited colonial legislatures from issuing paper currency that would be legal tender—in other words, that creditors would be legally required to accept to satisfy outstanding debts. Because the absence of cash of any sort made it difficult to conduct business in Virginia, in 1765 and again in 1767 the House of Burgesses voted to issue paper money that would not be legal tender—and thus was not technically in violation of the Currency Act—but the Board of Trade stopped it anyway. Nelson and the legislators were well aware of these precedents when they devised the 1771 statute, but he and others shrewdly argued that, in this case, the availability of paper money would significantly benefit British merchants, to whom Virginia planters sold their tobacco and to whom they also owed enormous sums, and thereby promote imperial economic interests generally. Without the proposed emissions, Nelson declared, the "Credit of many Merchants in Great Britain as well as Virginia would have been ruined."[46]

Something else happened in Williamsburg during the legislative session that may have softened the response of the Board of Trade to the Virginia relief statute. On Monday, 15 July, members of the Virginia Association met to reconsider the stringent nonimportation measures they had adopted in 1768 to protest the Townshend Duties Act. Although the meeting occurred ostensibly in response to complaints from Fairfax and Fauquier counties about the allegedly unequal enforcement of these measures, the end result was that the associators scaled back their nonimportation program, agreeing to boycott only "Tea, Paper, Glass, and Painters Colours of foreign Manufacture, upon which a Duty is laid for the Purpose of raising a Revenue in America." George Washington likely attended this meeting, and, if his response was typical, the associators' decision was a boon for London merchants. A few days later, Washington sent orders to several English trading houses, from whom he purchased various leather goods, fine clothing, two seals made of "Topaz or some other handsome stone ... w[it]h the Washington Arms neatly engraved thereon," and "a man's very best Bear Hat."[47]

That summer, the king received the news from Virginia with a combination of sympathy and condescension, as did Lord Hillsborough, the man most responsible for colonial affairs during these troubled times. Both men recognized that—as Hillsborough put it in a letter to Virginia's newly arrived royal governor, the Earl of Dunmore, in December—"the Distress brought upon a part of His Majestys Subjects in Virginia by the unexpected Inundation ... must have been very great, & as it was evident that some speedy & effectual Measures were necessary for their Relief, the Step taken by Mr President Nelson upon that Occasion of convening the General Assembly met with the King's Approbation," as did "the Justice & Liberality of the House of Burgesses in the Provision they have made for that purpose." At the same time, however, Hillsborough warned, that "Provision" might be disallowed on the grounds that "the Clause by which the Treasurer's Notes are made a Tender . . . in Payment of Taxes, may be judged to contravene" the Currency Act, though he himself hoped that "the Mode in which the Relief has been given, shall be found unexceptionable."[48]

As it turned out, the Board of Trade did not respond to the Virginia relief statute, and its inaction amounted to what one scholar has called "a type of in-kind disaster relief." While the Virginians capitalized on the crisis of the flood to get their paper currency—which might have set a precedent of some sort had the Revolution not intervened—the king and his imperial functionaries used the occasion to stage a subtle performance of benevolent condescension for the benefit of Virginia's disgruntled but potentially redeemable planter elite. The fact that most of those same Virginians turned irrevocably against the Crown after November 1775, when Dunmore offered their slaves freedom in exchange for joining the king's forces, should not obscure the possibility of reconciliation in 1771 and the tacit use of disaster relief to attain that objective.[49]

The deployment of imperial benevolence was, if anything, even more understated in the aftermath of the ruinous hurricane that devastated the Leeward Islands in 1772. Hurricanes occurred routinely in the Caribbean, but the storms were unusually severe in the 1760s and 1770s, and most notably so in 1772, when sixteen landfalls brought unprecedented destruction to the West Indies and the Gulf Coast of North America. The hurricane that hit the Leeward Islands—Antigua, Nevis, St. Christopher, St. Croix, and others— on 31 August was the fifth major hurricane of the season. Eyewitnesses described that storm as "the most terrible Hurricane of Wind and Rain that was known in the Memory of the oldest Man living," and some believed that it would take at least fifty years to repair the damage it caused. Hundreds of people died, though casualty figures remained sketchy. Financial losses were huge. In Antigua, "not one in ten houses was . . . standing," and the year's sugar crop was lost. One resident of St. Christopher believed that the losses suffered on that island alone "cannot, on the most moderate calculation, be computed at less than 500,000£." At least twenty-one ships and their cargoes were destroyed at the port of St. Kitts, and there was "scarce a Mill or [sugar] boiling House left standing" on that island.[50]

Press coverage of the storm was unusually prolific, due to the sugar planters' dense commercial and personal connections both with the mainland colonies and with London, where some absentee planters lived and others regularly visited. News of the hurricane arrived in three successive waves: brief notices that a storm had occurred, followed by assessments of losses, and then affecting personal narratives. Readers learned about the "company of Comedians" who lost their scenery, and the many more unfortunate souls who lost their houses, limbs, or lives. They read about Mr. Philpot, who "died of fright," and also about the hospital where all ten patients and their nurse perished in the wind and rain. News from St. Christopher included the plight of the widowed Mrs. Bibby and her daughters, "young ladies of reputation, [who] had their house in an instant reduced to atoms, and their wearing apparel whirled into the air, insomuch as to leave them destitute of a second suit of clothes," and of John Fahy, the tavern keeper, who lost his "large stock of liquors" and all his household goods when his dwelling suddenly collapsed, leaving him "scarce time to remove his wife and daughter, before the walls gave way and crushed all within them to shivers."[51]

For some, the experience of this hurricane was so profound, the devastation so extreme, that they could only understand its severity as an act of God, a divine corrective for their sinfulness. "No state, though ever so happily circumstanced, can promise itself a duration of felicity," wrote one resident of St. Christopher, because "vain is that flattery if the hand of Providence interferes to blast our hopes." Thomas Howe, the editor of the *St. Christopher Advertiser*, who called the hurricane a dreadful "visitation of Providence," marveled at the ameliorating effects of the "universal destruction," which opened "all hearts . . . to the soft influence of humanity and tenderness" and banished discord and rancor from "every breast" as islanders banded together to aid their fellow sufferers. Sir Ralph Payne, the royal governor of the British Leeward Islands, declared a day of fasting after the hurricane to "render thanks to Almighty GOD for their great deliverance, and to deprecate the infliction of any further miseries from the divine vengeance." The Reverend Hugh Knox, minister to the Presbyterian congregation on the Danish island of St. Croix, characterized the storm as a providential act designed to spur repentance among a population who, despite their suffering, still enjoyed "numberless undeserved mercies" from God.[52]

The "frightful and melancholy occasion" of the hurricane inspired intense piety and introspection in fifteen-year-old Alexander Hamilton, who was employed as a clerk in a St. Croix trading house when the storm annihilated much of the island. Hamilton described the hurricane and his own deeply emotional response to it in a letter to the *Royal Danish American*

Gazette, St. Croix's English-language newspaper. The horror of the storm, he explained, led him to feel as if he were a "vile worm" who was powerless when confronted by the "Omnipotence" of "He who gave the winds to blow, and the lightnings to rage," and who justly threatened to plunge the terrified young man into the "gulph of eternal misery" to punish his "vileness." Hamilton wrote his essay not because he believed himself to be either uniquely sinful or unusually pious — quite the opposite. "The scenes of horror exhibited around us, naturally awakened such ideas in every thinking breast, and aggravated the deformity of every failing of our lives," he observed, adding tellingly, "It were a lamentable insensibility indeed, not to have had such feelings, and I think inconsistent with human nature."[53]

Hamilton and others also saw the hurricane as an occasion for benevolence. He urged those "who revel in affluence" to "see the afflictions of humanity and bestow your superfluity to ease them." Some islanders heeded the call to action. One widely published report from St. Christopher praised the "generous spirits [who] have manifested their humanity in contributing liberally for the relief of the poor who have suffered" as a result of the storm. The editor of that island's local newspaper singled out for special praise "those worthy men" who contributed to the relief of widows and orphans. But most reports from the region described devastation so widespread and losses so massive that the situation clearly necessitated outside help.[54]

That relief never really materialized, mostly due to an economic crisis in Britain and perhaps also as a result of mainland colonists' preoccupation with their own deteriorating relations with London. On the one hand, although London merchants — arguably colonists' most dependable source of disaster relief during this period — may have initiated a subscription "for the Relief of the late dreadful Hurricane in the Leeward Islands," this effort apparently failed, largely because of a financial crisis caused by overextension of credit, which, in turn, resulted in several bank failures and many private bankruptcies. Merchants were themselves in dire straits, and the fact that credit extended to colonial planters was a key source of their travails likely lessened the chances of their sending hurricane relief. On the other hand, when Sir Ralph Payne requested assistance from his fellow governors, only Pennsylvania's Richard Penn responded, issuing a proclamation calling on local merchants to "give immediate Assistance to the afflicted Inhabitants . . . by sending Vessels with Provisions" to help avert an expected famine, which some apparently did. As a St. Christopher native, Payne was not especially well connected with other imperial functionaries. Though he had spent much of the previous decade in London, his political connections were mainly in the House of Commons, where he held a seat between 1768 and 1771.[55]

By all accounts, Payne worked hard to orchestrate government-sponsored relief both in the Leeward Islands and in London. Soon after the hurricane, he convened the legislature in Antigua, where he led efforts to undertake a two-part locally organized disaster relief program. First, Payne encouraged the assembly to pass a bill to raise £20,000 in taxes to be used to repay private citizens who were willing to advance funds as loans to the provincial government "in Order to supply the present Exigencies of the Island." Although this plan must have seemed like a creative way to mobilize local capital quickly in a time of crisis, it failed for lack of donors. Second, as we have seen, on the advice of his council, Payne wrote to other governors, asking them specifically to appeal to merchants to send grain and other provisions. Payne was a popular governor, and islanders appreciated his efforts. The author of one published account of the hurricane dedicated his tract to Payne, praising his "zeal in the service of the King, and regard for the people committed to his care," and crediting him with "deliverance from a quick approaching famine."[56]

Payne duly reported his efforts, and the many challenges he faced, to his superiors in London. Days after the storm, he described the horrific destruction at Antigua to Lord Hillsborough, whom he likely expected to share his letters with the king and others in London. Payne recounted the loss of his own "Papers, furniture, Habitation, and Necessaries" and observed that the storm had "destroy'd many Lives, ruin'd Numbers of useful Members, and respectable Families of the Community." He told of "Persons who were buried in the Ruins of their Houses" and others who were "blown, maim'd and wounded, about the fields," as they tried to escape, instead enduring "a Degree of Misery and Distress from the Fury of the Storm, unknown ... to any Part of the human Creation." The melancholy effects of the hurricane, he declared, were altogether "such as might provoke the keenest Sensibility, from the most obdurate Heart." Payne also worried about the likelihood of famine. While he did not explicitly request assistance from London, he pointedly conveyed the enormity of the task ahead and his sense of his own responsibility, as governor, to "resist the Struggles of Sensibility, and ... endeavor to merit His Majesty's gracious Approbation, and your Lordship's Applause, by an inflexible Constancy, and indefatigable Industry, in healing, to the best of my Power, the Wounds, of this miserable Country."[57]

In his post-hurricane interactions with imperial officials, Payne also took a more pragmatic and targeted approach, advocating on behalf of the island's legislators, who petitioned the king for £2,500 to repair and rebuild the military barracks and hospital in Antigua's capital. The petitioners ingratiatingly appealed to George III as their "Humane and Gracious Sovereign whose desire of alleviating Affliction, has ever Accompanied his Power." According to Hillsborough's successor, Lord Dartmouth, the king "graciously received" the petition and assented to providing £2,000. (No explanation was forthcoming from London as to why the petitioners received £500 less than they requested.) For his part, Dartmouth believed the situation in the Leeward Islands to be less dire than Payne reported. "I am not without Hope," he wrote, "that, by Industry and Oeconomy, the private Losses of the Inhabitants may in time be repaired, and by a prudent and frugal Application of the Revenue, the public Buildings may be restored to their former respectable Condition."[58]

Colonists' interest in news about disaster relief in the Danish island colony of St. Croix suggests that they expected more from their own supposedly benevolent imperial governors. On 2 September 1772, Ulrich Wilhelm von Roepstorff, the royal governor of St. Croix, issued a proclamation in which he pledged to energetically address the needs of his hurricane-ravaged colony. Von Roepstorff estimated that the storm destroyed half the buildings on the island, leaving many homeless. He also worried about the possibility of famine and the unruliness of the island's large enslaved population. Acting briskly and emphatically, Von Roepstorff pledged that his government would keep order and provide free bread to the "poorest White Persons." He also insisted, "None will be dispirited with the Misfortunes they may have suffered" because storm victims could "expect every Thing from a gracious Sovereign," the king of Denmark, who would make every effort to assist the "needful." Complete translations of Von Roepstorff's proclamation appeared in newspapers from New England to Virginia, a tacit rebuke to the comparatively stingy British imperial administration. This attention was noteworthy. Newspapers in the mainland colonies infrequently reported news from Danish St. Croix, despite the island's large English population.[59]

In the aftermath of the deadly hurricane, prominent residents of St. Croix praised Von Roepstorff as a man of feeling, as well as a colonial official of unusual initiative and competence. Days after the governor issued his proclamation, the Reverend Hugh Knox dedicated the sermon he delivered at St. Croix's Presbyterian church to the island's "Chief ruler" in appreciation of his "peculiar attention to . . . soothing the calamities and alleviating the distresses, and supplying the wants of its suffering, ruined inhabitants, by a series of humane edicts, wholesome regulations, and private charities,

Benevolent Empire

which do honour to human nature, and to Christianity itself." Alexander Hamilton approvingly reported that Von Roepstorff had "issued very salutary and humane regulations" after the hurricane. Another St. Croix resident, Dr. Cullen, informed a friend in London that the governor had shown "an extraordinary share of good sense, good nature, and fatherly tenderness to us all" in that time of crisis.[60]

These accolades made their way to the mainland colonies and to the seat of empire. One particular report from St. Croix appeared in several colonial newspapers, sometimes alongside articles detailing the unalloyed devastation in the British island colonies. "On this melancholy Occasion, his Excellency the [Governor] General has devised every Thing for the Relief of the suffering Poor that Humanity and Goodness of Heart which so eminently distinguish his Character could suggest," an unnamed observer noted, specifically praising Von Roepstorff's efforts to procure and dispense provisions among St. Croix's "distressed" inhabitants. A more explicit comparison between Von Roepstorff's compassion and effectiveness and the lackluster performance of his British imperial counterparts appeared at the end of Dr. Cullen's letter, which was published in at least one London newspaper. Cullen hoped to see a statue erected to honor Von Roepstorff for his "wisdom and courage" in guiding St. Croix through the aftermath of the hurricane. "I wish you could say as much," he concluded tartly, "for any of your [British] governors."[61]

Memories of Von Roepstorff's effort to provide comprehensive disaster relief likely influenced both the rhetoric and reality of Britons' approach to Caribbean hurricanes in the ensuing decade. While residents of the British West Indies continued to look to London for assistance, at least some idealized Von Roepstorff as the personification of a benevolent (Danish) empire. In 1774, two years after the hurricane, the local newspaper on the British island of St. Christopher published a poem extolling the virtues of St. Croix's governor:

O! be that Name forever dear
While age to age shall roll
When Storms and Plagues and Famines near
Think on his generous Soul.[62]

Perhaps not coincidentally, the next time a major hurricane hit the British islands the king and Parliament forcefully and visibly stepped in to join the committees of merchants and philanthropists that rushed to aid the "unhappy sufferers." In early October 1780, in the midst of America's War of Independence, two unusually severe hurricanes struck Jamaica and Barbados, killing thousands and resulting in unprecedented property losses. In London, Parliament responded to colonists' petitions for aid by sending a total of £120,000 to the two islands; the king personally donated 5,000 pairs of shoes for poor men who served in Jamaica's militia.[63]

§ The example of Von Roepstorff was neither solely nor even primarily responsible for this outpouring of disaster relief from London to its island colonies. Indeed, in the short term, hurricane relief was one of several political dividends that colonists in the British West Indies received from London as a result of their loyalty during the American Revolution. In the somewhat longer term, humanitarian benevolence, coupled with centralized hierarchical governance, would become the twin pillars of a rejuvenated British imperialism, the principal features of what one scholar has called the "spirit of 1783."[64] Those colonists who declared their independence in 1776, by contrast, established political institutions that were unable or unwilling to provide relief to those who suffered the devastation of hurricanes, fires, and other calamities in the postrevolutionary era.

{ 5 }

DISASTER NATION

Although hurricanes and earthquakes occurred from time to time after the Revolution, their cultural impact paled in comparison to that of the fires and epidemics that ravaged the growing cities of the early republic. Because few Americans lived in urban places, only a tiny subset of the nation's inhabitants experienced these disasters directly. But because cities were the political, commercial, social, and communications hubs of the United States, such episodes were widely reported and sometimes assumed national significance. The yellow fever epidemic that devastated Philadelphia in 1793 brought business and politics to a standstill in the nation's second largest city, which was also its temporary capital, while spreading fears of pestilence up and down the Eastern Seaboard. And in 1811, citizens throughout the nation mourned the victims of a deadly theater fire in Richmond, Virginia, which inspired vigorous debates on topics ranging from the supposed evils of the theater to the need for improvements in building standards and public safety.

Disasters like these also gave rise to public conversations about benevolence, religion, and the respective responsibilities of citizens and government. Debating the relative weight of religion and science in explaining—and perhaps preventing—calamities was part of that process, as was determining the appropriate sources, extent, and objectives of post-disaster relief. Disasters also tested the cherished belief that sympathy, benevolence, and public virtue were essential and even unique attributes of citizens of the American republic, both individually and collectively.

In the early American republic, narratives that emphasized citizens' philanthropic responses to disaster dovetailed nicely with a political culture that was distrustful of government, as did emotionally laden stories of individual suffering, which construed disasters more as personal tragedies than as public problems. While certain elements of the colonial culture of calamity survived the Revolution, government-sponsored disaster relief did not. Responses to disasters in the early American republic were mostly voluntary, ephemeral, and local.

§ The Philadelphia yellow fever epidemic of 1793 was the republic's first disaster of national significance, as well as a test case for how disasters might work in an independent America. Historians have shown how the discourse surrounding the epidemic both reflected and contributed to ongoing debates about national identity. Scientists and physicians pondered not only the biological causes of yellow fever but also its geographical origins and their larger implications. Did yellow fever come to Philadelphia with refugees from Haiti's revolution or with other interlopers, or was it a product of the city's unclean (and hence corrupt) environment? Should American physicians adopt the practices of their European counterparts, or, as one contemporary urged, should they shed their "provincial shackles, no less in the science of medicine than of government"? Some observers worried that yellow fever, which appeared in 1793 and then returned in subsequent years, signified moral failing on the part of the United States and its citizens. Others saw the fever as a providential visitation by a wrathful God. Many worried about the seeming lack of sensibility and compassion toward the fever's victims during this time of crisis. Did those who fled the infected city or those who remained behind to tend the sick and dying better represent the American character?[1]

The cause of yellow fever remained a mystery until the twentieth century. A virus spread by the bite of *Aedes aegypti* mosquitoes, it first appeared in North America in 1693, resurfacing periodically in the port cities of British America throughout the colonial era. Epidemiological evidence suggests that the virus and its mosquito vectors originated in Africa, came to the West Indies via the slave trade, and then spread to mainland North American ports with the trade in sugar and slaves. The virus's symptoms are flu-like, but in serious cases they escalate and cause jaundice, delirium, bleeding—both internally and from the nose and ears—and violent vomiting. In terminal cases, the afflicted becomes comatose, the organs and circulatory system fail, and death results.[2]

Beginning in 1793, a time when bitter partisan divisions over both fiscal and foreign policy generated deep anxieties about the future of the republic, yellow fever returned with a vengeance after nearly a thirty-year absence. These later epidemics were more frequent and often more severe than their colonial predecessors. Each year between 1793 and 1805, yellow fever struck three or more American cities; it returned often, most especially to southern ports, through the Civil War era. News of these epidemics and their casualties spread quickly, thanks to the creation of a national postal service that carried newspapers and letters with unprecedented efficiency to every corner of the republic. Overwhelmingly an urban problem, yellow fever likely amplified the anti-urban bias of those who, like Thomas Jefferson, condemned cities as "pestilential to the morals, the health and the liberties of man."[3]

In 1793, the first fatalities from what Philadelphia's leading physician, Benjamin Rush, called the "bilious remitting yellow fever" occurred in early August, and within weeks the city was experiencing a major medical emergency. By mid-September, Henry Knox, the secretary of war—the only high-ranking government official still in Philadelphia, whose own departure was imminent—informed President Washington that at least a hundred people were being buried every day, that commerce and shipping had ceased, and that the streets of one of the most populous and prosperous cities in the United States were now "lonely to a melancholy degree." The blow, Knox lamented, was "as heavy as if an army of enemies had possessed the city without plundering it." When it was all over in mid-November, nearly 5,000 people had perished. Fatalities were highest among young- and middle-aged adults, and especially among the poor.[4]

Previous epidemics had been as bad or worse, but their cultural impact was comparatively minimal. In 1699, when yellow fever killed 220 Philadelphians, the city lost 15 percent of its people—compared with 10 percent in 1793—but the later epidemic had a more profound cultural impact because the arrival of the pestilence, after a thirty-one year absence, during which health and longevity improved significantly overall, made the sudden pervasiveness of so much suffering and death especially shocking. In 1699, moreover, Pennsylvania had no newspaper and its provincial government suppressed information about the epidemic. When the fever returned in 1762, though there were two newspapers in Philadelphia, the press was silent about the epidemic, perhaps because the disease was mostly confined to the city's southern fringe, relatively far removed from its wealthier and more densely populated neighborhoods. In 1793, by contrast, the onset of yellow fever was widely publicized, and since Philadelphia was now America's pre-eminent political, cultural, and commercial center, many people viewed the epidemic as a national emergency. Because the city attracted so many visitors, including refugees from the revolutions in France and Haiti, outsiders who believed (incorrectly) that yellow fever spread by human contact also perceived Philadelphia's crisis as a direct threat to their own communities.[5]

In 1793, Philadelphia was the seat of three governments, none of which responded effectively to yellow fever and its challenges. At the federal level, Congress adjourned in early March and did not reconvene until December. President Washington, who had returned to Mount Vernon, considered calling Congress into session in another city in November, but Attorney General Edmund Randolph advised him that such a "call of congress from the executive" would be unconstitutional. At any rate, correspondence between Washington and his cabinet indicates that the nation's political leaders saw responding to the war in Europe, not the fever in Philadelphia, as their most pressing business. Meanwhile, Pennsylvania's state legislators gradually fled the city, after reviving a colonial law that mandated the quarantining of all ships arriving from the West Indies; Governor Thomas Mifflin promised $1,000 to fund inspections of incoming vessels, but then he, too, promptly abandoned the capital. Although Mayor Matthew Clarkson remained in town, most of the city's aldermen, judges, and other officials joined an exodus of some 17,000 mostly affluent urban dwellers who left for the surrounding countryside.[6]

In fever-ridden Philadelphia, efforts to retain order and relieve the afflicted were therefore necessarily ad hoc, unofficial, and unsupported by any level of government. The Philadelphia College of Physicians, established six years earlier to "advance the Science of Medicine, and thereby lessen human misery, by investigating the diseases and remedies which are peculiar to our country," met to discuss the fever and offered an eleven-point program—advocating cleanliness and the use of vinegar and other chemical deterrents—to defeat or at least contain it. Physicians offered competing cures to the afflicted, with Benjamin Rush advocating purging the body by extensive bleeding and vomiting, while Edward Stevens (a recent arrival from St. Croix) preferred a gentler regimen of quinine, cold baths, and herbs. While the doctors debated, Mayor Clarkson took the bold step of appealing directly "to the benevolent citizens" of his city, soliciting volunteers for a committee that would assume the newly expanded responsibilities of the Overseers of the Poor, most of whose members themselves had become ill or left town.[7]

On 12 September, twenty-seven men, mostly artisans and other middling sorts, attended the committee's first meeting. Addressing the dire need for hospital space to house the ailing poor, they unanimously agreed to secure a bank loan of $1,500 "for the purpose of furnishing suitable accommodation and supplies for the use of the afflicted under the prevailing malignant fever" at Bush Hill, an abandoned loyalist estate that the city previously commandeered for use as a hospital. For the duration of the crisis, the committee focused on four major tasks. One subcommittee "undertook the extreme hazardous part of attending at and managing" the hospital at Bush Hill, while a second oversaw the admission of new fever victims to Bush Hill and the interment of the dead. As the crisis deepened, the committee also confronted the growing challenge of housing and feeding hundreds of newly orphaned children, as well as the need to provide food, firewood, and other necessities to some 200 indigent families. To accomplish these essential tasks, the committee met nearly every day. With Clarkson, the twelve men whom "death and other causes" did not prevent from attending to committee business were, for the duration of the crisis, Philadelphia's de facto government.[8]

Among the committee's members, only Clarkson, a longtime member of the American Philosophical Society and a native New Yorker who had both family and business contacts in Manhattan, likely had significant connections outside Philadelphia. Churches, which had been so active in collecting donations in the aftermath of Boston's great fire, were closed due to the fever. Local government, which sometimes provided relief or at least organized relief efforts in such situations, had left town. For his part, Governor Mifflin did not follow the example of his colonial predecessors by issuing a call for relief from his fellow governors. In this case at least, the institutional networks that delivered disaster relief to colonists before 1776 no longer functioned in the postrevolutionary era.[9]

The mostly unsolicited sum of roughly $34,000 in cash donations—plus contributions of food, clothing, and firewood—that the Philadelphia committee nonetheless received fell into three main categories. Nearly $6,000 came from Philadelphians who had fled to Germantown, Darby, and other towns in Pennsylvania and neighboring Delaware. An additional $19,000 came from the inhabitants of nearby communities in Pennsylvania, New Jersey, and Delaware, many of whom also sent provisions. Finally, the common council of the city of New York and a committee of citizens in Boston, port cities that were Philadelphia's main commercial rivals, sent contributions of $5,000 and $2,651, respectively. Scattered small donations came from elsewhere. A combination of guilt and benevolence toward sick and indigent fellow Philadelphians likely motivated the wealthy exiles. For other donors, even those who professed sympathy and benevolence, their utmost concern was to keep Philadelphians at home in their infected city and away from their own communities. States from Massachusetts to North Carolina imposed quarantines for ships coming from Philadelphia, and many towns, especially in nearby New Jersey and New York, posted guards to prevent those traveling by land from Philadelphia from entering their communities.[10]

New York's response to the epidemic explicitly embraced these dual priorities. The first communication that Clarkson's committee received from New Yorkers came from a self-described committee "to prevent the introduction and spreading of infectious diseases" composed of fourteen men, half appointed by New York's city council and the rest chosen "by the citizens at large." The committee's chairman, John Broome, asserted that their main strategy for preventing the spread of fever to New York would be to provide "such aid as in their power, for the relief of the poor and most distressed citizens" of Philadelphia. New York's mayor, Richard Varick, later fulfilled this promise with a donation of $5,000 from his city's common council, the largest single donation Clarkson's committee reported receiving. In his letter to Clarkson, Varick invoked both providential and patriotic themes, noting that New Yorkers were "deeply impressed with the awful judgment of the Almighty on the American Nation, in permitting a pestilential disease to lay waste to that once populous, well regulated and flourishing sister city, the seat of Empire." At the same time, however, New Yorkers cut themselves off from their suffering "sister city." Governor George Clinton closed his state's ports to people and goods from Philadelphia, and armed militia deterred travelers from entering New York City, where angry crowds intimidated newcomers suspected of being infected, even if they were not.[11]

Alexander Hamilton experienced firsthand the hostility and fear that gripped many communities. He and his wife, Eliza, contracted yellow fever in Philadelphia, survived the disease, and then set off to join their children, who were staying with Eliza's parents in Albany. Along the way, citizens and armed militia prevented the Hamiltons from entering their towns. Barred from New York City, they traveled northward along the east bank of the Hudson River. When they tried to cross the river to Albany, however, they learned that city officials prohibited ferrymen from transporting passengers who had been in infected places. Only the intervention of Eliza's powerful father, General Philip Schuyler, enabled them to reach their destination, though local authorities insisted that they leave their baggage behind, submit to medical examinations, and then stay effectively in quarantine at the Schuyler estate. Hamilton protested these conditions as "derogatory to my rights, as a citizen of this State," arguing that a man could not "be deprived by arbitrary and tyrannical means of the essential rights of a member of Society merely because it has been his lot to have had a dangerous disease." Albany's mayor was not persuaded. "You may rest assured," he avowed, "that those are absolutely mistaken who may conceive that intimations of this nature and menaces can prevent us from fulfilling our duties to our constituents, or divert our Attention from the welfare of our Citizens."[12]

More than fires or earthquakes, disease created tensions between the rights of individuals and the good of the community while often straining the bonds of sympathy between those who gave and received benevolence. Fearful and sometimes hostile actions often belied the sympathetic words of those who masked the reality of physical distance with rhetoric of emotional closeness. Although a few towns welcomed the fleeing Philadelphians, many more kept them at bay with eloquent performances of benevolence that reflected contemporary ideals of sympathy and citizenship, or the optimistic notion that the American republic was exceptional precisely because of the warm social bonds among its citizens.[13]

The statement of Henry Wynkoop, a former congressman who chaired a committee in Bucks County, Pennsylvania, for "procuring relief for the poor and sick inhabitants of Philadelphia," exemplified this approach. Wynkoop insisted that he and his colleagues "as citizens of the same common country" were morally bound to "share the honors of benevolence, and partake with [Philadelphians] in the offices of social affection." Impelled by civic obligation, Christian charity, and what they called "the social tie" and its "common principle of benevolence," the inhabitants of Bucks County collected more than $2,000 for Philadelphia's sick and indigent.[14]

When Wynkoop praised Clarkson and his committee for their "laudable and unremitted exertions in the cause of humanity," he echoed the more widely publicized accolades of Mathew Carey, a prominent and civic-minded publisher and bookseller who penned his first brief account of the epidemic at its height in mid-October. Carey disapprovingly tallied the various state and local measures aimed at isolating Philadelphians and expressed his "deep regret, that the dread of this disorder has so far extinguished the feelings of humanity" among his countrymen. He excoriated the unfounded rumors and "extravagant stories" that fanned the fires of fear and hostility. Carey also criticized his fellow Philadelphians who had abandoned their city, as well as those who remained behind but treated the afflicted with neglect or malevolence. The plague, he declared, had ruptured social bonds within families, as well as in the wider community. The only bright spot in this otherwise troubling portrait, Carey asserted, was made up of the "patriotic citizens" of the committee who "erected a standard for the benevolent citizens to rally round." By acting with "disinterested humanity," these men, he declared, "merited the unceasing gratitude of their fellow citizens."[15]

Carey elaborated on these themes in his more substantial *Short Account of the Malignant Fever, lately prevalent in Philadelphia*, first published in mid-November, particularly lamenting the "total dissolution of the bonds of society" that the fever engendered. One consequence of this development that saddened him deeply was the refusal of men to shake hands, an old custom that had become an increasingly popular alternative to bowing in the more egalitarian climate of the postrevolutionary era. Because of the fever, Carey observed critically, "many were affronted at even the offer of a hand," while anyone who wore mourning clothes "was shunned like a viper." Still, Carey vigorously applauded those who risked their own lives to help the suffering, reserving his highest praise for the model citizens of Clarkson's committee, especially the hospital managers, who at great personal risk to themselves and "without any possible inducement but the purest motives of humanity . . . came forward, and offered themselves as the forlorn hope" of the community.[16]

While Carey praised humanity and public service as hallmarks of good citizenship, he made those attributes race-specific by disparaging Philadelphia's African Americans, who mostly remained in the city during the epidemic. At the suggestion of Benjamin Rush, who shared the popular (but incorrect) belief that African Americans were immune from yellow fever, free black Philadelphians mobilized to nurse the sick and bury the dead. Rush had advised Richard Allen and Absalom Jones, both influential clergy in the local African Methodist Episcopal Church, that providing such hazardous and essential services would earn them the gratitude of white Philadelphians and thereby enhance the status of the city's African American community. As it turned out, Rush was doubly wrong. At least 198 black Philadelphians died from yellow fever, and Carey, who so extravagantly lauded the contributions of white volunteers, condemned the city's African Americans, claiming that the "vilest of blacks" charged extortionate fees for their nursing services and "were even detected in plundering the houses of the sick," though he conceded that Allen and Jones had themselves behaved admirably. Allen and Jones penned a spirited response to Carey, but the damage had been done. Allen and Jones's *Narrative of the Proceedings of the Black People* was published once in January 1794, whereas Carey's *Short Account* went through ten Philadelphia printings, including German and French translations, besides separate editions published in London and Dublin in the 1790s.[17]

Carey's enormously influential pamphlet was a notable salvo in an ongoing offensive to identify American citizenship and national identity with whiteness, but it also emphatically and unequivocally defined disaster relief as a function of community, not government. Carey mentioned government only to note that it had "vacated" the city, leaving the field to Clarkson's committee of citizen volunteers. "Never, perhaps," he mused, "was there a city in the situation of Philadelphia at this period." It is true that after the crisis Governor Mifflin asked the committee to recommend "general precautions . . . to guard against a similar calamity in the future" and that local officials in Philadelphia and elsewhere gradually implemented efforts to promote cleanliness to advance the intertwined agendas of civic morality and public health. But while local officials were mildly interested in preventing epidemics, they showed no interest in helping victims of disease once they started. As the leading authority on the history of American epidemics has aptly concluded, "Leadership during epidemics [came] almost invariably from outside of established administrative circles" well into the nineteenth century. In cholera-stricken mid-nineteenth-century New York as in Philadelphia in 1793, "temporary committees, organized and led by the more courageous members of the community," provided relief and effectively performed the functions abdicated by local and state governments.[18]

As for the newly installed national government, the men who drafted, supported, and implemented the Constitution of 1787 did not envision disaster relief or assistance for suffering citizens as part of its charge, despite the fact that they endowed that new government with capacious powers. Those powers chiefly pertained to military and fiscal matters; their main purpose was to enable the government to fight wars and protect American trade and commerce. As one scholar observes, "The founders never designed their government to deal with . . . the regulation of the economy and the health, morals, and general welfare of the citizens." In theory at least, those were jobs for the states, but they, too, mostly left the business of disaster relief to citizen volunteers.[19]

A telling episode in the spring and summer of 1789 afforded an early indication of how American officials would respond to disasters and how their approach differed from that of an evolving British Empire. That year, unusually cold weather and the Hessian fly caused grain shortages in the northeastern United States and southern Canada, which distribution problems, arising primarily from market demands, severely aggravated. Although few, if any, people died as a result of the shortages, the situation was dire, with white settlers and Native Americans alike on the brink of starvation on both sides of the newly established border. The American government did nothing to aid the suffering. Of the effected states, only New York offered some paltry aid — as a loan, not a gift — which was too little and too late to help. By contrast, the British government suspended its trade laws, opened ports to foreign grain to ease the shortage, and sent thousands of bushels of wheat, flour, and peas to Canada. In subsequent decades, the imperial government also adopted highly interventionist policies to address famines in India, sent money and provisions to Canadian victims of fires and other disasters, and provided generous assistance to hurricane victims in storm-plagued island colonies.[20]

This publicly funded performance of imperial paternalism and benevolence stood in marked contrast to the political culture of the American republic, which imagined such matters as personal or local problems. The point is not that the British were kind and generous and the Americans were not but rather that their constitutional and political imperatives differed significantly. The increasing paternalism of the British Empire contrasted markedly with the American ideal of limited, even invisible, government—an ideal most citizens embraced—which made disaster relief the voluntary function of virtuous and enlightened citizens who shared a social bond rather than a power or responsibility of a distant government.

Consequently, on those rare occasions when Congress enacted laws pertaining to disaster prevention, protecting and promoting commerce was typically legislators' chief priority. For instance, "An Act for the establishment and support of Lighthouses, Beacons, Buoys, and Public Piers" was one of the first laws that Congress passed under the new constitution. Lighthouses could save lives by preventing maritime disasters, but the context in which the law passed shows that Congress saw it as part of a larger legislative program to support American trade and shipping, an objective that many deemed one of the foremost tasks of the newly empowered central government. Aside from establishing administrative departments and a federal judiciary, the business of the first session of the first Congress focused overwhelmingly on economic and fiscal matters, with Congress enacting the Lighthouse Act as part of a commercial agenda that included the first federal tariff, tonnage duties, and laws that regulated incoming vessels and the coastal trade. The centrality of trade to the American economy and the fact that tariffs would furnish the bulk of the government's revenue meant that lighthouses were hugely important to the nation's prosperity and political stability—so much so that, according to his biographer, Alexander Hamilton "scrawled more mundane letters about lighthouse construction than about any other single topic" during his more than five years as secretary of the treasury.[21]

When Congress considered adopting a national quarantine law amid the recurring yellow fever epidemics of the 1790s, its debates centered on the proposed statute's constitutionality, not the effectiveness of quarantines in saving lives. Supporters of a bill that empowered the president to establish quarantines and federal customs officers to enforce them argued that quarantines were primarily commercial regulations and therefore within the purview of the national government. Opponents saw quarantines as policing powers that only states could exercise. In the end, Congress enacted a law mandating federal enforcement of state quarantine laws, leaving the decision of when and where to impose quarantines to state authorities.[22]

When it came to providing relief for citizens, Congress acted on only sixteen occasions between 1789 and 1860, most of which did not involve plagues, hurricanes, or other calamities but rather arose from concerns about national security and the United States' increasingly expansionist geopolitical objectives.[23] The first case occurred after the Whiskey Rebellion of 1794, when Congress provided $16,500 in "relief" for citizens in western Pennsylvania who had incurred losses as a result of their loyalty during a revolt that many in the ruling Federalist party believed aimed to overthrow the Philadelphia-based national government. In four later cases, Congress sought to strengthen U.S. power on the southern and western frontiers by sending provisions to "friendly Indians" and relief to Indian fighters and also by allowing white settlers and speculators whose landholdings were destroyed by the New Madrid earthquakes of 1811–12 to swap them for acreage elsewhere. In 1852, Congress allocated $6,000 in relief to American citizens who had been captured and imprisoned in Cuba — but since pardoned and returned home — for involvement in a pro-annexation revolt. A year later, the legislature allocated funds to General Bennet Riley, California's last military governor, to reimburse him for the "relief of destitute overland emigrants" who helped settle and thereby secure that western territory.[24]

Congress also occasionally delivered impressive and carefully targeted gifts to assuage suffering outside U.S. borders. The people of Venezuela became the first recipients of U.S. foreign aid after an earthquake destroyed Caracas in March 1812. Enthralled by the revolutionary spirit of the South Americans, Congress sent $50,000 in provisions to Venezuelans who had declared their independence from Spain in July 1811 and launched their republic, only to have the earthquake imperil and defeat them eight months later. (In the same session, Congress considered, but did not fund, relief for people "suffering from famine, occasioned by the ravages of locusts," in the Canary Islands, a nonrevolutionary Spanish colony.) In 1847, Congress donated the services of two U.S. Navy vessels to transport more than $2,000,000 in citizens' contributions to a massive international effort to relieve Irish famine victims. This action served the dual purpose of pleasing

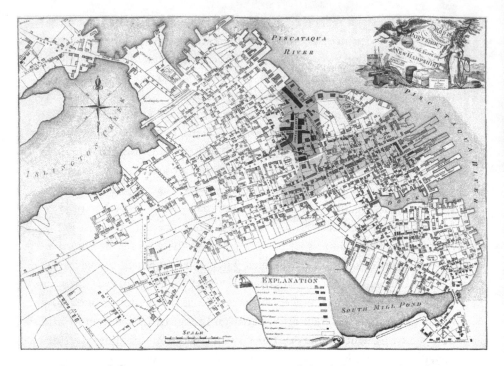

Portsmouth fire map. Fires were common in crowded early American cities, where building with wood was common. New Hampshire's largest city suffered three major fires in the early nineteenth century. On this map, the darkest shading indicates the area destroyed by fire in 1802; a second conflagration, in 1806, occurred in the more lightly shaded area immediately to the east of the first fire. The largest shaded area, stretching from Court Street to the city wharves, burned in 1813. *Portsmouth Athenaeum.*

Irish American voters and stemming the tide of impoverished immigrants arriving in American cities, objectives that appealed, respectively, to Democrats and Whigs.[25]

Closer to home, Congress sometimes considered a specific commercially oriented sort of disaster relief in the aftermath of urban fires because cities and their ports were so essential to the nation's fiscal and economic health. When citizens in Portsmouth, New Hampshire (1802, 1806), Norfolk, Virginia (1804), and New York City (1835) asked for relief after major fires, Congress authorized moratoria on the collection of customs duties to help merchants in these coastal communities. Congress's 1803 "Act for the relief of the sufferers by fire, in the town of Portsmouth," which some see as the first American disaster relief legislation, merely protected the local merchant elite by delaying the collection of debts they owed to U.S. Customs. There was no provision for humanitarian aid in the wake of a fire that destroyed a substantial portion of the city and left hundreds of "widows and orphans . . . destitute of every necessity of life."[26]

Fires were commonplace in the growing cities of the early republic, but with one notable exception, humanitarian relief efforts for fire victims, as for victims of epidemics and other domestic calamities, were locally organized and ad hoc. That exception occurred in 1827, when Congress granted the city of Alexandria $20,000 after a fire caused more than $100,000 in property losses and destroyed fifty-three buildings, leaving many homeless. This fire was not even close to being the worst of the era, but Alexandria, though now in Virginia, was then part of the District of Columbia, which Congress governed. Even so, disaster relief for Alexandrians proved controversial. In 1831, when considering a plea from the mayor of Georgetown—also part of the District—to furnish firewood for the poor during a particularly brutal winter, Congressman James K. Polk of Tennessee condemned the measure, arguing that the Alexandria case had set a dangerous precedent. "Was the obligation to contribute to the relief of sufferers [there] . . . greater than to those of other parts of the Union?" he asked, adding that on "the very same day that the fire occurred in Alexandria," Cincinnati suffered a more ruinous blaze, but Ohio's fire victims did not receive, and had not applied for, relief from Congress.[27]

Nor could survivors expect much aid from their states in the aftermath of fires and other disasters. New York's city government received the state legislature's permission to raise $6,000,000 in bonds after a fire destroyed more than seventeen city blocks in lower Manhattan in 1835, but that money, which amounted to a loan, not a gift, was earmarked not for humanitarian aid but rather for the relief of local insurance companies and other businesses. A decade later, when citizens in fire-ravaged Pittsburgh boldly asserted, "Charity and benevolence are as much the duty of States as individuals," the Pennsylvania assembly responded by taking the unusual step of allocating $50,000 to the ruined city for relief. The Pittsburgh fire, which consumed nearly half the city, resulted in millions of dollars in lost property, including nearly $800,000 in losses by more than a thousand individual claimants. After the fire, Pittsburgh's citizens' committee followed what was by then an established tradition of seeking assistance from towns, churches, and individual donors, collecting nearly $200,000, not including the unusual contribution from the state government.[28]

In 1802, leading men in Portsmouth, New Hampshire, who were the first to petition Congress for assistance after a devastating fire, also moved quickly to use their personal and occupational connections and the power of a pervasive press to mobilize their own local relief effort. Densely populated and home to five of the nation's twelve largest cities—Portsmouth itself ranked eleventh—New England was the ideal place for such a project. Highly literate and relatively homogeneous, New Englanders shared long traditions of local governance and more recent success, honed during the imperial crisis, using circular letters and committees of correspondence to mobilize people beyond their own communities. Ultimately, Portsmouth's effort netted some $45,000, or roughly one-fourth of the city's fire-related losses, the same proportion that colonial Bostonians had recouped in 1760 via their transatlantic commercial ties and the prodigious efforts of their energetic and well-connected royal governor.[29]

At a time when women were increasingly prominent in organized benevolence, especially in efforts to assist widows and orphans, disaster relief remained the province of men who had the connections and public influence needed to raise comparatively large sums of money in a relatively short time. Two days after the fire, on the morning of Tuesday, 28 December, Portsmouth's board of selectmen met and appointed five of the city's most prominent men to a committee to receive and distribute "any donations which the Charitable may be disposed to make to those who have suffered by the late distressing fire . . . whereby many persons have lost their ALL." The *New Hampshire Gazette* published the committee's appeal for contributions, concluding with a request that "the printers of Newspapers . . . insert the foregoing, in aid of the cause of humanity." Not content to rely on newspapers alone, however, the committee also prepared a circular letter, which members sent to influential men throughout New England. These letters were handwritten, but the use of mass-produced printed form letters soon became common in post-disaster fund-raising efforts. When the next great fire devastated Portsmouth in 1806, its selectmen addressed a generic printed appeal to clergy throughout the United States. A committee of citizens in nearby Newburyport also circulated a printed plea for aid to the "Selectmen of the Town of _____," filling in the names of municipalities throughout New England, when fire destroyed a large section of their city in 1811.[30]

After the December 1802 fire, though few newspapers published the Portsmouth committee's appeal in full, the story spread quickly, reaching Philadelphia by 7 January and making its way as far as Ohio in the coming weeks. Press coverage led some communities to collect money for Portsmouth, and it also inspired individual donations. A "Sincear Republican" in Rhode Island who read about the fire felt obliged to "cast in my mite, towards relieving such of them as are the most needy." An anonymous donor from Savannah, Georgia, contributed $20 "towards the relief of the sufferers" but asked that the committee return the money "should the paper have given a false account" of it. Phineas Dana was a New England native and Norfolk, Virginia, merchant who sent the committee $100 after learning about the fire from a Philadelphia newspaper. "I truly feel for the Town," he declared, "and particularly so for those that have been burnt." These cases attest to the ease with which both information and sentiment could move up and down the Eastern Seaboard in the aftermath of disaster.[31]

A day after news of the fire appeared in Washington's *National Intelligencer*, President Thomas Jefferson wrote to his friend former senator John Langdon, chairman of Portsmouth's relief committee, enclosing $100 for the "distressed sufferers." Unlike George III, whose widely publicized donation after the Montreal fire in 1765 was a performance of both kingly virtue and imperial benevolence, Jefferson offered assistance as a private citizen, not as a representative of the United States government. Indeed, perhaps to avoid creating the impression of government involvement in the relief effort, the president asked that his contribution remain anonymous. "I observe the trustees say in the papers that they will make a record of the donations," he wrote, but "I pray that in my case it may be of the sum only, without the name." Jefferson's anonymous gift aimed only to help those who lost their property in the fire, not to enhance the power or reputation of either the presidency or the national government.[32]

Portsmouth's leaders also targeted certain prospective donors and lobbied them aggressively. Taking advantage of New England's compact geography, the committee dispatched two emissaries to nearby port towns as roving fund-raisers. Edmund Quincy spent much of January visiting important men in Salem, Marblehead, and other Massachusetts trading communities. Daniel Waldron was in Boston in January overseeing a subscription drive that eventually brought in $2,400; in February, he was in Newport, Rhode Island, where he collected at least $800. The fact that Waldron was a merchant, appealing primarily to fellow merchants for support, likely eased his task in both locales. Meanwhile, Charles Pearce, a Portsmouth bookseller and printer, wrote to his counterparts in Philadelphia, describing the devastation at his printshop and his family's living quarters and requesting help. Within days, Philadelphia bookseller W. W. Woodward had placed a newspaper notice soliciting contributions. The Company of Philadelphia Booksellers soon took up a collection, and its members encouraged their colleagues in Boston and Baltimore to do likewise.[33]

Although the efforts of the Portsmouth committee were perhaps unusually proactive, forming a temporary committee to seek outside assistance in the aftermath of fires and some other disasters became standard practice in New England and elsewhere. In October 1807, for instance, after a fire destroyed roughly half of the town of Fredericksburg, Virginia, a committee of prominent citizens undertook a letter-writing campaign to solicit relief. The committee collected more than $7,000, more than $5,000 of which came from fellow Virginians, including $100 from President Jefferson. The only donation from beyond the Chesapeake region (Virginia, Maryland, and the District of Columbia) was a $100 contribution from New York firms with business connections in Fredericksburg. The Fredericksburg committee was structurally similar to its Portsmouth counterpart, but it was far less successful. While newspaper reports estimated Fredericksburg's losses at $200,000, the local town committee collected less than 4 percent of that amount. Virginia's dispersed population and the economic hardships caused by the Embargo Act of 1807 likely hampered its efforts.[34]

In all, the Portsmouth committee received contributions from thirty-six localities in which people organized fund-raising drives on behalf of fire victims. Of these, all but five were in New England, with two donations each from towns in New York and New Jersey, and also more than $7,700 from Philadelphia, by far the largest sum provided by any single contributor. A comparison of three relatively well-documented local efforts to aid Portsmouth shows how towns and cities used varying methods to collect money, depending on the size and composition of their respective communities.[35]

In Philadelphia, a sprawling city of more than 40,000, city officials appear to have provided unofficial leadership for the fund-raising effort. Moses Levy, the city recorder, informed the Portsmouth committee that, on hearing of "the disastrous Event . . . a Tale of woe . . . calculated to excite the Sympathy of benevolence," he and other prominent Philadelphians sprang to action. "A Town-meeting was invited and held, a general Contribution organized," he reported, "and Subscribers appointed a Committee to ascertain its amount, and receive and transmit it to such persons [in Portsmouth] who might be authorized to receive it." In mid-January, Levy sent $3,000 to Portsmouth to provide relief for people whose needs were "urgent," though his committee continued collecting money, eventually sending an additional $4,100 in February and $619.72 more in May. Levy attributed the generosity of Philadelphians at least in part to their memory of "the charitable hand the Inhabitants of Portsmouth . . . held out for their Relief" during a recent outbreak of yellow fever.[36]

While Philadelphians learned of the situation in Portsmouth primarily by reading their local newspapers, news of the fire and of efforts to assist its victims came to Newburyport, Massachusetts, via the committee's letter to leading merchants in that thriving trading community. Newburyport, a coastal city of some 6,000 inhabitants, was only about twenty miles from Portsmouth, whose committee members likely knew merchants William Bartlett and Moses Brown, as well as the other prominent men to whom they appealed for help. Those men, in turn, knew the wealthiest and most influential people in Newburyport, and their initial efforts to raise money for Portsmouth drew exclusively on these personal networks of the rich and powerful. "We embraced the earliest opportunity to wait personally on the more wealthy," they explained, and then "solicited of the several Clergymen to procure a Contribution on Sunday in their respective Congregations." Within days, they collected more than $1,400 by these two methods. Additional church contributions and an individual donation of a "Box of Goods" worth $30 later arrived in Portsmouth separately.[37]

The fund-raising effort in Portland, Maine, underscores the continuing importance of churches in civic and benevolence work in postrevolutionary communities. In 1802, Portland had some 3,700 people and at least six congregations of various Christian denominations. When the Portsmouth committee wrote to Samuel Freeman, one of the town's most influential citizens, he consulted "a number of Gentlemen" about what steps to take, and the group agreed that the most effective means of soliciting contributions would be to have local ministers ask for donations at Sabbath services, just as the Massachusetts clergy had done so effectively after Boston's fire in 1760. By the following week, all of Portland's congregations had responded, with donations totaling more than $900. By contrast, the public collection that another Portland resident offered to spearhead, independent of the churches, never seems to have happened.[38]

In all of these cases, contributors identified with victims of the Portsmouth fire, whom they regarded as fellow members of their own religious, regional, occupational, or national communities. Familiarity and shared identity engendered not only sympathy for the sufferers but also a belief in their worthiness. As one resident of Salem, Massachusetts, observed—in a letter that appeared in at least two New England newspapers—"To charity, it is always the strongest motive, that they are worthy for whom we are to do good actions." This attitude was very different from the ideal of universal benevolence, which held that aiding strangers was more admirable than helping friends, family, coreligionists, or others who might reciprocate and with whom the donors shared common interests and values, an ideal that had inspired Jonas Hanway and other Protestant Britons to send aid to Montreal in 1765. In the early American republic, the absence of an established church and other institutions that typically attended to the general welfare meant that disaster relief would be a matter for private citizens, while the nation's participatory public culture enlisted citizens of every sort, from President Jefferson and one of Baltimore's wealthiest merchants (who sent twenty barrels of flour) to David Ray of Cheshire, Connecticut, who donated twelve cents to the Portsmouth fire relief effort. As one donor put it, they sympathized with the sufferers as "members of the same great national family, link'd together by every endearing principle of duty, Interest, and Inclination."[39]

Disaster relief (and benevolence generally) came with somewhat different strings attached in the American republic, where social distinctions between donors and recipients were more fluid and less hierarchical. In the colonial period, the benevolent acts of transatlantic philanthropists had dramatized the superior wealth and status of contributors and colonists' dependence on these British benefactors. When contributors sent money to their fellow citizens in Portsmouth, by contrast, donors of every rank addressed the gentlemen of the committee as equals and sometimes offered strong opinions about how best to use their funds. Despite their own elite status, committee members expected to be accountable to contributors. In their initial published call for contributions, they reassured prospective givers that "all donations of the compassionate will be . . . faithfully appropriated agreeable to the benevolent intention of the donors." They also promised that their ledger, showing "receipts and distributions," would be "open for inspection" by the public.[40]

Donors most commonly instructed relief committees to use their contributions to help those who were most in need. While some generically cited widows and orphans as the most innocent and helpless — and therefore the most deserving — recipients, others specified that their donations go to "those who are Rendered destitute of Property or are Real Objects of Charity" as a result of the fire. "Altho' we Sincerely lament the misfortune which has occurred to those whose remaining property places them on higher ground," declared the wealthy Salem merchant George Crowninshield, "we think there may be others of their fellow Citizens, whose Sufferings demand more immediate relief." Townspeople in Peacham, Vermont, informed the committee that they had earmarked the forty-two dollars they collected specifically for Elizabeth Mackey, a widow who resided in Peacham but whose sole income came from rent on a house she owned in Portsmouth, where she used to live. "We know not whether it be consistent with your arrangements to make those sufferers . . . who reside out of Portsmouth sharers in the Contributions . . . or not," they wrote. "If it be, you will consider Mrs. Mackey as having received the above Some [*sic*]. . . . If otherwise, it may be considered as contributed to her relief."[41]

One church group from Haverhill emphasized that they wanted their $102 donation to go to "sufferers by the late fire in Portsmouth who are *really poor*," an instruction they added in part because they believed that Boston's wealthiest residents had received too much compensation for their losses after the fire in 1760. "It is said that the charities entrusted to the Committee in Boston after their great fire, were distributed by this rule—that every sufferer, rich and poor, received a dividend in proportion to the property, which he had lost," they explained, though the needs of the poor were most dire. The Haverhill donors, who described themselves as "persons by no means in affluent circumstances," informed the Portsmouth committee that they would not have contributed their "mites" without reassurance that "the money collected should be restricted to the *poor* only . . . [and] entirely appropriated to . . . widows, or orphans, & other really poor persons."[42]

When community leaders organized local fund-raising efforts, prospective donors sometimes questioned the worthiness of the project and those who stood to benefit from it. Michael McClary, a state senator and former Continental Army officer and one of the most influential citizens of Epsom, New Hampshire, convened a town meeting to collect money for fire victims after he received the circular letter from the Portsmouth committee. McClary was surprised to find that some townspeople opposed his subscription plan on the grounds that the people in Portsmouth "neglected to use proper means to extinguish the fire, that their [fire] Engines were plug'd up, and that the greater part of the buildings destroyed were insured in Boston." These critics resolutely refused to support McClary, who nevertheless managed to collect nearly $100 from other donors. Days after McClary related the townspeople's criticisms to the Portsmouth committee, an item in the *New Hampshire Gazette* attempted to quash this potential public relations nightmare by reporting that "the Fire Engines in this town were all in compleat repair when the fired called [them] into action, but in consequence of the great exertions and lack of water, two of them were soon injured, the others remain sound."[43]

If the Portsmouth fire of 1802 exemplified a carefully orchestrated approach to obtaining material relief in the aftermath of disaster, the response to the Richmond fire of 1811 shows how sympathy and melodrama could dominate the response to an unusually traumatic loss, generating nationally meaningful public discussions in the process. In an era when a dearth of tall buildings made fire-related deaths comparatively uncommon, at least seventy-six people died in the Richmond theater fire, making it at that time the deadliest in American history, a distinction it retained until the Chicago and Peshtigo fires of 1871. Among the dead were some who were already well known, including the state's governor, and others who became familiar as their sad stories circulated in newspapers, sermons, poems, and even children's books in the United States and beyond. Shocking and dramatic, the Richmond theater fire was a cultural event that exposed ideological tensions and social divisions, eliciting widespread public sympathy (and some censure), as civic and religious leaders sought to explain the calamity and mourn its casualties.[44]

On the evening of 26 December 1811, some 600 people flocked to Richmond's three-story brick theater to see a popular touring company perform a play called *The Father, or Family Feuds*, followed by a pantomime called *Raymond and Agnes, or The Bleeding Nun*. The audience included free and enslaved workers, Governor George William Smith and other well-heeled patrons from across Virginia, and visitors from Europe and out of state. Tragedy struck when a stagehand raised the chandelier between acts and some scenery caught fire. The flames spread rapidly, and people struggled to escape the burning building. Many were trampled to death in the confusion, while others who jumped out windows to escape the blaze "were dashed to pieces on the ground." Those who were unable to leave the fiery playhouse were burned to death in theater boxes or crowded stairways. Richmond's city council called the fire "a calamity unknown in the annals of our Country." Legislators in Massachusetts agreed, passing a resolution lamenting the "awful calamity which has deprived the State of Virginia . . . and the City of Richmond of many distinguished inhabitants by a conflagration in its effects unexampled in the history of their country." Heartfelt expressions of sympathy poured in from throughout the United States. Members of Congress wore black armbands to mourn the dead. "The sympathy which was excited was as general as the calamity was awful," one Virginian observed. The fire "drew forth the feelings of a nation. . . . We were all one family — from Boston to Savannah."[45]

Sympathy, however, did not bring relief to the afflicted. Although the Richmond theater fire was America's most widely and demonstratively mourned calamity of the early nineteenth century, material assistance for its victims was negligible. Unlike the citizens of nearby Fredericksburg in 1807, Richmonders formed no committee to solicit aid; their city's two clergymen—Episcopal and Presbyterian—focused their efforts on comforting survivors and planning for and officiating at the mass funeral on 29 December and official day of prayer and humiliation three days later. While it is true that this particular fire, which destroyed only a single public building, left no one in Richmond homeless, many survivors needed medical attention and supplies, and the loss of a breadwinner to injury or death left some families newly impoverished. Some businesses closed; the widow of a carpenter who had perished in the blaze faced eviction from her home. A month after the fire, the governor's widow held an auction to sell three slaves, along with furniture and other household goods, though she alone received a modest sum as relief from Virginia's state legislature.[46]

The fact that so many people died—suddenly, shockingly, violently, and visibly—distinguished what happened in Richmond from other contemporary disasters. Although death tolls from yellow fever were higher, disease was an expected fact of life. (Yellow fever filled the epidemiological gap between the age of smallpox and that of cholera, which devastated cities throughout the United States after 1832, while tuberculosis and malaria took many lives during this entire period.) Urban fires were common, too, and even some who experienced them regarded them as routine. In its first issue after the Portsmouth fire, the headline in the *New Hampshire Gazette* was "Distressing Conflagration! Unparalleled in America! (OF LATE)."[47]

But death by fire was comparatively rare, and the death of so many, most of whom were female and many of whom were young, was rarer still. When donors sent money or provisions to Portsmouth, pithy and often formulaic expressions of sympathy accompanied their cash or bank drafts, but the money was the main point of the exchange, which aimed to provide material assistance for those who lost their homes and means of sustenance. In contrast, whatever financial hardships survivors in Richmond incurred, their fire story was mostly about physical and emotional pain, not material loss, and outsiders reacted accordingly. George Hay, who knew many people in Richmond and was in the city at the time of the fire, spent subsequent days visiting survivors, whom he attempted to comfort. Hay described Richmond as a scene of "unexampled calamity & Suffering.... I have never experienced So terrible a Shock," adding, "I have attended to nothing but distress."[48]

Expressions of emotional community, rather than economic support, poured into Richmond after the fire. One particularly telling example came from Raleigh, North Carolina, where citizens passed a series of resolutions to affirm that the "calamity that has recently visited the City of Richmond had excited our warmest sensibility" and to solicit contributions to be used to purchase a marble tablet as "a durable monument to our participation in their sorrow." A marble tablet was a more appropriate gift than money or provisions because virtue and civility, in the words of one scholar, "required a shocked spectatorial sympathy in response to pain." Although it is not clear whether the tablet was ever made and sent to Richmond, the plan and the sympathetic fellow feeling that inspired it were duly reported in the *Richmond Enquirer*.[49]

For all of these reasons, the Richmond theater fire became a cultural event and not just another fire story of the sort routinely reported in the nation's newspapers. Public fascination with the fire stemmed at least partly from dramatic and widely circulated accounts of individual suffering and heroics. These narratives strongly resonated with audiences already immersed in a world of affective, sensational, and inspiring personal narratives, which they consumed not only in the form of sentimental novels but also in the newly popular genres of lurid Gothic fiction, autobiography, and memoirs. Although scholars generally associate the advent of sensational journalism with mid-nineteenth-century crime reportage, similarly graphic narratives were common in the wake of the Richmond fire. Rendered variously as first- and third-person narratives, these stories appeared in newspapers and broadsides, as well as in compilations of eyewitness accounts, such as John O'Lynch's *Narrative . . . of the Deplorable Conflagration at Richmond from Letters and Authentic Documents*.[50]

These narratives boasted an unusually affecting cast of characters. Louis Hue Girardin, veteran of the French Revolution and proprietor of a popular local academy, rushed to the theater to try to save his wife and son, who nonetheless died in the blaze. Their deaths so traumatized him that he abruptly closed his school and left town. The beautiful Sally Conyers, "one of the fairest flowers of Virginia," perished with her beau, Lieutenant James Gibbon, a gallant soldier who had survived imprisonment by pirates in Tripoli only to die at home trying to save his beloved. Benjamin Botts had by "his integrity, his industry, & his talents" risen from humble origins to be an esteemed member of Richmond's legal community. "Prosperous in his affairs, happy in his family, beloved by many, and respected by all," Botts and his wife, Jane, died in the theater that night, leaving five orphans behind. Governor George William Smith, a father of eight, had been in office only three weeks when he reentered the burning theater and died heroically while attempting to rescue others.[51]

With two significant exceptions—a crude illustration on a broadside titled *Theatre on Fire. Awful Calamity!* and a print by the Philadelphia engraver Benjamin Tanner—accounts of the fire relied on words, not pictures, to convey its victims' horrific experiences. The editor of Richmond's *American Standard* newspaper, who had attended the theater that night and survived the ordeal, published this vivid description of the tragic scene, which was soon reprinted in Washington, D.C., and elsewhere:

> There was but one door for the greatest part of the audience to pass. Men, women, and children were pressing upon each other, while the flames were seizing upon those behind. . . . Those nearest to the windows, ignorant of their great danger, were afraid to leap down, whilst those behind them, were seen catching on fire and writhing in the greatest agonies of pain and distress. At length those behind, urged by the pressing flames, pushed those out who were nearest to the windows, and people of every description began to fall, one upon another, some with their clothes on fire; some half roasted. . . . One lady jumped out when all her clothes were on fire. [The editor] tore them, burning, from her; stripped her of her last rags and protecting her nakedness with his coat, carried her from the fire.

Another frequently reprinted first-person account, written by the schoolmaster Leroy Anderson, told of his inability to save his teenage daughter, Margaret, and her three "amiable" friends on "that fatal night." An understandably grief-stricken Anderson reported that only a gold locket with an inscription from her grandfather made it possible to identify his daughter's charred remains.[52]

As these two examples suggest, sensational narratives of the Richmond theater fire initiated discourses on topics ranging from fire safety to gender, even as they engaged readers' imaginations and aroused their emotions. All contemporary published accounts of the fire were written by white men, most of whom dwelled on the brave exertions of Richmond's gentlemen to rescue white ladies and children. These authors were acutely conscious of the deeply held ideal of masculinity that afforded them patriarchal power while also obliging them to protect the women and children they lorded over.

The fact that three-quarters of the dead were women made these men justifiably defensive while also drawing attention from outsiders, who shared their notion of idealized ladies and their children as dependent innocents and saw men's ability to safeguard them—and the cherished values they represented—as an essential attribute of American national identity. When one

Theatre on Fire.

AWFUL CALAMITY!

A letter from Richmond, Virginia dated Dec. 27, fays, "Laft night the theatre took fire and was confumed, together with about 80 people, with the governor Smith—many were trampled to death under foot, others threw themfelves out of the windows, and were dafhed to pieces on the ground, fome with legs arms broken. Many were burnt to death in the boxes, and others on the ftairways."

Later accounts fay, 160 fkull bones have been found.

OH ! what a painful, dreadful tafk,
  Which we are call'd to pen,
When will the anguifh of our hearts—
And forrows have an end ?

Thoughtlefs of every cheerful air —
  Grief's filenc'd ev'ry tongue ;
The tidings from a fifter ftate,
Have all our harps unftrung.

Oh ! we lament with flowing tears—
  Our hearts with forrow fwell,
At the d ftreffing, awful fcene,
At Richmond late befell.

An evening in December laft,
  Th' fix and twentieth day,
The people there with joyful hafte,
Did go to fee a play.

When in the midft of joy and mirth,
  The houfe it caught on fire,
Hundreds envelop'd in the flames—
There many did expire.

Dear parents fond, and lovely babes,
  Did meet their folemn doom—
And lovers too did perifh there,
And virgins in their bloom.

People of ev'ry fect and age,
  Of dignity and ftate,
Were hurried from this mortal ftage—
How dreadful to relate !

Oh ! the cries—the piercing cries,
  'Twould melt a heart of ftone,
Such difmal fcreams were heard for aid,
But help now there was none.

Ah ! we lament their awful fate,
  Yes. from our very foul,
The fympathetic tears burft forth,
And down our cheeks doth roll.

May theatres all be done away,
  Thro' all Columbia's fhore,
The buildings put to better ufe,
And plays be feen no more.

Father of mercy, grant thy aid,
  Relieve thofe in diftrefs ;
Heal all the maimed of their wounds—
Do thou the mourners blefs.

Ye thoughtlefs, gay, both old and young—
  To facred things attend ;
And think how many ways death comes,
To bring us to our end.

One moment all is blooming health,
  Expecting years to come,
The next, fome fudden fatal ftroke,
Which fend us to the tomb.

Since life is fo uncertain then,
  Let's ftrive our ways to mend ;
Forfake every vicious way,
And God will be our friend.

Theatre on Fire. Awful Calamity! This sensational anti-theater broadside was published in Boston shortly after the Richmond theater fire. Its author, Joseph White, inflated the fire's death toll, claiming that "160 Skull bones" had been found in the rubble. White despised the theater. He attributed the Richmond fire to human sinfulness and urged his readers to repent and be saved. The theater, he believed, should be abolished, "the buildings put to better use, / And plays be seen no more." *American Antiquarian Society.*

The Burning of the Theatre in Richmond, Virginia. This engraving was made by Benjamin Tanner in Philadelphia shortly after the deadly fire. Tanner's image captured the horror conveyed in print accounts of conflagration. People jump from open windows to flee the burning building, while entangled bodies of anguished theatergoers block the escape of others. Those outside the building attend to the injured, clutch rescued children, or cry out in grief for lost loved ones. *Library of Congress Prints and Photographs Division.*

Baltimore newspaper pointed out that so few men died in a blaze that killed so many women and children, its editor sniffed derisively, "We make no other comment upon these proportions, than that a similar conflagration in this City, would have been infinitely less fatal." Not surprisingly, the *Richmond Enquirer* denounced the Baltimore report as "a most illiberal insinuation . . . against the generosity and gallantry of the gentlemen of Richmond." The editor of the *Enquirer*, Thomas Ritchie, retorted that ladies mostly occupied the theater's boxes, to shield themselves (and their reputations) from the rowdy people in the pits, a rule of etiquette that made it more difficult, when fire ensued, for them to flee to save their lives. While Ritchie conceded that some men may have "too readily listened to the laws of self-preservation," he insisted that many others had courageously tried to save the ladies.[53]

Gilbert Hunt. This enslaved blacksmith rushed to Richmond's theater and saved
at least a dozen people as they leaped from the burning building. Twelve years
later, as a member of the city's volunteer fire brigade, Hunt saved even more
lives when a fire started at the state penitentiary. While newspapers touted the
bravery of white men who did far less, Hunt received no such recognition for
his heroics. By 1829, he had purchased his freedom and immigrated to Liberia,
though he later returned to Richmond, where he died in 1863. *Library of Virginia.*

Significantly, no one publicly acknowledged the truly heroic actions of Gilbert Hunt, an enslaved blacksmith, who caught many women as they leapt from the burning building and also carried the injured physician James McCaw to safety. Nor did any published accounts mention the ordeals of African American women, at least four of whom were among the theater-goers who died that night. Rumors that the fire was either the result of slaves' arson or the prelude to insurrection were quickly silenced or disproven, though some enslaved people may have used the fire's chaos as an opportunity to escape bondage. Neither African American heroes like Hunt nor black fire victims were part of the post-fire discussion, though the latter were included on lists of the dead that appeared in newspapers and also as an inscription on a monument erected in 1814. Placement of the names of the free and enslaved African American dead, at the base of the monument, separate from those of white fire victims, attested to both their inclusion and inferior status in Richmond, and in the American republic generally.[54]

Just as some Virginians parsed their identities as white men through the lens of the disaster, others used the occasion to ponder the state of the American nation and the character of its citizens. Those who expressed sympathy for suffering Richmonders esteemed sensibility as an attribute of virtuous and civilized people. In Richmond and beyond, black armbands, lowered flags, tolling bells, and other solemn tributes fostered a sense of national unity and helped to solidify a distinctively American style of public mourning that celebrated ordinary citizens as well as presidents (or kings) and transcended state and regional boundaries. The city of Norfolk, for instance, held a funeral procession for the fire's victims eight days after the main ceremony took place in Richmond. "Never did we behold so great a concourse of people assembled at once on any former occasion in this Borough," one participant observed, "and since the funeral rites in honor of WASHINGTON, the nation's savior and benefactor, never on so mournful a one." The procession was "not the empty pageant of a volatile crowd, fond of novelty and parade, but . . . the solemn ritual of real mourners," complete with a large urn—it took eight men to carry it—inscribed to commemorate "the Citizens who were victims of the conflagration."[55]

Amid the mourners, however, some of the loudest cries came from those who interpreted the fire as a providential rebuke to the American nation and who saw it more appropriately as an occasion for repentance than for doleful sensibility. The author of the aptly named *Repent! Repent! Or Likewise Perish* argued that the fire was one of a series of calamities—including yellow fever outbreaks and attacks by "savage tribes"—that were "signs and tokens of approaching national judgment." Another author, writing under the pseudonym "A Theocrate," agreed that such "awful and vindictive providences of this nature are sure tokens of national guilt, if not of national condemnation," and urged Americans "to discover what are the crimes we are guilty of, which according to the infallible rules laid down, equally criminate every citizen." A minister in Ipswich, Massachusetts, asserted that the fire in Richmond occurred in part because the ruinous — but death-free — fire in Newburyport the preceding May did not inspire Americans to repent and reform. "Now," he declared, "the Lord calls on us in a way yet more impressive." Across the Atlantic, the English Quaker Ann Tuke Alexander agreed that the fire was God's judgment against Americans, but she believed that their main offense was "their traffic in negroes . . . still held in oppression, and . . . cruel bondage." At least one American commentator shared this view. "Has eternal justice no claims in behalf of twelve million of Africans," he asked, "who have been annually sacrificed, for almost a century past, to the demon of commercial avarice; the spirit of European luxury; and the genius of American indolence?"[56]

Apocalyptic interpretations of the fire often emphasized the immorality of frivolous amusements and of the theater in particular. Colonial Puritans and their cultural descendants had long condemned theatrical performances, and, though the number of American playhouses increased after the Revolution, in evangelical circles the theater remained controversial. Evangelicals regarded actors and plays as wicked; they charged that theatergoers spent money they could ill afford on such vile entertainments and that time expended watching shows was better devoted to work, prayer, and other wholesome activities. Some critics published lengthy lists of historical theater fires — from ancient times to the present — as evidence that Richmond was one of many "visitations from God . . . which have befallen public Theatres" as signs of his displeasure. The theatre "in its origin and history . . . has been a public nuisance. . . . In its present constitution it is criminal, under every form useless, and it must necessarily tend to demoralize any people who give it their support," some New York clergy opined. "The theatre," warned a pious Philadelphian, "at best, leads down to moral death. . . . Happy are they, who never tread this fatal round, where morals, manners, sentiment, and taste, are all ingulphed within the vortex of surrounding vice."[57]

Others rejected these contentions, sometimes defending the theater and occasionally questioning this particularly pessimistic assessment of the American character. More than one commentator observed that horrific fires struck churches as well as theaters, both of which tended to be tall edifices that accommodated large crowds but lacked sufficient means of egress. At least one observer noted that, though the Richmond fire was "unequalled" in American history, it was "not without a parallel" in Europe, where many theaters, opera houses, and churches had suffered deadly conflagrations. The Reverend Samuel Gilman, a Boston Unitarian, penned a sympathetic and sentimental poem mourning the fire's victims and denouncing those who believed that they and their loved ones had deservingly suffered the wrath of God.[58]

Nevertheless, use of the Richmond theater fire as a cautionary tale persisted for decades in the popular culture of American evangelicals. In 1842, the American Sunday School Union published *A Voice from Richmond: And Other Addresses to Children and Youth*, part of which drew on a lecture delivered in Philadelphia a few weeks after the fire in January 1812. The author emphasized that many "young persons, in the prime of life," and some "dear little children" numbered among the dead and urged his readers to prepare their souls for divine judgment because death could be sudden, even for children, as the story of the Richmond fire sadly showed. Evangelical writers also deployed the fire story in their continuing attacks on the theater in the antebellum decades. At least one evangelical tract reprinted Leroy Anderson's tearful account of his daughter's gruesome death with an added editorial admonition that readers frequent only places in which they would be prepared to die and from whence they would unashamedly proceed to "the Bar of God." In 1857, the *Presbyterian Magazine* rejected the notion that attending the theater could be an innocent pleasure by republishing accounts of the Richmond story to vindicate its anti-theater views.[59]

Although some Richmonders shared this animus against the theater, harsh fire-and-brimstone assertions about the meaning of the fire in its immediate aftermath came overwhelmingly from elsewhere. While stern ministers in other places — mostly New York and Philadelphia — purposefully used the episode as sensational and compelling evidence of human sinfulness and divine wrath, Richmond's clergy encouraged their congregants to look to religion as a source comfort, not fear, as they pulled together in the weeks following the tragedy.

The sermon preached by the Episcopal minister John Durbarrow Blair on the city's official day of public prayer and humiliation was a case in point. Unlike evangelical preachers who sought to replicate the horrors of the fire to impel sinners to feel the wrath of God, Blair neither forced his listeners to recall the pain and suffering of the recent past nor enjoined them to give up their innocent pleasures, condemning neither the theater nor its patrons.

Although he preached a Christian lesson about repentance and salvation, Blair offered a gentler and more compassionate version of that message. "In the memory of the oldest of us, there never has been a more awful warning of the uncertainty of human life than this which is given us now," he observed. "A large number of our relatives, friends & neighbours have been torn from us by the most furious of all the elements, & in a moment hurried into eternity. Can anything present to our minds a more striking memento of the precarious tenure on which we hold our lives, or a more powerful motive for us to comply with the admonition in the text, to be upon our guard & 'prepare,' as we know neither the day nor the hour in which the Son of Man cometh?"[60]

As befitted his charge to minister to a diverse community of some 10,000 souls, Blair's approach straddled the spectrum of local opinion concerning the fire and its causes. Thomas B. Hewitt, a resident of Alexandria who was enjoying the "splendid attractions" of Virginia's capital in late December, found that the city's residents included both those who did and those who did not interpret the disaster as a providential act of God. "The memorably distressing calamity which late overtook the citizens of Richmond in a moment of festivity was for some days almost the Sole subject of Converse," he observed, "as well as among those gloomy religionists who viewed it in the light of Special visitation of divine vengeance, as those less confined minds that mourned the loss of valuable lives destroyed by a most unfortunate accident."[61]

Local political leaders also took a nondogmatic approach to the fire and its causes. Almost immediately, Richmond's municipal council proclaimed a citywide day of prayer and humiliation and organized a collective Christian funeral for fire victims, but council members did so without characterizing the fire as punishment for theatergoing or any other sinful activities. At the same meeting, the councilmen appointed a committee of investigators to discern the fire's physical causes and to ascertain what made it so especially deadly, with the express purpose that the findings might benefit their countrymen by ensuring that "no theatres should be permitted to open in the other cities of the U. States until every facility has been procured for the escape of the audience" in case of fire. That committee included Thomas Ritchie, editor of the *Richmond Enquirer*, who published the committee's conclusion that "defects in the *construction* of our theatre," and particularly the fact that there were so few exits, had caused heavy losses once the building caught fire. Although committee members could not decide who exactly was responsible for those defects, or for raising the chandelier that started the fire, they averred that human error — not sin and divine vengeance — was its ultimate cause.[62]

More than most other major fires of the era, the deadly Richmond theater fire initiated a revealing public discussion about building standards and public safety. That discussion featured probing questions and cogent analysis. Why was there only one exit to the theater, and why was the staircase descending from the galleries so narrow and overcrowded? Why was Richmond's ability to fight fires seemingly so inadequate, despite the "great exertions made for the improvement of our city" in other areas? After the fire, the theater company expressed its willingness to have its buildings "examined by the guardians of public safety," and the city's committee of investigators recommended that theaters throughout the United States be inspected to prevent future fires and especially to improve the audience's chances of escape in the event of another deadly conflagration.[63]

Yet Richmond, like so many other localities that experienced devastating fires, adopted no new building or fire safety regulations. The Portsmouth fire of 1802 was the first of three that destroyed parts of the central district of that thriving port before the state legislature prohibited the erection of new wooden structures more than twelve feet high because of their susceptibility to fire and the difficulty of fighting fires in multistory buildings. Only in 1860 did New York become the first American city to adopt a comprehensive building code, which initially applied only to tenements. In part for that reason, fire insurance — which had been available locally in Richmond since the mid-1790s — was an increasingly attractive option for those who could afford it. Insurance, like sentimental narratives of human suffering, reinforced the cultural predisposition to see disaster-related losses as private tragedies rather than as public problems.[64]

A committed deist and theater aficionado who spearheaded the official investigation of the fire's causes and promoted the committee's recommendations, Thomas Ritchie pushed for new building codes and ridiculed the "language of superstition" of those who attributed the fire to divine intervention. A month after the fire, undoubtedly frustrated by popular disdain for science and continual talk of God's wrath, Ritchie lashed out against such "absurdities" in the pages of the *Enquirer*. "These are indeed times of wonder," he began caustically. "Comets — eclipses — tornadoes — earthquakes — in the age of superstition, they were held to be portentous signs. . . . Does not the conflagration of the theatre verify your superstitious auguries?" Ritchie charged that faith in divine portents of this sort was akin to belief in witchcraft. "To the eye of the bigot," he sneered, "there seems to be a mysterious sympathy between the revolutions of the moral and physical world." Ritchie's outburst initiated a public debate with contributors to two other local newspapers. While his *Enquirer* remained the most influential newspaper in the state, and he as editor remained politically powerful, men like Ritchie lost the battle to supplant divine providence with scientifically based public policy.[65]

In fact, the theater fire either caused or accelerated a religious revival in Virginia's genteel and cosmopolitan capital. In 1811, Richmond, the twelfth largest city in the United States, had only two ministers, who alternated offering ecumenical services in the hall of the state's capitol. Small Baptist and Methodist congregations had church buildings but no regular clergy. In the decade or so after the fire, the Baptists, Methodists, and Presbyterians enjoyed significant growth in the city, and the Episcopal Church became more demonstratively pious. Even the affable Reverend Blair, who was by then no longer a leading ecclesiastical force in the city, distanced himself from his earlier tolerant stance on the theater and other forms of amusement.[66]

At the same time, the use of Richmond's urban space in the years after the fire suggests that fires and other disasters would continue to expose tensions between faith and reason, religion and science, God's will and human agency. On the one hand, the erection of Monumental Church on the site of the incinerated theater to commemorate the fire and its victims was, despite its Enlightenment-inflected neoclassical architecture, a potent material representation of Richmonders' desire to make things right with God. For decades after the fire, guidebooks directed tourists to that "handsome octagonal edifice" that stood on the site of the famous fire where the victims' remains "are deposited in a marble urn . . . in the front portico of the church." On the other hand, a new playhouse opened in Richmond in 1818, funded by a subscription supported by many influential citizens, including Thomas Ritchie and some who had lost loved ones in the fire in 1811. Although evangelicals continued to revile the theater, it remained a fixture of cultural life in American cities, in Richmond and elsewhere.[67]

§ The contours of an American approach to disasters and disaster relief coalesced in the postrevolutionary decades. A republican political culture that celebrated voluntarism and limited government informed disaster relief and prevention in the United States, where institutions that solicited and delivered disaster relief were local, voluntary, and ephemeral. No level of government actively engaged in dealing with disasters of any sort, and proactive regulations that aimed to prevent or lessen the impact of fires, diseases, or other calamities were minimal, even at the local level.

At the same time, because Americans valued sympathy and benevolence, real and rhetorical sentiment figured prominently in their rationales for offering aid to those they deemed blameless sufferers. Narratives of suffering and loss cast disasters and their effects as personal tragedies and disaster relief as a voluntary expression of sympathetic social bonds — as Americans, as Christians — between donors and sufferers. The result of neither policy nor convention, funds for Portsmouth and sympathy for Richmond, like the carrot-and-stick combination of money and quarantines for Philadelphia in 1793, were efforts tailored, by both sufferers and their benefactors, to fit the perceived and often contested needs of each specific afflicted community. These approaches would prove to be both enduring and insufficient as disaster, and disaster stories, became a part of everyday life in the coming decades.

{ 6 }

EXPLODING
STEAMBOATS AND
THE CULTURE
OF CALAMITY

The steamboat revolutionized travel and trade, facilitated the settlement and prosperity of the American West, and made it possible for more people to take trips for social and recreational purposes. Steamboats were emblems of progress, but they were also agents of violent and visible destruction. Their boilers exploded dramatically and with horrific frequency, leaving a trail of burned and disfigured corpses across the continent. This juxtaposition of the steamboat as a source of opportunity and pleasure as well as of suffering and devastation fascinated nineteenth-century Americans.

The growing accessibility of steam travel and the seemingly constant reports of steamboat explosions and collisions led many Americans not only to sympathize with their victims but also to imagine themselves as prospective steamboat casualties. Public preoccupation with steamboat disasters was evident on the front pages of newspapers, in scientific inquiries and reports, and in the popular culture of the era. The sheer number and violence of steamboat explosions ensured public interest in them, while technological improvements in printing and lithography made their memorialization in words and images swift, ubiquitous, and sensational by the 1840s.

Community and institutional responses to steamboat disasters differed qualitatively from Americans' approach to urban fires, hurricanes, and other calamities. Because a single steamboat voyage typically moved between states and carried passengers from many points of origin, when a vessel exploded, its impact was not confined to the specific locality in which it happened. Although benevolence had a role to play in the immediate aftermath of steamboat explosions, those passengers who managed to survive the ordeal dispersed, returning home to nurse their injuries. But far more than storms and earthquakes, or even fires, this new and dangerous steam technology raised the specter of human agency—and therefore also of human culpability. Consequently, unlike most other disasters, steamboat explosions garnered public attention that resulted in citizens' meetings, coroners' inquests, and scientific investigations to assess blame and propose improvements, which eventually gave rise to modest but precedent-setting changes in public policy.

§ In August 1787, delegates to the Constitutional Convention in Philadelphia gathered on the banks of the Delaware River to witness the first successful trial run of an American steam-powered vessel. For a variety of legal and financial reasons, however, steamboats did not become profitable as business ventures until after 1807, when Robert Fulton began his service on New York's Hudson River. Powered by a low-pressure steam engine, Fulton's first ship, the *North River Steamboat* (later known as the *Clermont*), carried passengers from New York City to Albany in thirty-two hours, making the return trip downriver in two hours less. Five years later, Fulton and his partner, Robert R. Livingston, established a shipyard in Pittsburgh to take waterborne steam transportation to what they expected to be an even more lucrative western market. Their ship, the *New Orleans*, became the first steamboat on the western waters when it traveled the 1,100 miles from Pittsburgh to New Orleans—a journey that took as much as four months by land—in fourteen days in 1812. The *New Orleans* later covered the roughly 250 miles from New Orleans to Natchez, Mississippi, in six days, six hours, and forty minutes; a steamboat could complete that route in less than a day by 1844. A demonstrably faster and less expensive way to transport goods and people, steamboats crowded waterways throughout the United States in the early nineteenth century. By 1838, there were more than 700 steamboats operating on the nation's rivers, lakes, and coastal waters. By 1850, that number had doubled.[1]

For many, and most especially for white Americans looking westward, the steamboat was a source of opportunity. Steamboats made it possible to travel upriver, offering a faster, cheaper, and more direct route to Mississippi valley farmers seeking to transport their produce to thriving midwestern and eastern markets. Important steamboat depots stimulated the growth of modest towns into booming metropolises; Cincinnati and Louisville became, respectively, the sixth and sixteenth largest cities in the United States by 1840. By promoting settlement and commerce, steamboats made the West a white man's country, facilitating both the eradication of Native American peoples and the spread of King Cotton (and hence the expansion of slavery). Those who benefited saw the steamboat as an agent of progress and civilization. "A simple mechanical device ha[s] made life both possible and comfortable in regions which heretofore have been a wilderness," one traveler explained, at a time when a desire to conquer and tame the continent was becoming a defining feature of American national identity.[2]

Steamboats fascinated Americans because of their enormity and power. Ships were probably the largest objects that most people ever encountered, and, though steamboats were neither the first nor the only steam-powered mechanisms in the United States, relatively few Americans witnessed first-hand the operation of new steam-based technologies that increased the speed and efficiency of tasks such as printing and textile production. When Robert Fulton's *Clermont* made its first trip from New York to Albany in 1807, those ashore watched the vessel's "huge black vomiting and smoke" and heard its "hoarse breathing," which "filled the imagination with all the dark pictures of goblins that romancers have invented since the foundation of the world," according to one observer. People panicked as the 142-foot-long craft noisily moved through the waters of the mighty Hudson River. While some thought the *Clermont* was "an unheard of monster of the sea," others feared it was a "herald of the final conflagration" that would precede the Day of Judgment. Fulton and some other early steamboat owners reveled in their vessels' awe-inspiring power. Ships with names like *Aetna, Volcano*, and *Vesuvius*—Fulton's third steamboat, built in Pittsburgh in 1814 and burned near New Orleans two years later—powered along American waterways in the 1810s and 1820s.[3]

Indeed, contemporaries often described steamboats, like volcanoes, as "sublime" because they juxtaposed beauty and power, civilization and savagery, and—in cases of steamboat explosions—the power of technology and the fragility of human life. Harriet Beecher Stowe compared the "almost sublime" steamboat to a "fabled monster of the wave, breathing fire," with its "mysterious, even awful" power. Edward Flagg admired the "truly sublime" spectacle of "the mighty steam rolling . . . this noble fabric of man's workmanship" as it triumphantly conquered "the terrible Mississippi." Anyone who saw the steamboat, Flagg believed, would acknowledge "its sublimity of power, with astonishment and admiration." When steamboats exploded, however, emotions pivoted from delight to terror. *Lloyd's Steamboat Directory* described the burning of the *Phoenix* on Lake Michigan in 1847 as "a most awful and sublime spectacle." This doomed vessel "was a complete bed of fire, which, bursting in flames from the sides, at times streamed far out over the waters, and then curled aloft, till flame meeting flame, the combined fiery current rushed furiously upward till it appeared to be lost in the clouds." Rapt onlookers watched the "sad catastrophe" that took the lives of all but 8 of the 218 people aboard the ship. "As the flames advanced, one voice after another was hushed in death, and finally a stillness, awful and profound, told the spectator that the scene of suffering was finished."[4]

The coexistence of celebratory and mournful ruminations on the power of steamboats betokened Americans' occasional ambivalence toward technology and industrialization. On the one hand, for most people, boarding a steamboat or seeing one operate was their initiation into the exciting world of modern technology, which many associated with progress and unprecedented opportunities for adventure, mobility, efficiency, and the reduction of physical labor. On the other hand, the transformation of travel from process to commodity—increasingly produced and marketed by remote capitalist entrepreneurs and corporations—resulted in the individual's loss of control over the transportation experience. Unregulated competition and the desire to garner public attention and maximize profits led ship owners to build ever-bigger ships, overload their vessels with flammable cargoes, travel at excessive speeds and under unsafe conditions, and hire inexperienced engineers—all of which made American steamboats uniquely dangerous, with far more explosions and fatalities than their European counterparts. Although some lauded the comparative safety of steamboat travel, explosions were highly visible and widely publicized, and they had spectacularly fatal consequences.[5]

Beginning in the 1820s, as reports of steamboat explosions jammed the pages of newspapers, these dramatic and deadly affairs became the archetypical American disaster in the most literal sense. The use of the word "disaster" remained remarkably uncommon before the nineteenth century. A full-text search of the Washington-based *National Intelligencer* newspaper reveals a sharp increase in the use of term, however, coinciding with the spread of steam travel and steamboat explosions in the 1820s and after. Moreover, for the entire period between 1816 (the date of the first reported steamboat explosion) and 1840, the *Intelligencer* used the term "disaster" almost exclusively in articles pertaining to steamboats (with its usage in articles about the

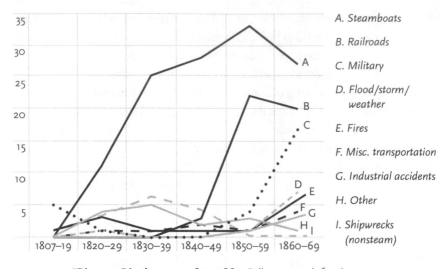

"Disasters" in the news, 1807–1869. Full-text search for the term "disaster" in the Washington *National Intelligencer*, N=263.

destruction of non-steam-powered ships a distant second). In the 1840s, railroads wrecks replaced non-steamer shipwrecks in second place, but steamboat calamities remained the most widely reported "disasters."[6]

The explosion of the *Washington* on 5 June 1816 marked the beginning of America's public discourse on steamboat calamities. Shortly after its departure from Marietta, Ohio, the *Washington* became the nation's first reported steamboat disaster when its boiler exploded, drenching passengers in scalding water and launching them violently through the air, leaving eight dead and others injured. Those ashore saw the "melancholy sight" and heard "the screams and groans of agonizing sufferers, rendering the scene horrible, beyond description." The deck of the *Washington* was "strewn with mangled and writhing human beings, uttering screams and groans of intense suffering." The Ohio River carried one scalded corpse fourteen miles downriver to Parkersburgh, Virginia (now West Virginia), where townspeople found the body three days later.[7]

The *Washington* was the first of 233 steamboats to explode in the United States between 1816 and 1848, leaving some 2,563 verifiably dead, 2,097 injured, and—as surviving accounts make abundantly clear—the bodies of many other casualties unrecovered and uncounted. According to one estimate, roughly 30 percent of all steamboats built in the United States before 1849 were destroyed in explosions or other accidents.[8] The sheer number of steamboat wrecks guaranteed their prominence in the press and their impact

Exploding Steamboats and the Culture of Calamity

in the wider culture, but some steamboat explosions had more impact than others. Major explosions in the New York City area in 1824 and 1840 drew unprecedented national attention, in part due to New York's significance as a commercial and publishing center. In 1838 and again in 1852, unusually deadly wrecks at opposite ends of the country spurred important, and hotly contested, changes in public policy.

In 1824, the wreck of the ominously named *Aetna* became the first steamboat disaster to make national news when its boiler burst on Raritan Bay en route to New York from Washington, New Jersey, killing at least thirteen people, "spreading instant destruction among the passengers, machinery, &c. and filling the minds of the survivors with undescribable misery." William C. Redfield, a steamboat operator who spent years experimenting with boilers, gauges, and other mechanisms to promote steamboat safety, noted that "the public was astounded" by the *Aetna* explosion, in part because the ship had a high-pressure engine, a more powerful but also more volatile type of engine found mainly on western riverboats. The use of this seemingly dangerous technology in the East, where low-pressure engines had predominated and where steamboat fatalities had been uncommon, made the fate of the *Aetna* especially shocking and prompted an early admonition against Americans' seemingly uncritical celebration of both speed and steam power. "Instead of speaking in terms of approbation of astonishing instances of despatch in stages and steamboats . . . which in all cases jeopardize the lives of the passengers," asked the editor of the *New York Commercial Advertiser*, "ought we not rather to censure them loudly and boldly, and point our pens steadily against every thing of the kind?"[9]

The response to the *Aetna* explosion by both press and public set important and enduring precedents for subsequent steamboat disasters. In what became the standard format for the genre, newspaper reports, reaching an increasingly far-flung readership, described the horrors of the explosion and listed its victims, who, in this case as in so many others, represented a cross-section of the American population. Those who died aboard the *Aetna* included a middle-class white family, a young Irish immigrant, and the wife of an "amiable young gentleman." They also included three African American members of the ship's crew: two men (a fireman and a waiter) and a cook named Ann Thomas.[10]

The *Aetna* explosion resulted in local relief efforts, public mourning, and calls for government action. People near the site of the wreck attended to the injured and held a solemn funeral for four dead passengers, whom they buried together in one large collective grave. They then transported the seriously injured, on litters or in coaches, to New York City Hospital, where "every exertion, which the dictate of humanity, or the medical talent could produce, were employed for their relief." Perhaps benevolent citizens collected money to aid the injured, as was the case after some later steamboat wrecks. Meanwhile, public outcry in the wake of the *Aetna* explosion led Congress to instruct the secretary of the treasury to "call to his assistance the knowledge and experience" of men "skilled in navigating and constructing vessels propelled by fire or steam" to learn "the material causes of those fatal disasters which have so frequently occurred on board steamboats in the waters of the United States, and what regulations may . . . afford better security to the lives of passengers and crews." Most respondents emphasized the overall safety of steamboats and their technology, attributing accidents primarily to the ignorance or negligence of the engineer or other crew members. Blaming workers, not owners or their equipment, would become the standard operators' response to steamboat explosions, just as reports that tearfully recounted passenger fatalities were notably less distraught about the deaths of crew members. In any event, efforts to pass a proposed bill to improve steamboat safety after the *Aetna* disaster failed in Congress.[11]

The *Aetna* explosion also initiated a tentative consideration of the causes of steamboat explosions within America's loosely organized scientific community. In 1824, people who engaged in scientific inquiry came from all walks of life. The closest thing to a professional scientist—the term "scientist" was first used in the 1830s—would have been college faculty, but even they were broadly learned and did not specialize in a single field or discipline. In 1824, the founding members of the nation's single most important scientific organization, the Philadelphia-based Franklin Institute, included merchants, mechanics, and manufacturers and sponsored lectures and publications that aimed to promote scientific and technical knowledge and expertise among the general public. Vernacular science, wide-ranging empiricism, and the involvement of nonspecialists were hallmarks of intellectual exchange, innovation, and invention in the early republic. Before he launched the first American steamboat in 1787, John Fitch had worked as a clockmaker and a gunsmith. Robert Fulton painted landscapes and portraits and patented several unrelated inventions before his steamboat made its initial trip on the Hudson River in 1807.[12]

Although full-time scientists became increasingly prominent in both the activities of the Franklin Institute and in American intellectual life overall, a diverse group of technologically minded men attempted to understand the causes of steamboat explosions and improve steamboat safety. Immediately after the *Aetna* explosion, the Franklin Institute solicited contributions on the subject, which Robert Hare, a professor of chemistry at the University of Pennsylvania, addressed in a letter published in an early issue of the *Franklin Journal, and American Mechanics' Magazine*. Other publications followed. Steam power and steamboat safety were such compelling topics that some of America's most innovative minds — men better known for scientific or technological achievements in other areas — attempted to tackle the problem. William Redfield, who investigated the causes of the *Aetna* explosion and became an acknowledged authority on boiler construction, was also a self-taught meteorologist who, based on his analysis of the patterns of fallen trees after the Great September Gale of 1821, was among the first to argue that hurricanes were "giant whirlwinds that hurtled across the sky like flying discs." Robert Mills, the famed architect who was an enthusiastic promoter and designer of fireproof buildings, experimented with designs for steam furnaces, which, he believed, would provide "a *simple* and *economical means* of *preventing* a steamer from taking fire."[13]

Inventions that aimed to save lives at sea also proliferated in the age of steam, building on earlier improvements in shipbuilding and flotation devices and also informed by the humane society movement, which employed an array of gadgets — drags and grapnels for snaring bodies, bellows and fumigators to stimulate lungs and administer tobacco enemas — to rescue and resuscitate drowning people, including some victims of maritime disasters. Massachusetts native Joseph Francis was one inventor who spent his life perfecting "Life-Saving Appliances," the most important of which were the durable and fireproof metal lifeboats and "life-cars." In pitching his products, Francis praised technology and commerce as engines of American prosperity and lauded the "gigantic strides" made by science and industry, the "iron arms of progressive civilization." At the same time, however, he appealed to the "benevolence and mercy" of his prospective customers, bemoaning the "too often fatal occurrences" that arose from steamboat explosions, and offered his lifeboats as humanitarian innovations. "If competition and custom has introduced into our passenger vessels all the comforts and luxuries of home, for the pleasure of the travelling public," Francis queried, "does not humanity and self-interest also require that the most approved means of safety should be provided in case of accident?"[14]

As death tolls escalated, some of the worst explosions of the 1830s evoked increasingly vigorous public outrage and became important turning points on the road to public engagement and modest government intervention in the steamboat industry. The loss of the *Helen McGregor* in Memphis in Feb-

Two Hundred Lives Saved . . . by Francis' Patent Corrugated Life-Car. Invented by Joseph Francis, the "life-car" became one of the most widely used life-saving devices of its era. To initiate a life-saving operation, people on shore fired a cannon-like gun to send ropes out to the vessel. Once the ropes were attached to the ship, the life-car was suspended from the ropes and traveled back and forth, using a pulley system. No more than four people could fit in the life-car. The *Ayrshire* rescue, shown here, in 1850, was the first recorded use of Joseph's device, which, over the course of two days, saved many lives. *Library of Congress.*

ruary 1830 caused the deaths of at least forty people—the highest number of casualties from a single steamboat disaster to date—and badly wounded many others as a result of a powerful explosion that could be seen from the shore by citizens in this growing riverside community. One eyewitness described the gruesome scene, which included a corpse whose "forehead had been blown away [though] the brains were still beating" and "tufts of hair, shreds of clothing, and splotches of blood" propelled "in every direction" by the force of the steam expelled from the bursting boiler. The editor of Virginia's *Richmond Enquirer* spoke for many when he affirmed, "The Steam-Engine is a powerful, most useful agent, but it is still far from the point of perfection. The principal defect remaining for mechanical Ingenuity to overcome, and for which humanity most loudly demands a remedy, is its liability to accidents of a truly distressing nature."[15]

The *Helen McGregor* explosion led the secretary of the treasury to commission a Franklin Institute study of the causes of steamboat disasters, the first federally funded scientific research in U.S. history. Alexander Dallas

Exploding Steamboats and the Culture of Calamity

Bache, an army man turned professor of natural philosophy and chemistry and great-grandson of Benjamin Franklin, oversaw these experiments and prepared the final report, which Congress received in 1836. By then, both President Andrew Jackson, a Democrat, and one of his leading Whig adversaries, Senator Daniel Webster of Massachusetts, had expressed support for federal intervention in certain aspects of the steamboat industry. In 1833, Jackson, noting that "the number of those fatal disasters is constantly increasing," charged "criminal negligence on the part of those by whom the vessels are navigated and to whose care and attention the lives and property of our citizens are so extensively intrusted" and urged Congress to enact "precautionary and penal legislation" to protect the public. Webster, too, cited a "very highly criminal degree of negligence" as the root of the problem and advocated legislation requiring both inspections and stiff financial penalties for the operation of unsafe equipment, racing, and other practices that endangered passengers. Congress took no action, however, even after receiving the Franklin Institute's detailed report, complete with recommendations for changes in boiler design and construction to improve steamboat safety.[16]

The effect of the even more deadly wrecks of the *Moselle* near Cincinnati in April 1838 and of the *Pulaski* off the Carolina coast less than two months later was more substantive. By then, five states had enacted steamboat safety laws (which applied only to the relatively small portion of steamboat traffic that did not cross state lines), and the federal government had allocated funds to remove submerged tree trunks and other dangerous debris (known as "snags") that caused collisions on western rivers as part of a more general program of internal improvements. In December 1837, however, noting the continuing escalation of steamboat-related casualties, President Martin Van Buren reiterated Jackson's call for regulatory legislation. A Senate committee immediately began drafting what one historian has called "a collage of what had been proposed in the three preceding attempts," none of which had been successful. Although this new bill would have mandated periodic inspections, limits on boiler pressure, firefighting and safety standards, and civil liabilities and financial penalties for negligent steamboat owners and operators, most of its provisions were deleted or diluted as it made its way through the upper house. Even so, passage in the House of Representatives seemed unlikely. Then, the explosions of the *Moselle* and the *Pulaski* generated an outpouring of public anger, likely ensuring passage of the "Act to provide for the better security of the lives of passengers on board of vessels propelled in whole or in part by steam" on 7 July 1838.[17]

Occurring less than a week after at least 100 people died when the *Oronoko* exploded in Mississippi, the *Moselle* disaster reportedly "shroud[ed] the whole country in mourning." Many still considered this disaster, which took at least 150 lives, "almost without a parallel in the annals of steamboat calamities" as late as the 1850s. One widely reprinted account, first published as an extra edition of the *Cincinnati Whig*, described a powerful explosion that resulted in "heads, limbs, and bodies . . . flying through the air in every direction, attended by the most horrible shrieks and groans from the wounded and the dying." Some passengers jumped off the ship to escape the flames, only to drown "before they could be rescued from a watery grave." Citizens who watched the grisly drama could do little to help, though the ship was only thirty yards from shore. One boy who had somehow made it to shore "was seen wringing his hands in agony, imploring those present to save his father, mother, and three sisters . . . whom the poor little fellow had the awful misfortune to see perish, one by one, almost within his reach." The force of the explosion propelled the ship's captain from the deck of the vessel to a city street, where he was found "dead and dreadfully mangled."[18]

The fact that the *Moselle* was a "brag boat" whose ambitious young captain had recently boasted having made some "exceedingly quick" trips especially inflamed public opinion and made the disaster unusually newsworthy. The *Cincinnati Whig* asserted that the debacle "unquestionably occurred *through sheer imprudence and carelessness*," with the captain clearly "desirous of showing off her great speed" by passing another boat that had left the wharf shortly before the *Moselle*. Others agreed. An Iowa newspaper angrily denounced the *Moselle* explosion as the result of the "most silly and culpable vanity" of its captain and advised the public to patronize "no boat which is valued only for its speed, and especially when that speed is indispensably connected with danger and death."[19]

As the steamboat bill foundered in Congress, another equally stunning disaster occurred in June, when the *Pulaski* exploded off the coast of North Carolina. Although the death toll was comparable to that of the *Moselle*, the carnage was less visible because the ship, which was en route to Baltimore from Savannah, was thirty miles from the shore when it was "torn in pieces" by its bursting boiler. Nearly fifty passengers survived the wreck, making their way across the perilous sea in two lifeboats, but the fate of the *Pulaski* was nonetheless shocking. For one thing, the overwhelming majority of American steamboat disasters involved ships with high-pressure boilers traveling on rivers and lakes, especially in the West, but the *Pulaski*, which exploded during a voyage on the Atlantic Ocean, was powered by a low-pressure engine. Moreover, the *Pulaski* was built by southerners for residents of the southern states who were wary of steam travel after the fatal loss of the New-York-based *Home* near Cape Hatteras in 1837. Advertisements for the *Pulaski,* which had made its first trip a few weeks earlier, touted its "ease, safety and speed" and assured prospective passengers that the new ship's boilers were "of the best copper and of great strength."[20]

One *Pulaski* survivor recalled that the disaster evoked "universal sorrow throughout the United States" in part because "almost every section of the country was represented on that fatal boat." A Philadelphia newspaper agreed that news of the *Pulaski* was of continuing interest to its readers, who shared bonds of kinship and friendship with "many persons in the South." The editor of the *Rhode-Island Republican* likewise reported that people in Newport felt "sick at heart" about the *Pulaski,* whose ill-fated passengers included many southerners who were voyaging northward to begin their annual summer sojourns in their coastal resort community.[21]

Some critics of current laissez-faire political arrangements emphasized that public pressure was an essential precondition for congressional action. A South Carolinian writing under the pseudonym "PUBLIC OPINION" warned readers that once the "excitement" over the *Pulaski* died down, that tragedy, like that of the *Home,* would soon be forgotten if the public did not act. "Prevention and punishment, aided by public opinion can produce the desired reform," insisted one Philadelphian, adding, "It only remains for Congress to act" to save lives. The ideal legislation, many believed, would mandate minimum standards for equipment and training, empower authorities to prosecute negligent captains and engineers, and hold managers and stockholders of steamboat companies financially liable for losses of lives and property.[22]

In Charleston and Savannah—the cities that lost the most people in the *Pulaski* disaster—as in Cincinnati after the *Moselle* explosion, citizens held public meetings and appointed committees to demand government-mandated improvements in steamboat safety. After the wreck of the *Pulaski,* newspapers from up and down the Eastern Seaboard also weighed in on the subject with unprecedented vigor. "Will the Congress of the United States, with a disgraceful apathy for the waste of human life, continue to be occupied in party squabbles and personal altercation, while a bill now sleeps on the table of the House of Representatives, which will ensure security to the lives of thousands against the cupidity of mercenary men and their pitiful ambition?" asked the Charleston-based *Southern Patriot.* "It really appears to us that there is about as much regard for the lives of passengers aboard steamboats as there is for those of so many blind puppies," one Philadelphia editor declared, denouncing the "harangues about states' rights and civil immunities" that often stymied congressional action, acerbically adding, "It should be remembered that there is no liberty for the citizen on board many steamboats as now managed. . . . He is under the worst of despotisms, that which can deprive him of existence."[23]

The wreck of the *Moselle*, and especially that of the *Pulaski*, thus resulted in unprecedented public agitation for federal intervention to protect citizens' lives. Spurred by public outrage, Congress passed the proposed steamboat bill, which President Van Buren immediately signed into law. The new statute set an important precedent for federal oversight of private corporations by mandating inspections of ships' hulls, boilers, and other machinery. It also stipulated that steamboat employees whose negligence resulted in loss of life would be charged with manslaughter and that injured parties could sue steamboat owners and operators in civil court, where "the fact of such bursting [boilers] . . . or injurious escape of steam, shall be taken as prima facie evidence, sufficient to charge the defendant with negligence, until he shall show that no negligence has been committed by him or those in this employment." Nevertheless, the 1838 law was full of omissions and loopholes; it specified neither the requisite qualifications for the poorly paid inspectors nor the criteria for evaluating the fitness of vessels or the engineers who ran them. When the Cincinnati citizens' committee presented its final report on the causes of the *Moselle* explosion in September, its members criticized the law as "totally inadequate" and recommended that additional action be taken at the state and local levels. Citizens in both Cincinnati and Savannah also regretted, in the words of the latter, "the frightful destruction of life here as compared with European boats," which were subject to stricter statutory regulation.[24]

If the *Moselle* and the *Pulaski* were pivotal events in the evolution of public policy aimed at disaster prevention, the explosion of the *Lexington* in January 1840 was the key turning point in the development of a pervasive and influential popular culture of disaster. Before the *Lexington* disaster, it is true that sermons, poems, stories, songs, and an occasional image had conveyed the drama of events such as the Richmond theater fire; at least one American disaster site—the New Hampshire home of the Willey family, all of whom died in an avalanche in 1826—became a major tourist destination. After the *Lexington*, however, exploding steamboats came to dominate what was fast becoming an expansive, diverse, and increasingly visual American popular culture of disaster.[25]

Most Americans likely first learned about the *Lexington* by reading a newspaper article describing the vessel's ill-fated trip from New York to Stonington, Connecticut, from whence many passengers expected to continue their trip, by train, to Boston. Within four hours of its departure the ship's boiler exploded and its cargo (mostly bales of cotton) burst into flames. These first reports included a preliminary list of victims and a statement from Chester Hilliard, one of only three known survivors—another, badly frostbitten, was discovered later—who confirmed that the ship's fire engine did not work and that its three lifeboats were undersized and ineffectually deployed. Hilliard survived by clinging to a cotton bale that floated perilously on the icy waters. His fellow passengers were not as fortunate. As one New York newspaper put it, those who escaped the fiery ship, "having no means of bailing out the water, and doubtless chilled with cold and exposure, ... were sustained with their faces above the surface, and finally, when their strength failed, their heads fell upon the cross seas" and they died.[26]

For several reasons, the wreck of the *Lexington*—one of the largest, fastest, and most luxurious ships that sailed on the Long Island Sound—was a bigger story than most. For one thing, boarding the ship was a virtual death sentence for unwitting passengers of every description, all but one of whom perished in the explosion and its aftermath (though three members of the ship's crew also survived the flames and freezing waters). For another, the *Lexington* story featured some famous and well-connected characters: Cornelius Vanderbilt, who made his fortune in the steamboat business, had been the vessel's original owner; casualties included Dr. Charles Follen, a German-born Harvard professor and antislavery activist, and Henry James William Finn, a popular playwright and comic actor whose demise, one editor predicted, "will dim the sunshine of every heart." As the *Baltimore Sun* reported, "The persons destroyed were mostly members of society who held extensive acquaintances with their fellow citizens in many sections of our country. They embraced a good portion of the enterprise of the communities in which they were located, and for that reason is their untimely loss the more severely felt."[27]

Equally significant, the *Lexington* story played out in public over several months, as local newspapers and benevolent citizens sought aid for victims' families, as more bodies washed ashore, and as survivors and experts rehashed the gruesome episode in a well-publicized eight-day coroner's inquest. In New York, some "philanthropic young men" visited the widows of workingmen who had died aboard the *Lexington* and, finding them destitute, began raising money that was, in turn, distributed by the Female Assistance

Society, a local women's charitable association. Others offered rewards for the recovery of bodies so that distraught citizens could ascertain the fate of loved ones. The author of one newspaper article called "The Widow's Mite" appealed to "benevolent individuals" to donate funds to provide assistance to a poor New York woman who could spare only five dollars to pay for the return of her presumably dead husband. Meanwhile, those who followed the proceedings of the ultimately inconclusive coroner's inquest were moved by sad tales of the anguished mother who tried unsuccessfully to save her drowning child and of the man who floated on a cotton bale in freezing water for eight long hours until, weak with hypothermia, he slipped off the bale and drowned. Many must have felt both sorrow and outrage when they learned that Captain William Tirrell, whose ship was only six miles away from the *Lexington*, might have saved many lives, if he had only jettisoned his schedule, changed course, and tried to help.[28]

For all these reasons, in addition to its proximity to both New York and Boston, the *Lexington* disaster received unusually detailed and extensive press coverage, both locally and nationally. News of the *Lexington* explosion appeared first in the next day's *Republican Standard* (published in Bridgeport, Connecticut, near the site of the wreck) and then a day later in the New York City papers. In the coming weeks, the story traversed the country. The *Ohio State Journal* reprinted the Bridgeport paper's story on 22 January, and the news appeared in the *Kalamazoo Gazette* in Michigan three days later. By the end of the month, the *Lexington* story had reached New Orleans, where the *Daily Picayune* reported, "The shrieks, the screams of human beings hunted by one element to perish in another — driven by fire into the sea in night, and in the depths of winter. Mothers with their babes, fathers, brothers, expired in the waves, giving their last cries to the unpitying wind." News of the disaster reached readers in Madison, Wisconsin, a week later.[29]

But the signal innovation in coverage of the *Lexington* debacle was the creation of timely visual representations. New York lithographer Nathaniel Currier (who would form a famous partnership with James Merritt Ives in 1852) produced at least fourteen images of the *Lexington*, the first of which appeared only three days after the explosion. Early versions of Currier's print spanned the width of the front page of post-disaster extra editions of the *New York Sun* newspaper. Currier then produced a separate color lithograph of the exploding steamboat, to be sold in New York and other cities, which was enormously popular. Currier's *Lexington* prints were among the earliest near-contemporaneous depictions of newsworthy events, as well as the

Exploding Steamboats and the Culture of Calamity

first representation of a steamboat explosion immediately after it happened. These images fueled fascination with the *Lexington* disaster among the general public. One New Yorker reported that, more than a week after the explosion, "the sensation is prolonged, and the force of it is in nothing lost. . . . Already are machinery and lithography picturing the scenes. . . . Nothing else is talked of in society." People far removed from the site of the explosion shared this avid interest in it. "The melancholy affair of the Lexington Steam Boat has made a great impression on the people here," observed one resident of South Carolina.[30]

Visual representations of exploding steamboats — and of disasters generally — became accessible to more people as lithography provided quick, inexpensive, and compelling depictions of sensational news events beginning in the 1830s. In 1835, members of the public paid 25 cents to visit an exhibit hall where they could view a painting of the "Great Gale" that had devastated Providence, Rhode Island, twenty years earlier. That same year, the *New York Herald* ran an engraving of its home city's recent fire on its front page just five days after it happened, and Nathaniel Currier sold his first disaster prints, which depicted fires in New York and New Orleans, for a cost of 12½ to 50 cents, an important early step en route to establishing his firm as the self-described "Grand Central Depot for Cheap and Popular Prints," which prospered for decades by producing "engravings for the people." Two years later, in 1837, Currier published his first shipwreck print, the *Dreadful Wreck of the Mexico*, a sail-powered ship bound from Liverpool to New York, in which 112 people perished when the vessel capsized near Hempstead, Long Island.[31]

Disaster prints worked in tandem with representations of fires and shipwrecks in other visual formats, which were increasingly accessible to a paying public. Currier's images of New York's Great Fire appeared on transferware plates, made in England for export to the United States. Both the New York fire and the wreck of the *Mexico* were subjects of contemporary dioramas, a proto-cinematic genre in which audiences viewed a succession of large images, accompanied by music and sound effects. Another diorama featured the explosion of the *Royal Tar*, a Canadian circus ship, which took the lives of thirty-two human passengers and many more animals. In 1840, shortly after the publication of Currier's lithograph of the *Lexington*, Boston's New England Museum exhibited a "panoramic of this awful tragedy."[32]

Disaster stories and their visual representations were part of a larger popular culture of sensationalism, which, beginning with the emergence of the so-called penny press in the 1830s, pervaded the antebellum era. While older, more established newspapers reported mainly staid political and com-

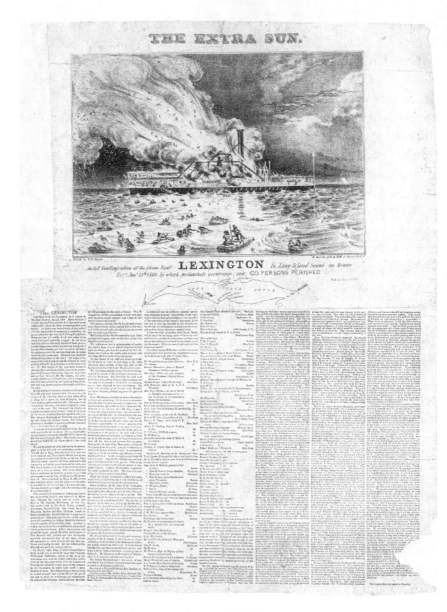

The Extra Sun. The *New York Sun* published this extra edition to report the *Lexington* explosion. The illustration, unusual for both its size and timeliness, was Nathaniel Currier's first rendering of the "Awful Conflagration." A map of the Long Island Sound, located directly beneath Currier's image of the flaming vessel, shows the location of Eaton's Neck, east of New York City, where the fire aboard the ship was first discovered. The text describes the explosion's ghastly aftermath, lists names of those known to have died, and reports the early proceedings of the coroner's jury convened to investigate the disaster. *William K. Hewitt (1818–1892) and N. Currier (Firm) / Museum of the City of New York. 56.300.4.*

RUINS OF THE MERCHANTS' EXCHANGE, WALL STREET, NEW YORK—BURNT ON THE MORNING OF THE 17TH DEC. 1835.

THE MERCHANT'S EXCHANGE.

Above we give a delineation of the ruins of the Merchant's Exchange, as they now appear to the spectator. We were struck with the magnificence of the view on beholding it after the desolating flame had swept over it, and left it as it now stands. We cannot present this representation in a more proper manner than with the following description from the Commercial Advertiser:—

This edifice, which was consumed by the flames on Wednesday night, was one of the largest in the city, situated on the south side of Wall street, and embracing 115 feet of the front between William and Hanover street.

It was three stories high, exclusive of the basement which was considerably elevated. Its south-west front 114 feet on Exchange street. The south-west of the front was of Westchester marble. The first and second stories of the Ionic order, from the temple of Minerva Polias, at Prigne, in Ionia. A recessed elliptical portico of forty feet wide introduced in front. A screen of four columns and two antæ, each thirty feet high, and three feet four inches in diameter above the base, composed of a single block of marble, extended across the front of the portico, supporting an entablature of six feet in height, on which rested the third story, making a height of sixty feet from the ground.

The principal entrance to the rotunda and exchange room was by a flight of ten marble steps with a pedestal at each end. On ascending to the portico, three doors opened to offices. The vestibule was of the Ionic order, from the little Ionic temple of Illyssus. The exchange room, which was the rotunda, was 75 feet long, 55 feet wide, and 45 feet high, to which were attached four principal rooms, and in the rear of the rotunda, another, used for the auction sales of real estate, shipping, and stocks.

The building was begun on the 1st of April, 1825, and occupied 27 months in its erection, having first been occupied in July, 1827. The plan was that of the architect, Mr. E. Thompson.

THE BURNING.—The Exchange long resisted the flames. It did not catch till 2 o'clock on Thursday morning. The end in which the spire seems to house, in the back ground, was the spot where it caught. It extended from that point to the cupola and dome. Between the two central Ionic columns in front, the statue of Hamilton was for a long time seen surrounded with the blazing light—a transient flood of awful glory. About four o'clock, the magnificent dome fell in with a terrible crash, and one lurid glare ascended to heaven. In the foreground the print represents the patrol, citizens, and spectators, as it appeared on Thursday last, throughout the day. At the eastern end is an immense pile of rubbish, and people clambering over. We desire all our readers to preserve this paper among the archives of their family. Fifty thousand copies only are printed.

THE FOLLOWING IS A CORRECT PLAN OF THE CONFLAGRATION OF NEW YORK, ON THE EVENING OF THE 16TH DEC. 1835.—BY A. A. LANSING.

EXPLANATION OF THE MAP.—The Map covers a space equal to one-third of the First Ward. F. M. T. represents the locality of the Franklin Market. E. X. on Wall street, the Exchange. The black blocks are those parts burned down, and now in ruins. In the second black from Pearl in Water, east, there is a white indentation; this represents the store of Vernet, Saloman & Benson, the modern Shadrach, Meshech and Abednego, which was preserved entire. On the black block in Wall street, between Pearl and the Exchange, large white rectangular spot, which is seen is the the new stores still smoking—behind is a round white spot where the fire began, and extended, south, east, and west, covering nearly fifty acres of ground, burning 670 buildings, and 15,000,000 of millions of property. The time occupied in the devastation was from 9 o'clock on Wednesday night of the 16th December, 1835, until 12 o'clock next day—only fifteen hours—a million an hour. From five to ten thousand persons have been thrown out of employment. The calamity will be felt throughout the United States from the Saint Croix to the Sabine.

Ruins of the Merchants' Exchange after the Destructive Conflagration of December 16–17, 1835. On 21 December 1835, James Gordon Bennett's *New York Herald* published this illustration, just five days after a major fire engulfed lower Manhattan. The accompanying map shows the area the fire destroyed. New York's Great Fire was the first disaster depicted in a U.S. newspaper. Bennett made 50,000 copies of this edition, which he urged his readers to preserve "in the archives of their family." John H. Bufford, 9 x 12¼, New-York Historical Society. *Photography © New-York Historical Society.*

New York fire transferware plate. This Staffordshire plate is one of three manufactured by an unidentified English pottery bearing views of New York's Great Fire. This plate's center reproduces Nathaniel Currier's lithograph *Ruins of the Merchants' Exchange*, which was drawn by John H. Bufford. Its border features fire engines and the American eagle. English potteries produced many pieces with American scenes for export, though the New York fire plates appear to have been unique in portraying a contemporary American disaster. *American Antiquarian Society.*

mercial news, the new and cheaper publications cultivated a mass audience by pursuing human-interest stories that often included visceral accounts of lurid crimes and horrific tragedies. The *New York Sun*, which featured Currier's image of the *Lexington* on its front page in 1840, was also the first newspaper to publish reports of suicides, divorces, and other traumatic personal stories. As its editor observed candidly, he and his fellow penny-press editors "thrive best on the calamities of others."[33]

Exploding Steamboats and the Culture of Calamity

Although the appeal of disaster stories was part of what one historian has called "a popular voyeuristic taste for scenarios of death," it also represented fascination with the darker side of a rapidly changing world. While many of Currier's better-known lithographs celebrated American industry, prosperity, and growth with images of orderly cities, western vistas, ships, and later railroads, others depicted the destruction of these same technological and topographic marvels. Steamboats were central to this ambivalence toward modernity and Currier's representation of it. On his own and later in partnership with Ives, Currier published at least 200 lithographs of steamboats, more than one-fourth of which portrayed explosions or collisions, the first of which was the *Lexington*.[34]

By the 1840s, descriptions of steamboat explosions were available to mass audiences in a variety of literary formats, besides the omnipresent newspaper. Folk songs and ballads recounted stories of maritime disasters, including that of the *Lexington*, which was commemorated in a song published in New York and sold throughout the eastern United States. Clergy preached sermons that drew lessons from steamboat disasters, memorialized victims, and comforted survivors while emphasizing the omnipotence of God, the prudence of preparing for sudden and unexpected death, and the need for faith and benevolent works. "Yes, my friends," the Reverend W. H. Furness of Philadelphia insisted, "this sore calamity is full of moral significance." Accounts of individuals who perished in steamboat explosions also taught moral lessons. The chillingly titled *Warning Voice from a Watery Grave!* presented the story of the abrupt and grisly death of the amiable and pious eighteen-year-old Sophia Wheeler as "Solemn Proof of the Uncertainty of Life, and the Importance of an Early Preparation for Death," cautioning "youthful readers" against the "the present prevailing thrust for worldly wealth" and reminding them that riches became "worthless dross" to those on the verge of destruction, though their faith remained a comfort.[35]

Like earlier narratives of the Lisbon earthquake or the Richmond theater fire, many of these steamboat stories were appallingly—but also appealingly—graphic in their description of human carnage, even when they lacked accompanying illustrations. When the steamboat *Louisiana* exploded in New Orleans in November 1849, local journalists described the scene in typically gory detail, in an account that was reprinted in other newspapers, as well as in *Lloyd's Steamboat Directory*. "The sight of the mangled bodies on every side, the groans of the dying, and the shrieks of the agonized sufferers, produced a general thrill of horror among the multitude," this eyewitness reported. "The body of a man was seen, with the head and one leg off, and the entrails torn out. A woman, whose long hair lay wet and matted by her side, had one leg off, and her body was shockingly mangled. A large man, having his skull mashed in, lay dead on the levee; his face looked as though it had been painted red, having been completely flayed by the scalding water. Others of both sexes, crushed, scalded, burned, mutilated and dismembered, lay about in every direction. Two bodies were found locked together, brought by death into a sudden and close embrace."[36]

A quarter-century after the *Washington* explosion, steamboat stories remained popular and, if anything, more voyeuristic than ever. Indeed, one historian has noted that these narratives were designed to "materialize the unimaginable," and to that end, along with the narratives of escaped slaves, they constituted some of the most graphically violent literature of the antebellum era. The continuing appeal of these stories, which invited readers to be vicarious spectators at scenes of destruction and death, spurred the publication of compilations of accounts of past maritime disasters, which repurposed newspaper reports as sources of entertainment and moral instruction.[37]

In 1840, just months after the *Lexington* debacle, Southworth Allen Howland of Worcester, Massachusetts, published *Steamboat Disasters and Railroad Accidents in the United States*, a 408-page compendium that went through three editions in six years and that, despite its title, focused overwhelmingly on steamboat explosions and other shipwrecks. Howland explained that the purpose of his book was not only to catalog "the many disasters that have occurred on our waters since the introduction of steam navigation, and, as far as practicable, [explain] the principle causes that led to such disasters," but also "to perpetuate the memory of those who have been the innocent sufferers thereby." Doing so, he believed, would inspire moral improvement in his readers, rendering them more benevolent and compassionate. After pondering the sad fates of those who perished aboard the *Moselle* and the *Lexington*, he declared, "That heart must be callous, indeed, that turns not from scenes like these . . . and looking back on past sufferings as beyond the reach of help, extends not the hand of charity to relieve those of the present—sufficient of which ever exist around us."[38]

Charles Ellms, who published two illustrated compilations of maritime disaster stories in the 1830s and 1840s, agreed that such narratives were morally uplifting because of their emotional power. Readers would find his stories appealing, he believed, because the "natural desire to know the fate of their fellow creatures seems implanted in the breast of mankind, and the most powerful sympathies are excited by listening to the misfortunes of the innocent." Rousing "the dormant powers of sympathy," in turn, "serves at

The Burning of the Steamer Royal Tar. This engagingly melancholy woodcut
was one of many illustrations in *The Tragedy of the Seas*, a compilation of
maritime disaster stories by Charles Ellms. The *Royal Tar* was carrying "a
valuable Menagerie of Wild Beasts," as well as twenty-one crew members and
seventy passengers, when it exploded off the coast of New Brunswick in 1836.
Seeking to evoke feelings of sympathy and benevolence, Ellms's rendering of
the wreck foregrounds female passengers and animals—especially horses—
struggling to stay afloat in the perilous sea. *American Antiquarian Society*.

once to mend the heart, and to exercise one of its most amenable propensi-
ties . . . till we feel an inclination to lessen the mass of ills within our reach."
Ellms asserted that his "authentic and true narratives of the most affecting
and thrilling description" would be "not only read with avidity, but in our
opinion, with advantage" because they would engender sentimental feelings
that would promote kindness and benevolence.[39]

There were steam-themed children's stories, too, from "The Balloon and
the Steamboat," in which two brothers debate the relative merits of steamboats and hot air balloons, to the more somber nonfiction *Disasters by Steam,
Fire, and Water: With Elegant Engravings*. Based on real-life events, the latter
brought together four shipwreck stories—two of which involved steamboats—to entertain "young readers" and also to present them with moral
exemplars. The saga of the *Byron* highlighted the leadership of its brave and
manly captain, whose ability to maintain order and discipline saved the lives
of panicking passengers after his ship collided with an iceberg off the coast
of Newfoundland in 1836. The story of the *Pulaski* focused on a male passenger who went to extraordinary lengths to save a "young lady," with whom he

was marooned at sea for days after the wreck. The castaways agreed to marry, though once they were rescued the man, admitting that he lost all his property in the explosion, offered to dissolve the engagement. The story ended happily, however, with the valiant man being rewarded for his candor when his betrothed informed him that she was "an heiress with an estate worth $200,000" and would marry him nonetheless.[40]

Eye-catching illustrations, showing ships tossed amid the churning seas and bodies propelled from the decks of exploding vessels, made such stories even more vivid and emotionally powerful. As the author of *Disasters by Steam, Fire, and Water* observed, his stories were "illustrated by superior engravings, which will add much interest to the narratives." Works aimed primarily at adult readers, if they were published after 1840, were also replete with images — new illustrations added to older stories — from crude woodcuts that showed bodies flying through the air as they were expelled from convulsing ships to the "one hundred fine engravings and forty-six maps" that adorned such popular compilations as *Lloyd's Steamboat Directory, and Disasters on the Western Waters*. Published in 1856, *Lloyd's Steamboat Directory* was produced ostensibly to celebrate the role of the steamboat in opening the West to white settlement and tourism and making western agriculture profitable; its author, James T. Lloyd, maintained that there had been "more real danger and more actual loss of life" on the western waters before the advent of steamboats, in the era of keel boats and barges. But Lloyd also knew that steamboat disasters fascinated his readers. As a result, he devoted 157 of his book's 326 pages to detailed illustrated accounts of explosions, collisions, and other steamboat disasters.[41]

These stories were compelling in part because of the apparent ubiquity of the events they described, which made it possible for almost anyone to imagine themselves as potential steamboat casualties — or, conversely, to feel gratitude for having been spared the gruesome fate that so many people like them suffered. The power of steamboats, the mobility and apparent freedom they offered, and the suddenness with which the vessels and their passengers could be reduced to dismembered and smoldering rubble also spoke to equally profound anxieties about conventions and hierarchies of class, gender, and race in a quickly changing world.

At a time when territorial expansion fractured long-established families and communities, immigrants thronged the streets of growing cities, industrialization transformed the means of both production and consumption, and workingmen asserted their right to equal suffrage, conservative elites like the New York diarist Philip Hone refused to believe that steamboat (and

Exploding Steamboats and the Culture of Calamity

LLOYD'S

STEAMBOAT DIRECTORY,

AND

DISASTERS ON THE WESTERN WATERS,

CONTAINING THE HISTORY OF THE

FIRST APPLICATION OF STEAM,
AS A MOTIVE POWER;

THE LIVES OF

JOHN FITCH AND ROBERT FULTON,

LIKENESSES & ENGRAVINGS OF THEIR FIRST STEAMBOATS.

EARLY SCENES ON THE WESTERN WATERS, FROM 1798 TO 1812---HISTORY OF THE EARLY STEAMBOAT NAVIGATION ON WESTERN WATERS--ENGRAVINGS OF THE BOATS.

FULL ACCOUNTS OF ALL THE STEAMBOAT DISASTERS SINCE THE FIRST APPLICATION OF STEAM DOWN TO THE PRESENT DATE, WITH LISTS OF THE KILLED AND WOUNDED—A COMPLETE LIST OF STEAMBOATS AND ALL OTHER VESSELS NOW AFLOAT ON THE WESTERN RIVERS AND LAKES—WHEN AND WHERE BUILT, AND THEIR TONNAGE:

Maps of the Ohio and Mississippi Rivers,

Towns, Cities, Landings, Population and Distances correctly laid down on the Ohio, Mississippi, Missouri, Tennessee, Cumberland, Kentucky, Green, Illinois, Arkansas, White, Red and Yazoo Rivers.

LIST OF

PLANTATIONS ON THE MISSISSIPPI RIVER;

Daguerrean Views and Sketches of

Pittsburgh, Wheeling, Cincinnati, Louisville, Falls of Ohio, Nashville, Cairo, Falls of St. Anthony, Gates of the Rocky Mountains, St. Louis, New Orleans, and Mobile—Sketches of the Ohio and Mississippi Rivers, and their Tributaries, Sources, Length, Area of country drained, &c. Names of all the U. S. Licensed Pilots and Engineers—Fast Time of Boats,

THE EARTHQUAKE IN 1812, &c., &c.

ONE HUNDRED FINE ENGRAVINGS, AND FORTY-SIX MAPS,

Being a Valuable Statistical Work, as well as a Guide-Book for the Travelling Public.

BY JAMES T. LLOYD.

5358.

CINCINNATI, OHIO:
JAMES T. LLOYD & CO.
1856.

Lloyd's Steamboat Directory. James T. Lloyd was a steamboat enthusiast who compiled his directory mainly to celebrate the dramatic growth in population and prosperity that steamers brought to the American West. He described his book as "a Valuable Statistical Work, as well as a Guide-Book for the Travelling Public." Despite its overall tone of boosterism, Lloyd's book included many accounts of steamboat explosions, reprinted from newspapers, which he embellished with new illustrations. *American Antiquarian Society.*

later railroad) disasters were mere accidents. "I never take up a paper that does not contain accounts of loss of life, dreadful mutilation of limbs, and destruction of property, with which these dangerous, murderous modes of locomotion are attended," he wrote. Hone attributed these deadly episodes to the fact that Americans "have become the most careless, reckless, headlong people on the face of the earth," with lawless disorder driving his countrymen ever "ahead with a vengeance, regardless of consequences and indifferent about the value of human life." Travel by steamboat, even a safe passage, would have been a jarring experience to Hone and his peers, who increasingly resided in socially homogeneous elite enclaves, remote from the "vulgar and uneducated masses." Despite their own luxurious shipboard accommodations, elite passengers punctuated accounts of their voyages with derogatory and uneasy observations about the sights, sounds, and smells of unruly folk who traveled uncomfortably on the steamboats' crowded decks.[42]

In this era of confidence men and painted women, the geographic mobility of Americans posed problems and risks, as well as opportunities. Removed from the defining context of family and community, people could reinvent themselves, and the steamboat, the site of a transient gathering of strangers, was the ideal venue for such a project. Con men, gamblers, and faux aristocrats flourished on antebellum steamboats, as did escaped slaves passing as free people and those with African blood and light skin claiming the privileges of whiteness.[43]

Gender, specifically conventions governing the proper roles of respectable men and ladies, posed other problems. Steamboat explosions repeatedly belied the fiction that men were willing and able to protect women, a conceit that lay at the core of contemporary ideals of masculinity and white male authority. The architecture and etiquette of steamboats, like those of theaters, enclosed respectable women in spaces that were both secluded — to shield them from corruption by the licentious hoards — and difficult to escape. Cumbersome clothing, along with confinement in the "ladies' cabin," helped account for the fact that women, who always constituted a minority of steamboat passengers, consistently numbered disproportionately among their fatalities. While a gender-skewed death toll had led to critical scrutiny and defensive protestations in the wake of the Richmond theater fire, that discussion was short-lived because it revolved around a singular event. By contrast, lists of steamboat fatalities accompanied by descriptions of the ghastly deaths of virtuous young ladies were the stuff of many heartrending popular stories. The belief that men would save "women and children first," a notion that originated in the early nineteenth century, was a myth that defensively sustained an ideal of male sacrifice and gallantry that had little basis in reality. Women and children were often the last to be rescued in part because men viewed them as impediments to saving their own lives and their ship's valuable cargoes.[44]

Although Americans were not alone in embracing the myth of "women and children first," the loss of so many women at sea clearly clashed with emerging notions of national identity and American exceptionalism. "The relative success of crew and male passengers to ensure the safety of women and children became a gauge of national moral character at a time when individualism threatened the ideal of a national community," one scholar has argued, adding that in American shipwreck stories, men who saved women in maritime disasters were depicted as "saving faith in God, loyalty to family, and commitment to community."[45]

Among the many American steamboat disasters of the era, the explosion of the *Arctic* in 1854 resonated more than most because, though eighty-six people survived, all of the women and children on board died. The contrast with the wreck of the British steamboat *Birkenhead*, two years earlier, made the *Arctic* incident especially galling. Only 192 of 650 people aboard the *Birkenhead* survived, but nearly all of the women and children were rescued. One widely circulating press account of the *Arctic* disaster decried the "unmanly spectacle" of so many "robust cowards . . . treacherously deserting feeble and delicate women, and shutting their ears to cries from little children," as they fled the scene in the ship's lifeboats. This scene, and the values it represented, differed dramatically—and distressingly—from the conduct of the "heroic band" of British men aboard the *Birkenhead*, who stoically accepted death, "shoulder to shoulder," as the women and children were saved."[46]

Lists of the dead, published in the aftermath of each steamboat tragedy, included men, women, and children—rich and poor, native-born and foreign, free and enslaved—segregated by class, gender, and race aboard the ship but now companions in death. As readers perused these lists, they would have noticed people like themselves among the casualties. Among those who died aboard the *Lexington*, one minister observed, "there was the humble and toilful *laborer*; the active and enterprising *man of business*; the learned and accomplished *scholar and divine*; the young *betrothed*, who had just left the beloved one amidst the joys of happy affection; the *husband*, . . . [the] *tender woman*," and trusting children who followed their parents onto the ship, "not dreaming that there *could* be danger in a *mother's* arms." Although this litany of the lost failed to include the seventeen African Ameri-

Published by J. Pharazin 103 South River.

TERRIBLE CONFLAGRATION AND DESTRUCTION OF THE STEAM-BOAT "NEW-JERSEY."

On the River Delaware, opposite Philadelphia, on the Night of Saturday, March 15th, 1856, between 2 and 9 o'clock, by which Dreadful Calamity Sixty-One Lives were lost. Names of all on Board.

The Dead.—Abo. Janney, John Little, James M. Skreiner, John S Newton, Mrs. Shade, Alex. Claxton, James McCoffey, Francis Fitzpatrick, Francis Baird, Fredk. A. Thompson, Myre Reinbeck. Van. Nixon, Charles Weatherby, Henry Lafarge, Mary Massey, Charles Sharpe, Samuel Briggs, Ann Bullard, Thomas Smith, John Fidell. *Colored*—Emory Riley, Mary Ann Diggs, James Williams, Jacob Campbell, James A. Kennard, Morris Bairy, Henry Johnson, Lother Otery, Elijah Hatchinson, B. H. Simons, Edw. Manorky.—Total 31. *Entered According to Act of Congress in the District Court for Eastern District of Pa. by A Pharazin.*

The Missing.—Miss E. Fullerton, Thomas Allen, Miss Sally Caxman, John T. Parsons, Edw. Mershamp, Charles Hollandsend, Charles Keyser, John Primer, Charles Beale, — Ehlman, Miss St. Jones, J. W. Wainwright. — Quinn, — Barbanca's German boy, — Riddle, Mrs Wagstaff, Ann Oakman, Saml. Gilberman's child, Miss Sarah Fremsell, Miss S. W. Gwinn, A. W. Freeman. *Colored*—Maj. Snively's boy, J. Wesley Stewart, — Bourden, — Smith, James Mitchell, Edward Simson, Peter Monely.—Total 30.

The Saved.—W. H. Yeaton, Jacob Eazilo, Alfred Beadley, Miss Stow, Mrs. Nixon and child, Mr. Hewing, Mr. Edwards, Mr. Crispo, Mr. Ferguson, Capt. Corner, Carrey Carter, Edw. Hoopes, Chas. P. Dickson, Thos. Storms, J. Bevring, Gotlelb Erkhart, Alfred Brebary, Mrs. Giberman, Mr. Shade, Capt. J. B. Howe, Wm. Copeland, May. Snively, — Patterson, T. B. Dudley, R. W. Mitchell, Mrs. Stearns, Mrs Fidel, L. Newton, Mr. Nagel, Mr. Howard, David Jeator, Wm. Young, John Springer, Wm. P. Wilson, James M. Sterling, Jas. Thompson, Wm. F. Agnew, Mr. Barlow, Saml. Gibreson, Godfrey Ostenhart, Mr. Hayward, Chas. Dixey, Restore Corsaman, N. E. Chase, Chas. Keyser.—Total 46.

Terrible Conflagration and Destruction of the Steam-Boat "New-Jersey." This lithograph depicts efforts to save people from the burning ship, which exploded on the Delaware River in March 1856. Its creator, A. Pharazin, employed the common practice of identifying disaster casualties by name and by race. "Colored" passengers are listed separately at the bottom of the first two columns, labeled "The Dead" and "The Missing," respectively. Although a black man is shown swimming toward the wharf, no "Colored" passengers were listed among "The Saved." *Library of Congress Prints and Photographs Division.*

cans—three passengers and fourteen crew members—who also numbered among the dead, newspapers also identified black victims by name, often placing them all together at the end of the list of casualties.[47]

Most Americans could blithely presume their own immunity from other newsworthy disasters, dismissing fires as urban problems and taking comfort in knowing that earthquakes, tornadoes, and even hurricanes (in most regions) were fascinating precisely because they were relatively uncommon. By contrast, steamboats traversed every American waterway, from eastern cities to the newer western territories, and they were increasingly essential for the transportation of goods and people in both rural and urban areas. As lists of the dead that were published in the aftermath of virtually every steamboat tragedy revealed, passengers came from everywhere, and they included men, women, and children of every social rank. Whether people read about steamboat explosions, witnessed them as spectators, or gathered in their aftermath to attend to the dead and dying, they could therefore readily imagine themselves in similar circumstances. As one clergyman observed, the "dismal history" of the *Lexington* and so many other steamboats "shows a long, sad list of the honored and loved, filling every position in human society, and touching a thousand hearts . . . and so it will be in the future." Edward W. Bancroft, who heard of the *Lexington* explosion not long after traveling by steamer from Boston to South Carolina, agreed. "I could ask but why the 100 passengers aboard [my own ship]," he mused, "were not buried beneath the waves of the boisterous ocean."[48]

The fact that so many bodies were either lost or unidentified compounded the problem, depriving the dead of funeral rituals and their loved ones of the comfort that such rituals could bring. Newspaper accounts of steamboat disasters typically included the names of casualties not only to memorialize the victims but also to convey the magnitude of the loss to an empathetic public. This practice of listing disaster victims by name was not new—accounts of hurricanes and fires had often included such information—but the lists of steamboat casualties were longer, more frequent, and probably more likely to be incomplete or erroneous. As the anthologist James T. Lloyd noted, "A large proportion of the passengers on western steamboats are persons from distant parts of the country, or emigrants, perhaps, from the old world, whose journeyings are unknown to their friends, and whose fate often excites no inquiry. When such persons are the victims of a steamboat calamity, their names, and frequently their numbers, are beyond all powers of research." Nor were eastern routes immune to such uncertainties. After the *Lexington* explosion, people across New York and New England scoured newspapers to see if they had family and friends among the victims, but, though reporters had "ascertained the names of the greater part of the passengers," they did not believe that the list was either complete or free of errors.[49]

In part because the 1838 steamboat safety law had proven so ineffective, the *Lexington* disaster occasioned more than the usual debates about culpability and government's appropriate role. As the inquest continued, some newspapers defended the steamboat company, though at least one New York paper boldly characterized the owners of the *Lexington* as "nothing less than homicides," a charge reprinted approvingly elsewhere. The pages of Washington's *National Intelligencer* featured a weeks-long debate between a defender of the steamboat operators and "J. E. D."—most likely Senator John Davis of Massachusetts, a longtime supporter of stronger government oversight—who argued forcefully in favor of reform. "Let . . . the steamers be regulated, let the owners, crew, and *inspectors* be made to feel their responsibility, let the passengers see that they are not placed in jeopardy by carelessness or intoxication," he declared, asserting the "right" of passengers to travel safely. Citizens at a Boston town meeting called on Congress to impose strict regulations to improve steamboat safety, though the *Boston Courier* remained skeptical about the ability of "public execrations" to vanquish the power of greedy steamboat owners. Conversely, editors of the *Spirit of the Times: A Chronicle of the Turf, Field Sports, Literature and the Stage*, which catered to the upper classes, protested, "It is impossible to discover any ground for the fierce denunciations of the steamboat company," whose officers produced a "Review of the Presentment" to explicate the inquest's inconclusive verdict and emphasize their own blamelessness in hopes of discouraging survivors' families from filing civil suits against them.[50]

In the protracted aftermath of the *Lexington* explosion, some critics noted that the United States lagged far behind some European countries in protecting the lives of the traveling public, revealing what one Philadelphian called "an alarming and increasing recklessness of human life." The Reverend Samuel Kirkland Lothrop, who attributed the *Lexington* tragedy to "either the selfishness and cupidity of the owners, who, greedy of gain, insisted upon overloading their boat with a dangerous and inflammable freight, or to the culpable carelessness . . . of the masters and officers . . . to which hundreds had entrusted their lives," angrily asserted that "there is no country upon earth, where proprietors, managers and conductors of these public conveyances, are so little responsible, so slightly amenable to law, so far beyond the reach of public rebuke or public punishment." The Reverend William Henry Furness concurred but sadly conceded that even new legislation was unlikely to help because laws in "this country can do little, if the governing spirit of all classes is hostile to it." Southworth Howland, the Worcester author, avowed the need for reform in his compendium, *Steamboat Disasters and Railroad Accidents*, published within months of the *Lexington* explosion. "Although the laws of the land, with strange apathy, refuse to award the condign punishment such aggravated cases demand," he wrote, "yet the stern voice of an indignant public should denounce the reckless indifference, the gross carelessness, and the criminal neglect, through which so many of their fellow-beings are suddenly swept into eternity."[51]

Such protests had little impact in Congress, where owners and managers of steamboat companies pressed to thwart passage of a bill proposed

Collins and Cunard. Raising the Wind; or, Both Sides of the Story. This 1852
Frank Bellew cartoon, published in the *Lantern* magazine, depicts transoceanic
steamship magnates Edward Knight Collins (backed by a complacent Uncle Sam)
and Samuel Cunard (actively supported by John Bull). Presented here as an unfair
contest between a U.S. entrepreneur and his government-subsidized foreign
competitor, the Collins-Cunard rivalry also pitted American speed against British
safety. By 1858, after two highly publicized disasters—one of which was the *Arctic*
debacle—Collins was out of business, while Cunard thrived and prospered.
Library of Congress Rare Book and Special Collections Division.

by Senator John Ruggles, a Democrat from Maine, that March. Noting the
many shortcomings of the 1838 law and the success of France's recently
adopted regulatory program, Ruggles presented a bill that included a total
of twenty-one provisions, including compulsory and detailed inspections
of ships' engines, boilers, and hulls; specific qualifications and training programs for engineers; minimum requirements for foghorns, lifeboats, and
other safety equipment aboard ships; and continued criminalization of crew
members' negligence and financial liability for ships' owners and masters. In
response, the steamboat companies sent a memorial to Congress in which
they affirmed the relative safety of steam travel, asserted that overseeing the
design and inspection of ships' engines and boilers were best left to those
familiar with the steamboat business, and demanded the repeal of the lia-

bility clause in the 1838 law on the grounds that it was "so much at variance with their fundamental rights and privileges as American citizens." In March 1840, Ruggles introduced his bill in the Senate, only to have consideration of it postponed indefinitely.[52]

Between 1841 and 1851, a period during which at least 1,218 people died in American maritime explosions, Congress revisited the issue of steamboat regulation from time to time without acting decisively, despite receiving a new report from the U.S. Commissioner of Patents that reiterated the scientific findings of the Franklin Institute and characterized the current system of inspection and post-disaster litigation as ineffective and corrupt. Experienced engineers, who had organized in many cities to promote steamboat safety, also increasingly supported the passage of a new law to improve inspection practices and require all engineers to be certified as qualified by knowledgeable boards of experts. Scientists were near-universal in rejecting the notion that holding people and corporations liable for disasters was sufficient to prevent them, arguing in favor of specific standards for the construction and operation of boilers and other apparatuses and viable means to enforce them.[53]

Between 1849 and 1851, steamboat-related deaths actually increased to an average of 200 per year — compared with roughly 80 per year between 1841 and 1848 — and, perhaps for that reason, in early 1851, both the Senate and the House considered steamboat safety bills, though the proposed legislation never came to a vote that year in either house. In January 1852, Secretary of the Treasury Thomas Corwin submitted his report, "Statistics and History of the Steam Marine in the United States." After tallying the total lives and property lost between 1816 and 1848 in steamboat disasters, the secretary was remarkably sanguine. "The array of numbers is appalling, and calls for every remedy that can be applied," he asserted before adding, "But, on the other hand, if we take a full view of the case, it is but a small matter, and should produce little alarm." According to Corwin's calculations, approximately 1 of every 5,013 steamboat passengers died as a result of partaking of the "great public convenience" of steam travel. "Can any mode of conveyance," he asked, "compare with this for safety?"[54]

Notwithstanding the secretary's report, three deadly explosions in the spring and summer of 1852 may have provided the extra impetus needed for Congress to act. In April 1852, the *Glencoe* exploded at St. Louis, killing at least 60 people; four days later, the explosion of the *Saluda* at Lexington, Missouri, claimed as many as 100 more lives. The *Saluda* was the thirteenth major steamboat disaster of 1852. Altogether, these explosions and wrecks had claimed a total of 327 lives. But that year's most highly publicized wreck occurred in late July, when at least 70 people — and likely many more — died in the conflagration of the *Henry Clay* near Riverdale, just north of New York City on the Hudson River.[55]

The *Henry Clay* story checked all the boxes needed to guarantee its cultural resonance, as coverage in the recently established *New York Times* amply shows. The *Times* reported that the captain of the *Henry Clay* was racing with another ship, the *Armenia*, and that his recklessness terrified passengers even before the boiler's explosion engulfed the ship and its 400 to 500 passengers in fiery chaos and people scrambled to escape the vessel, which had no usable lifeboats. No one knew for sure how many passengers were onboard, but the *Times* was "quite certain" that many bodies remained missing more than a week after the explosion. Equally certain was the fact that women and children numbered disproportionately among the casualties and that many lives were lost due to a lack of lifeboats and life preservers. The dead included some well-known people, including a granddaughter of President John Adams, Nathaniel Hawthorne's sister, a former mayor of New York, and the landscape architect Andrew Jackson Downing. Citizens' committees angrily denounced the owners and operators of the *Henry Clay* and insisted that only the "indignant voice of the public" could ensure punishment for their "criminal recklessness." Although the coroner's jury quickly indicted those men for manslaughter, they were all found not guilty in the U.S. district court.[56]

In the weeks following the wreck of the *Henry Clay*, Congress devoted considerable time to debating and amending the previously stalled steamboat safety bill proposed by John Davis, the Whig senator from Massachusetts. Petitioners ranging from steamboat engineers in Pittsburgh and Cincinnati to the Humane Society of Boston implored the legislators to act. The New Orleans Chamber of Commerce even sent a draft bill — mandating regular inspections by salaried experts, specifications for boilers and engines, and other safety requirements — and urged "the passage of an act in conformity therewith, which will greatly lessen, if not entirely obviate, the casualties, which it is the object of the Chamber to prevent." Another petition circulated in New York City and its environs, citing the wreck of the *Henry Clay* and other recent "fearful and appalling disasters," which had resulted in such a "dreadful waste of human life." More than 1,500 people signed a total of eighty-five copies of the New York petition, all of which were sent to Washington. The New York petitioners pressed Congress to pass Davis's bill "without amendment, that any further delay may be at once obviated." The

New York petitioners included presidents of eight insurance companies and other business leaders, along with General Frederick Ellsworth Mather, who identified himself as a survivor of the *Swallow* disaster in 1845, a steamboat explosion that had claimed the life of his only son.[57]

Perhaps impelled by citizens' assertions that Congress must—in the words of the Pittsburgh engineers—"pass such laws as may be necessary to give protection to the lives and property of those thus exposed," both houses passed the bill by large bipartisan majorities, over the protests of steamboat owners and operators. President Millard Fillmore, who previously had not weighed in officially on either side of the issue, signed the bill into law on 30 August 1852. The most careful student of the history of the Steamboat Act of 1852 concludes that the "final step toward positive regulation found support from congressmen of all political postures and from all geographical areas . . . [who were] prompted by the recognition of the inadequacy of the 1838 law as evidenced by the continued severe loss of life, and . . . by constituents who were able to recognize how the problem could be solved." The same legislative session also approved the largest federal appropriation to date for the eradication of snags and other river hazards that caused steamboat collisions on western rivers.[58]

Landmark legislation that established the first federal regulatory agency, the Steamboat Act of 1852 had forty-one sections that imposed specific requirements on steamboats and the men who ran them. Among its most important provisions were the first-ever technical standards for the design, construction, and operation of boilers, gauges, and other machinery. Other sections of the law established standards for the training and certification of engineers and new rules for safely transporting gunpowder, cotton, and other highly flammable cargoes. Still others stipulated specific procedures for annual inspections, to be completed by salaried men "selected for their knowledge, skill, and experience in the uses of steam power" and who had no personal connection to or financial interest in the vessels they evaluated. The law also enumerated the types and numbers of lifeboats, life preservers, and hoses and other firefighting equipment that steamboats would now be required to carry. The law addressed other public concerns by mandating that documents certifying a ship's successful attainment of inspection criteria be on display and plainly visible to passengers and that the ship's master keep "a correct list of all the passengers . . . noting the places where received and where landed." Congress imposed stiff fines for violations of any of the law's provisions. Although the 1852 law did not end steamboat explosions in the United States, it did help to reduce them, and lives were saved as a result.[59]

Exploding Steamboats and the Culture of Calamity

Unlike the 1838 law, the 1852 law sought to attain the desired safety standards via administrative remedies rather than common law or criminal sanctions. In cases of negligence or malfeasance, the new law—like the 1838 act—stipulated that crew members could be tried for manslaughter and that ship owners could be sued and held financially liable. In practice, however, there had been only nine criminal convictions under the old law, and even those found guilty in those cases received only nominal punishment. Because coroners' reports were often inconclusive, successful civil suits against steamboat owners were uncommon, and even in winning cases, damages tended to be minimal. Indeed, the growing use of steam technology brought significant changes in the legal definition of negligence, as liability became less associated with the actions of a specific individual than with an overall situation that posed risks that courts tended to view as reasonable and necessary in an expanding and industrializing economy. This acceptance of vulnerability and risk, which in part accounted for the rise of an American insurance industry during this period, is a hallmark of modern capitalism.[60]

§ Efforts to promote and enforce steamboat safety were ultimately successful in part because vivid representations of horrific maritime disasters gave rise to public conversations about passengers' vulnerability, human culpability, and the role of the state in preventing disasters and protecting the lives of its citizens. The cultural and political history of steamboat explosions and efforts to curtail them foreshadowed later discussions about railroad safety in response to the growing frequency and visibility of train disasters, though in that case state governments and railroad owners adopted regulations and technological improvements to address passengers' concerns and largely avert federal safety regulation. The lives of railroad workers on freight lines, however, continued to be in jeopardy, just as American factory workers—many of whom were women and children—labored in close proximity to steam boilers and other machinery.[61] While many Americans could imagine themselves as passengers on steamboats or on trains, even the most sympathetic members of the middle class could not identify with the systemic problems of industrial workers, who were far more vulnerable than their employers and received scant protection from government at any level.

EPILOGUE

The half century or so following the passage of the Steamboat Act of 1852 was something of a golden age for American disasters. Exploding steamboats continued to make news, now accompanied, but not entirely displaced, by sensational accounts of railroad wrecks, the deadliest of which, in Ashtabula, Ohio, in 1876, resulted in the loss of ninety-two lives.[1] Other disasters of the post–Civil War decades had far more fatalities. The Peshtigo fire in 1871, the Johnstown flood in 1889, and the Galveston hurricane in 1900 all set successive records for U.S. disaster-related deaths, with Galveston's loss of at least 6,000 people—and perhaps many more—still standing today as the deadliest in U.S. history. Some late nineteenth- and early twentieth-century disasters were truly iconic. The Chicago fire and the San Francisco earthquake captured the public's attention for weeks, even months, as relief workers and local authorities sorted through the wreckage and debated ambitious rebuilding efforts.

Although the scope of these disasters could be unprecedented, responses to them would have been largely familiar to anyone who remembered the *Lexington* explosion—or who lived through Hurricane Katrina. Journalists reported quantitative losses in lives and property and soon added vivid eyewitness accounts and moving stories of suffering and survival. Relief committees scrambled to bury the dead and collect donations of money, provisions, and expertise to aid the injured, hungry, and homeless. Investigations and litigation sometimes followed. Like the Richmond theater fire and so many exploding steamboats, these post–Civil War disasters also became subjects for sentimental stories, poetry, pictures, and other popular culture representations.

But official and popular responses to these later calamities also revealed the continuing evolution of an increasingly expansive American culture of disaster. One aspect of that evolution was the growing presence of the federal government and of national organizations, such as the Red Cross, in disaster relief efforts, reflecting what one scholar has called "a clear principle of *national* obligation" that had not existed in the antebellum decades. Another was the result of technological changes—the growing use of telegraphs, railroads, and photography—that made the news more immediate, more vivid, and more uniform throughout the country. Although this "truly *national* politics of disaster" arguably originated in the Civil War era, this study takes a longer view, casting these developments less as a dramatic break with the past than as elaborations of processes and practices that emerged over the course of two centuries.[2]

§ What happened at Johnstown, Pennsylvania, is emblematic of this general story of continuity and change. On 31 May 1889, torrential rains led to the collapse of a poorly constructed dam on the Little Conemaugh River, unleashing its surging waters to level four square miles of downtown Johnstown, killing at least 2,209 people and making western Pennsylvania the site of what was, at the time, America's deadliest-ever calamity. A careful examination of the horrific flood and its aftermath suggests that by the time Johnstown fell prey to the river's raging waters and the greed of the dam's negligent proprietors—wealthy men from Pittsburgh who constituted the membership of the South Fork Fishing and Hunting Club—the modern culture of disaster was an established fact of life.

In 1889, as in 1811 or 1840, newspaper reports shaped the disaster's cultural resonance beyond its home community. Words and pictures conveying shocking news from Johnstown conformed to older conventions of disaster reportage, though they were more timely and voluminous than they would have been in the antebellum era. Employed commercially as early as the 1840s, the telegraph became pervasive during the Civil War, both for coordinating complex military operations and for facilitating the delivery of war news to the public. After the war, newspapers and magazines continued to rely on telegraphs for immediate news from across the country, and journalists' access to such quick and detailed information enabled readers to follow disaster stories in real time as they happened. On Saturday, the day after the flood engulfed Johnstown, newspapers reported the disaster and estimated its death toll. More substantive stories soon followed as reporters arrived in Johnstown. The proliferation of railroads, including the completion of three transcontinental lines, enabled journalists to flock to the scene. The flood began on Friday morning; by evening, reporters from Pittsburgh, Philadelphia, New York, and elsewhere were on their way, with others soon arriving from as far away as California.[3]

Reporting on the flood, newspapers broke all circulation records, with many publishing extra editions to meet unprecedented demand, a business strategy often used by sensational antebellum penny-press newspapers. Disasters, like war, sold newspapers, especially when reports featured stories that stimulated readers' emotions and validated their prejudices. Reports from Johnstown provided detailed accounts of the "Slaughter of Innocents" — virtuous women and children — as well as affecting stories about people who lost their homes and families. Newspapers also published lurid tales of "foul deeds" supposedly perpetrated by "Hungarians" and other immigrants. Stigmatizing marginal minority populations was nothing new: Mathew Carey had decried the supposed misconduct of Philadelphia's free blacks during the yellow fever epidemic in 1793 and, in so doing, undermined their claim to full citizenship. This sort of reporting became standard practice in the late nineteenth century, when elites (and a press that largely reflected their views and interests) used disasters as opportunities to disparage working-class people and thereby reassert their own dominance.[4]

In northern communities like Johnstown, immigrants were the main subjects of post-disaster crime and conspiracy stories, while white southerners typically unleashed their anxiety-laden vitriol on newly emancipated Africans Americans. In 1871, journalists played to elite Chicagoans' fear and distrust of the so-called dangerous lower classes when they invented the legend of Mrs. O'Leary and her cow, blaming their city's great fire on the carelessness or ignorance of a working-class Irish immigrant woman. After an earthquake in Charleston, South Carolina, in 1886, and the hurricane in Galveston in 1900, the white press demonized African Americans as looters and worse, which helped to justify post-disaster changes that curtailed economic opportunities for black citizens and eventually extinguished their political and civil rights.[5]

Sensational reporting became even more riveting when accompanied by pictures, and here again the Civil War era was a pivotal moment in American journalism history. New York's penny press had pioneered the publication of newsworthy images with the *Herald*'s depiction of the Great Fire of 1835 and Nathaniel Currier's lithograph of the *Lexington*, which appeared on the *Sun*'s front page five years later. Newspapers soon discontinued the use of woodcut engravings because of the time and expense of producing them, but the popular image-heavy news magazines *Frank Leslie's Illustrated Newspaper* and *Harper's Weekly* began publishing in 1855 and 1857, respectively, and a few years later the Civil War dramatically increased their circulation. Not surprisingly, death and destruction figured prominently both in prints featured in news magazines and in photographs by Mathew Brady and others, which were widely viewed during the war, especially in the North. By the 1870s, many consumers of news expected pictures with their words. *Frank Leslie's, Harper's Weekly,* and some other magazines sent sketch artists to Johnstown—as they had to fire-ravaged Chicago in 1871—and, like many newspapers, the illustrated magazines published special flood-themed editions. With the first Kodak cameras having hit the market in 1888, Johnstown also attracted hundreds of amateur photographers, along with the professionals.[6]

Like the Richmond theater fire and the exploding steamboats of the antebellum era, the Johnstown flood story moved beyond newspapers and magazines into an array of popular culture forms. Songs about the flood appeared almost immediately. One called "Her Last Message" was based on the plight of a local telegraph operator, a Civil War widow named Hettie Ogle, who sent distress messages to Pittsburgh until the rising floodwaters disabled the telegraph and drowned both her and her daughter. Another song, "That Valley of Tears," was about a baby who was drowned in its cradle by the "cruel waters" of the flood. Like earlier disasters, the Johnstown flood was also the subject of many poems, including one by Walt Whitman, which the *New York World* commissioned to run on its front page. The first book about the flood was published only a week after it happened, and others soon followed. Prints and photographs, many of which were the work of tourists, were soon for sale nationally. Also available were stereographs, side-by-side images that created a three-dimensional effect when viewed through a binocular-like device, the nineteenth century's popular version of virtual reality.[7]

Relief in the aftermath of the Johnstown flood likewise featured a combination of old and new. Following an American tradition of grassroots disaster management that went back at least to the Boston fire of 1760, citizens in both Johnstown and nearby Pittsburgh immediately formed relief committees to address the needs of flood survivors. In the coming months, the Johnstown committee received some $335,000 in donations, which arrived from every U.S. state and territory, plus six foreign countries. Donations came from towns, churches, schools, voluntary associations (such as lodges and temperance clubs), and individual donors. The Johnstown committee used these funds mainly to rebuild bridges, bury the dead, and pay for fire, police, and morgue services. The Pittsburgh committee collected more than $831,000 "for the direct aid of Johnstown," plus an impressive haul of provisions and volunteer labor, from an equally diverse group of sources, includ-

The Johnstown Calamity: Main Street after the Flood. This stereographic view of downtown Johnstown was made by George Barker of Niagara Falls, New York, one of many commercial photographers who flocked to the flood-ravaged community. When viewed through a stereoscope viewer, the side-by-side images looked three-dimensional. Realistic conveyers of both news and entertainment, stereographs were hugely popular among late nineteenth-century Americans. *Library of Congress Prints and Photographs Division.*

ing several local newspapers that initiated their own fund-raising efforts. As the committee's treasurer observed, "There are two great floods suggested by the thought of Johnstown. The first swift, pitiless, never to be adequately described . . . the second, a great wave of human sympathy and magnificent generosity." This wave of munificence for Johnstown was not unique. Private donations from across the nation, and across the world, poured into other suffering communities in the aftermath of widely publicized disasters.[8]

While the telegraph and railroads expedited the arrival of these donations in Johnstown, institutional changes associated with the Civil War and its aftermath added new players to the mix, diluting the traditionally local administration of post-disaster relief. One was the state government, which called for troops to maintain order and enforce sanitary practices. (A larger and more controversial army had been sent to Chicago at the Illinois governor's behest after the fire in 1871, despite the opposition of municipal authorities.) Pennsylvania governor James A. Beaver arrived in Johnstown on 9 June and, seeing the enormity of the task at hand, determined that the state would assume responsibility for coordinating the collection and dispersal of relief, though the Pittsburgh and Johnstown committees would continue to accept donations. Contributions to the various Johnstown relief funds, which did not include government money, eventually totaled $3,742,818.78.[9]

The most important outsider involved in disaster relief in Johnstown was Clara Barton, president of the recently established American Red Cross. Famous for orchestrating heroic efforts to care for sick and wounded soldiers during the Civil War, Barton sought to continue her work in the postwar era. In the 1870s, though some European Red Cross organizations occasionally participated in disaster relief, their chief purpose was to provide medical attention and other forms of assistance in times of war. When the U.S. government rejected Barton's plan to create an American Red Cross as a permanent voluntary medical military auxiliary, she decided to establish the organization on her own, as a private charity, and to make disaster relief central to its humanitarian mission. Founded in 1881, the fledgling organization and its president went to Ohio and Texas for floods, South Carolina for the Charleston earthquake, Illinois for a tornado, and Florida for an outbreak of yellow fever in the 1880s. Johnstown was Barton's greatest challenge to date and her organization's first of many major disaster relief efforts. She quickly arrived there with fifty doctors and nurses, set up tents as hospitals, established temporary "Red Cross hotels" for the homeless, and distributed much-needed provisions and supplies. When she left Johnstown five months later, local newspapers sang her praises and townspeople gave her a diamond locket to express their profound gratitude.[10]

Although the federal government played no role in the Johnstown disaster, its absence belied a modest but significant expansion of federal involvement in disaster relief in the postwar years. Historian Gareth Davies, the leading authority on national disaster politics during this period, argues persuasively that the Civil War—or, more specifically, the need to address the challenges of postwar Reconstruction in the southern states—set important precedents that made federal disaster relief far more common than it had been before the war (though also not nearly as frequent or expansive as it would become a century later). The most significant precedent was the creation of the Freedmen's Bureau, which provided economic and educational support for newly emancipated African Americans to ease their transition to citizenship. A combination of wartime devastation and virulent white racism—coupled with crop failures, floods, insect infestations, and yellow fever—led Congress to allocate an additional $500,000 for southern famine relief in 1867.[11]

After Congress disbanded the Freedmen's Bureau in 1870, other government entities sometimes dispensed disaster relief on an ad hoc basis. Between 1870 and 1889, on ten occasions, Congress allocated funds for food, clothing, and army tents to assist relief and recovery efforts after floods caused by the overflow of the Mississippi and Ohio rivers. Two allocations in 1875 covered the costs of buying and distributing food, clothing, and seeds among "sufferers from the grasshopper ravages" in Nebraska and Kansas. Other allocations supplied army tents to the governor of Missouri after several tornadoes tore through his state in April 1880 and army rations to feed "sufferers from cyclone" in Macon, Mississippi, in February 1882. In many cases, the U.S. Army was charged with delivering congressional gifts and with overseeing disaster relief efforts.[12]

There were likely two reasons why the federal government did not step in to assist the people of Johnstown, though their flood was far more deadly and destructive than those others that had occurred in mostly rural areas. First, Congress was not in session when the dam on the Little Conemaugh burst in May, and the legislators did not reconvene until December. Second, by the time Congress reassembled in Washington, the relief committees and the Red Cross had everything under control in Johnstown—so much so that the Red Cross had left the area in October and President Benjamin Harrison held a celebratory dinner to honor Clara Barton when she arrived in Washington shortly thereafter. In 1889, philanthropy and ad hoc local fund-raising remained the default strategies for disaster relief in the United States, and these strategies worked reasonably well in Johnstown. A community that had sustained an estimated $17,000,000 in property losses received nearly $4,000,000 in cash, plus more in in-kind donations. This recovery of approximately one-quarter of the community's losses via private donations was a rate of support that was comparable to that achieved by relief efforts in the wake of the Boston and Portsmouth fires of 1760 and 1802, respectively.[13]

The normalization and expansion of federal involvement in disaster relief and prevention was nonetheless one important change that transpired in the post-Johnstown decades. Between 1889 and the enactment of the first comprehensive national disaster legislation in 1950, a mixture of private philanthropy, Red Cross initiatives, and congressional action provided assistance to communities and individuals on a case-by-case basis. After the San Francisco earthquake in 1906, there was a significant federal presence in that city, with locally stationed U.S. Army units deployed in law enforcement, the U.S. Marine Hospital Service involved in the eradication of disease, and Congress allocating an unprecedented $2.5 million for provisions and other supplies. Other disaster-specific legislation enacted by Congress during this period included flood prevention measures, direct relief to victims of floods and storms, loans for rebuilding public facilities in the aftermath of disasters, and assistance to farmers in drought-stricken areas.[14]

Although the Disaster Relief Act of 1950 did not result in an immediate and dramatic expansion of federal involvement in disaster relief and prevention, it was an important first step in that direction. The Disaster Relief Act established a regular process for determining what qualified as a disaster—the president would decide—and stipulated that, in such cases, the federal government would supplement relief provided by the state and local governments. In the coming decades, federal responsibility gradually expanded overall, with the establishment of permanent bureaucracies and funding for disaster relief and the creation of the National Flood Insurance Program in 1968. Although the Red Cross and other voluntary relief organizations remained significant actors, their roles diminished relative to that of the federal government. The increasing visibility of the president as "consoler-in-chief"—a marked contrast to the anonymity or aloofness of most earlier presidents—signified not only changing expectations for the American executive but also the politicization of hurricanes, floods, and other disasters.[15]

A second significant difference between the periods before and after Johnstown was the advent of increasingly sensational disaster-themed entertainments, first in amusement parks and then later on film (and still later in video games). The popularity of these new cultural forms attested to the technological and commercial innovations of the times and also to the persistent appeal of sensational depictions of real-life calamities. As early as 1882, *The Last Days of Pompeii*, a show at James and Henry Pain's Coney Island amphitheater, recreated the destruction of that ancient city by the erupting volcano Vesuvius. Beginning in the 1890s, staged reenactments of urban fires, the Johnstown flood, and the Galveston hurricane—which, in 1900, supplanted Johnstown as America's deadliest disaster—drew crowds in the big new amusement parks that opened in Coney Island, Atlantic City, and elsewhere. Fires, floods, and other disasters were also staples of early films. An hour-long silent movie called *The Johnstown Flood* was made in 1926, starring Janet Gaynor and featuring Clark Gable and Carole Lombard in minor roles.[16]

Movies and amusement park novelties were new ways to bring disaster stories to mass audiences, but they also changed the meaning of those narratives. Like the sermons and pious shipwreck stories of earlier centuries, modern disaster spectacles encouraged viewers to look inward, to experi-

Johnstown flood amusement postcard. This postcard shows the massive building that housed a mechanical reenactment of the Johnstown flood on the boardwalk in Atlantic City. The "Original Pan-American Production" premiered at the Pan-American Exposition in Buffalo in 1901, moving first to Coney Island and then to Atlantic City after the Buffalo fair closed. Its promoters claimed that it was the most popular attraction at the Buffalo exposition and "the greatest electrical scenic production in the world." *Author's collection.*

ence for themselves the horror of fires or floods. But unlike clergy who told disaster stories in the hopes of inspiring permanent spiritual transformations, those who staged these elaborate entertainments aimed only for temporary titillation.

While they were not unique in using disaster stories for commercial ends, the sensationalism of these new amusements appealed to thrill-seekers who sought to experience trauma without risk, a telling way in which they also differed from earlier secular narratives, which were outward-looking and designed to evoke sympathy for genuine sufferers. Timely human-interest stories about fires and exploding steamboats and their victims had inspired sympathy and benevolence, but these new commercial amusements, which set the tone for Hollywood movies, portrayed disasters more as sites of violence and terror than as scenes of suffering innocents. That more sinister reimagining of disasters and their victims could engender antipathy and suspicion, teaching viewers to trust coercive outsiders—armies, police, governments—to save them from horrific calamities and their equally insidious social consequences.[17]

§ Science, sentiment, and information constituted the foundational triumvirate at the heart of the culture of calamity whose origins and subsequent development this book has examined, charting the influence of Enlightenment ideals and their practical applications over roughly two centuries. Science, sentiment, and information remain essential components of our own contemporary culture of calamity, though all three play out somewhat differently in twenty-first century America.

Once confidently esteemed as the solution to all of humanity's problems, the authority and veracity of science is now widely contested. In the United States especially, it is increasingly acceptable to reject scientific findings—climate change is the premier example—particularly when acting on them seems too expensive, inconvenient, or politically unpopular. While Enlightenment polymaths and antebellum tinkerers strove mightily to understand hurricanes, earthquakes, fires, and other destructive forces, the main problems faced by their twenty-first-century counterparts is not a lack of scientific understanding but rather a surprisingly widespread unwillingness to accept science and, following its prescriptions, to implement and enforce policies that could stem the ruin wrought by environmental degradation and other hazards.

The adoption of regulations to prevent deadly fires and protect vulnerable coastlines, for instance, are both sensible and necessary, but corporations and developers often deem criminal and civil penalties worth risking to garner bigger profits, while political leaders overlook lapses in compliance in heedless pursuit of economic growth. The Hamlet, North Carolina, fire of 1991, which killed twenty-five workers and injured fifty-five others—all of whom were illegally locked in a flaming chicken processing factory—was one of the deadliest industrial fires in U.S. history, a horrific industrial debacle made both more likely and more fatal by the willful negligence of the factory's owners and the complicity of state and local governments. Political leaders and engineers likewise ignored the widely known fact that the levees in New Orleans were insufficient to protect the city and its people, accepting that risk and leaving thousands of its poorest citizens particularly vulnerable to Katrina, one of the deadliest hurricanes in U.S. history, with the deaths of more than 1,800 people as the tragic result.[18]

At the same time, many experts are now concluding that innovations in science, technology, and engineering have ultimately proven unable to realize the Enlightenment-inspired conceit that humans could—and should—wield complete mastery over the natural world. In some circles at least, greater understanding of the causes of so-called natural disasters has led to growing recognition of both the limits of humans' ability to control nature and the potential problems that even well-meaning interventions in the natural environment can cause. The leveling of hills and the filling in of waterways may have created welcome new neighborhoods for residents of San Francisco, but these areas became death traps when the earthquake pummeled that city in 1906. Federally sponsored engineers and experts built levees to constrain the mighty Mississippi River, converting natural wetlands into cotton-producing plantations, but their efforts also created a "pathological landscape" that featured recurring droughts and frequent floods—the worst of which was in 1927—and intensified outbreaks of malaria, yellow fever, and other deadly diseases. In 2018, six years after Superstorm Sandy, the Army Corps of Engineers proposed erecting a giant steel and concrete barrier to shield the coasts of New York and New Jersey from future storms, a plan that critics believe would cause significant environmental damage without attaining the desired objective.[19]

Sentiment, or the emotional response to disasters and their victims, also functions somewhat differently in a twenty-first-century context. Almost from the beginning, sympathy, together with a desire to preserve order, fueled disaster relief efforts. Sincere sensibility and Christian charity motivated Jonas Hanway's fund-raising campaign on behalf of Montreal's fire victims, a group he also hoped to convert into loyal subjects of the British Empire by virtue of his efforts. Generous assistance to Philadelphia's yellow fever victims aimed to ease their suffering while also keeping afflicted populations off the streets and out of trouble. But while earlier relief efforts at least rhetorically privileged sensibility over social control, these priorities now seem reversed. Government officials and media outlets almost reflexively construe disasters as sites of mob violence and disorder, though studies of specific disasters—by historians, journalists, sociologists, and others—have repeatedly proven that not to be the case and, indeed, suggest that paramilitary-style interventions often exacerbate problems in disaster-ravaged communities.[20]

Spectacularly unsuccessful federal efforts at disaster relief after Katrina and after Hurricane Maria in Puerto Rico have led some critics of the status quo to argue that, regardless of their undeniable need for outside assistance in the form of money and provisions, communities in crisis benefit more from grassroots relief programs, which can be more effective and less wasteful than their overly bureaucratized official counterparts. Citing evidence that communities pull together in mutual aid in times of crisis, such critics advocate a return to older forms of locally administered disaster relief, as well as to a culture of calamity that makes humanitarian concerns its chief priority. That vision is appealing, and the example of the nonprofit World Central Kitchen's impressive effort to help Puerto Ricans feed themselves after Hurricane Maria is both inspiring and instructive. Yet other examples of community-based disaster relief reveal an uglier side of local control: blatant discrimination, often racially based, as when San Francisco's civic leaders schemed to snatch prime real estate from their city's Chinese residents after the earthquake and when white southerners successfully used disasters in Charleston in 1886, Galveston in 1900, and New Orleans after Hurricane Betsy in 1965 (and forty years later after Katrina) as pretexts to further dispossess or disenfranchise African Americans.[21]

Access to information, the main precondition for the sympathetic feelings and benevolent acts that characterized the culture of disaster in the Atlantic world, also functions somewhat differently in a twenty-first-century context. Information used to be scarce and carefully curated; now it is free-flowing and abundant. The untrammeled spread of information, and the speed with which it travels, can help address inequities that are inherent in the politics of location. In 2017, for instance, horrific wildfires on the Great Plains received scant news coverage — especially in comparison to their California counterparts — despite the fact that they destroyed almost two million acres and killed at least seven people. But as locals employed social media to spread stories about the fires in Kansas and Oklahoma, relief poured into the area from across the country, especially from rural Americans who sent food, bottled water, feed for livestock, and other agricultural supplies. "The government didn't help us, but America did," one young woman observed, though FEMA, the U.S. Department of Agriculture, and state governments also eventually played important roles in responding to this ruinous disaster.[22]

Yet information that is immediate and abundant also has its downside. When disaster strikes, we are bombarded with stories — some accurate, some not — from a bewildering array of legitimate and spurious sources. Access to so much information can be an empowering force for good, inspiring international relief efforts for the famine in Ethiopia in the 1980s and, closer to home, significant changes in how FEMA operated after the Katrina debacle. But an excess of information in an age of seemingly unending disasters, coupled with an inability or unwillingness to critically assess its veracity, can also engender paralytic feelings of helplessness, apathy, and despair, or even antipathy, particularly toward sufferers whose culture, identity, or politics seems alien to our own. Overwhelmed by the enormity of the task at hand, especially when options for change appear problematic, it is tempting for many—either genuinely or cynically—to equate disaster prevention, amelioration, and relief with glibly ritualized offerings of thoughts and prayers.

ACKNOWLEDGMENTS

As a newcomer to the field of disaster history, I have benefited from the experience and insights of many people. Although it might be hyperbole to say that the project would have been a disaster without their advice and assistance, *Inventing Disaster* is surely much better because of it.

At the top of the list are Matthew Mulcahy and Gareth Davies, both important historians in the field of disaster studies whose work has informed my own and whom I was fortunate to have as readers for this project. *Inventing Disaster* improved as a result of the careful assessments of both readers, whose enthusiasm for the project and its potential significance is deeply gratifying. A historian of public policy who has written extensively on federal disaster relief, Gareth Davies offered useful insights from a perspective very different from my own. Matt Mulcahy read pieces of the book at various stages and eventually the entire manuscript. His detailed suggestions and comments, based on vast knowledge of the cultural and environmental history both of disasters and of early America generally, were uniquely valuable.

Others have read chapters or related work, providing helpful suggestions along the way. Susan Branson, Catherine Kerrison, and Jennifer Ritterhouse commented on several versions of my then quasi-baked research proposals. Emily Clark, who co-teaches a disaster history course at Tulane, provided helpful comments on an early ill-fated essay. Also in the early stages, Debbie Gershenowitz offered good advice about some chapters. Susan Branson's response to my introduction was a perfect combination of reassurance and criticism as the project neared completion.

Students, both graduates and undergraduates, in my disaster history seminars at George Mason University deserve more than the usual pro forma acknowledgment. Professorial nirvana happens when research informs our teaching and teaching informs our research. I have never had that experience more than in these classes, in which students researched and wrote about specific disasters—a Welsh mining explosion, an Alabama tornado, a recent oil spill in Maryland—and I learned from their projects. Some of these students' work is featured in an online Disaster History Archive (http://disasterhistoryarchive.cynthiakierner.org), a growing collection that also includes some of this book's illustrations. Thanks are also due to Megan Brett, doctoral student and queen of Omeka, for walking the students (and me) through that excellent open-source web-publishing platform developed and supported by my colleagues at the Roy Rosenzweig Center for History and New Media.

While writing syllabi and teaching courses helped me to puzzle out the narrative arc of *Inventing Disaster*, giving talks and presentations on specific themes and topics helped to refine the arguments in my chapters. Conference papers on shipwrecks, exploding steamboats, and imperial benevolence occasioned thoughtful questions and suggestions that informed my revisions of the manuscript's successive drafts. Insights from Susan Branson, Arthur Burns, Toby Ditz, Richard John, Alicia Maggard, Sarah Hand Meacham, Greg Nobles, Zachary Schrag, and Karin Wulf were especially valuable. And I am grateful to Megan Taylor Shockley, who invited me to give the annual lecture for the Southern Association for Women Historians at the Southern Historical Association meeting in 2017. Talking about the Richmond theater fire was great fun, and it also forced me to think more systematically about the deeply gendered nature of disasters, both as lived experiences and as culturally constructed narratives.

Over the years, telling people that I was writing a book about disasters has elicited an interesting range of reactions. Some asked if the book would include a hurricane, flood, or industrial accident that interested them particularly. Others wondered if my focus was only on "natural" disasters, prompting an impromptu lecture about how scholars now pretty much reject the idea that any disaster is entirely, and unavoidably, "natural."

The best responses came from those who, in the course of their own work, encountered disaster-related material, which they kindly passed on to me. Jon Kukla sent an eyewitness account of the 1755 New England earthquake. Angel Luke O'Donnell alerted me to a newspaper article about a fire in Barbados, which I would not have found myself. At the Virginia Historical Society, I first learned of the Great Fresh from archivist Lee Shepard. Cassandra Good sent letters about the Richmond theater fire from the papers of James Monroe, and Lee Benson offered citations from guidebooks that mentioned the fire's site as a possible tourist destination. Zach Schrag shared a reference about Philadelphia merchants collecting food for starving people in Cape Verde. Whitney Martinko told me about a painting depicting a hurricane that people paid to see in the 1830s. Susan Branson sent amazing, and sometimes bizarre, stories about and pictures of steam-powered devices. Sheri Huerta gave me an obscure book about historical disasters. George Oberle, who was always on the lookout for new disaster-related acquisitions at Mason's Fenwick Library, also told me about an 1848 cyclorama depicting the Lisbon earthquake. Finally, and maybe best of all, at the American Antiquarian Society Nan Wolverton showed me those remarkable English transferware plates bearing images of New York's Great Fire.

This project received institutional support from an impressive array of sources, for which I am truly grateful. A Mellon Research Fellowship from the Virginia Historical Society funded early work on the Richmond theater fire and the Great Fresh. Support from the American Antiquarian Society enabled me to immerse myself in its unparalleled collections of newspapers, broadsides, sermons, and other printed material that constitute the book's core research. As a Georgian Papers Fellow, I benefited from the support of the Omohundro Institute of Early American History and Culture, in partnership with the Royal Collection Trust and King's College London. Although I did not find exactly what I was looking for in the Round Tower at Windsor, what I did find there led me to think about imperial benevolence from different perspectives. Thanks go especially to Oliver Walton, Georgian Papers project manager and curator, and Rachael Krier, metadata creator, for guiding me toward relevant sources and for an utterly amazing experience, and to Her Majesty The Queen Elizabeth II for permission to use and cite them. At the International Center for Jefferson Studies at Monticello, Andrew Jackson O'Shaughnessy welcomed me with a fellowship and a quiet office where I wrote my fifth chapter. A study leave from the College of Humanities and Social Sciences at George Mason University gave me the time I needed to complete a draft of the entire book and to begin the first round of revisions.

Inventing Disaster includes many pictures—at least for a scholarly book—from a total of seventeen different libraries, museums, or other sources. Repositories that furnish digital images for publication at little or no cost to academic authors deserve praise and gratitude for the essential service they provide to both scholars and readers. The Library of Congress and the American Antiquarian Society are particularly rich, and generous, sources of images for historians of early America. In gathering the images for this book, Jan Kozak (Kozak Collection, NISEE Library), Marie Lamoureux (American Antiquarian Society), Christopher Lyons (McGill University), Carolyn Marvin (Portsmouth Athenaeum), and Meghan Townes (Library of Virginia) were especially helpful.

This book is my second project with the University of North Carolina Press. This time, even more than last, Chuck Grench's advice has been invaluable. At a time when I was unsure what exactly my project was and whether it was even doable, Chuck wisely urged me to produce a chapter outline to plan the book's trajectory. Although my overall plan has changed a fair amount since then, Chuck consistently has been an enthusiastic supporter of this project. I hope his confidence is well founded. Also at UNC, Dylan White has answered my questions promptly and given good practical advice, especially about those troublesome details that always seem to arise at the end of any project.

Finally, my family has lived with this project at least since Superstorm Sandy invaded the Jersey Shore. Tom, Zack, and Anders (and Brutus and Floyd) are all terrific, as are the members of my shore-centric extended family (Mom, Dad, Bob, Sandy, Danielle, Mike, and Ami). This book is dedicated to Anders not because I like him best but because he is probably the only one who will write his own book any time soon. I can't wait to read it.

Ocean Beach, N.J.
November 2018

NOTES

PREFACE

1. Ritchie and Roser, "Natural Disasters"; "Natural Disasters in 2017."
2. U.S. Government Accountability Office, *Federal Disaster Assistance* and *2017 Hurricanes and Wildfires*.

INTRODUCTION

1. The classic scholarly discussion of this problem of definition is Quarantelli, *What Is a Disaster?* For a recent example of FEMA officials' attempts to grapple with the issue by drawing on the scholarly literature on the subject, see Federal Emergency Management Agency, "Session 6: Defining Disaster."
2. Scholars working in a variety of fields cite this consensus. See, for instance, Hewitt, *Interpretations of Calamity*; Kent and Ratcliffe, *Responding to Catastrophes*; Anthony Oliver-Smith, "Theorizing Disaster: Nature, Culture, Power," in Hoffman and Oliver-Smith, *Catastrophe and Culture*, 23–47; and Milleti, *Disasters by Design*. See also the useful discussion in Steven Biel, introduction to Biel, *American Disasters*, 4–6.
3. Steinberg, *Acts of God*, 4.
4. McCullough, *Johnstown Flood*; Godbey, "Disaster Tourism and the Melodrama of Authenticity"; Hartnell, "Katrina Tourism and a Tale of Two Cities."
5. Lefebvre, *Introduction to Modernity*, 1–4.
6. "An Act To authorize Federal assistance to States and local governments in major disasters, and for other purposes," 30 Sept. 1950, *U.S. Statutes at Large*, 81st Cong., 2nd sess., 64:1109–11; G. Davies, "Emergence of a National Politics of Disaster"; Rozario, *Culture of Calamity*, 11–12, 150–55. The Mississippi flood of 1927 was the first disaster whose "mediascape" included radio, which Susan Scott Parrish observes provided the first bona fide "real-time virtual disaster coverage." Other changes that Parrish characterizes as "distinctly new" in 1927 — the vividness of news stories, the expression of critical and dissenting views, the commemoration of the disaster in music and other cultural forms — were to varying degrees equally applicable to Johnstown and other contemporary disasters. See Parrish, *Flood Year 1927*, esp. 11–12, 69–71.
7. Beck, *Risk Society*, esp. chaps. 1–2; Lübken and Mauch, "Uncertain Environments," 1–12. Gareth Davies argues that "a substantial body of routinized disaster politics already existed by 1950"; see his "Pre-modern Disaster Politics," 261–63.
8. Rozario, *Culture of Calamity*, 152–53; Lübken and Mauch, "Uncertain Environments," 4.

9. Rozario, *Culture of Calamity*, 10, 75–76. This cheery response did not go uncontested. See Dyl, *Seismic City*, esp. chap. 4.

10. Steinberg, *Acts of God*, xiv, xxi–xxv.

11. Steinberg, xvii–xix and chaps. 4–5; M. Davis, *Ecology of Fear*, esp. 50–55, 109, 143–47. For a specific case, see Horowitz, "Hurricane Betsy."

12. Sawislak, *Smoldering City*, 6–8, 16–17; Tierney et al., "Metaphors Matter"; Remes, *Disaster Citizenship*, 4–20; Andrés, *We Fed an Island*.

13. Neither Mulcahy nor Schwartz explicitly makes the connection between the unusual richness of their sources and the commercial and geopolitical value of these island colonies, but it strikes me as not coincidental that their excellent books, on similar topics, are by far the most detailed scholarly treatments we have of how early colonial settlers, governments, and societies responded to New World disasters. See Mulcahy, *Hurricanes and Society*; and Schwartz, *Sea of Storms*.

14. Sawislak, *Smoldering City*, 21–22. Conevery Bolton Valencius details the circulation of both oral and written accounts of the earthquakes and argues persuasively for their cultural and scientific significance (*Lost History of the New Madrid Earthquakes*, esp. chaps. 1 and 5). My point is simply that discussions about the Richmond theater fire, which occurred at roughly the same time, were far more pervasive and had a greater overall cultural impact.

15. M. Davis, *Ecology of Fear*, 5, 17–19.

CHAPTER 1

1. Anthony Oliver-Smith, "Theorizing Disasters: Nature, Power, and Culture," in Hoffman and Oliver-Smith, *Catastrophe and Culture*, 28–30.

2. The shipboard mortality rate for free passengers on the Atlantic crossing in the seventeenth century was approximately 10 percent. See Gemery, "Emigration from the British Isles to the New World," 187. On early English ventures in Ireland and the Americas, see Kupperman, *Jamestown Project*, chap. 6.

3. Percy, "True Relation," 266–67; Fiske, *Old Virginia and Her Neighbors*, 1:250–51. Population figures for the colony vary, but see Morgan, *American Slavery*, 101; Vaughan, *American Genesis*, 31–32, 60, 105, 120, 161; and Kupperman, "Apathy and Death," 24.

4. Vaughan, *American Genesis*, 25, 30; Morgan, *American Slavery*, 63–75.

5. White, *Cold Welcome*, 9–19, 98, 110–14; Fagan, *Little Ice Age*, chap. 6; Blanton, "Drought as a Factor in the Jamestown Colony," 76; Parker, *Global Crisis* and "Crisis and Catastrophe."

6. White, *Cold Welcome*, chap. 6; Carville V. Earle, "Environment, Disease, and Mortality in Early Virginia," in Tate and Ammerman, *Chesapeake in the Seventeenth Century*, 96–102; Kupperman, "Apathy and Death," 25, 32–35.

7. On the cultural work of modern disasters, see, for instance, Rozario, *Culture of Calamity*, 3, 10–14, 32; Knowles, "Lessons in the Rubble." On conflict among settlers in Jamestown specifically, see Horn, *Land as God Made It*, esp. 87–88, 99–100, 110–13, 129–30, 171–74; and Percy, "True Relation," 266–67, 268–69. On the Jamestown fire, see the letter from Francis Perkins, 28 Mar. 1608, in A. Brown, *Genesis of the United States*, 1:173.

8. Horn, *Land as God Made It*, 87–88, 99–100, 104–39, 171–80; Vaughan, *American Genesis*, chaps. 3–4.

9. Reported use of the related words "calamity" and "catastrophe" date to 1490 and 1579,

respectively. "Calamity" was often used in reference to an individual's misfortune, while "catastrophe" sometimes had humorous connotations. For historical uses of these terms, as well as of the word "disaster," see *Oxford English Dictionary Online*, Mar. 2019, http://www.oed.com/view/Entry/26161?redirectedFrom=calamity, http://www.oed.com/view/Entry/28794?redirectedFrom=catastrophe, and http://www.oed.com/view/Entry/53561?rskey=xSZ75n&result=1. Additional information on the use of the word "disaster" is based on a full-text search of the database Early English Books Online, but see also the discussion in Rozario, *Culture of Calamity*, 11–14.

10. See especially Steinberg, *Acts of God*, xiv. The quotations are from *Romeo and Juliet*, 3.2; *Hamlet*, 1.1; and *King Lear*, 1.2.

11. William Strachey, *True Reportory*, in Wright, *Voyage to Virginia in 1609*, 66; Culloford, *William Strachey*, 57–58; Betty Wood, "Strachey, William," *Oxford Dictionary of National Biography*, 2004, https://doi.org/10.1093/ref:odnb/26623; John Smith, *The Generall Historie of Virginia, New-England, and the Summer Isles*, in Barbour, *Complete Works of Captain John Smith*, 2:129, 137, 265, 299, 324–25, 331, 435, 436 37, 462.

12. John Smith, *A True Relation of Such Occurrences and Accidents of Noate as Hath Hapnd in Virginia . . .* , in Barbour, *Complete Works of Captain John Smith*, 1:33, 41, 97. On Smith's presidency of the colony, see Vaughan, *American Genesis*, chap. 3.

13. John Smith, *A Map of Virginia . . .* , in Barbour, *Complete Works of Captain John Smith*, 1:175, 176–77, 212, 278.

14. J. Smith, *Generall Historie*, 2:143–45, 169, 255–56, 327–32.

15. Letter of Gabriel Archer, 31 Aug. 1609, in A. Brown, *Genesis of the United States*, 1:328–32; Lord De La Warr and the council in Virginia to the Virginia Company of London, 7 July 1610, in A. Brown, 1:404–5; Sir Thomas Dale to Salisbury, 17 Aug. 1611, in A. Brown, 1:501–7; *The Relation of Lord De-la-ware*, in Tyler, *Narratives of Early Virginia*, 213; "Virginia Planters' Answer to Captain Butler," 1623, in Tyler, 409–19; "The Tragical Relation of the Virginia Assembly," 1624, in Tyler, 422–26; Silvester Jourdain, *Discovery of the Bermudas*, in Wright, *Voyage to Virginia in 1609*, 66–67, 73, 82.

16. Walsham, *Providence in Early Modern England*, 2–3, 9, 116–42; Thomas, *Religion and the Decline of Magic*, chap. 4; M. Todd, "Providence, Chance and the New Science," 701–2; Witmore, *Culture of Accidents*, 42–44, 90–91.

17. On Bermuda's bad reputation, see Glover and Smith, *Shipwreck That Saved Jamestown*, 125–28.

18. Strachey, *True Reportory*, esp. 8–9, 12, 16, 60, 66–70.

19. Strachey, *True Reportory*, 64–70, 95.

20. Council for Virginia, *True Declaration*, 46–47; William Crashaw, "Dedicatorie" to Whitaker, *Good Newes From Virginia*; Glover and Smith, *Shipwreck That Saved Jamestown*, 196–210.

21. Douglas Bradburn, "The Eschatological Origins of the English Empire," in Bradburn and Coombs, *Early Modern Virginia*, 28–32; P. Miller, "Religious Impulse," 509–14, 521–22; John Parker, "Religion and the Virginia Colony," 1607–1610," in Andrews et al., *Westward Enterprise*, 247–54, 269–70; Vaughn, "'Expulsion of the Salvages,'" 60–62, 68–74.

22. Quoted in P. Miller, "Religious Impulse," 506.

23. Crashaw, *Sermon preached in London*, esp. F4 recto, G2 recto, I3 recto and verso; W. H. Kelliher, "Crashawe [Crashaw], William," *Oxford Dictionary of National Biography*, 2009, https://doi.org/10.1093/ref:odnb/6623; Porter, "Alexander Whitaker," 332.

24. Alexander Whitaker to William Crashaw, 9 Aug. 1611, in A. Brown, *Genesis of the*

United States, 1:497–500; Whitaker, *Good Newes From Virginia*, 22–24; Porter, "Alexander Whitaker."

25. Council for Virginia, *True and Sincere Declaration*, esp. 4, 10, 15; Council for Virginia, *Briefe Declaration*, 2–3, 4.

26. Donegan, *Seasons of Misery*, 72; Marx, *Machine in the Garden*, 36–46; Lovejoy, "Satanizing the American Indian."

27. Donegan, *Seasons of Misery*, esp. 2–6, 72, 88; Wingfield, *Discourse of Virginia*, 29; letter of John Pory, 1619, in Tyler, *Narratives of Early Virginia*, 282, 283, 286. On plows and cattle as perceived evidence of order and English cultural superiority, see V. Anderson, *Creatures of Empire*, esp. chap. 3.

28. Morgan, *American Slavery*, 126–29; Kingsbury, *Records of the Virginia Company*, 4:38, 58–62.

29. Donegan, *Seasons of Misery*, 69–72, 90–96, 101–5; Percy, "True Relation," 260–61.

30. Slack, *Impact of Plague*, 2–37, 199, 216; Slack, "Dearth and Social Policy"; Outhwaite, *Dearth, Public Policy and Social Disturbance*, 32–35; White, *Cold Welcome*, 132–34; Witmore, *Culture of Accidents*, 132–33; Thomas, *Religion and the Decline of Magic*, 79–81, 85–87; M. Todd, "Providence, Chance and the New Science," 700, 706–8. Among corporate and proprietary colonies, Jamestown was not unique in this regard. See Schwartz, *Sea of Storms*, 49, 63–69.

31. Earle, "Environment, Disease," 106–9; Donegan, *Seasons of Misery*, 79–80.

32. Pettegree, *Invention of News*, 220; McMurtrie, *First Printing in Virginia*, 3–4, 8. The press established by William Nuthead in Jamestown in 1682 was unauthorized and soon shut down by the government.

33. Morgan, *American Slavery*, 93–101; 68–74; Vaughan, "'Expulsion of the Salvages'"; Kupperman, *Jamestown Project*, 267–73, 278–304; Copland, *Virginia's God be Thanked*, 10, 25–26. Detailed accounts of the Opechancanough-led attack can be found in Horn, *Land as God Made It*, chap. 9; and Rountree, *Pocahontas*, chap. 16.

34. *Oxford English Dictionary Online*, Mar. 2019, http://www.oed.com/view/Entry/114675?rskey=TUEQ7L&result=1. Information on the use of the word "massacre" is based on a full-text search of the database Early English Books Online. On the St. Bartholomew's Day Massacre, see generally Diefendorf, *Beneath the Cross*, esp. chap. 6. On the Marian martyrs, see Freeman, "Foxe's Marian Martyrs." Games, "Violence on the Fringes," examines the evolution of the term among the English in a global context after 1622.

35. Horn, *Land as God Made It*, chap. 9; Rountree, *Pocahontas*, chap. 17.

36. *The Virginia Planters' Answer to Captain Butler*, in Tyler, *Narratives of Early Virginia*, 409–19; *The Discourse of the Old Company*, in Tyler, 437–42. On the defense and dissolution of the company, see Vaughan, *American Genesis*, chap. 9; and Craven, *Dissolution of the Virginia Company*, chaps. 9–10.

37. Purchas, *Hakluytus Posthumus*, 19:224–25, 228–31; David Armitage, "Purchas, Samuel," *Oxford Dictionary of National Biography*, 2007, https://doi.org/10.1093/ref:odnb/22898.

38. Waterhouse, *Declaration of the State of the Colony*, 14–15, 18–19, 20, 22.

39. This catalog of cultural production pertaining to the massacre is from Games, "Violence on the Fringes," 519–20.

40. Brooke, "Poem on the Late Massacre," 263–64, 280–81.

41. Brooke, "Poem on the Late Massacre," 264–65, 283–84; Waterhouse, *Declaration of the State of the Colony*, 15–17.

42. Brooke, "Poem on the Late Massacre," 276.

43. Waterhouse, *Declaration of the State of the Colony*, 34.

44. Brooke, "Poem on the Late Massacre," 269, 274, 276, 285–92; Waterhouse, *Declaration of the State of the Colony*, 34. On the didactic uses of horror, see N. Davis, "Rites of Violence," 55–56.

CHAPTER 2

1. Greene's use of the word "disaster" was also only the third recorded instance overall, according to a full-text search of the database Early English Books Online (EEBO).

2. Morrison, *Shipwrecked*, esp. 4–7; Landow, *Images of Crisis*, 75–84. Between 1762 and 1800, Falconer's poem appeared in twenty-one separate London editions; it was also published twice in Philadelphia (in 1774 and 1788) and Dublin (1777 and 1790), as well as once in Baltimore (1796) and New York (1800). Sometimes its title varied slightly. The poem was also frequently republished, either alone or in anthologies, during the nineteenth century. See Jones, *Poetical Works of William Falconer*, 13–45.

3. Scholarly studies of shipwreck narratives include Duffy, *Shipwreck and Empire*; Huntress, *Narratives of Shipwrecks*; Lincoln, "Shipwreck Narratives"; Blackmore, *Manifest Perdition*; Sievers, "Drowned Pens and Shaking Hands"; and Mitchell-Cook, *Sea of Misadventures*.

4. Ratcliffe, "Bells, Barrels, and Bullion," 35–36, 44–45; *Maryland Gazette*, 24 Feb.–3 Mar. 1730; Mitchell-Cook, *Sea of Misadventures*, 30.

5. Chetwood, *Voyages and Adventures of Captain Robert Boyle*, 333; Wilkinson, *Seaman's Preservation*, 3–4; Wilkinson, *Tutamen Nauticum*, 1; Mitchell-Cook, *Sea of Misadventures*, 30.

6. Berry, *Path in Mighty Waters*, 2, 208, 210, 243; Colley, *Britons*, 71, 88–94; Purvis, *Colonial America*, 134, 145, 152, 161, 165; Fogelman, "Migrations to the Thirteen British North American Colonies," 698; D. Vickers, *Young Men and the Sea*, 8, 24, 77–80, 145.

7. Duffy, *Shipwreck and Empire*, 4–10, 22–25, 37, 47; Blackmore, *Manifest Perdition*, x–xxiii, 26, 116–17. See also Mancall's introduction to his *Travel Narratives*, 3–48.

8. Huntress, *Narratives of Shipwrecks*, 220; Wright, *Voyage to Virginia in 1609*, xxii, xxvii.

9. Sievers, "Drowned Pens and Shaking Hands," 752–54.

10. Publication data is based on searches in the Early English Books Online and Early American Imprints databases. Oddly, Cotton Mather's *A Token, for the Children of New-England . . .* (Boston, 1700), appears only in EEBO. See also Harold Love, "Parkhurst, Thomas," *Oxford Dictionary of National Biography*, 2004, https://doi.org/10.1093/ref :odnb/21366. Parkhurst was listed as bookseller on the title page of many of Janeway's publications, as well as on that of the 1687 edition of Mather's book. On the colonial book trade, see James Raven, "The Importation of Books in the Eighteenth Century," in Amory and Hall, *History of the Book in America*, 183–97.

11. The latter, 1708, London edition of *A Token for Mariners: Containing Many Famous and Wonderful Instances of God's Providence in Sea Dangers and Deliverances, in Mercifully Preserving the Lives of His Poor Creatures . . .* does not appear in EEBO.

12. Janeway, *Mr. James Janeway's Legacy*, esp. A2–A3, 103–4.

13. Janeway, *Mr. James Janeway's Legacy*, 1–9; I. Mather, *Essay for the Recording of Illustrious Providences*, 15–17; C. Mather, *Magnalia Christi Americana*, 2:345–46. The legal scholar A. W. Brian Simpson has argued that this sort of "survival cannibalism" was the "custom of the sea" and that stories of maritime cannibalism that featured the drawing of

lots remained common into the nineteenth century. See Simpson, *Cannibalism and the Common Law*, esp. 141, 144–45.

14. Janeway, *Mr. James Janeway's Legacy*, 9, 128–30.

15. I. Mather, *Essay for the Recording of Illustrious Providences*, preface; Sievers, "Drowned Pens and Shaking Hands," 743–44, 759, 775–77. See also P. Miller, "Errand into the Wilderness."

16. I. Mather, *Essay for the Recording of Illustrious Providences*, 1–15; Sievers, "Drowned Pens and Shaking Hands, 744.

17. I. Mather, *Essay for the Recording of Illustrious Providences*, chap. 10; D. Anderson, *William Bradford's Books*, 177–78; Bradford, *Of Plymouth Plantation*, 313; C. Mather, *Magnalia Christi Americana*, 1:366. More generally, see Middlekauff, *Mathers*, 139–48, 291–300; Hall, *Worlds of Wonder*, chap. 2.

18. C. Mather, *Compassions Called For*, 10–11.

19. Lawson, *Threnodia*.

20. C. Mather, *Compassions Called For*, 7–11, 18–21, 58–60. On the controversial wreck of the *Nottingham Galley*, see Erickson, "'To Obviate a Scandalous Reflection'"; Simpson, *Cannibalism and the Common Law*, 114–16.

21. On sensibility, see, for instance, J. Todd, *Sensibility*, 6–8, 10–14, 21–28; Barker-Benfield, *Culture of Sensibility*, esp. xviii–xxviii; and Eustace, *Passion Is the Gale*, esp. 259–66, 483.

22. Dickinson, *God's Protecting Providence*, 1–6, 11–14, 15–28, 46. On the common, but also complicated, identification of cleanliness with Englishness and filth with savagery, see K. Brown, *Foul Bodies*, esp. 70–80, 152–58.

23. Dickinson, *God's Protecting Providence*, preface (unpaginated). On the production of the Philadelphia edition, see Andrews and Andrews, *Jonathan Dickinson's Journal*, 204–5.

24. For the various editions of Dickinson's narrative, with images of their title pages, see Andrews and Andrews, *Jonathan Dickinson's Journal*, 163–96.

25. Huntress, *Narratives of Shipwrecks*, 221–25. No new narratives appeared until 1780, but thirteen were published in the ensuing decade, the hiatus coinciding more or less with the duration of the British-American war.

26. Vanek, "Uses of Travel"; Morrison, *Shipwrecked*, 102–22; Mitchell-Cook, *Sea of Misadventures*, 100–101; *Catalogue of the books belonging to the Library Company of Philadelphia*, 97–99. Literary criticism pertaining to *Robinson Crusoe* is vast, but for a representative sampling, see the essays in the Norton Critical Edition of Defoe's work, edited by Michael Shinagel.

27. Bailey, *God's Wonders*, 3. Bailey's narrative was reprinted in Boston, also in 1750.

28. [Webb], *Authentic Narrative*; *Gentleman's Magazine* 27 (1757): 553–59, 599–603. Webb's account was also included in Plaisted, *Journal from Calcutta*; and Barrow, *Collection of Authentic, Useful, and Entertaining Voyages*. The quotations here are from a newspaper account of the incident, which will be discussed below (*London Evening Post*, 7–9 June 1757).

29. [Webb], *Authentic Narrative*, esp. 5–7, 6–18, 20, 25, 28. The New York edition cited here also bears a quotation from the Psalms on its title page: "They that go down to the Sea in Ships . . . see the Works of the Lord, and his Wonders in the Deep." This epigraph does not appear in the original London publication. On the man of feeling, see J. Todd, *Sensibility*, chap. 6; and Barker-Benfield, *Culture of Sensibility*, 247–50.

30. [Webb], *Authentic Narrative*, 8–9. On women as victims of shipwrecks in life and literature, see, for instance, Mitchell-Cook, *Sea of Misadventures*, 100–101, 105; Burg, "'Women and Children First'"; and Stilgoe, *Lifeboat*, 234–42.

31. *London Evening Post*, 7–9 June 1757.

32. A presumably incomplete list of the periodicals that published Jones's account includes *Boston News-Letter*, 25 Aug. 1757; *Virginia Gazette*, 2 Sept. 1757; *New-York Gazette, or Weekly Post-Boy*, 5 Sept. 1757; and *Universal Magazine* 20 (1757): 276–77. On newspapers as vehicles for the spread of polite culture in provincial America, see Charles E. Clark, "Periodicals and Politics," in Amory and Hall, *History of the Book in America*, 355.

33. Pettegree, *Invention of News*, 167–68, 220, 238–47; Steele, *English Atlantic*, chap. 8; Clark, "Periodicals and Politics," 350–53.

34. Pettegree, *Invention of News*, 246–47; Clark, "Periodicals and Politics," 354; *Boston News-Letter*, 17–24 Apr., 24–31 July 1704.

35. Based on full-text searches for "hurricane" and "tempest" (a common contemporary synonym for "hurricane") in the America's Historical Newspapers database.

36. *American Weekly Mercury* (Philadelphia), 14 Nov. 1723; *Boston Gazette*, 30 July–6 Aug. 1733, 13 Nov. 1738; *Boston News-Letter*, 16 Nov. 1738.

37. *American Weekly Mercury*, 7 July 1720; *Maryland Gazette*, 24 June–1 July 1729.

38. See Nord, "Teleology and News." Both Matthew Mulcahy and Stuart B. Schwartz argue persuasively that the frequency of hurricanes in the Caribbean divested them of their potentially providential meaning. See Mulcahy, *Hurricanes and Society*, chap. 1; and Schwartz, *Sea of Storms*, 31–32, 38–42.

39. *Boston News-Letter*, 11–18 Aug. 1737; *Pennsylvania Gazette*, 25 Aug.–1 Sept. 1737; P. Griffin, *People with No Name*, esp. chaps. 3–4.

40. *Boston News-Letter*, 11–18 Aug. 1737; *Pennsylvania Gazette*, 25 Aug.–1 Sept. 1737.

41. *Boston News-Letter*, 11–18 Aug. 1737; *Pennsylvania Gazette*, 25 Aug.–1 Sept. 1737; J. Todd, *Sensibility*, 21–23.

42. *Boston Post-Boy*, 20 June 1743; "An Account of the Misfortune of the Ship *Dolphin*," *Gentleman's Magazine* 1 (1731): 406; "Letters Concerning the Burning of the *Prince George*," *Gentleman's Magazine* 28 (1758): 228. Eyewitness accounts of the wreck of the *Prince George* also appeared in *Annual Register* 1 (1759): 306; *Scots Magazine* 20 (1758): 272; *Boston Weekly Advertiser*, 31 July 1758.

43. On the Robinsonades, some of which appeared within months of Defoe's novel, see Fisher, "Innovation and Imitation," 99–103, 108–9; and also "Daniel Defoe's *Robinson Crusoe* and the Robinsonades."

44. W. Jones, *Poetical Works of William Falconer*, 1–14; Joseph, "William Falconer"; review of *The Shipwreck*, in *Critical Review* 13 (1762): 440. The 1774 Philadelphia edition featured the expanded subtitle.

45. *American Weekly Mercury*, 3 Aug. 1721.

46. I. Vickers, *Defoe and the New Sciences*, 65–68, 132–34; Guilhamet, *Defoe and the Whig Novel*, 15, 18–19, 133–35, 142, 144–47; G. A. Starr, "Defoe and Disasters," in Johns, *Dreadful Visitations*, 35–38, 46–47; Defoe, *Journal of the Plague Year*, 11.

47. Defoe, *Journal of the Plague Year*, 3–4, 226; Mayer, "Reception of a Journal of the Plague Year"; Starr, "Defoe and Disasters," 38–39.

48. Levy, *Freaks of Fortune*, 1–3, 29–30, 43–45; Thomas, *Religion and the Decline of Magic*, 649–56; Kingston, "Marine Insurance," 392–93; Kingston, "Governance and Institutional

Change in Marine Insurance," 2–3, 12–13, 15; Crothers, "Commercial Risk," 610–11. Some shipwreck narratives may have dwelled on technical details in part because their authors needed to furnish insurers with precise information about the wreck and its causes.

49. Stevenson, *World's Lighthouses*, 5–10, 17–21, 36–38, 97–109, 133–41, 155–58.

50. Lindberg, "From Private to Public Provision."

51. Stevenson, *World's Lighthouses*, 173–80, 183.

52. *Charter Granted By Their Majesties King William and Queen Mary*, 184; Scott, "Sandy Hook Lighthouse"; *New-York Gazette*, 7 Feb. 1757; *American Weekly Mercury*, 26 Nov.–3 Dec. 1741. The Stono Rebellion, which occurred in September–October 1739, was the largest slave uprising in the British mainland colonies, resulting in the deaths of about twenty whites and forty blacks (Mark M. Smith, "Introduction: Finding Stono," in M. Smith, *Stono*, xiv). On white South Carolinians' desire to expand slavery southward and their antipathy toward the Georgia trustees, see McIlvenna, *Short Life of Free Georgia*, 84–91. In 1752, the Crown abolished the trusteeship and Georgia became a royal colony.

53. Stevenson, *World's Lighthouses*, 31–58.

54. "A Method for Preventing Ships from Sinking," *Universal Magazine of Knowledge and Pleasure* 24 (1759): 211–12.

55. "Account of the Hydraspis," *Gentleman's Magazine* 17 (1747): 387–89; Zohn and Davis, "Johann Christoph Wagenseil."

56. "Account of the Hydraspis," 388; "Substance of the Memorial which M. de Graffin has laid before the Royal Academy of Sciences," *Gentleman's Magazine* 20 (1750): 246; *Pennsylvania Gazette*, 5 Oct. 1752; *New-York Gazette*, 9 Oct. 1752; *Boston Post-Boy*, 23 Oct. 1752.

57. Wilkinson, *Seaman's Preservation*, xi–xx, 3–4; Wilkinson, *Tutamen Nauticum*, ii, xiv; M. Wesley, "Early Lifesavers."

CHAPTER 3

1. The most complete accounts of the Lisbon earthquake are Molesky, *This Gulf of Fire*; Shrady, *Last Day*; and Kendrick, *Lisbon Earthquake*. On the estimated death toll, see also Aguirre, "Better Disaster Statistics." For John Adams and the Cape Ann, Massachusetts, earthquake of 18 November, see Ebel, "Cape Ann, Massachusetts Earthquake"; and Butterfield et al., *Diary and Autobiography of John Adams*, 1:1.

2. On Lisbon as the "first modern disaster," see, for instance, Dynes, "Lisbon Earthquake"; A. Betâmio de Almeida, "The 1755 Lisbon Earthquake and the Genesis of the Risk Management Concept," in Mendes-Victor et al., *Lisbon Earthquake*, 147–48, 153–57; and Rozario, *Culture of Calamity*, 13–20.

3. Musson, "History of British Seismology," 717–24, 727–34; Grey, *Chronological and Historical Account*; Grey, *Farther Account*. On the cultural impact of the 1580 earthquake, see Walsham, *Providence in Early Modern England*, 130–35.

4. Parrish, *American Curiosity*, esp. 15–21; Rappaport, "Hooke on Earthquakes"; Mulcahy, "Port Royal Earthquake," 405–6; Charles Walker, "Shaking the Unstable Empire: The Lima, Quito, and Arequipa Earthquakes, 1746, 1783, and 1797," in Johns, *Dreadful Visitations*, 115–16. The English edition of this account, wrongly attributed to the Jesuit Pedro Lozano, is *True and Particular Relation of the Dreadful Earthquake Which Happen'd at Lima*, which was published first in London (1748) and then in Philadelphia (1749). See also Walker, *Shaky Colonialism*, 6–7, 17.

5. Golinski, *British Weather*, 54–55, 79–80; Macadam, "English Weather," 245; Chenoweth et al., "Pioneer in Tropical Meteorology," 1957–59; Kupperman, "Puzzle of the American Climate"; White, "Unpuzzling American Climate," 548–49. More generally, see Appleby, *Shores of Knowledge*; and Parrish, *American Curiosity*.

6. [Crouch], *General History of Earthquakes*, esp. 3–4, 6–10, 171–77.

7. Mulcahy, "Port Royal Earthquake."

8. Winiarski, *Darkness Falls on the Land of Light*, 53–57; Seeman, *Pious Persuasions*, 149–52; W. Andrews, "Literature of the 1727 New England Earthquake," 281–89.

9. Davison, *History of British Earthquakes*, 333–36; Chandler, *Scripture Account*, esp. 6, 42. On Chandler, see also John Stephens, "Chandler, Samuel," *Oxford Dictionary of National Biography*, 2009, https://doi.org/10.1093/ref:odnb/5109.

10. Davison, *History of British Earthquakes*, 1–2; McCormmach, *Weighing the World*, 78–79; Flowers et al., "18th-Century Earthquakes"; *Gentleman's Magazine* 20 (Apr. 1750): 169–72; *Advice to England; or, Resolution*, esp. pp. 7–12. On Leibniz, Pope, and philosophical optimism, see Kendrick, *Lisbon Earthquake*, chap. 7.

11. Walker, *Shaky Colonialism*, 17–18, 68–69; *True and Particular Relation of the Dreadful Earthquake Which Happen'd at Lima*, esp. 117–31, 182–97.

12. Araújo, "Lisbon Earthquake of 1755," 1; Boxer, *Some Contemporary Reactions*, 11. Mark Molesky's exhaustive bibliography includes sixty-seven titles for stand-alone volumes in seven languages (Portuguese, English, Spanish, French, German, Italian, and Dutch). See Molesky, *This Gulf of Fire*, 438–45.

13. Molesky, *This Gulf of Fire*, chap. 7; Kendrick, *Lisbon Earthquake*, 213–14; *Whitehall Evening Post or London Intelligencer*, 22–25 Nov. 1755.

14. *Boston Gazette*, 22 Dec. 1755; *Boston Evening-Post*, 22 Dec. 1755; *New-York Mercury*, 29 Dec. 1755; *Pennsylvania Gazette*, 8 Jan. 1756; *Maryland Gazette*, 15 Jan. 1756; *South Carolina Gazette*, 29 Jan. 1756; Robert Hunter Morris to Jonathan Belcher, 29 Dec. 1755, *Pennsylvania Archives*, 2:530.

15. *New-York Mercury*, 9, 16, 23 Feb., 22 Mar., 5, 12, 19, 26 Apr., 10, 24 May, 25 Oct. 1756; 9 Oct., 11 Dec. 1758. The king's chief minister, Pombal, amassed dictatorial powers in the aftermath of the earthquake, in part by earning gratitude for his efforts to restore order and rebuild the ruined city. On Pombal's "reign of terror" and the expulsion of the Jesuits, see Molesky, *This Gulf of Fire*, 343–53; and more generally Maxwell, *Pombal*.

16. Araújo, "Lisbon Earthquake of 1755," 3–8; Boxer, *Some Contemporary Reactions*, 17; D'Haen, "On How Not to Be Lisbon"; Larsen, "Lisbon Earthquake"; Molesky, *This Gulf of Fire*, 322–43.

17. Abrams, *Natural Supernaturalism*, 98–102; Kozak and James, "Historical Depictions." See also the excellent Earthquake Engineering Online Archive, NISEE e-Library, which includes forty-eight contemporary European images of the Lisbon earthquake and its aftermath. Another print, not in the NISEE collection, is *An Authentic VIEW of LISBON, just as the Dreadful Earthquake began and as it ended*, in the Picture Collection of the Royal Library, Windsor. For images of London fire, see "The Great Fire of London, 1666."

18. Hunter, *Historical Account of Earthquakes*, esp. 1–12, 56, 68–71, 76–80.

19. *Boston Gazette*, 8 Jan. 1756; *Pennsylvania Gazette*, 6 May 1756; *Maryland Gazette*, 20 May 1756; Samuel Davies, "The Religious Improvement of the Late Earthquake," in S. Davies, *Sermons on Important Subjects*, 79–93; K. Murphy, "Prodigies and Portents," 401–7, 412–15. For the proclamation of George II, which appeared in both English and colonial newspapers, see, for instance, *London Gazette*, 16–20 Dec. 1755; *Whitehall Evening*

Post or London Intelligencer, 20–23 Dec. 1755; *Maryland Gazette,* 8 Apr. 1756; and *New-York Mercury,* 12 Apr. 1756.

20. Flowers et al., "18th-Century Earthquakes"; Wesley and Wesley, *Hymns occasioned by the earthquake;* J. Wesley, *Some Serious Thoughts,* 11–15, 24–26; Whitefield, *Letter from a Clergyman,* 5–8, 11, 15–17.

21. Ashton, *Sermon Preached on Occasion of the General Fast,* 14; *True and Particular Account of the Late Dreadful Earthquake at Lisbon;* Hunter, *National Wickedness,* 12–13, 18; *Address to the Inhabitants of Great-Britain,* 2, 4. See also S. Clark, *Sermon Preached at Daventry,* 14–17; and Alcock, *Sermon on the Late Earthquakes,* 1–5.

22. *Lines Made After the Great Earthquake;* Dexter, *Extracts from the Itineraries and Other Miscellanies of Ezra Stiles,* 1; John Winthrop to Ezra Stiles, 17 Apr. 1756, in Dexter, 595; Robles, "Atlantic Disaster."

23. Freke, *Plain Account of the Cause of Earthquakes,* 2–16; Alcock, *Sermon on the Late Earthquakes,* 21.

24. Pennington, *Serious Call to Repentance,* 4, 10.

25. Burt, *Earthquakes,* 7; Mayhew, *Expected Dissolution of All Things,* 57–58; Chauncy, *Earthquakes a Token of the righteous Anger of God,* 8–9; Biddulph, *Poem on the Earthquake at Lisbon,* 9.

26. Halifax, *Sermon Preach'd in St. John's Chapel,* 14–15; Moss, *Sermon Preached at the Parish Church of St. James,* 8–9; Foxcroft, *Earthquake, A Divine Visitation,* 41; *Reflections Physical and Moral,* esp. 1–10, 30–33.

27. Molesky, *This Gulf of Fire,* 335–43; Almeida, "The 1755 Lisbon Earthquake and the Genesis of the Risk Management Concept," 147–59; Maria do Rosário Themudo Barata, "The Lisbon Earthquake of November 1st, 1755: An Historical Overview of Its Approach," in Mendes-Victor et al., *Lisbon Earthquake,* 26–38; Montluzin, "'Every Body Apprehended an Earthquake'"; Winthrop, *Lecture on Earthquakes;* Ebel, "Cape Ann, Massachusetts Earthquake."

28. Shapiro, *Culture of Fact,* esp. 112–27, 165–67; McCormmach, *Weighing the World,* 82–94, 113–15; Graham, "Scientific Piety of John Winthrop," 112–16; Winthrop, *Lecture on Earthquakes.* See also Tilton, "Lightning-Rods and the Earthquake of 1755."

29. Voltaire, *Poem upon the Lisbon Disaster,* 13; Rozario, *Culture of Calamity,* 13–17; Kendrick, *Lisbon Earthquake,* chap. 2.

30. Thomas W. Lacqueur, "Bodies, Details, and the Humanitarian Narrative," in Hunt, *New Cultural History,* 176–204; Halttunen, "Humanitarianism and the Pornography of Pain," 303–10.

31. *Whitehall Evening Post or London Intelligencer,* 22–25 Nov. 1755; *Boston Gazette,* 22 Dec. 1755; *Boston Evening-Post,* 22 Dec. 1755.

32. *Boston Gazette, or Country Journal,* 12 Jan. 1756; *New-York Mercury,* 19 Jan. 1756; *Pennsylvania Gazette,* 22 Jan. 1756; *South Carolina Gazette,* 5 Feb. 1756.

33. Figueiredo, *Narrative of the earthquake and fire of Lisbon,* 5–6, 13–14, 17–18.

34. "Letter from a Gentleman, dated Lisbon Harbour," "Other Letters from Lisbon Harbour," "Effects of the Earthquake . . . ," and "Farther Particulars relating to the Earthquake at Lisbon," all in *Gentleman's Magazine* 25 (Dec. 1755): 558, 561, 564, 592; Lacqueur, *Work of the Dead,* 4, 102–3.

35. "Farther Particulars relating to the Earthquake at Lisbon," 592; "Other Letters from Lisbon Harbour," 560; "Letter from a Gentleman, dated Lisbon Harbour," 558; "Account of the Earthquake at Lisbon," *Gentleman's Magazine* 25 (Dec. 1755): 594; "An Account of

the late Earthquake at Lisbon," *Miscellaneous Correspondence in Prose & Verse* 1 (Dec. 1755): 220–22.

36. *Account of the late Dreadful Earthquake and Fire.* On this aspect of captivity narratives, see Ben-Zvi, "Ethnography and the Production of Foreignness."

37. *Account of the late Dreadful Earthquake and Fire*, 5, 11–12, 21–22.

38. *Account of the late Dreadful Earthquake and Fire*, 13–17. See also *Two Very Circumstantial Accounts of the Late Dreadful Earthquake at Lisbon*, 5–7, 11–12; *Boston News-Letter*, 19 Feb. 1756; and *South Carolina Gazette*, 18 Mar. 1756.

39. Molesky, *This Gulf of Fire*, 266–67; *Satirical Review of the Manifold Falshoods*, 76–77.

40. *Account of the late Dreadful Earthquake and Fire*, 11–12; "Farther Particulars relating to the Earthquake at Lisbon," 591; *Address to the Inhabitants of Great-Britain*, 28–30; Hunter, *Historical Account of Earthquakes*, 76–79; *An Authentic VIEW of LISBON* (text).

41. "Account of the late Earthquake at Lisbon," 221; *New-York Mercury*, 26 Apr. 1756; *Pennsylvania Gazette*, 6 May 1756.

42. Sirota, *Christian Monitors*; Prochaska, *Royal Bounty*, 2–19; Moniz, *From Empire to Humanity*, chap. 1; P. Clark, *British Clubs and Societies*, 80–83, 105–9, 352–54; Colley, *Britons*, 88–98; Hancock, *Citizens of the World*, chap. 9; Bridenbaugh, *Cities in Revolt*, 319–25.

43. Mulcahy, "'Great Fire' of 1740," 136–41.

44. Cobbett, *Cobbett's Parliamentary History of England*, 15:543–44; *Whitehall Evening Post or London Intelligencer*, 27–29 Nov., 29 Nov.–2 Dec. 1755; "His Majesty's most Gracious Message to the House of Lords," *London Magazine: or, Gentleman's Monthly Intelligencer* 24 (Dec. 1755): 587; "The following Message from his Majesty . . . ," *Miscellaneous Correspondence in Prose & Verse* 1 (Dec. 1755): 206.

45. *Poem on the Late Earthquake at Lisbon*, 7–8; "On the Late Earthquake at Lisbon," *Universal Magazine of Knowledge and Pleasure* 19 (Dec. 1756): 319–20. For British government expenditures, see Brewer, *Sinews of Power*, 40–42.

46. Gibbons, *Sermon Preached at Haberdashers-Hall*, 16–17, 32.

47. Gibbons, *Sermon Preached at Haberdashers-Hall*, 32. On British patriotism after the defeat of the Stuart rebellion in 1745, see Colley, *Britons*, 85–98. A recent revisionist biography of George II emphasizes his adeptness in matters of foreign policy. See Thompson, *George II*.

48. Anguish, *Sermon preached at St. Nicholas*, 6–7. See also Anguish, *Allegiance and Support*.

49. Clark, *Sermon Preached at Daventry*, 8–9, 18; Nowell, *Sermon preached at the Parish Church of Wolsingham*, 6–7; *Poem on the Late Earthquake at Lisbon*, 8; *Satirical Review of the Manifold Falshoods*, 5–7, 78–82, 93.

50. *Pennsylvania Gazette*, 12 Feb., 8 Apr., 6 May 1756; *Boston Evening-Post*, 9 Feb., 22 Mar. 1756; *New-York Mercury*, 16 Feb., 12 Apr. 1756; *South Carolina Gazette*, 12 Feb., 18 Mar. 1756.

51. McConville, *King's Three Faces*, esp. 75–78, 131–38; Colley, *Britons*, 85–98, 202–3.

52. Colley, *Britons*, 228–29; Chandler, *Character of a Great and Good King*, 27; Haven, *Supreme Influence of the Son of God, in . . . terminating the reign of Princes*, 19; S. Cooper, *Sermon upon the Occasion of the Death of our Late Sovereign*, 26. See also Jewel Spangler, "American Mourning: Catastrophe, Public Grief, and the Making of Civic Identity in the Early National South," in Friend and Glover, *Death and the American South*, 90–91.

53. S. Davies, *Sermon Delivered at Nassau-Hall*, 13, 19–20. Other editions of this sermon were published in New York and Philadelphia.

54. "A Remarkable Preservation in the Great Earthquake at Lisbon," *Moral & Entertaining Magazine* 1 (June 1777): 171; *Account of the Earthquake Which Destroyed the City of Lisbon*; Cato, "To the Public," in *Poughkeepsie Country Journal* (supplement), 19 Dec. 1787, in Kaminski et al., *Documentary History of the Ratification of the Constitution*; "The Cyclorama," *Illustrated London News*, 30 Dec. 1848, 428.

55. Coelho and Howard, "The Image of Portugal in British Travel Literature"; Baretti, *Journey from London to Genoa*, 1:137, 144–45. On the role of such representations in popularizing another disaster site, see Kovacs, "Pompeii and Its Material Reproductions."

CHAPTER 4

1. Marshall, "Who Cared About the Thirteen Colonies?"; Armstrong, "Dissenting Deputies"; Sirota, *Christian Monitors*, esp. 4–7, 249–50; Prochaska, *Royal Bounty*, 2–19; Moniz, *From Empire to Humanity*, chap. 1; P. Clark, *British Clubs and Societies*, 82–83, 105–9, 303–4, 404–10; Mulcahy, "'Great Fire' of 1740."

2. McConville, *King's Three Faces*, esp. chap. 4; Mulcahy, "'Great Fire of 1740,'" 139; [Hanway], *Case of the Canadians at Montreal*, 34–35; Mulcahy, *Hurricanes and Society*, chap. 7.

3. Reports about the fire in Boston, which occurred on 20 March 1760, first appeared in the *Boston News-Letter* the next day and in other Boston papers (all of which were weeklies that published on Mondays) on 24 March. Both the *New-York Mercury* and Rhode Island's *Newport Mercury* published their accounts, presumably based on the story in the *News-Letter*, on 25 March. For estimated losses of life and property resulting from the 1780 hurricanes, see Mulcahy, *Hurricanes and Society*, 165.

4. Kammen, *Rope of Sand*, esp. 4, 16–21; Flavell, *When London Was the Capital of America*; Moniz, *From Empire to Humanity*, esp. chap. 1; O'Brien, "Transatlantic Community of Saints"; Parrish, *American Curiosity*, esp. chap. 3; Gronim, "What Jane Knew."

5. *Boston Evening-Post*, 24 Mar. 1760. See also *Boston News-Letter*, 21 Mar. 1760.

6. Bridenbaugh, *Cities in the Wilderness*, 55–60; Hoffer, *Seven Fires*, 36; *Boston News-Letter*, 21 Mar. 1760; *Boston Evening-Post*, 24 Mar. 1760.

7. *Boston News-Letter*, 21 Mar. 1760; *Boston Evening-Post*, 24 Mar. 1760.

8. *Volume of Records Relating to the Early History of Boston*, 126–27; *Acts and Resolves . . . of the Province of Massachusetts Bay*, 4:337, 440. See also Hoffer, *Seven Fires*, 48–51, on the local "politics of recovery."

9. *By His Excellency Thomas Pownall, Esq.; . . . A Brief*; *Boston Evening-Post*, 31 Mar. 1760. On the use of charity briefs in Britain and British colonial America, see Mulcahy, *Hurricanes and Society*, 144–45.

10. Mayhew, *God's Hand and Providence*, esp. 9–11, 15–18, 25–27, 35–36.

11. Janeway, *Seasonable and Earnest Address*, 3–5; D. Jones, *Discourse upon the Great Fire of London*; J[ohonnot], *Poem on the Rebuke of God's Hand*.

12. *Volume of Records Relating to the Early History of Boston*, 100. At the time, a sum of £200 sterling was the equivalent of £266.13.4 in Massachusetts local money.

13. *Volume of Records Relating to the Early History of Boston*, 100; Hancock, *Citizens of the World*, 283, 308–9; Sirota, *Christian Monitors*, 231–32; *New-York Mercury*, 4 Apr., 12 May 1760; *Pennsylvania Gazette*, 17 Apr., 19 May 1760; *Boston Evening-Post*, 18 May 1761. News

of the Boston fire appeared in London newspapers in early June. See, for instance, *Public Advertiser*, 7 June 1760.

14. Schutz, *Thomas Pownall*, 34–35, 133–35; Ward, *"Unite or Die,"* 57–65; Shannon, *Indians and Colonists*, 52–56, 131–33.

15. *Volume of Records Relating to the Early History of Boston*, 100; *By His Excellency Horatio Sharpe*. New Hampshire's governor also issued a charity brief on Boston's behalf; Virginia's council members supported the preparation of a "suitable brief" to be read in all the churches in their province to solicit donations. See *By His Excellency Benning Wentworth*; McIlwaine et al., *Executive Journals of the Council of Virginia*, 6:157; and Francis Bernard to Francis Fauquier, 7 Feb. 1761, in Nicholson, *Papers of Francis Bernard*, 1:98.

16. *Volume of Records Relating to the Early History of Boston*, iv–vi, 1–101. The original document is in the Treasury Board Papers of the British National Archives. See Petition of Sarah Ayers, et al., Treasury 1/412/96–99.

17. Petition of Sarah Ayers et al., Treasury 1/412/96–99, verso.

18. Brewer, *Sinews of Power*, 114; Calloway, *Scratch of a Pen*, 12–13; Bushman, *King and People*, 139–55; *Boston Evening-Post*, 18 May 1761.

19. *Quebec Gazette*, 30 May 1765; Young, *Patrician Families*, 123–24; A. Cooper, *Hanging of Angélique*, 193–94, 203; Report of Adam Mabane and Benjamin Price, 27 June 1765, Colonial Office Records 42/3/433, British National Archives (hereafter CO); Calloway, *Scratch of a Pen*, 114–21; W. Smith, *History of Canada*, 2:8. Montreal's first printing press was established in 1776.

20. Calloway, *Scratch of a Pen*, 118–21; G. P. Browne, "Murray, James," *Dictionary of Canadian Biography*, 2003, http://www.biographi.ca/en/bio/murray_james_4E .html; W. Smith, *History of Canada*, 2:15–26. Walker's assailants escaped and were not apprehended until November 1766; they were tried and acquitted in March 1767.

21. Council minutes, 22 May 1765, CO 42/4/220; Report of Adam Mabane and Benjamin Price, 27 June 1765, CO 42/3/433.

22. Report of Adam Mabane and Benjamin Price, 27 June 1765, CO 42/3/433.

23. *Journal of the Honourable House of Representatives*, 139–40. For Bostonians' response to the Stamp Act, see Morgan and Morgan, *Stamp Act Crisis*, chap. 8. On New Englanders' deep hatred for French Canadians, see McConville, *King's Three Faces*, esp. 261–66.

24. James Murray to Horatio Sharpe, 29 June 1765, in *Votes and Proceedings of the Lower House*, 21; *Pennsylvania Gazette*, 28 Nov., 5 Dec. 1765.

25. Kukla, *Patrick Henry*, chap. 7; Morgan and Morgan, *Stamp Act Crisis*, chaps. 5 and 7; *Pennsylvania Gazette*, 28 Nov., 5 Dec. 1765.

26. Kukla, *Patrick Henry*, 73–75, 95–96; *Virginia Gazette* (Purdie and Dixon), 8 Aug. 1766.

27. Council minutes, 26 June 1765, CO 42/3/161–63; Petition of John Welles et al., [June 1765], CO 42/3/447–49; Petition of the French Inhabitants of Montreal, [June 1765], CO 42/3/451–53.

28. Early reports in the London press include *Public Advertiser*, 12 July 1765, and *Public Ledger*, 16 July 1765. Both papers' coverage extended into October, as did that of some of their London competitors. For coverage outside of London, see, for instance, *Bath Chronicle and Weekly Gazette*, 18 July, 25 July, 15 Aug., 12 Sept. 1765; *Derby Mercury*, 19 July, 26 July, 2 Aug. 1765; *Caledonian Mercury*, 17 July, 10 Aug. 1765; and *Aberdeen Press and Journal*, 22 July, 29 July, 5 Aug., 19 Aug. 1765. For trade-related stories, see *London Chronicle*, 6–8 Aug. 1765, and *Public Ledger*, 31 Oct. 1765.

29. [Hanway], *Case of the Canadians at Montreal*, 28–32; *Public Advertiser*, 30 July, 10 Oct., 14 Oct. 1765; *Public Ledger*, 30 July, 10 Oct., 14 Oct. 1765; *Gazetteer and New Daily Advertiser* (London), 14 Oct. 1765; Contu, "Philanthropy and Propaganda," 59, 62; Edwin Welch, "Thornton, John," *Oxford Dictionary of National Biography*, 2004, https://doi.org /10.1093/ref:odnb/27358.

30. James Stephen Taylor, "Hanway, Jonas," *Oxford Dictionary of National Biography*, 2008, https://doi.org/10.1093/ref:odnb/12230; [Hanway], *Summary of the Case of the Sufferers* and *Case of the Canadians at Montreal*. These pamphlets are similar but not identical.

31. [Hanway], *Case of the Canadians at Montreal*, 18.

32. [Hanway], *Case of the Canadians at Montreal*, 12–13, 21–22; [Hanway], *Summary of the Case of the Sufferers*, 6–8, 14–15.

33. [Hanway], *Summary of the Case of the Sufferers*, 6–9.

34. [Hanway], *Summary of the Case of the Sufferers*, 12–14; [Hanway], *Case of the Canadians at Montreal*, 9; *Public Advertiser*, 20 Sept. 1765; *Public Ledger*, 12 Aug., 20 Sept., 30 Sept. 1765; *Gazetteer and New Daily Advertiser*, 21 Sept., 18 Nov., 25 Nov. 1765; *Lloyd's Evening Post*, (London), 18–20 Nov. 1765. See also Moniz, *From Empire to Humanity*, 33–36. On insurance, see Oviatt, "Historical Study of Fire Insurance," 335–38.

35. *Lloyd's Evening Post*, 28–30 Aug., 9–11 Sept. 1765; *London Chronicle*, 29–31 Aug., 10–12 Sept. 1765; *Public Ledger*, 11 Sept. 1765; *Stamford [Eng.] Mercury*, 5 Sept. 1765; *Pennsylvania Gazette*, 31 Oct. 1765; *South-Carolina Gazette*, 31 Dec. 1765; [Hanway], *Case of the Canadians at Montreal*, 34–35.

36. Prochaska, *Royal Bounty*, esp. 2–3, 12–17; Augusta, Princess of Wales, Accounts, 1737–45, Royal Archives, Windsor Castle (hereafter RA), GEO/MAIN/55422–55430; George III, Privy Purse, RA GEO/MAIN/17110, 17126, 17144, 17162, 17166, 17190, 17211, 17230, 17249, 17269, 17288, 17292. On the use of the royal touch and its demise after the death of Queen Anne in 1714, see Bloch, *Royal Touch*, 56–60, 65–67, 216–17, 219–23; and H. Smith, *Georgian Monarchy*, 95–96.

37. Essays of George III, RA GEO/ADD/32, 1480–81, 1731, 1995, 2003, 2006; Private memorandum of the king, n.d., George III Private Correspondence, RA GEO/MAIN /15673.

38. Contu, *Persuasion and Propaganda*, chap. 6; Contu, "Philanthropy and Propaganda," 59–60, 64.

39. *Pennsylvania Gazette*, 10 July 1766; Mulcahy, *Hurricanes and Society*, 147; Contu, "Philanthropy and Propaganda," 62. On Barbadians' response to the Stamp Act, see O'Shaughnessy, *Empire Divided*, 92–95.

40. Hillsborough to George III, 22 July 1768, George III Official Correspondence, RA GEO/MAIN/792. An excellent recent account is K. Murphy, "Virginia's Great Fresh." Murphy also sees this relief effort as serving the interests of planters and merchants, though she does not situate it in a larger context of imperial statecraft or benevolence.

41. Richard Bland to Thomas Adams, 1 Aug. 1771, in "Virginia in 1771," 128; *Virginia Gazette* (Rind), 30 May 1771; *Virginia Gazette* (Purdie and Dixon), 30 May, 6 June 1771; William Nelson to Secretary of State, 14 June 1771, in Van Horne, *Correspondence of William Nelson*, 144; Coleman, "Great Fresh of 1771," 20; "Forty Foot High (and Risin'?)."

42. *Virginia Gazette* (Purdie and Dixon), 30 May, 20 June 1771. For coverage outside Virginia, see *Pennsylvania Gazette*, 20 June 1771; *Connecticut Journal*, 21 June 1771; *Boston*

Evening-Post 24 June, 1 July 1771; *Boston News-Letter,* 27 June, 4 July 1771; *Providence Gazette,* 22–29 June 1771; *Essex [Mass.] Gazette,* 2 July 1771; *Massachusetts Spy,* 4 July 1771; *South Carolina Gazette,* 4 July, 9 Aug. 1771; *Scots Magazine* 33 (July 1771): 380–82; and *Gentleman's Magazine* 41 (July 1771): 233.

43. Memorial of Merchants and Others, [c. 12 June 1771], in Van Horne, *Correspondence of William Nelson,* 145–47; Nelson to Secretary of State, 14 June 1771, in Van Horne, 144; Mulcahy, "Port Royal Earthquake." On previous James River floods, see William Byrd to "my father Horsmanden," 5 June 1685, in "Capt. Byrd's Letters Continued," 81; Roger Atkinson to Lyonel and Samuel Lynde, 10 June 1771, in "Letters of Roger Atkinson," 350–52; *Virginia Gazette* (Rind), 30 May 1771; and *Virginia Gazette* (Purdie and Dixon), 6 June 1771. A tropical storm may have caused the unusual severity of the 1771 flood. See Dennis B. Blanton, Michael Chenoweth, and Cary J. Mock, "The Great Flood of 1771: An Explanation of Natural Causes and Social Effects," in Dupigny-Girox and Mock, *Historical Climate Variability,* 11–15. For a list of eighteenth-century Virginia fast days, see K. Murphy, "Prodigies and Portents," 413.

44. Nelson to Secretary of State, 14 June 1771, in Van Horne, *Correspondence of William Nelson,* 144; Kammen, *Rope of Sand,* 140.

45. "Enclosure A: Address of the President to the General Assembly," William Nelson to the Earl of Hillsborough, 11 Jul. 1771, in Van Horne, *Correspondence of William Nelson,* 158–59; Kennedy, *Journals of the House of Burgesses,* 119–140; Hening, *Statutes at Large,* 8:493–503; *Virginia Gazette* (Purdie and Dixon), 6 June, 11 July, 18 July, 25 July 1771; *Virginia Gazette* (Rind), 18 July, 1 Aug. 1771; K. Murphy, "Virginia's Great Fresh."

46. "Enclosure A: Address of the President to the General Assembly," William Nelson to the Earl of Hillsborough, 11 July 1771, in Van Horne, *Correspondence of William Nelson,* 158–59; Holton, *Forced Founders,* 60–65.

47. *Virginia Gazette* (Purdie and Dixon), 18 July 1771; Jackson and Twohig, *Diaries of George Washington,* 3:38–42.

48. John Pownall to William Nelson, 7 Aug. (2), 4 Sept. 1771, CO 5/1375/78; Hillsborough to Dunmore, 4 Dec. 1771, CO 5/1375/81–82.

49. K. Murphy, "Virginia's Great Fresh," 323; Holton, *Forced Founders,* chap. 5.

50. S. Johnson, *Climate and Catastrophe,* 93–94, 101; *Pennsylvania Packet; and General Advertiser,* 21 Sept. 1772; *Massachusetts Gazette, and the Boston Post-Boy and Advertiser,* 5 Oct. 1772; *Pennsylvania Gazette,* 7 Oct. 1772; *London Chronicle,* 5–7 Nov. 1772; *London Evening Post,* 10–12 Nov. 1772; *Gazetteer and New Daily Advertiser,* 4 Dec. 1772. For a modern estimate of the death toll, see "Deadliest Atlantic Tropical Cyclones."

51. *Massachusetts Gazette, and the Boston Post-Boy and Advertiser,* 5 Oct. 1772; *Massachusetts Spy,* 8 Oct. 1772; *New-York Journal,* 8 Oct. 1772; *New London [Conn.] Gazette,* 9 Oct. 1772; *New Hampshire Gazette,* 9 Oct. 1772; *Providence Gazette, and Country Journal,* 10 Oct. 1772; *Newport Mercury,* 12 Oct. 1772.

52. Mulcahy, *Hurricanes and Society,* 55–56; [Howe], *Account of the Late Dreadful Hurricane,* 2–4; *Massachusetts Gazette, and the Boston Post-Boy and Advertiser,* 5 Oct. 1772; *Massachusetts Spy,* 20 Oct. 1772; Knox, *Discourse Delivered on the 6th of September,* 24.

53. Alexander Hamilton to the *Royal Danish American Gazette,* 6 Sept. 1772, in Syrett, *Papers of Alexander Hamilton,* 1:34–38.

54. Alexander Hamilton to the *Royal Danish American Gazette,* 6 Sept. 1772, in Syrett, *Papers of Alexander Hamilton,* 1:34–38; *Connecticut Journal, and the New-Haven Post-Boy,*

9 Oct. 1772; *Essex Gazette*, 13 Oct. 1772; *Pennsylvania Gazette*, 14 Oct. 1772; *New-Hampshire Gazette, and Historical Chronicle*, 16 Oct. 1772; *Providence Gazette, and Country Journal*, 24 Oct. 1772; [Howe], *Account of the Late Dreadful Hurricane*, 49–50.

55. Mulcahy, *Hurricanes and Society*, 84–86; *Account of the Late Dreadful Hurricane*, 50–51; *Pennsylvania Gazette*, 7 Oct. 1772; *Pennsylvania Chronicle*, 3–10 Oct. 1772; *South-Carolina Gazette, and Country Journal*, 17 Nov. 1772; Hoppit, "Financial Crises," 45, 51–52, 54, 57. The London merchants' subscription effort may have been more rumor than reality. Unlike the highly publicized effort to send disaster relief to Montreal in 1765, this one received virtually no press coverage, but see *Northampton [Eng.] Mercury*, 23 Nov. 1772. On Payne, see Andrew J. O'Shaughnessy and W. P. Courtney, "Payne, Ralph, Baron Lavington," *Oxford Dictionary of National Biography*, 2008, https://doi.org/10.1093/ref :odnb/21652.

56. Sir Ralph Payne to Lord Hillsborough, 18 Sept. 1772, CO 152/52/105–8; [Howe], *Account of the Late Dreadful Hurricane*. See also *General Evening Post* (London), 24–26 Nov. 1772.

57. Sir Ralph Payne to Lord Hillsborough, 5 Sept. 1772, CO 152/52/101–4.

58. Sir Ralph Payne to Lord Hillsborough, 18 Sept. 1772, CO 152/52/105–8; Petition of the Council and Assembly of Antigua, Sept. 1772, CO 152/52/109; Lord Dartmouth to Sir Ralph Payne, 9 Dec. 1772, CO 152/52/114.

59. Newspapers in the mainland North American colonies that published Von Roepstorff's proclamation included, in chronological order, *Boston Evening-Post*, 5 Oct. 1772; *Pennsylvania Gazette*, 7 Oct. 1772; *New-York Journal*, 8 Oct. 1772; *Pennsylvania Packet*, 12 Oct. 1772; *Massachusetts Spy*, 22 Oct. 1772; and *Virginia Gazette*, 29 Oct. 1772. On English colonists in the eighteenth-century Danish West Indies, see Mulcahy, *Hubs of Empire*, 13.

60. Knox, *Discourse Delivered on the 6th of September*, ii; Alexander Hamilton to the *Royal Danish American Gazette*, 6 Sept. 1772, in Syrett, *Papers of Alexander Hamilton*, 1:38; *Morning Chronicle and London Advertiser*, 4 Dec. 1772.

61. *Morning Chronicle and London Advertiser*, 4 Dec. 1772; *Boston Evening-Post*, 5 Oct. 1772; *South-Carolina Gazette, and Country Journal*, 6 Oct. 1772; *Pennsylvania Gazette*, 7 Oct. 1772; *Virginia Gazette*, 29 Oct. 1772; *South Carolina Gazette*, 2 Nov. 1772.

62. Westergaard, *Danish West Indies*, 245.

63. Mulcahy, *Hurricanes and Society*, 154–55, 165–68; O'Shaughnessy, *Empire Divided*, 207.

64. Jasanoff, *Liberty's Exiles*, 12–13; Mulcahy, *Hurricanes and Society*, 191–93; O'Shaughnessy, *Empire Divided*, 206–7.

CHAPTER 5

1. See, for instance, Kornfeld, "Crisis in the Capital," 199–200; Sally F. Griffith, "'A Total Dissolution of the Bonds of Society': Community Death and Regeneration in Mathew Carey's *Short Account of the Malignant Fever*," in Estes and Smith, *Melancholy Scene of Devastation*, 47, 55–56; Susan E. Klepp, "'How Many Precious Souls Are Fled?' The Magnitude of the 1793 Yellow Fever Epidemic," in Estes and Smith, 173–75; Waterman, *Republic of Intellect*, chap. 5; Finger, *Contagious City*, esp. 104–10, 120–27, 156–57; Apel, "Thucydidean Moment," 321–27, 340–42; and Caldwell, *Reply to Dr. Haygarth's "Letter to Dr. Percival*,*"* 1–12. On the perceived connection between physical and moral cleanliness, see also K. Brown, *Foul Bodies*, esp. 195–212.

2. Patterson, "Yellow Fever Epidemics"; McNeill, *Mosquito Empires*, 32–52.

3. Patterson, "Yellow Fever Epidemics"; John, *Spreading the News*, 37–42; Thomas Jefferson to Benjamin Rush, 23 Sept. 1800, in Boyd et al., *Papers of Thomas Jefferson*, 32: 166–69; Conn, *Americans against the City*, chap. 1.

4. Powell, *Bring Out Your Dead*, 8–28, 280–82; Klepp, "'How Many Precious Souls Are Fled?,'" 171; Henry Knox to George Washington, 18 Sept. 1798, in Twohig et al., *Papers of George Washington*, 14:112–14.

5. Klepp, "'How Many Precious Souls Are Fled?,'" 166–75; G. Nash, *First City*, 122, 140–43. For the remarkably underdocumented 1762 epidemic, see Redman, *Account of the Yellow Fever*, 3, 10–13.

6. George Washington to William Pearce, 26 Aug. 1793, in Twohig et al., *Papers of George Washington*, 13:558–60; Washington to Thomas Jefferson, 7 Oct. 1793, in Twohig et al., 14: 179–180; Edmund Randolph to George Washington, 24 Oct. 1793, in Twohig et al., 14: 281–84; Powell, *Bring Out Your Dead*, 21–22, 54–72; Thomas A. Horrocks and John C. Van Horne, foreword to Estes and Smith, *Melancholy Scene of Devastation*, vii.

7. Powell, *Bring Out Your Dead*, 29–44, 75–80, 151–52; Finger, *Contagious City*, 110–14; J. Worth Estes, "Introduction: The Yellow Fever Syndrome and Its Treatment in Philadelphia, 1793," in Estes and Smith, *Melancholy Scene of Devastation*, 7–14; *Minutes of the Proceedings of the Committee*, A.

8. *Minutes of the Proceedings of the Committee*, esp. 7–11, 128–30; Powell, *Bring Out Your Dead*, 151–52, 185–88.

9. On Clarkson, see Matthew Clarkson to Thomas Jefferson, 3 June 1793, editor's note, in Boyd et al., *Papers of Thomas Jefferson*, 26:172. For examples of local governments providing or orchestrating relief before 1776, see Burton, "'Awful Judgments of God,'" 498, 501–2; and Clarfield, "Salem's Great Inoculation Controversy."

10. *Minutes of the Proceedings of the Committee*, 217–23; Powell, *Bring Out Your Dead*, 220–27.

11. *Minutes of the Proceedings of the Committee*, 41, 63–64; *By George Clinton, Governor of the State of New-York . . . a Proclamation*; Henry Knox to George Washington, 24 Sept. 1793, in Twohig et al., *Papers of George Washington*, 14:129–31.

12. Chernow, *Alexander Hamilton*, 448–52; Alexander Hamilton to Abraham Yates, 26 Sept. 1793, in Syrett, *Papers of Alexander Hamilton*, 15:343–48; Yates to Alexander Hamilton, 27 Sept. 1793, in Syrett, 349–51.

13. Powell, *Bring Out Your Dead*, 228; Knott, *Sensibility and the American Revolution*, 1–3, 199–201, 237, 260.

14. *Minutes of the Proceedings of the Committee*, 86–88, 218.

15. Carey, *Desultory Account of the Yellow Fever*, esp. 3–4, 6–7.

16. Carey, *Short Account of the Malignant Fever*, 32–42. The last quotation is from S. Fisher, *Philadelphia, 11th Month*. On handshaking and the extent to which it may have signified a shift toward more democratic manners in postrevolutionary America, see Hemphill, *Bowing to Necessities*, 151, 272; and Allgor, *Parlor Politics*, 19, 79, 201.

17. Phillip Lapsansky, "'Abigail, a Negress': The Role and Legacy of African Americans in the Yellow Fever Epidemic," in Estes and Smith, *Melancholy Scene of Devastation*, 61–69; Griffith, "'Total Dissolution of the Bonds of Society,'" 54–56; Winch, *Philadelphia's Black Elite*, 15–17; Newman, *Freedom's Prophet*, 87–89, 93–95; Hardy, "Figures of Authorship." On the more general contemporary effort to equate American identity with whiteness, see Waldstreicher, *In the Midst of Perpetual Fetes*, chap. 6; and Parkinson, *Common Cause*.

18. Carey, *Short Account of the Malignant Fever*, 58; *Minutes of the Proceedings of the Committee*, 126–32; Rosenberg, *Cholera Years*, esp. 2, 18–21, 31, 82; Finger, *Contagious City*, 148–51; Golinski, "Debating the Atmospheric Constitution."

19. Edling, *Hercules in the Cradle*, esp. 13, 19, 33; Edling, *Revolution in Favor of Government*. On the specific issue of disaster relief, see G. Davies, "Dealing with Disaster."

20. Alan Taylor, "'The Hungry Year': 1789 on the Northern Border of Revolutionary America," in Biel, *American Disasters*, 39–41, 56–62; Weaver and de Lottinville, "Conflagration and the City," 439–40; Kinealy, *Great Irish Famine*, 32; Louis-Charles, "State Sovereignty," esp. 106–17. By the 1840s, the British government would adopt noninterventionist policies before formally acknowledging "the duty of the state to save life" in 1880. See Edgerton-Tarpley, "Tough Choices," 144–45, 151–59.

21. Chernow, *Alexander Hamilton*, 339–40; "List of the Public Acts of Congress," *Public Statutes at Large of the United States of America*, 1:xvii–xviii.

22. An excellent summary of this debate is in Finger, *Contagious City*, chap. 9.

23. A list of "Acts of Congress Granting . . . Relief to Sufferers from Floods, Fires, Earthquakes, and So Forth" was inserted into the congressional record during the debates that led to the National Emergencies Act (*Congressional Record*, 7 Aug. 1950, 11900–02). The list included eight pre-1860 examples, which I have supplemented with eight more found by searching for keywords such as "relief" and "sufferers" in the congressional journals.

24. "Acts of Congress Granting . . . Relief to Sufferers"; *U.S. Statutes at Large*, 3rd Cong., 2nd Sess., 1:423; 19th Cong., 1st Sess., 4:194; 22nd Cong., 1st Sess., 4:532–33; 32nd Cong., 1st Sess., 10:2; 32nd Cong., 2nd Sess., 10:155. On New Madrid and the resulting expansion of white citizens' speculative landholdings, see also Valencius, *Lost History of the New Madrid Earthquakes*, 43–44, 98–99.

25. "Acts of Congress Granting . . . Relief to Sufferers"; Fitz, *Our Sister Republics*, 1–14; Bierick, "First Instance of U.S. Foreign Aid"; "Famine in the Canary Islands," *American State Papers*, 12th Cong., 1st sess., Miscellaneous, 2:184; Kinealy, *Charity and the Great Hunger*, 1–9, 221–50. Indeed, the treasurer of the relief committee in New York warned that the arrival of many poor immigrants from Ireland would reduce American contributions.

26. *New Hampshire Gazette*, 26 Dec. 1802; *U.S. Statutes at Large*, 7th Congress, 2nd sess., 2:201; Candee, "Social Conflict and Urban Rebuilding," 120–21; Hogan, "Origins of U.S. Emergency Management"; Moss, *When All Else Fails*, 234.

27. "Acts of Congress Granting . . . Relief to Sufferers"; Landis, "Let Me Next Time Be Tried by Fire," 1000–1002; *Alexandria Gazette*, 23 Jan. 1827; *National Intelligencer* (Washington), 20 Jan. 1827, 2 Feb. 1831.

28. Foster, *Full Account of the Great Fire at Pittsburgh*, 20–27, 48–52; Cook, "Great Fire of Pittsburgh," 143; *Journal of the Assembly of the State of New York*, 67–69, 116, 139–40, 149.

29. U.S. Census Bureau, "Population of the 33 Urban Places"; Adams, *Annals of Portsmouth*, 324–25, 364; Labaree, *Patriots and Partisans*, 94–98, 104, 131–33. Colonists' use of committees of correspondence began during the Stamp Act crisis. See Maier, *From Resistance to Revolution*, 78–81.

30. *New Hampshire Gazette*, 28 Dec. 1802. Letters from four towns either allude to this letter or mention it explicitly. See Robert Means (Amherst) to Nathaniel Parker, 19 Jan. 1803; Michael McClary (Epsom) to Nathaniel Adams, 16 Jan. 1803; William Coombs (Newburyport) to the committee, 11 Jan. 1803; and Samuel Freeman (Portland) to John Langdon, 11 Jan. 1803, all in Portsmouth Fire Collection, Portsmouth Athenaeum,

Portsmouth, N.H. For examples of early generic form letters from Portsmouth and Newburyport, respectively, see *Addressed to the Reverend the Clergy*; and *To the Selectmen of the Town of [blank]*.

31. *Gazette of the United States* (Philadelphia), 7 Jan. 1803; *National Intelligencer*, 10 Jan. 1803; *Scioto [Ohio] Gazette*, 22 Jan. 1803; A Sincear Republican to John Langdon, 20 Jan. 1803, Portsmouth Fire Collection; Phineas Dana to John Wardrobe, 15 Jan. 1803, Portsmouth Fire Collection; An Orphan to the committee, 5 Feb. 1803, Portsmouth Fire Collection.

32. Thomas Jefferson to John Langdon, 11 Jan. 1803, in Boyd et al., *Papers of Thomas Jefferson*, 39:311–12.

33. Edmund Quincy to Nathaniel Adams, 9 Jan., 13 Jan. 1803; Daniel Waldron to John Langdon, 13 Jan., 14 Jan., 16 Jan. 1803; George Champless to John Langdon, 12 Feb. 1803, all in Portsmouth Fire Collection; Charles Pearce to Thomas and William Bradford, 7 Jan. 180[3]; Charles Pearce to William Bradford, 1 Feb. 1803; Thomas Andrews to William Bradford, 24 Jan. 1803; Vincent Bonsal to William Bradford, 29 Jan. 1803, all in Bradford Family Papers, Historical Society of Pennsylvania, Philadelphia; *Gazette of the United States*, 11 Jan. 1803.

34. Alvey, *Fredericksburg Fire of 1807*, 18–24, 31–35; *Alexandria Advertiser*, 23 Oct. 1807; *New-York Gazette*, 24 Oct. 1807; *Salem Register*, 26 Oct. 1807; *Connecticut Courant*, 28 Oct. 1807; *Virginia Telegraph*, 28 Oct. 1807. Listed in his account books as "charity for Fredsbg" given to Daniel C. Brent, Jefferson's donation was likely again anonymous as it was not reported in the newspapers. See Bear and Stanton, *Jefferson's Memorandum Books*, 2:1214.

35. Trenton and Perth Amboy, both in New Jersey, contributed $508 and $50, respectively. Poughkeepsie and New Lebanon, New York, sent $37 and $250, respectively. My assessment of sources of donations is based on donors' letters in the Portsmouth Fire Collection.

36. Moses Levy to the committee, 19 Jan. 1803; and Moses Levy, Samuel Coates, and James Milnor to the committee, 21 Feb., 9 May 1803, all in Portsmouth Fire Collection.

37. William Coombs et al. to the committee, 11 Jan. 1803; William Bartlett to the committee, 17 Jan. 1803; Moses Brown to the committee, 29 Jan. 1803, all in Portsmouth Fire Collection. On Bartlett and Brown, see Labaree, *Patriots and Partisans*, 94–95, 207–8.

38. Samuel Freeman to John Langdon, 17 Jan., 21 Jan. 1803 (2); Hugh McLellan to John Langdon, 15 Jan. 1803; John Waite to John Langdon, 21 Jan. 1803; Samuel Hussey and James Neal to the committee, 21 Jan. 1803, all in Portsmouth Fire Collection. There were five churches in Portland in 1803, in addition to the local meeting of the Society of Friends (Quakers), which donated $65. See Willis, *History of Portland*, 2:224–49. A biographical sketch of Freeman is in Willis, 272n.

39. *Salem Register*, 3 Jan. 1803; *Farmer's Cabinet* (Amherst, N.H.), 13 Jan. 1803; Jeremiah Yellott to John Langdon, 7 Feb. 1803, Portsmouth Fire Collection; Moses Levy to the committee, 19 Jan. 1803, Portsmouth Fire Collection; "The Collection from Cheshire in Connecticut," Portsmouth Fire Collection. See also Yellott, "Jeremiah Yellott." On the decline of the ideal of universal benevolence and the evolution of American benevolence during this period, see Opal, "Labors of Liberality," 1084–87, 1093–98, 1105–7; and Moniz, *From Empire to Humanity*, chap. 7. K. McCarthy, *American Creed*, focuses on the emergence of permanent voluntary philanthropic associations.

40. *New Hampshire Gazette*, 28 Dec. 1802. These sorts of stipulations were articulated occasionally during the colonial era. See Mulcahy, *Hurricanes and Society*, 149.

41. George Crowninshield to the committee, 17 Jan. 1803; A Sincear Republican to John Langdon, 20 Jan. 1803; David Goodall to John Langdon, 20 Feb. 1803; David Meacham to John Langdon, 28 Mar. 1803; Daniel Goodrich to John Langdon, 29 Mar. 1803; Leonard Worcester to the committee, 11 May 1803, all in Portsmouth Fire Collection.

42. Abiel Abbot to Nathaniel Adams, 22 Jan. 1803, Portsmouth Fire Collection.

43. Michael McClary to Nathaniel Adams, 16 Jan. 1803, Portsmouth Fire Collection; *New Hampshire Gazette*, 18 Jan. 1803. On McClary, see Whiton, *Sketches from the History of New-Hampshire*, 204.

44. A good morning-after account of the fire is Isaac Coplin to Prudence Coplin, 27 Dec. 1811, Isaac Coplin Letters, Library of Virginia, Richmond. The definitive list of known deaths is Baker, "1811 Theater Fire Victim List."

45. *Theatre on Fire*; *Richmond Enquirer*, 28 Dec. 1811, 30 Jan., 6 Feb. 1812. Baker, *Richmond Theater Fire*, is an excellent book-length account.

46. Baker, *Richmond Theater Fire*, 90–98, details the suffering of individual families and the limited, and mostly unsuccessful, efforts to encourage donations locally.

47. *New Hampshire Gazette*, 28 Dec. 1802; Rosenberg, *Cholera Years*, 1–4; Pyle, "Diffusion of Cholera."

48. George Hay to James Monroe, 31 Dec. 1811, in Preston et al., *Papers of James Monroe*, 6:103.

49. Halttunen, "Humanitarianism and the Pornography of Pain," 327, 330; *Richmond Enquirer*, 14 Jan. 1812.

50. Baker, *Richmond Theater Fire*, 64–67; Davidson, *Revolution and the Word*; Julia Stern, "The Politics of Tears: Death in the Early Novel," in Isenberg and Burstein, *Mortal Remains*, 109–13; Appleby, *Inheriting the Revolution*; Halttunen, "Humanitarianism and the Pornography of Pain," 310–12; Halttunen, *Murder Most Foul*; Trotti, *Body in the Reservoir*.

51. Baker, *Richmond Theater Fire*, 20–22, 28–31, 36–37, 41–42, 112; *Virginia Argus*, 2 Jan. 1812. On Sally Conyers, see also *Richmond Enquirer*, 21 Jan. 1812; and Caroline Homassel Thornton, "Notes on the Richmond theatre fire," n.d., Greene Family Papers, Virginia Historical Society, Richmond. For Botts, see also *Richmond Enquirer*, 4 Jan. 1812.

52. *National Intelligencer*, 31 Dec. 1811; *Maryland Gazette*, 2 Jan. 1812; *Martinsburg [Va.] Gazette*, 3 Jan. 1812; *Richmond Enquirer*, 11 Jan. 1812. Anderson's account was also reprinted in O'Lynch, *Narrative . . . of the Deplorable Conflagration*; and in *Full Account of the Burning of the Richmond Theatre*, 61–62.

53. *Federal Republican* (Baltimore), 2 Jan. 1812; *Richmond Enquirer*, 11 Jan. 1812; Kann, *Republic of Men*, 159–70. On theater seating, see Cohen, *They Will Have Their Game*, 135–37. The fact that the Baltimore editor, Alexander Contee Hanson, was a staunch Federalist and *Enquirer* editor Thomas Ritchie was a prominent Republican likely influenced the remarkable exchange between them. For representative eyewitness and third-person accounts, along with lists of fatalities, see *Richmond Enquirer*, 2 Jan., 4 Jan., 11 Jan., 18 Jan., 21 Jan. 1812.

54. [Mordecai], *Richmond in By-Gone Days*, 142–47; Barrett, *Gilbert Hunt*, chap. 2; Baker, *Richmond Theater Fire*, 43, 71–72, 167.

55. Jewel Spangler, "American Mourning: Catastrophe, Public Grief, and the Making of Civic Identity in the Early National South," in Friend and Glover, *Death and the American South*, 86–109; *Richmond Enquirer*, 9 Jan. 1812.

56. Richards, *Repent!*, esp. 19–25; Theocrate, *Five Important Questions*, 16; *Concise*

Statement of the Awful Conflagration of the Theatre, 3; Dana, *Tribute of Sympathy*, 13; [Alexander], *Remarks on the Theatre*, 10–12.

57. Richards, *Repent!*, 30; Edwards, *Warning to Sinners*, esp. 2–6; *Serious Inquiry into the Nature and Effects of the Stage*, 6–22; Dana, *Tribute of Sympathy*, v–viii; Ashton, *Awful Calamity Occasioned by the Conflagration of the Theatre at Richmond*, ix–xii. On anti-theater sentiment in early America generally, see Kierner, *Contrast*, 15–18. On the history of theater in Richmond specifically, see Shockley, *Richmond Stage*, esp. 392–408.

58. *Richmond Enquirer*, 11 Jan., 23 Jan. 1812; Gilman, *Monody on the Victims*.

59. R. May, *Voice from Richmond*, 9–17; S. Miller, *Theatrical Exhibitions*, 11–12; "Burning of the Richmond Theatre in 1811, and Observations on Theatrical Amusements," *Presbyterian Magazine* 7 (July 1857): 301–12. See also Lloyd, *Richmond Alarm*.

60. John Durbarrow Blair, "A sermon occasioned by the dreadful calamity . . . ," in John Durbarrow Blair Papers, Library of Virginia, Richmond.

61. Thomas B. Hewitt to Samuel Arell Marsteller, 15 Jan. 1812, Thomas B. Hewitt Letter, Library of Virginia, Richmond.

62. *Richmond Enquirer*, 28 Dec., 31 Dec. 1811, 9 Jan., 11 Jan., 14 Jan. 1812. See also O'Lynch, *Narrative and Report . . . of the Deplorable Conflagration*, esp. 35–38.

63. *Richmond Enquirer*, 23 Jan., 30 Jan. 1812.

64. Rosen, *Limits of Power*, esp. 3–5.

65. *Richmond Enquirer*, 25 Jan. 1812. See also the excellent discussion in Baker, *Richmond Theater Fire*, 146–50. On Ritchie as a political force, see Ambler, *Thomas Ritchie*, esp. chaps. 3–4.

66. Baker, *Richmond Theater Fire*, chap. 8; U.S. Census Bureau, "Population of 46 Urban Places."

67. Baker, *Richmond Theater Fire*, 222–36; G. Fisher, *History and Reminiscences of the Monumental Church*, 1–6, 38–41; *North American Tourist*, 433; C. McCarthy, *Walks about Richmond*, 61–62; *Visitor's Guide to Richmond*, 18.

CHAPTER 6

1. Philip, *Robert Fulton*, 198–205, 270–81; J. Lloyd, *Lloyd's Steamboat Directory*, 17–41; W. Johnson, *River of Dark Dreams*, 6, 79; J. K. Brown, *Limbs on the Levee*, 10–11.

2. W. Johnson, *River of Dark Dreams*, 74–79; U.S. Census Bureau, "Population of the 100 Largest Urban Places."

3. Benson John Lossing quoted in Howell and Tenney, *Bi-centennial History of Albany*, 312. For the *Volcano* and *Vesuvius*, respectively, see *New York Gazette & General Advertiser*, 16 June 1818; and J. Lloyd, *Lloyd's Steamboat Directory*, 42–43. For onshore rescues as spectacles, see, for instance, J. Lloyd, 56–57, 225–31.

4. Stowe, "Canal Boat," 167; Flagg, *Far West*, 18, 34, 78; J. Lloyd, *Lloyd's Steamboat Directory*, 181–83. On "steamboat sublime," see W. Johnson, *River of Dark Dreams*, chap. 3. For the postrevolutionary search for sublimity in the American wilderness, see Sears, *Sacred Places*, 13–16, 78; R. Nash, *Wilderness and the American Mind*, 44–46, 67–68; Rozario, *Culture of Calamity*, 108–11; and Fuller, *From Battlefields Rising*, 6–8.

5. Marx, *Machine in the Garden*, 190–209, emphasizes the celebratory attitude toward machines and technology in early nineteenth-century America. On changes in the travel experience due to corporatization, see Mackintosh, "'Ticketed Through.'" For assertions

of the relative safety of American steamboats, see, for instance, *Memorial of the Sundry Proprietors and Managers of American Steam Vessels*, 1, 47; *Report of the Secretary of the Treasury*; and J. Lloyd, *Lloyd's Steamboat Directory*, 57.

6. A full-text search of the America's Historical Newspapers database, series 1 and 2, found only 63 instances of the use of the word "disaster" between 1690 and 1750; for the period between 1750 and 1780, the term appeared 245 times, an increase attributable at least in part to the greater number of newspapers published during this later period. A search of Google Books, using Google Ngram, shows a gradual increase in the use of the word "disaster" after 1740, though "calamity" was consistently more widely used than either "disaster" or "catastrophe" (https://books.google.com/ngrams/graph?content =disaster%2C+calamity%2C+catastrophe&year_start=1650&year_end=1850&corpus =15&smoothing=3&share=&direct_url=t1%3B%2Cdisaster%3B%2Cc0%3B.t1%3B%2 Ccalamity%3B%2Cc0%3B.t1%3B%2Ccatastrophe%3B%2Cc0).

7. On the *Washington*, see Showalter, "First Steamboat Explosion in the West"; *The Union* (Washington, Ky.), 21 June 1816; and J. Lloyd, *Lloyd's Steamboat Directory*, 55–57.

8. Hunter and Hunter, *Steamboats on the Western Rivers*, 272–85; Burke, "Bursting Boilers and the Federal Power"; Brockmann, *Exploding Steamboats*.

9. *New York Commercial Advertiser*, 17 May 1824; *Daily National Advertiser* (Washington), 20 May 1824; *Richmond Enquirer*, 21 May 1824; *Trenton [N.J.] Federalist*, 24 May 1824; *Public Advertiser* (Hagerstown, Md.), 25 May 1824; *Kentucky Gazette*, 3 June 1824; Hunter and Hunter, *Steamboats on the Western Rivers*, 121–33, 284; Redfield to secretary of the treasury, 26 Dec. 1838, in *Memorial of the Sundry Proprietors and Managers of American Steam Vessels*, 30, 31.

10. *New York Commercial Advertiser*, 17 May 1824; Stanford, *Aetna*, 13–20.

11. Stanford, *Aetna*, 13–15; Brockmann, *Exploding Steamboats*, 11–16, 55; Burke, "Bursting Boilers and the Federal Power," 8–11; *National Intelligencer*, 20 May 1824; *Richmond Enquirer*, 24 May 1824; *Journal of the House of Representatives*, 25 May 1824, 8: 579. See also Cox, "Gibbons v. Ogden," *Law, and Society*, 151–52.

12. Valencius, *Lost History of the New Madrid Earthquakes*, chap. 5; John C. Greene, "Science, Learning, and Utility: Patterns of Organization in the Early Republic," in Oleson, *Pursuit of Knowledge*, 1–20; Sutcliffe, *Steam*, 21–22, 165–67, 200–204; Philip, *Robert Fulton*, 36–44, 89–92.

13. Bruce Sinclair, "Science, Technology, and the Franklin Institute," in Oleson, *Pursuit of Knowledge*, 194–99; "Letter from Robert Hare," *Franklin Journal, and American Mechanics' Magazine* 2 (Sept. 1826): 147–48; Moore, *Weather Experiment*, 11–15; Redfield, "On the Supposed Collapse of Steam Boilers," 190–91; *Memorial of the Sundry Proprietors and Managers of American Steam Vessels*; *Dictionary of American Biography*, s.v. "Redfield, William Charles"; Liscombe, *Altogether American*, esp. 114–18, 136, 147; Robert Mills to [?], 6 Aug. 1852, Robert Mills Papers, South Carolina Historical Society, Charleston.

14. *Francis' Metallic Lifeboat Company*, 3, 8, 20–23; Pond, *History of Life-Saving Appliances*. Humane societies originated in northern Europe; founded in 1780, the Philadelphia Humane Society was the first such group established in North America. See Moniz, "Saving the Lives of Strangers," 610, 614. On contemporary inventions related to steamboat safety generally, see J. Smith, *Causes of Steamboat Explosions*, 3–4, 7, 9, 12, 21–23.

15. Ellms, *Shipwrecks and Disasters at Sea*, 153–58; J. Lloyd, *Lloyd's Steamboat Directory*, 69–73; *Richmond Enquirer*, 23 Mar., 9 Apr. 1830. Another early example of community relief

for steamboat casualties occurred when the *Oliver Ellsworth* exploded near Saybrook, Connecticut, in 1827 (*New York Spectator*, 26 Mar. 1827).

16. Burke, "Bursting Boilers and the Federal Power," 8–14; Brockmann, *Exploding Steamboats*, 33–37, 43–46, 60–67; Sinclair, "Science, Technology, and the Franklin Institute," 199–200; Andrew Jackson, "Fifth Annual Message," 3 Dec. 1833, *Messages and Papers of the Presidents*; "Remarks on Steamboat Accidents," 23 Dec. 1833, in Everett, *Writings and Speeches of Daniel Webster*, 14:172–76; Hugh Richard Slotten, "Bache, Alexander Dallas," *American National Biography*, 2000, https://doi-org.mutex.gmu.edu /10.1093/anb/9780198606697.article.1300059.

17. Martin Van Buren, "First Annual Message," 5 Dec. 1837, *Messages and Papers of the Presidents*; Paskoff, *Troubled Waters*, 28–60; Brockmann, *Exploding Steamboats*, 109–15; "An Act to provide for the better security of the lives of passengers on board of vessels propelled in whole or in part by steam," 7 July 1838, *U.S. Statutes-at-Large*, 25th Cong., 2nd sess., 5:304. For the larger legal and constitutional context, see also Sandukas, "Gently Down the Stream," 22–27. The states that had enacted safety laws were New York, Alabama, Louisiana, Kentucky, and Missouri. See Gudmestad, *Steamboats and the Rise of the Cotton Kingdom*, 113–15; *Revised Statutes of the State of New York*, 1:681–84.

18. *Cincinnati Whig*, 25 Apr. 1838. See also *Richmond Enquirer*, 1 May 1838; *Salem Gazette*, 4 May 1838; *Newport Mercury*, 5 May 1838; and J. Lloyd, *Lloyd's Steamboat Directory*, 89–93, 105–7.

19. *Cincinnati Whig*, 25 Apr. 1838; *Burlington [Iowa] Gazette*, 6 May 1838.

20. *Charleston Courier*, 24 Aug., 20 Oct. 1837, 12 Apr. 1838; *Southern Patriot* (Charleston), 20 Apr. 1838; *American Commercial and Daily Advertiser* (Baltimore), 1 June 1838; McLeod, "Loss of the Steamer Pulaski," 65–66. One authority counted a total of 178 steamboat wrecks in the United States between 1830 and 1840. Of the 79 wrecks in which people died, only 14 occurred on the East Coast. In most cases, the death toll in these eastern wrecks was comparatively light. See *Steamboat Accidents, Loss of Life*, which listed the death toll from the *Pulaski* as 138, though some other estimates were lower.

21. McLeod, "Loss of the Steamer Pulaski," 90–91; *National Gazette and Literary Register* (Philadelphia), 25 June 1838; *Rhode-Island Republican*, 27 June 1838.

22. *Charleston Courier*, 21 June 1838; *National Gazette and Literary Register*, 23 June 1838.

23. See especially *Southern Patriot* (Charleston), 19 June 1838; and *National Gazette and Literary Register (Philadelphia)*, 23 June 1838. On the public citizens' meetings, see *Report of the Committee Appointed by the Citizens of Cincinnati*, 2–8; *Charleston Courier*, 23 June 1838; and *Savannah Republican*, 27 June 1838.

24. Mashaw, *Creating the Administrative Constitution*, 187–90; Brockman, *Exploding Steamboats*, 124–26; Burke, "Bursting Boilers and the Federal Power," 8–17; "An Act to provide for the better security of the lives of passengers"; *Report of the Committee Appointed by the Citizens of Cincinnati*, 69–75; *Savannah Republican*, 27 June 1838.

25. On the Willey avalanche, which was also the subject of a short story by Nathaniel Hawthorne and paintings by Henry C. Pratt and Thomas Cole, see Sears, "Hawthorne's 'The Ambitious Guest'"; and Sears, *Sacred Places*, chap. 4.

26. See, for instance, *New York Commercial Advertiser*, 15 Jan., 18 Jan. 1840; and *New York Journal of Commerce*, 23 Jan. 1840.

27. For newspaper coverage of the proceedings, see, for instance, *New York Commercial Advertiser*, 20–23 Jan., 25 Jan., 28 Jan., 30 Jan., 31 Jan., 1 Feb. 1840; and *Baltimore Sun*, 18 Jan.

1840. On Follen and Finn, respectively, see *The Emancipator*, 23 Jan. 1840; and *Charleston Courier*, 27 Jan. 1840. In general, see also Dunbaugh, *Night Boat to New England*, 41–64.

28. *Proceedings of the Coroner*, 3–7, 22, 23–29, 37, 42, 49; *New York Commercial Advertiser*, 22 Jan., 25 Jan., 31 Jan. 1840. For the ongoing search for—and recovery of—bodies, see *New York Journal of Commerce*, 23 Jan. 1840; *Connecticut Courant*, 1 Feb. 1840; *New York Commercial Advertiser*, 24 Feb., 25 Feb., 27 Feb. 1840; and "The Lexington," *American Masonic Register*, 13 Aug. 1842, 398.

29. *New York Commercial Advertiser*, 15 Jan. 1840; *Ohio State Journal*, 22 Jan. 1840; *Kalamazoo Gazette*, 25 Jan. 1840; *Daily Picayune* (New Orleans), 31 Jan., 1 Feb. 1840; *Wisconsin Enquirer*, 8 Feb. 1840.

30. Brust and Shadwell, "Many Versions and States"; LeBeau, *Currier and Ives*, 8–13; *New York Sun*, 20 Jan. 1840; *National Daily Intelligencer*, 23 Jan. 1840; Edward W. Bancroft to Fabius Bancroft, [25–26 Jan. 1840], Edward W. Bancroft Letter, South Carolina Historical Society, Charleston.

31. Emlen, "Great Gale of 1815"; J. Brown, *Beyond the Lines*, 12–14; Butterfield, "Pictures in the Papers"; Shepley, "By Which Melancholy Occurrence"; Erica Piola, "Drawn on the Spot," in Piola, *Philadelphia on Stone*, 181–82.

32. Weinberg, "Great New York City Fire"; Shepley, "By Which Melancholy Occurrence"; *New Hampshire Gazette*, 3 Nov. 1836, 2 Jan. 1838; *New Bedford [Mass.] Mercury*, 11 May 1838; *Boston Courier*, 20 Jan. 1840. A New York theater company staged the reenactment of another local shipwreck, the *Bristol*, shortly after it happened (*New York Herald*, 10 Jan. 1837).

33. Lehuu, *Carnival on the Page*, 37–58; Spencer, *Yellow Journalism*, 25–27; Shepley, "By Which Melancholy Occurrence."

34. Halttunen, *Murder Most Foul*, 67; LeBeau, *Currier and Ives*, 292–300.

35. Carr, "'We Will Never Forget,'" 36–37; Kunihara, "Voice of God"; Furness, *Discourse . . . Occasioned by the Loss of the Lexington*, 4–5; "Steamer Lexington—Particular Providence," *Youth's Cabinet*, 1 Mar. 1843, 34; [Weild], *Warning Voice from a Watery Grave!*, 9, 15–16.

36. J. Lloyd, *Lloyd's Steamboat Directory*, 225–31. The original story appeared in the New Orleans *Daily Picayune* on 16 Nov. 1849, the day after the explosion occurred. For reprints of the *Picayune* article, see, for instance, *Richmond Enquirer*, 27 Nov. 1849; and *Wisconsin Democrat*, 1 Dec. 1849.

37. W. Johnson, *River of Dark Dreams*, 110–11.

38. Howland, *Steamboat Disasters*, v–vi. Howland's table of contents lists forty-four "Steamboat Disasters," twelve "Railroad Accidents," and thirty-one "Shipwrecks, Fires at Sea, &c.," all but three of which occurred between 1830 and 1840.

39. Ellms, *Shipwrecks and Disasters at Sea*, iii. On Ellms's career and literary output, see also "Ellms, Charles," in Searchable Sea Literature.

40. "The Balloon and the Steamboat," in A Lady, *Child's Gem*, 68–69; Howland, *Disasters by Steam, Fire, and Water*, 6, 10–13, 17–23.

41. Howland, *Disasters by Steam, Fire, and Water*, 5; J. Lloyd, *Lloyd's Steamboat Directory*, 57; W. Johnson, *River of Dark Dreams*, 107–11.

42. Philip Hone quoted in Levine, *Highbrow*, 172–75; W. Johnson, *River of Dark Dreams*, 129–35; Blackmar, *Manhattan for Rent*, chaps. 3 and 4.

43. Halttunen, *Confidence Men and Painted Women*, xv–xvii, 23–32, 117–18; W. Johnson, *River of Dark Dreams*, 135–42.

44. Burg, "'Women and Children First,'" 8; Miskolcze, *Women and Children First*, xvi; Stilgoe, *Lifeboat*, 242–43; Lardner, *Steam Engine Explained and Illustrated*, 495.

45. Miskolcze, *Women and Children First*, xvi.

46. Miskolcze, *Women and Children First*, 29–43, 50–55; Stilgoe, *Lifeboat*, 146–48. For news reports, see, for instance, *Newburyport [Mass.] Morning Herald*, 13 Oct. 1854; *Daily Telegraph* (Jersey City, N.J.), 17 Oct. 1854; *National Daily Intelligencer*, 18 Oct. 1854; *Alexandria Gazette*, 20 Oct. 1854; and *Georgia Weekly Telegraph*, 7 Nov. 1854.

47. Stone, *Sermon, Occasioned by the Burning of the Steamer Lexington*, 10–11; Piola, "Drawn on the Spot," 187–88; W. Johnson, *River of Dark Dreams*, 129–32.

48. Edward W. Bancroft to Fabius Bancroft, [25–26 Jan. 1840], Edward W. Bancroft Letter; Rogers, *Sermon, Occasioned by the Loss of the Harold and the Lexington*, 8–9.

49. J. Lloyd, *Lloyd's Steamboat Directory*, 87; *Albany Argus*, 21 Jan. 1840.

50. For defenses of the company, see *New York Commercial Advertiser*, 18 Jan. 1840; *New York Spectator*, 20 Jan. 1840; *Albany Evening Journal*, 23 Jan. 1840; *National Intelligencer*, 23 Jan. 1823; and *Spirit of the Times* (New York), 25 Jan. 1840. For criticism of the company and support for government regulation, see *Baltimore Sun*, 18 Jan. 1840; *Boston Courier*, 20 Jan., 6 Feb. 1840; *Connecticut Courant*, 1 Feb. 1840; and *National Intelligencer*, 14 Feb. 1840. See also *Proceedings of the Coroner*, 49–89.

51. Furness, *Discourse . . . Occasioned by the Loss of the Lexington*, 12, 14; Lothrop, *Sermon . . . on the Destruction of the Lexington*, 17–19; Howland, *Steamboat Disasters*, 46–47, 92, 114, 154. On Davis, see Burke, "Bursting Boilers and the Federal Power," 16, 19.

52. "Committee Report on the resolution to inquire whether law regulating vessels propelled by steam does not require amendment, together with sundry petitions and memorials on same," 2 Mar. 1840, in *Public Documents, Printed by Order of the Senate of the United States*, 5:1–3, 11–13; *Memorial of the Sundry Proprietors and Managers of American Steam Vessels*, 1–3; *Congressional Globe*, 26th Cong., 1st sess., 1, 2 Mar. 1840, 229.

53. Burke, "Bursting Boilers and the Federal Power," 18–19; Brockmann, *Exploding Steamboats*, 22–27. For bills proposed in the Senate and the House, see H.R. 71, 18 Jan. 1844; H.R. 305, 27 Mar. 1846; S. 284, 17 July 1850; and H.R. 386, 7 Sept. 1850. Casualty figures are based on Burke, "Bursting Boilers and the Federal Power," 18–19 (for 1841–48 and 1850–51); and J. Lloyd, *Lloyd's Steamboat Directory*, 228, 252, 294, 296–97 (for 1849). Lloyd counted 186 deaths from steamboat explosions in the West alone in 1851.

54. *Report of the Secretary of the Treasury*, 114–15.

55. J. Lloyd, *Lloyd's Steamboat Directory*, 287–91; Hartley and Woods, "Explosion of the Steamboat *Saluda*"; *New York Times*, 29 July, 30 July 1852; *New York Herald*, 2 Aug. 1852.

56. For an overview of the *Henry Clay* explosion and its aftermath, see Hansen, *Death Passage on the Hudson*.

57. Petition of members of the Cincinnati and Pittsburgh association of steamboat engineers, 10 Feb. 1852, House of Representatives Collection, box 243, Library of Congress, Washington, D.C.; Memorial of Pittsburgh steamboat engineers, 5 Jan. 1852; Project of a Law, Drawn up in accordance with the Resolutions adopted by the New Orleans Chamber of Commerce, Apr. 1852; Petition of the Humane Society of Boston, Mass., 7 Aug. 1852; Petition of citizens of New York, 2–13 Aug. 1852 [eighty-five copies], all in House Committee on Commerce, 32nd Cong., H.R. 2A-G4.10, National Archives and Records Administration, Washington, D.C. On Mather, see Mather Family Trees, http://www.matherclan.com/trees/getperson.php?personID=I1404&tree=Mather.

58. Burke, "Bursting Boilers and the Federal Power," 19–22 (quote on 22n); Paskoff,

Troubled Waters, 83–84, 136. For owners' opposition to the law, see Memorial of citizens of Philadelphia, 15 July 1852, and Petition of citizens of Baltimore, 20 July 1852, both in House Committee on Commerce, 32nd Cong., H.R. 2A-G4.10.

59. "An Act to Amend 'An Act to provide for the better Security of the lives of Passengers on board of Vessels propelled in whole or in part by Steam,' and for other purposes," *U.S. Statutes-at-Large*, 32nd Cong., 1st sess., 10:61–75; Burke, "Bursting Boilers and the Federal Power," 22; Brockmann, *Exploding Steamboats*, 126; Mashaw, *Creating the Administrative Constitution*, 190–94. For another view, which sees the decline in casualties as owing more to federally sponsored river improvements, see Paskoff, *Troubled Waters*, 20–22, 186–87.

60. Mashaw, *Creating the Administrative Constitution*, 195, 202–8; Goodman, *Shifting the Blame*, 7–8; Levy, *Freaks of Fortune*, 3–6, 19–40; Burke, "Bursting Boilers and the Federal Power," 18. On life insurance generally, see also S. Murphy, *Investing in Life*.

61. Aldrich, *Death Rode the Rails*, esp. chap. 3; Schulman, *Work Sights*, 38–40; Bronstein, *Caught in the Machinery*, 60–73. For a useful summary of state laws and regulations pertaining to factory safety before 1900, see U.S. Department of Labor, "Factory Inspection Legislation."

EPILOGUE

1. Aldrich, *Death Rode the Rails*, chap. 3; Vogel, *Angola Horror*, 1–10, 145–61.

2. G. Davies, "Emergence of a National Politics of Disaster," 306, 313–14. Davies presents a thorough and nuanced overview of the changes in American disaster relief in the post–Civil War era, focusing primarily on federal involvement. I disagree mainly with his contention that "even a large disaster [was] primarily a local event" in the antebellum era (313).

3. G. Davies, "Emergence of a National Politics of Disaster," 312–14; John, *Network Nation*, 7, 77–81, 101–10; McCullough, *Johnstown Flood*, 203–7; Fahs, *Imagined Civil War*, 19, 55.

4. McCullough, *Johnstown Flood*, 208–19, 223.

5. Sawislak, *Smoldering City*, 42–49, 85–100; Williams and Hoffius, *Upheaval in Charleston*, esp. 109–11, 191–216, 249–57; Horowitz, "Complete Story of the Galveston Horror," 95–108.

6. Sawislak, *Smoldering City*, 217–18; Nelson, *Ruin Nation*, 166–67; Fahs, *Imagined Civil War*, 36, 50; Godbey, "Disaster Tourism," 285–90; J. Brown, *Beyond the Lines*, 8, 12–14, 46–57. Although photography was a significant technological innovation, magazines often continued to use engravings based on sketches that were "superior in clarity, detail, and contrast" to early halftone photo reproductions. See Schulman, *Work Sights*, 10–11.

7. McCullough, *Johnstown Flood*, 218, 223–24; Godbey, "Disaster Tourism," 286–90; "Remembering the Johnstown Flood"; Heil, *Art of Stereography*.

8. *Report of the Johnstown Flood Committee*, 14–41, 45–47; *Johnstown Flood: Report of the Citizens' Relief Committee*, 5, 7–8, 22, 28, 65–80, 109. See also Sawislak, *Smoldering City*, 70–72; Dyl, *Seismic City*, 87–88; Williams and Hoffius, *Upheaval in Charleston*, 107–8.

9. *Johnstown Flood: Report of the Citizens' Relief Committee*, 16; McCullough, *Johnstown Flood*, 201–2, 225–26, 229; Sawislak, *Smoldering City*, 49–67.

10. M. Jones, *American Red Cross*, 28–30; McCullough, *Johnstown Flood*, 229–31; G. Davies, "Emergence of a National Politics of Disaster," 314–15.

11. G. Davies, "Emergence of a National Politics of Disaster," 306–9.

12. G. Davies, "Emergence of a National Politics of Disaster," 309–12; "Acts of Congress Granting . . . Relief to Sufferers from Floods, Fires, Earthquakes, and So Forth," *Congressional Record*, 7 Aug. 1950, 11900–02.

13. McCullough, *Johnstown Flood*, 225, 264; G. Davies, "Emergence of a National Politics of Disaster," 315–16.

14. P. May, *Recovering from Catastrophes*, 9–11, 18–23; "Acts of Congress Granting . . . Relief to Sufferers from Floods, Fires, Earthquakes, and So Forth"; Dyl, *Seismic City*, 59–60, 64, 87, 199, 204, 210; Parrish, *Flood Year 1927*, 66–68.

15. P. May, *Recovering from Catastrophes*, 9–11, 18–40, 161–62; G. Davies, "Pre-modern Disaster Politics." For a convenient list of general (as opposed to disaster-specific) legislation, see U.S. Department of Housing and Urban Development, "History of Federal Disaster Policy."

16. Kasson, *Amusing the Million*, 71–72; Dennett and Warnke, "Disaster Spectacles"; Flood History, "Silent Era"; Luna Park, "The Johnstown Flood Show (1902–1905)" and "The Deluge (1906–1908)."

17. Solnit, *Paradise Built in Hell*, 120–32; Dennett and Warnke, "Disaster Spectacles"; Rozario, *Culture of Calamity*, 123–33.

18. Simon, *Hamlet Fire*; O'Neill, "Broken Levees," 89–93, 98–103; Tierney, "Hurricane in New Orleans?"

19. Dyl, *Seismic City*, 82–83, 279–80; Morris, *Big Muddy*, esp. 164–74, 206–13; Parrish, *Flood Year 1927*, 1–18, 56–57, 62; U.S. Army Corps of Engineers, *New York–New Jersey Harbor*; "Sierra Club."

20. Solnit, *Paradise Built in Hell*, esp. 2, 8, 21, 75–78, 123–25; Remes, *Disaster Citizenship*; Tierney et al., "Metaphors Matter."

21. Andrés, *We Fed an Island*; Williams and Hoffius, *Upheaval in Charleston*, 191–216, 249–57; Dyl, *Seismic City*, chap. 4; Horowitz, "Complete Story of the Galveston Horror"; Horowitz, "Hurricane Betsy."

22. Frazier, "Day the Great Plains Burned," 38–39.

BIBLIOGRAPHY

PRIMARY SOURCES

Manuscripts

British National Archives, Kew, U.K.
    Colonial Office Records, series 5, 42, 152
    Treasury Board Papers and In-Letters, series 1
Historical Society of Pennsylvania, Philadelphia
    Bradford Family Papers
Library of Congress, Washington, D.C.
    House of Representatives Collection
Library of Virginia, Richmond
    John Durbarrow Blair Papers (microfilm)
    Isaac Coplin Letters
    Thomas B. Hewitt Letter
National Archives and Records Administration, Washington, D.C.
    House Committee on Commerce Papers
Portsmouth Athenaeum, Portsmouth, N.H.
    Portsmouth Fire Collection
Royal Archives, Windsor Castle, Windsor, U.K.
    Augusta, Princess of Wales, Accounts
    Essays of George III
    George III Official Correspondence
    George III Private Correspondence
    George III, Privy Purse
Royal Library, Windsor Castle, Windsor, U.K.
    Picture Library
South Carolina Historical Society, Charleston
    Edward W. Bancroft Letter
    Robert Mills Papers
Virginia Historical Society, Richmond
    Greene Family Papers

Newspapers

Aberdeen Press and Journal (UK)
Albany Argus
Albany Evening Journal
Alexandria Advertiser
Alexandria Gazette
American Commercial and Daily
Advertiser (Baltimore)
American Weekly Mercury (Philadelphia)
Baltimore Sun
Bath (Eng.) Chronicle and
Weekly Gazette
Boston Courier
Boston Evening-Post
Boston Gazette
Boston Gazette, or Country Journal
Boston News-Letter
Boston Post-Boy
Boston Weekly Advertiser
Burlington (Iowa) Gazette
Caledonian Mercury (UK)
Charleston Courier
Cincinnati Whig
Connecticut Courant
Connecticut Journal
Connecticut Journal, and the
New-Haven Post-Boy
Daily National Advertiser (Washington)
Daily Picayune (New Orleans)
Daily Telegraph (Jersey City, N.J.)
Derby (Eng.) Mercury
The Emancipator
Essex (Mass.) Gazette
Farmer's Cabinet (Amherst, N.H.)
Federal Republican (Baltimore)
Gazetteer and New Daily
Advertiser (London)
Gazette of the United States (Philadelphia)
General Evening Post (London)
Georgia Weekly Telegraph
Kalamazoo Gazette
Kentucky Gazette
Lloyd's Evening Post (London)
London Chronicle
London Evening Post
London Gazette

Martinsburg (Va.) Gazette
Maryland Gazette
Massachusetts Gazette, and the
Boston Post-Boy and Advertiser
Massachusetts Spy
Morning Chronicle and London Advertiser
National Gazette and Literary
Register (Philadelphia)
National Intelligencer (Washington)
National Daily Intelligencer (Washington)
New Bedford (Mass.) Mercury
Newburyport (Mass.) Morning Herald
New Hampshire Gazette
New-Hampshire Gazette, and
Historical Chronicle
New London (Conn.) Gazette
Newport Mercury
New York Commercial Advertiser
New-York Gazette
New York Gazette & General Advertiser
New-York Gazette, or Weekly Post-Boy
New York Herald
New-York Journal
New York Journal of Commerce
New-York Mercury
New York Spectator
New York Sun
New York Times
Northampton (Eng.) Mercury
Ohio State Journal
Pennsylvania Chronicle
Pennsylvania Gazette
Pennsylvania Packet
Pennsylvania Packet; and
General Advertiser
Providence Gazette
Providence Gazette, and Country Journal
Public Advertiser (Hagerstown, Md.)
Public Advertiser (London)
Public Ledger (London)
Quebec Gazette
Rhode-Island Republican
Richmond Enquirer
Salem Gazette
Salem Register

Savannah Republican
Scioto (Ohio) Gazette
South Carolina Gazette
South-Carolina Gazette, and Country Journal
Southern Patriot (Charleston)
Spirit of the Times (New York)
Stamford (Eng.) Mercury
Trenton (N.J.) Federalist
The Union (Washington, Ky.)

Virginia Argus
Virginia Gazette
Virginia Telegraph
Washington Post
Whitehall Evening Post or
London Intelligencer
Wisconsin Democrat
Wisconsin Enquirer

Magazines

American Masonic Register
Annual Register
Critical Review
Franklin Journal, and American
Mechanics' Magazine
Gentleman's Magazine
Illustrated London News
London Magazine: or, Gentleman's
Monthly Intelligencer

Miscellaneous Correspondence
in Prose & Verse
Moral & Entertaining Magazine
Presbyterian Magazine
Scots Magazine
Universal Magazine
Universal Magazine of
Knowledge and Pleasure
Youth's Cabinet

Other Published Primary Sources

An Account of the Earthquake Which Destroyed the City of Lisbon . . . Illustrative of the Great Picture of the Earthquake . . . . London: W. Glendinning, 1800.

An Account of the late Dreadful Earthquake and Fire, which destroyed the City of Lisbon. 3rd ed. Boston: Green and Russell, 1756.

Acts and Resolves, Public and Private, of the Province of Massachusetts Bay. 21 vols. Boston: Wright and Potter, 1869–1922.

Adams, Nathaniel. Annals of Portsmouth: Comprising a Period of Two Hundred Years from the First Settlement of the Town. Portsmouth, N.H.: Published by the Author, 1825.

Addressed to the Reverend the Clergy, of All Religious Denominations, throughout the United States. Portsmouth, N.H.: n.p., 1807.

An Address to the Inhabitants of Great-Britain; Occasioned by the late earthquake at Lisbon. London: J. Buckland, 1755.

Advice to England; or, Resolution, a Poem, Occasioned by the Late Earthquake. London: John Hinton, 1750.

Alcock, Thomas. A Sermon on the Late Earthquakes, More particularly that at Lisbon. Oxford: Richard Clements, 1756.

[Alexander, Ann Tuke]. Remarks on the Theatre, and on the Late Fire in Richmond, Virginia. York, Eng.: T. Wilson and Son, 1812.

American State Papers. 38 vols. Washington, D.C.: Gales and Seaton, 1832–61.

Andrés, José. We Fed an Island: The True Story of Rebuilding Puerto Rico, One Meal at a Time. With Richard Wolffe. New York: Anthony Bourdain/Ecco, 2018.

Andrews, Evangeline Walker, and Charles McLean Andrews, eds. Jonathan Dickinson's Journal, or, God's Protecting Providence. New Haven: Yale University Press, 1945.

Anguish, Thomas. *Allegiance and Support, A Debt of Gratitude to His Majesty.* London: H. Whitridge, 1745.

————. *A Sermon preached at St. Nicholas, Deptford, on the Fast Day appointed by Royal Proclamation.* London: John Clarke, 1756.

Ashton, Thomas. *A Sermon Preached on Occasion of the General Fast Appointed by Royal Proclamation.* London: J. Kippax, 1756.

An Awful Calamity Occasioned by the Conflagration of the Theatre at Richmond. London: Darton, Harvey, and Co., 1812.

Bailey, Joseph. *God's Wonders in the Great Deep: or, A Narrative of the Shipwreck of the Brigantine Alida and Catharine.* New York: James Parker, 1750.

Barbour, Philip L., ed. *The Complete Works of Captain John Smith (1580–1630).* 3 vols. Chapel Hill: University of North Carolina Press, 1986.

Baretti, Joseph. *A Journey from London to Genoa; Through England, Portugal, Spain, and France.* 4 vols. London: T. Davis and L. Davis, 1770.

Barrett, Philip. *Gilbert Hunt, the City Blacksmith.* Richmond: James Woodhouse and Co., 1859.

Barrow, John. *A Collection of Authentic, Useful, and Entertaining Voyages.* 3 vols. London: J. Knox, 1765.

Bear, James A., Jr., and Lucia C. Stanton, eds. *Jefferson's Memorandum Books: Accounts, with Legal Records and Miscellany, 1767–1826.* 2 vols. Princeton: Princeton University Press, 1997.

Biddulph, John. *A Poem on the Earthquake at Lisbon.* London: W. Owen, 1755.

Boyd, Julian P., et al., eds. *The Papers of Thomas Jefferson.* 43 vols. to date. Princeton: Princeton University Press, 1954–.

Bradford, William. *Of Plymouth Plantation, 1620–1647.* Edited by Francis Murphy. New York: Modern Library, 1981.

[Brooke, Christopher.] *A Poem on the Late Massacre in Virginia, With particular mention of those men of note that suffered in that disaster.* London: G. Eld, 1622.

————. "A Poem on the Late Massacre in Virginia." Edited by Robert C. Johnson. *Virginia Magazine of History and Biography* 72 (1964): 259–92.

Burt, John. *Earthquakes, The Effects of God's Wrath.* Newport, R.I.: J. Franklin, 1755.

Butterfield, L. H., et al., eds. *The Diary and Autobiography of John Adams.* 4 vols. Cambridge, Mass.: Harvard University Press, 1961.

By George Clinton, governor of the state of New-York . . . a proclamation. New York: n.p., 1793.

By His Excellency Benning Wentworth, Esq.; . . . A brief. Portsmouth, N.H.: Daniel Fowle, 1760.

By His Excellency Horatio Sharpe, Esq.; . . . A brief. Annapolis: Jonas Green, 1760.

By His Excellency Thomas Pownall, Esq.; . . . A brief. Boston: John Draper, 1760.

Caldwell, Charles. *A Reply to Dr. Haygarth's "Letter to Dr. Percival, on Infectious Fevers," and His "Address to the College of Physicians at Philadelphia, on the Prevention of the American Pestilence."* Philadelphia: Thomas and William Bradford, 1802.

"Capt. Byrd's Letters Continued." *Virginia Historical Register* 2 (1849): 78–83.

Carey, Mathew. *A Desultory Account of the Yellow Fever, prevalent in Philadelphia.* Philadelphia: Mathew Carey, 1793.

————. *A Short Account of the Malignant Fever, lately prevalent in Philadelphia.* 3rd ed. Philadelphia: Mathew Carey, 1793.

A Catalogue of the books belonging to the Library Company of Philadelphia. Philadelphia: Zachariah Poulson, 1789.

Chandler, Samuel. *The Character of a Great and Good King Full of Days, Riches, and Honour.* London: J. Noon, 1760.

——. *The Scriptural Account of the Cause and Intention of Earthquakes.* London: John Noon, 1750.

The Charter Granted By Their Majesties King William and Queen Mary, to the Inhabitants of the Province of the Massachusetts-Bay in New-England. Boston: S. Kneeland, 1759.

Chauncy, Charles. *Earthquakes a Token of the righteous Anger of God.* Boston: Edes and Gill, 1755.

Chetwood, W. R. *The Voyages and Adventures of Captain Robert Boyle . . . To which is added, the Voyage, Shipwreck, and Miraculous Preservation, of Richard Castelman.* London: John Watts, 1726.

Clark, Samuel. *A Sermon Preached at Daventry . . . On Occasion of the Late Earthquake at Lisbon.* London: James Buckland, 1756.

Cobbett, William, ed. *Cobbett's Parliamentary History of England.* 36 vols. London: T. C. Hansard, 1806–20.

A Concise Statement of the Awful Conflagration of the Theatre, in the City of Richmond. Philadelphia: n.p., 1812.

Congressional Globe. 46 vols. Washington, D.C.: Blair and Rives, 1834–73.

Congressional Record. Washington, D.C.: Government Printing Office, 1874–.

Cooper, Samuel. *A Sermon upon the Occasion of the Death of our Late Sovereign.* Boston: John Draper, 1761.

Copland, Patrick. *Virginia's God be Thanked, or A sermon of thanksgiving for the happie successe of the affayres in Virginia this last yeare.* London: William Sheffard and John Bellamie, 1622.

Council for Virginia. *A Briefe Declaration of the Present State of Things in Virginia.* London: Thomas Snodham, 1616.

——. *A True and Sincere Declaration of the Purpose and Ends of the Plantation begun in Virginia.* London: George Eld, 1610.

——. *A True Declaration of the Estate of the Colony in Virginia.* London: Eliot's Court Press and William Stansby, 1610.

Crashaw, William. *A sermon preached in London before the right honorable the Lord LaWarre.* London: William Welby, 1610.

[Crouch, Nathaniel]. *The General History of Earthquakes.* 1694. Reprint, London: A. Bettesworth, 1734.

Dana, Joseph. *Tribute of Sympathy . . . on the late Overwhelming Calamity at Richmond, Virginia.* Newburyport, Mass.: E. W. Allen, 1812.

Davies, Samuel. *A Sermon Delivered at Nassau-Hall.* Boston: R. Draper, 1761.

——. *Sermons on Important Subjects.* Boston: Lincoln and Edmands, 1810.

Defoe, Daniel. *A Journal of the Plague Year.* Edited by George Rice Carpenter. New York: Longmans, Green, and Co., 1896.

——. *Robinson Crusoe.* Norton Critical Edition. 2nd ed. Edited by Michael Shinagel. New York: W. W. Norton, 1993.

——. *The Storm.* Edited by Richard Hamblyn. New York: Penguin Classics, 2005.

Dexter, Franklin Bowditch, ed. *Extracts from the Itineraries and Other Miscellanies of Ezra*

Stiles, D.D., LL.D., 1755–1794, with a Selection from His Correspondence. New Haven: Yale University Press, 1916.

Dickinson, Jonathan. *God's Protecting Providence Man's Surest Help and Defence in Times of Greatest Difficulty and Most Imminent Danger.* Philadelphia: Reinier Jansen, 1699.

The Earthquake Engineering Online Archive. NISEE e-Library. https://nisee.berkeley .edu/elibrary/. Accessed 12 Mar. 2019.

Earthquakes Improved, or Solemn Warning to the World. Boston: J. Green, 1755.

Edwards, John. *Warning to Sinners, or An Address to All Play-Actors . . . and the World at Large.* New York: published for the author, 1812.

Ellms, Charles. *Shipwrecks and Disasters at Sea, or Historical Narratives of the Most Noted Calamities, and Providential Deliverances from Fire and Famine, on the Ocean.* Boston: S. N. Dickinson, 1836.

———. *The Tragedy of the Seas; or, Sorrow on the Ocean, Lake, and River, from Shipwreck, Plague, Fire, and Famine.* New York: Israel Post, 1841.

Everett, Edward, ed. *The Writings and Speeches of Daniel Webster.* 18 vols. Boston: Little, Brown, 1903.

[Falconer, William]. *The Shipwreck: A Poem, In Three Cantos.* London: A. Millar, 1762.

Federal Emergency Management Agency. "Session 6: Defining Disaster." https://training .fema.gov/hiedu/aemrc/courses/coursesunderdev/hazdisusems.aspx. Accessed 23 Nov. 2018.

Figueiredo, Antonio Pereira de. *A narrative of the earthquake and fire of Lisbon by . . . an eyewitness thereof . . . Translated from the Latin.* London: G. Hawkins, 1756.

Fisher, George D. *History and Reminiscences of the Monumental Church, Richmond, Virginia, from 1814 to 1878.* Richmond: Whittet and Shepperson, 1880.

Fisher, Samuel Rowland. *Philadelphia, 11th Month, 18th, 1793, Respected Friend . . .* Philadelphia: n.p., 1793.

Flagg, Edmund. *Far West, or, A Tour beyond the Mountains.* New York: Harper and Brothers, 1838.

Foster, J. Heron. *A Full Account of the Great Fire at Pittsburgh . . . with the Individual Losses and Contributions for Relief.* Pittsburgh: J. W. Cook, 1845.

Foxcroft, Thomas. *The Earthquake, A Divine Visitation.* Boston: S. Kneeland, 1756.

Francis' Metallic Lifeboat Company. New York: W. C. Bryant and Co., 1852.

Freke, John. *A Plain Account of the Cause of Earthquakes.* London: W. Innys and J. Richardson, 1756.

A Full Account of the Burning of the Richmond Theatre. Richmond: J. Edwin Goode, 1858.

Furness, W. H. *A Discourse . . . Occasioned by the Loss of the Lexington.* Philadelphia: C. A. Elliott, 1840.

Gibbons, Thomas. *A Sermon Preached at Haberdashers-Hall . . . on Occasion of the tremendous Earthquake at Lisbon.* London: J. Buckland, 1756.

Gilman, Samuel. *A Monody on the Victims, and Sufferers by the Late Conflagration in the City of Richmond.* Boston: Charles Williams, T. B. Wait and Co., 1812.

Grey, Zachary. *A Chronological and Historical Account of the Most Memorable Earthquakes.* Cambridge: J. Bentham, 1750.

———. *A Farther Account of Memorable Earthquakes.* Cambridge: J. Bentham, 1756.

Halifax, James. *A Sermon Preach'd in St. John's Chapel in the Parish of St. Andrew Holborn.* London: J. Hughes, 1756.

[Hanway, Jonas]. *The Case of the Canadians at Montreal distressed by Fire: Motives for a subscription towards the relief of the sufferers at Montreal in Canada, by a dreadful fire.* London: n.p., 1766.

————. *A Summary of the Case of the Sufferers by fire at Montreal.* London: n.p., 1766.

Haven, Samuel. *The Supreme Influence of the Son of God, in appointing, directing, and terminating the reign of Princes: A Sermon Occasioned by the Death of King George the Second.* Portsmouth, N.H.: D. Fowle, 1761.

Hening, William Waller. *Statutes at Large: Being a Collection of All the Laws of Virginia . . .* 13 vols. Richmond: Samuel Pleasants Jr., 1809–23.

[Howe, Thomas]. *An Account of the Late Dreadful Hurricane, which happened on the 31st of August, 1772.* Basseterre, St. Christopher: Thomas Howe, 1772.

Howell, George Rogers, and Jonathan Tenney. *Bi-centennial History of Albany . . . from 1609 to 1886.* New York: W. W. Munsell and Co., 1886.

Howland, S. A. *Disasters by Steam, Fire, and Water: With Elegant Engravings.* Worcester, Mass.: Dorr, Howland and Co., 1842.

————. *Steamboat Disasters and Railroad Accidents in the United States.* Worcester, Mass.: Dorr, Howland and Co., 1840.

Hunter, Thomas. *An Historical Account of Earthquakes, Extracted from the most Authentic Historians.* Liverpool: R. Williamson, 1756.

————. *National Wickedness the Cause of National Misery.* Liverpool: R. Williamson, 1756.

Jackson, Donald, and Dorothy Twohig, eds. *The Diaries of George Washington.* 6 vols. Charlottesville: University of Virginia Press, 1976–79.

Janeway, James. *Mr. James Janeway's Legacy to his Friends, Containing Twenty Seven Famous Instances of Gods Providence in and about Sea Dangers and Deliverances.* London: Dorman Newman, 1674.

————. *A Seasonable and Earnest Address to the Citizens of London.* 1666. Reprint, Boston: Benjamin Mecom, 1760.

————. *A Token for Children . . . To which is added, A Token, for the Children of New England.* Boston: Nicholas Boone, 1700.

————. *A Token for Mariners.* London: Hugh Newman, 1698.

Johnstown Flood: Report of the Citizens' Relief Committee, of Pittsburgh. Pittsburgh: Myers, Shinkle, and Co., 1890.

J[ohonnot], A[ndrew]. *A Poem on the Rebuke of God's Hand in the Awful Desolation made by Fire in the Town of Boston.* Boston: Fowle and Draper, 1760.

Jones, David. *A Discourse upon the Great Fire of London.* 1666. Reprint, Boston: Fowle and Draper, 1760.

Journal of the Assembly of the State of New York, at Their Fifty-Ninth Session. Albany: E. Crowell, 1836.

Journal of the Honourable House of Representatives, of His Majesty's province of the Massachusetts-Bay . . . on . . . the twenty-ninth day of May . . . 1765. Boston: Green and Russell, 1765.

Kaminski, John P., et al., eds. *The Documentary History of the Ratification of the Constitution.* Digital ed. Charlottesville: Rotunda/University of Virginia Press, https://rotunda .upress.virginia.edu/founders/RNCN.html. Accessed 12 Mar. 2019.

Kennedy, John Pendleton, ed. *Journals of the House of Burgesses of Virginia, 1770–1772.* Richmond: Colonial Press, E. Wadley Co., 1906.

Kingsbury, Susan Myra, ed. *Records of the Virginia Company.* 4 vols. Washington D.C.: Government Printing Office, 1906–35.

Knox, Hugh. *A Discourse Delivered on the 6th of September, 1772, In the Dutch Church of St. Croix.* St. Croix: n.p., 1772.

A Lady. *The Child's Gem.* New York: Samuel Coleman, 1839.

Lardner, Dionysius. *The Steam Engine Explained and Illustrated: With an Account of Its Invention and Progressive Improvement, and Its Application to Navigation and Railways; Including Also a Memoir of Watt.* London: Taylor and Walton, 1840.

Lawson, Deodat. *Threnodia, or A Mournfull Remembrance.* Boston: Bartholomew Green, 1694.

"Letters of Roger Atkinson, 1769–1776." *Virginia Magazine of History and Biography* 15 (1908): 345–59.

Lines Made After the Great Earthquake. Boston: n.p., 1755.

Lloyd, James T. *Lloyd's Steamboat Directory, and Disasters on the Western Waters.* Cincinnati: James T. Lloyd and Co., 1856.

Lloyd, Rees. *The Richmond Alarm: A Plain and Familiar Discourse . . . between a Father and His Son.* Pittsburgh: Robert Ferguson and Co., 1815.

Lothrop, Samuel Kirkland. *A Sermon . . . on the Destruction of the Lexington by Fire.* Boston: John H. Eastburn, 1840.

Mancall, Peter C., ed. *Travel Narratives from the Age of Discovery.* New York: Oxford University Press, 2006.

Mather, Cotton. *Compassions Called For: An Essay of Profitable Reflections on Miserable Spectacles.* Boston: B. Green, 1711.

———. *Magnalia Christi Americana.* 2 vols. 1702. Reprint, Hartford, Conn.: Silas Andrus and Son, 1855.

Mather, Increase. *An Essay for the Recording of Illustrious Providences Wherein an Account Is Given of Many Remarkable and Very Memorable Events Which Have Happened This Last Age, Especially in New-England.* Boston: Samuel Green, 1684.

May, Robert. *A Voice from Richmond: And Other Addresses to Children and Youth.* Philadelphia: American Sunday School Union, 1842.

Mayhew, Jonathan. *The Expected Dissolution of All Things, a Motive to Universal Holiness.* Boston: Edes and Gill, 1755.

———. *God's Hand and Providence to be Religiously Acknowledged in Public Calamities.* Boston: Richard Draper, 1760.

McCarthy, Carlton. *Walks about Richmond: A Story for Boys, and a Guide to Persons Visiting the City, Desiring to See the Principle Points of Interest.* Richmond: McCarthy and Ellyson, 1870.

McIlwaine, Henry R., et al., eds. *Executive Journals of the Council of Virginia, 1680–1775.* 6 vols. Richmond: Virginia State Library, 1925–66.

McLeod, Mrs. Hugh [Rebecca Lamar]. "The Loss of the Steamer Pulaski." *Georgia Historical Quarterly* 3 (1919): 63–95.

Memorial of the Sundry Proprietors and Managers of American Steam Vessels. New York: n.p., 1840.

Messages and Papers of the Presidents. American Presidency Project. http://presidency.proxied.lsit.ucsb.edu/ws/. Accessed 23 Nov. 2018.

Miller, Samuel. *Theatrical Exhibitions.* New York: American Tract Society, ca. 1830.

Minutes of the Proceedings of the Committee, appointed on the 14th September, 1793. Philadelphia: R. Aitken and Son, 1794.

[Mordecai, Samuel]. *Richmond in By-Gone Days: Being Reminiscences of an Old Citizen.* Richmond: G. M. West, 1856.

Moss, Charles. *A Sermon Preached at the Parish Church of St. James, Westminster.* London: J. Whiston and B. White, 1756.

Nicholson, Colin, ed. *The Papers of Francis Bernard,* 5 vols. Charlottesville: University of Virginia Press, 2007–15.

The North American Tourist. New York: A. T. Goodrich, 1839.

Nowell, William. *A Sermon preached at the Parish Church of Wolsingham.* Newcastle: I. Thompson and Company, 1756.

O'Lynch, John. *Narrative and Report of the Causes and Circumstances of the Deplorable Conflagration.* Richmond: n.p., 1812.

Pennington, John. *A Serious Call to Repentance.* Cambridge: J. Bentham, 1756.

Pennsylvania Archives. 1st ser., 12 vols. Philadelphia: J. Severns, 1852–56.

Percy, George. "A True Relation." *Tyler's Quarterly Historical and Genealogical Magazine* 3 (1922): 259–82.

Plaisted, Bartholomew. *A Journal from Calcutta in Bengal . . . in the Year MDCCL.* 2nd ed. London: T. Kennersly, 1758.

A Poem on the Late Earthquake at Lisbon, to which is added, Thoughts in a Church-Yard. London: R. and J. Dodsley, 1755.

Pond, James L. *History of Life-Saving Appliances, and Military and Naval Constructions, Invented and Manufactured by Joseph Francis.* New York: E. D. Slater, 1885.

Preston, Daniel, et al., eds. *The Papers of James Monroe.* 6 vols. to date. Westport, Conn.: Greenwood Press, 2003–.

Proceedings of the Coroner in the Case of the Steamer Lexington. New York: n.p., 1840.

Public Documents, Printed by Order of the Senate of the United States: First Session of the Twenty-Sixth Congress. 8 vols. Washington, D.C.: Blair and Rives, 1840.

Public Statutes at Large of the United States of America. 8 vols. Boston: Charles C. Little and James Brown, 1845–67.

Purchas, Samuel. *Hakluytus Posthumus, or, Purchas His Pilgrimes.* 20 vols. Glasgow: J. MacLehose and Sons, 1905–7.

Redfield, W. C. "On the Supposed Collapse of Steam Boilers, and the Means of Preventing Explosions." *American Journal of Science and Arts* 21 (Jan. 1832): 149–91.

Redman, John. *An Account of the Yellow Fever as It Prevailed in Philadelphia in the Autumn of 1762: A Paper Presented to the College of Physicians of Philadelphia . . . September 7, 1793.* Philadelphia: n.p., 1865.

Reflections Physical and Moral, upon the Various and numerous uncommon Phenomena, . . . which have happened from the Earthquake at Lima, to the present Time. London: A. Millar, 1756.

Report of the Committee Appointed by the Citizens of Cincinnati. Cincinnati: Alexander Flash, 1838.

Report of the Johnstown Flood Committee. Pittsburgh: Geo. T. Swank, 1890.

Report of the Secretary of the Treasury, of the Statistics and History of the Steam Marine of the United States. 1852. Proquest Congressional. Accessed 23 Nov. 2018.

Revised Statutes of the State of New York . . . Passed from 1828 to 1835 Inclusive. 3 vols. Albany: Packard and Van Benthuysen, 1836.

Richards, George. *Repent! Repent! Or Likewise Perish!* Philadelphia: Lydia R. Bailey, 1812.

Rogers, William M. *A Sermon, Occasioned by the Loss of the Harold and the Lexington.* Boston: Perkins and Marvin, 1840.

A Satirical Review of the Manifold Falshoods and Absurdities hitherto publish'd concerning the Earthquake. London: A. and C. Corbett, 1756.

A Serious Inquiry into the Nature and Effects of the Stage . . . by the Rev. John Witherspoon, also A Sermon on the Burning of the Theatre at Richmond, &c. by Samuel Miller. New York: Whiting and Watson, 1812.

"Sierra Club: Massive Army Corp Project Threatens Hudson River & New York Bay: Won't Work," 11 July 2018. *New Jersey Insider.* https://www.insidernj.com/press-release/sierra-club-massive-army-corp-project-threatens-hudson-river-new-york-bay-wont-work/. Accessed 19 Mar. 2019.

Smith, J. R. *The Causes of Steamboat Explosions, and the Evils under which They Have Been Permitted to Occur.* New Orleans: True Delta, 1852.

Smith, William. *History of Canada: From Its First Discovery, to the Year 1791.* 2 vols. Quebec: J. Neilson, 1815.

Stanford, John. *Aetna, a Discourse . . . Intended as a Moral Improvement.* New York: E. Conrad, 1824.

Steamboat Accidents, Loss of Life, Etc.: Letter from J. P. Van Tyne to the Hon. J. R. Underwood. 1840. Proquest Congressional. Accessed 23 Nov. 2018.

Stone, John S. *A Sermon, Occasioned by the Burning of the Steamer Lexington.* Boston: Perkins and Marvin, 1840.

Stowe, Harriet Beecher. "The Canal Boat." *Godey's Lady's Book,* Oct. 1841, 167–69.

Theatre on Fire. Awful Calamity! Boston: n.p., 1812.

A Theocrate. *Five Important Questions . . . Occasioned by Serious Reflections on the Alarming and Awfully Severe Visitation of the Theatre in Richmond.* N.p., 1812.

To the Selectmen of the Town of [blank] 1811. Newburyport, Mass.: n.p., 1811.

A True and Particular Account of the Late Dreadful Earthquake at Lisbon to Which is Added a Mournful Copy of Verses on the Occasion: Also the Heads of a Sermon by the Reverend Mr. Hervey. London: n.p., 1756.

A True and Particular Relation of the Dreadful Earthquake Which Happen'd at Lima, the Capital of Peru, and the Neighbouring Port of Callao. London: T. Osborne, 1748.

Twohig, Dorothy, et al., eds. *The Papers of George Washington, Presidential Series.* 20 volumes to date.Charlottesville: University of Virginia Press, 1987–.

Two Very Circumstantial Accounts of the Late Dreadful Earthquake at Lisbon. Boston: D. Fowle and Z. Fowle, 1756.

Tyler, Lyon Gardiner, ed. *Narratives of Early Virginia, 1606–1625.* New York: C. Scribner's Sons, 1907.

U.S. Army Corps of Engineers. *New York–New Jersey Harbor and Tributaries Coastal Storm Risk Management Feasibility Study.* http://www.nan.usace.army.mil/Portals/37/docs/civilworks/projects/nj/coast/NYNJHATS/NJHatPres.pdf?ver=2017-10-16-141621-747. Accessed 23 Nov. 2018.

U.S. Congress. *Journal of the House of Representatives of the United States.* 43 vols. Washington, D.C.: Gales & Seaton; Government Printing Office, 1826–73.

U.S. Government Accountability Office. *Federal Disaster Assistance: Federal Departments and Agencies Obligated at Least $277.6 Billion during Fiscal Years 2005 through 2014.* Sept. 2016. https://www.gao.gov/assets/680/679977.pdf. Accessed 19 Mar. 2019.

———. *2017 Hurricanes and Wildfires: Initial Observations on the Federal Response and Key*

Recovery Challenges. Sept. 2018. https://www.gao.gov/assets/700/694231.pdf. Accessed 19 Mar. 2019.

U.S. Statutes at Large. 125 vols. Washington, D.C.: Government Printing Office, 1845–2011.

Van Horne, John C., ed. *Correspondence of William Nelson as Acting Governor of Virginia, 1770–71*. Charlottesville: University of Virginia Press, 1988.

"Virginia in 1771." *Virginia Magazine of History and Biography* 6 (1893): 124–28.

Visitor's Guide to Richmond and Vicinity. Richmond: B. Bates, 1871.

Voltaire. *Poem upon the Lisbon Disaster*. Trans. Anthony Hecht. Lincoln, Mass.: Penmaen Press, 1977.

A Volume of Records Relating to the Early History of Boston: Miscellaneous Papers. Boston: n.p., 1900.

Votes and Proceedings of the Lower House of the Assembly of . . . Maryland; November session, 1765. Annapolis: Jonas Green, 1766.

Waterhouse, Edward. *A Declaration of the State of the Colony and Affaires in Virginia With a Relation of the Barbarous Massacre*. London: G. Eld, 1622.

[Webb, William]. *An Authentic Narrative of the Loss of the Doddington Indiaman, and of the Surprising Adventures, and Distresses, of those on Board, who survived the Shipwreck; from the Journal of one of the Surviving Officers*. 1756. Reprint, New York: James Parker, 1762.

[Weild, C.]. *A Warning Voice from a Watery Grave! Solemn Proof of the Uncertainty of Life, and Importance of an Early Preparation for Death!* New York: Sacket and Sargent, 1840.

Wesley, John. *Some Serious Thoughts Occasioned by the Late Earthquake at Lisbon*. Dublin: n.p., 1756.

Wesley, John, and Charles Wesley. *Hymns occasioned by the earthquake, March 8, 1750 . . . and . . . Occasioned by the destruction of Lisbon*. 2nd ed. Bristol: E. Farley, 1756.

Whitaker, Alexander. *Good Newes From Virginia*. London: Felix Kyngston, 1613.

Whitefield, George. *A Letter from a Clergyman at London to the Remaining Disconsolate Inhabitants of Lisbon*. 4th ed. London: R. Griffiths, 1756.

Whiton, John M. *Sketches of the History of New-Hampshire, from its Settlement, in 1623, to 1833: Comprising Notices of the Memorable Events and Interesting Incidents of Two Hundred and Ten Years*. Concord, N.H.: Marsh, Capon, and Lyon, 1834.

Wilkinson, John. *The Seaman's Preservation: Or, Safety in Shipwreck*. London: T. Osborne, 1759.

———. *Tutamen Nauticum: or, the Seaman's Preservation from Shipwreck*. 2nd ed. London: n.p., 1763.

Willis, William. *The History of Portland from Its First Settlement*. 2 vols. Portland, Maine: Charles Day and Co., 1831–33.

Wingfield, Edward Maria. *A Discourse of Virginia*. 1608. Reprint, Boston: J. Wilson and Son, 1860.

Winthrop, John. *A Lecture on Earthquakes*. Boston: Edes and Gill, 1755.

Wright, Louis B., ed. *A Voyage to Virginia in 1609: Two Narratives*. Charlottesville: University of Virginia Press, 2013.

SECONDARY SOURCES

Abrams, M. H. *Natural Supernaturalism: Tradition and Revolution in Romantic Literature*. New York: W. W. Norton, 1971.

Aguirre, Benigno E. "Better Disaster Statistics: The Lisbon Earthquake." *Journal of Interdisciplinary History* 43 (2012): 27–42.

Aldrich, Mark. *Death Rode the Rails: American Railroad Accidents and Safety, 1828–1965.* Baltimore: Johns Hopkins University Press, 2006.

Allgor, Catherine. *Parlor Politics: In Which the Ladies of Washington Help Build a City and a Government.* Charlottesville: University of Virginia Press, 2000.

Alvey, Edward. *The Fredericksburg Fire of 1807.* Fredericksburg, Va.: Historic Fredericksburg Foundation, 1988.

Ambler, Charles Henry. *Thomas Ritchie: A Study in Virginia Politics.* Richmond: Bell Book and Stationery Co., 1913.

American National Biography. Online edition.

Amory, Hugh, and David D. Hall, eds. *A History of the Book in America.* Vol. 1, *The Colonial Book in the Atlantic World.* Chapel Hill: University of North Carolina Press, 2007.

Anderson, Douglas. *William Bradford's Books: Of Plimmoth Plantation and the Printed Word.* Baltimore: Johns Hopkins University Press, 2003.

Anderson, Virginia DeJohn. *Creatures of Empire: How Domestic Animals Transformed Early America.* New York: Oxford University Press, 2004.

Andrews, K. R., et al., eds. *The Westward Enterprise: English Activities in Ireland, the Atlantic, and America, 1480–1650.* Detroit: Wayne State University Press, 1979.

Andrews, William D. "The Literature of the 1727 New England Earthquake." *Early American Literature* 8 (1973): 281–94.

Apel, Thomas. *Feverish Bodies, Enlightened Minds: Science and the Yellow Fever Controversy in the Early American Republic.* Stanford: Stanford University Press, 2016.

———. "The Thucydidean Moment: History, Science, and the Yellow-Fever Controversy, 1793–1805." *Journal of the Early Republic* 34 (2014): 315–47.

Appleby, Joyce. *Inheriting the Revolution: The First Generation of Americans.* Cambridge, Mass.: Harvard University Press, 2000.

———. *Shores of Knowledge: New Work Discoveries and the Scientific Imagination.* New York: W. W. Norton, 2013.

Araújo, Ana Cristina. "The Lisbon Earthquake of 1755—Public Distress and Political Propaganda." *E-Journal of Portuguese History* 4 (2006): 1–25. https://digitalis.uc.pt/en/artigo/lisbon_earthquake_1755_public_distress_and_political_propaganda.

Armstrong, Maurice W. "The Dissenting Deputies and the American Colonies." *Church History* 29 (1960): 298–320.

Baker, Meredith Henne. "1811 Theater Fire Victim List." The Richmond Theater Fire. https://www.theaterfirebook.com/victims-list. Accessed 23 Nov. 2018.

———. *The Richmond Theater Fire: Early America's First Great Disaster.* Baton Rouge: Louisiana State University Press, 2012.

Barker-Benfield, G. J. *The Culture of Sensibility: Sex and Society in Eighteenth-Century Britain.* Chicago: University of Chicago Press, 1992.

Beck, Ulrich. *Risk Society: Toward a New Modernity.* London: SAGE, 1992.

Ben-Zvi, Yael. "Ethnography and the Production of Foreignness in Indian Captivity Narratives." *American Indian Quarterly* 32 (2008): 9–33.

Berry, Stephen R. *A Path in Mighty Waters: Shipboard Life and Atlantic Crossings to the New World.* New Haven: Yale University Press, 2015.

Biel, Steven, ed. *American Disasters.* New York: New York University Press, 2001.

Bierick, Harold A., Jr. "The First Instance of U.S. Foreign Aid: Venezuelan Relief in 1812."
  Inter-American Affairs 9 (1955): 47–59.
Blackmar, Elizabeth. *Manhattan for Rent, 1785–1850*. Ithaca: Cornell University Press, 1991.
Blackmore, Josiah. *Manifest Perdition: Shipwreck Narrative and the Disruption of Empire.*
  Minneapolis: University of Minnesota Press, 2002.
Blanton, Dennis B. "Drought as a Factor in the Jamestown Colony, 1607–1612." *Historical
  Archaeology* 34 (2000): 74–81.
Bloch, Marc. *Royal Touch: Sacred Monarchy and Scrofula in England and France.* London:
  Routledge and Kegan Paul, 1973.
Boorstin, Daniel J. *The Lost World of Thomas Jefferson.* Chicago: University of Chicago
  Press, 1948.
Boxer, C. R. *Some Contemporary Reactions to the Lisbon Earthquake of 1755.* Lisbon:
  Universidade de Lisboa Faculdade de Letras, 1956.
Bradburn, Douglas, and John C. Coombs, eds. *Early Modern Virginia: Reconsidering the Old
  Dominion.* Charlottesville: University of Virginia Press, 2011.
Brewer, John. *The Sinews of Power: War, Money, and the English State, 1688–1783.*
  Cambridge, Mass.: Harvard University Press, 1990.
Bridenbaugh, Carl. *Cities in Revolt: Urban Life in America, 1743–1776.* New York: Knopf,
  1955.
———. *Cities in the Wilderness: The First Century of Urban Life in America.* 2nd ed. New
  York: Knopf, 1955.
Brockmann, R. John. *Exploding Steamboats, Senate Debates, and Technical Reports: The
  Convergence of Technology, Politics, and Rhetoric in the Steamboat Bill of 1838.* Amityville,
  N.Y.: Baywood, 2002.
Bronstein, Jamie. *Caught in the Machinery: Workplace Accidents and Injured Workers in
  Nineteenth-Century Britain.* Stanford: Stanford University Press, 2007.
Brown, Alexander. *The Genesis of the United States.* 2 vols. Boston: Houghton Mifflin, 1890.
Brown, John Kennedy. *Limbs on the Levee: Steamboat Explosions and the Origins of Federal
  Public Welfare Regulation.* Middlebourne, W.V.: International Steamboat Society, 1989.
Brown, Joshua. *Beyond the Lines: Pictorial Reporting, Everyday Life, and the Crisis of Gilded
  Age America.* Berkeley: University of California Press, 2002.
Brown, Kathleen M. *Foul Bodies: Cleanliness in Early America.* New Haven: Yale University
  Press, 2009.
Brust, James, and Wendy Shadwell. "The Many Versions and States of *The Awful
  Conflagration of the Steam Boat Lexington.*" *Imprint* 15 (Autumn 1990): 27–31.
Burg, B. R. "'Women and Children First': Popular Mythology and Disaster at Sea, 1840–
  1860." *Journal of American Culture* 20 (1997): 1–9.
Burke, John G. "Bursting Boilers and the Federal Power." *Technology and Culture* 7 (1966):
  1–23.
Burton, John D. "'The Awful Judgments of God upon the Land': Smallpox in Colonial
  Cambridge, Massachusetts." *New England Quarterly* 74 (2001): 495–506.
Bushman, Richard L. *King and People in Provincial Massachusetts.* Chapel Hill: University
  of North Carolina Press, 1992.
Butterfield, Roger. "Pictures in the Papers." *American Heritage* 13 (June 1962): 96–97.
Calloway, Colin G. *Scratch of a Pen: 1763 and the Transformation of North America.* New
  York: Oxford University Press, 2006.

Candee, Richard M. "Social Conflict and Urban Rebuilding: The Portsmouth, New Hampshire, Brick Act of 1814." *Winterthur Portfolio* 32 (1997): 119–46.

Carr, Revell. "'We Will Never Forget': Disaster in American Folksong from the Nineteenth Century to September 11, 2001." *New York Folklore* 30 (2004): 36–41.

Chenoweth, M., et al., eds. "A Pioneer in Tropical Meteorology: William Sharpe's Barbados Weather Journal, April–August 1680." *Bulletin of the American Meteorological Society* 88 (2007): 1957–64.

Chernow, Ron. *Alexander Hamilton*. New York: Penguin Press, 2004.

Clarfield, Gerard H. "Salem's Great Inoculation Controversy, 1733–74." *Essex Institute Historical Collections* 106 (1970): 277–96.

Clark, Peter. *British Clubs and Societies, 1580–1800: The Origins of an Associational World*. New York: Oxford University Press, 2000.

Coelho, Teresa Pinto, and Donald D. Howard. "The Image of Portugal in British Travel Literature, 1750–1850." *Consortium on Revolutionary Europe, 1750–1850: Proceedings* 20 (1990): 508–15.

Coen, Deborah R. "Introduction: Witness to Disaster: Comparative Histories of Earthquake Science and Response." *Science in Context* 25 (March 2012): 1–15.

Cohen, Kenneth. *They Will Have Their Game: Sporting Culture and the Making of the Early American Republic*. Ithaca: Cornell University Press, 2017.

Coleman, Elizabeth Dabney. "The Great Fresh of 1771." *Virginia Cavalcade* 1 (Autumn 1951): 20–22.

Colley, Linda. *Britons: Forging a Nation, 1707–1837*. New Haven: Yale University Press, 1992.

Conn, Steven. *Americans against the City: Anti-urbanism in the Twentieth Century*. New York: Oxford University Press, 2014.

Contu, Joan. *Persuasion and Propaganda: Monuments and the Eighteenth-Century British Empire*. Montreal: McGill-Queens University Press, 2006.

———. "Philanthropy and Propaganda: The Bust of George III in Montréal." *RACAR: Revue d'Art Canadienne / Canadian Art Review* 19 (1992): 59–67.

Cook, Donald E., Jr. "The Great Fire of Pittsburgh in 1845, or How a Great American City Turned Disaster into Victory." *Western Pennsylvania History* 51 (1968): 127–53.

Cooper, Afua. *The Hanging of Angélique: The Untold Story of Canadian Slavery and the Burning of Old Montreal*. Athens: University of Georgia Press, 2007.

Cox, Thomas H. *"Gibbons v. Ogden", Law, and Society in the Early American Republic*. Athens: Ohio University Press, 2009.

Craven, Wesley Frank. *The Dissolution of the Virginia Company: The Failure of a Colonial Experiment*. New York: Oxford University Press, 1932.

Crothers, A. Glenn. "Commercial Risk and Capital Formation in Early America: Virginia Merchants and the Rise of American Marine Insurance, 1750–1815." *Business History Review* 78 (2004): 607–33.

Culloford, S. G. *William Strachey, 1572–1621*. Charlottesville: University of Virginia Press, 1965.

Curtis, Heather D. *Holy Humanitarians: American Evangelicals and Global Aid*. Cambridge, Mass.: Harvard University Press, 2018.

"Daniel Defoe's *Robinson Crusoe* & the Robinsonades." University of Florida Digital Collections. http://ufdc.ufl.edu/defoe. Accessed 12 Mar. 2019.

Dauber, Michele Landis. *The Sympathetic State: Disaster Relief and the Origins of the American Welfare State*. Chicago: University of Chicago Press, 2012.

Davidson, Cathy N. *Revolution and the Word: The Rise of the Novel in America*. New York: Oxford University Press, 1987.

Davies, Gareth. "Dealing with Disaster: The Politics of Catastrophe in the United States, 1789–1861." *American Nineteenth Century History* 14 (2013): 53–72.

———. "The Emergence of a National Politics of Disaster, 1865–1900." *Journal of Policy History* 26 (2014): 305–26.

———. "Pre-modern Disaster Politics: Combating Catastrophe in the 1950s." *Publius: The Journal of Federalism* 47 (2017): 260–81.

Davis, Mike. *Ecology of Fear: Los Angeles and the Imagination of Disaster*. New York: Metropolitan Books, 1998.

Davis, Natalie Z. "The Rites of Violence: Religious Riot in Sixteenth-Century France; A Rejoinder." *Past and Present* 67 (1975): 51–91.

Davison, Charles. *History of British Earthquakes*. Cambridge: Cambridge University Press, 1924.

"The Deadliest Atlantic Tropical Cyclones, 1492–1996." National Hurricane Center. http://www.nhc.noaa.gov/pastdeadlyapp1.shtml. Accessed 23 Nov. 2018.

Dean, Dennis R. "Benjamin Franklin and Earthquakes." *Annals of Science* 46 (1989): 481–95.

Dennett, Andrea Stulman, and Nina Warnke. "Disaster Spectacles at the Turn of the Century." *Film History* 4 (1990): 101–11.

D'Haen, Theo. "On How Not to Be Lisbon If You Want to Be Modern—Dutch Reactions to the Lisbon Earthquake." *European Review* 14 (2006): 351–58.

Dictionary of American Biography. 22 vols. New York: Scribner, 1922–48.

Dictionary of Canadian Biography. Online edition.

Diefendorf, Barbara C. *Beneath the Cross: Catholics and Huguenots in Sixteenth-Century Paris*. New York: Oxford University Press, 1991.

Ditz, Toby. "Shipwrecked; or, Masculinity Imperiled: Mercantile Representations of Failure and the Gendered Self in Eighteenth-Century Philadelphia." *Journal of American History* 81 (1994): 51–80.

Donagan, Barbara. "Providence, Chance, and Explanation: Some Paradoxical Aspects of Puritan Views of Causation." *Journal of Religious History* 11 (1981): 385–403.

Donegan, Kathleen. *Seasons of Misery: Catastrophe and Colonial Settlement in Early America*. Philadelphia: University of Pennsylvania Press, 2014.

Duffy, James. *Shipwreck and Empire, Being an Account of Portuguese Maritime Disasters in a Century of Decline*. Cambridge, Mass.: Harvard University Press, 1955.

Dunbaugh, Edwin W. *Night Boat to New England, 1815–1900*. New York: Greenwood Press, 1992.

Dupigny-Giroux, Lesley-Ann, and Cary J. Mock, eds. *Historical Climate Variability and Impacts in North America*. Dordrecht, Neth.: Springer, 2009.

Dyl, Joanna L. *Seismic City: An Environmental History of San Francisco's 1906 Earthquake*. Seattle: University of Washington Press, 2017.

Dynes, Russell R. "The Lisbon Earthquake in 1755: The First Modern Disaster." 2003. http://udspace.udel.edu/handle/19716/294. Accessed 23 Nov. 2018.

Ebel, John E. "The Cape Ann, Massachusetts Earthquake of 1755: A 250th Anniversary Perspective." *Seismological Research Letters* 77 (Feb. 2006): 74–76.

Edgerton-Tarpley, Kathryn. "Tough Choices: Grappling with Famine in Qing China, the British Empire, and Beyond." *Journal of World History* 24 (2013): 135–76.

Edling, Max M. *A Hercules in the Cradle: War, Money, and the American State, 1783–1867.* Chicago: University of Chicago Press, 2014.

———. *A Revolution in Favor of Government: Origins of the U.S. Constitution and the Making of an American State.* New York: Oxford University Press, 2003.

Emlen, Robert P. "The Great Gale of 1815: Artifactual Evidence of Rhode Island's First Hurricane." *Rhode Island History* 2 (1990): 50–61.

Erickson, Stephen. "'To Obviate a Scandalous Reflection': Revisiting the Wreck of the *Nottingham Galley*." *New England Quarterly* 83 (2010): 375–412.

Estes, J. Worth, and Billy Gordon Smith, eds. *A Melancholy Scene of Devastation: The Public Response to the 1793 Philadelphia Yellow Fever Epidemic.* Canton, Mass.: Science History Publications USA, 1997.

Eustace, Nicole. *Passion Is the Gale: Emotion, Power, and the Coming of the American Revolution.* Chapel Hill: University of North Carolina Press, 2008.

Fagan, Bryan. *The Little Ice Age: How Climate Made History.* New York: Basic Books, 2000.

Fahs, Alice. *The Imagined Civil War: Popular Literature of the North and South, 1861–1865.* Chapel Hill: University of North Carolina Press, 2001.

Fenn, Elizabeth. *Pox Americana: The Great Smallpox Epidemic of 1775–82.* New York: Hill and Wang, 2001.

Finger, Simon. *The Contagious City: The Politics of Public Health in Early Philadelphia.* Ithaca: Cornell University Press, 2012.

Fisher, Carl. "Innovation and Imitation in the Eighteenth-Century Robinsonade." In *The Cambridge Companion to Robinson Crusoe*, edited by John Richetti, 99–111. Cambridge: Cambridge University Press, 2018.

Fiske, John M. *Old Virginia and Her Neighbors.* 2 vols. Cambridge, Mass.: Riverside Press, 1902.

Fitz, Caitlin. *Our Sister Republics: The United States in an Age of American Revolutions.* New York: Liveright, 2016.

Flavell, Julie. *When London Was the Capital of America.* New Haven: Yale University Press, 2010.

"Flood History." The Johnstown Flood Museum. https://www.jaha.org/attractions/johnstown-flood-museum/flood-history/. Accessed 12 Mar. 2019.

Flowers, Margaret G., et al. "18th-Century Earthquakes and Apocalyptic Expectations: The Hymns of Charles Wesley." *Methodist History* 42 (2004): 222–35.

Fogelman, Aaron. "Migrations to the Thirteen British North American Colonies." *Journal of Interdisciplinary History* 22 (1992): 691–702.

"Forty Foot High (and Risin'?)." *Henrico County Historical Society Newsletter* 36 (Mar. 2011).

Frazier, Ian. "The Day the Great Plains Burned: A Devastating Wildfire and Its Aftermath." *New Yorker*, 5 Nov. 2018, 34–41.

Freeman, Thomas S. "Foxe's Marian Martyrs." In *The Unabridged Acts and Monuments Online.* http://www.johnfoxe.org/freeman-marion.pdf. Accessed 23 Nov. 2018.

Friend, Craig Thompson, and Lorri Glover, eds. *Death and the American South.* New York: Oxford University Press, 2015.

Fuller, Randall. *From Battlefields Rising: How the Civil War Transformed American Literature.* New York: Oxford University Press, 2011.

Games, Alison. "Violence on the Fringes: The Virginia (1622) and Aboyna (1624) Massacres." *History* 99 (2014): 505–26.

Gemery, Henry A. "Emigration from the British Isles to the New World, 1630–1700: Inferences from Colonial Populations." *Research in Economic History* 5 (n.d.): 179–231.

Glover, Lorri, and Daniel Blake Smith. *The Shipwreck That Saved Jamestown: The Sea Venture Castaways and the Fate of America.* New York: Henry Holt, 2008.

Godbey, Emily. "Disaster Tourism and the Melodrama of Authenticity: Revisiting the 1889 Johnstown Flood." *Pennsylvania History* 73 (2006): 273–315.

Golinski, Jan. *British Weather and the Climate of Enlightenment.* Chicago. University of Chicago Press, 2011.

———. "Debating the Atmospheric Constitution: Yellow Fever and the American Climate." *Eighteenth-Century Studies* 49 (2016): 151–61.

Goodman, Nan. *Shifting the Blame: Literature, Law, and the Theory of Accidents in Nineteenth-Century America.* Princeton: Princeton University Press, 1998.

Graham, Louis. "The Scientific Piety of John Winthrop of Harvard." *New England Quarterly* 46 (1973): 112–18.

Gray, Peter. "Famine Relief Policy in Comparative Perspective: Ireland, Scotland, and Northwestern Europe, 1845–1849." *Eire/Ireland* 32 (1997): 86–108.

"The Great Fire of London, 1666." Museum of London. https://www.museumoflondon .org.uk/discover/great-fire-london-1666. Accessed 12 Mar. 2019.

Griffin, Carl J. "The Great Famine in Colonial Context: Public Reaction and Responses in Britain before the 'Black '47.'" *Historical Geography* 42 (2014): 111–29.

Griffin, Patrick. *The People with No Name: Ireland's Ulster Scots, America's Scots Irish, and the Creation of a British Atlantic World, 1689–1764.* Princeton: Princeton University Press, 2001.

Gronim, Sara Stidstone. "What Jane Knew: A Woman Botanist in the Eighteenth Century." *Journal of Women's History* 19 (2007): 33–59.

Grubb, Farley. "Morbidity and Mortality on the North Atlantic Passage: Eighteenth-Century German Immigration." *Journal of Interdisciplinary History* 17 (1987): 565–85.

Gudmestad, Robert. *Steamboats and the Rise of the Cotton Kingdom.* Baton Rouge: Louisiana State University Press, 2011.

Guilhamet, Leon. *Defoe and the Whig Novel: A Reading of the Major Fiction.* Newark: University of Delaware Press, 2010.

Hall, David D. *Worlds of Wonder, Days of Judgment: Popular Religious Belief in Early New England.* Cambridge, Mass.: Harvard University Press, 1990.

Halttunen, Karen. *Confidence Men and Painted Women: A Study of Middle-Class Culture in America, 1830–1870.* New Haven: Yale University Press, 1983.

———. "Humanitarianism and the Pornography of Pain in Anglo-American Culture." *American Historical Review* 100 (1995): 303–34.

———. *Murder Most Foul: The Killer and the American Gothic Imagination.* Cambridge, Mass.: Harvard University Press, 1998.

Hancock, David. *Citizens of the World: London Merchants and the Integration of the British Atlantic Community, 1735–1785.* Cambridge: Cambridge University Press, 1997.

Hansen, Kris A. *Death Passage on the Hudson: The Wreck of the Henry Clay.* Fleischmanns, N.Y.: Purple Mountain Press, 2004.

Hardy, Molly O'Hagan. "Figures of Authorship in Mathew Carey's Transatlantic Yellow Fever Pamphlets." *Book History* 17 (2014): 221–49.

Hartley, William G., and Fred E. Woods. "Explosion of the Steamboat *Saluda*: Tragedy and Compassion at Lexington, Missouri, 1852." *Missouri Historical Review* 99 (2005): 281–305.

Hartnell, Anna. "Katrina Tourism and a Tale of Two Cities: Visualizing Race and Class in New Orleans." *American Quarterly* 61 (2009): 723–47.

Heil, Douglas. *The Art of Stereography: Rediscovering Vintage Three-Dimensional Images.* Jefferson, N.C.: McFarland, 2017.

Hemphill, C. Dallett. *Bowing to Necessities: A History of Manners in America, 1620–1860.* New York: Oxford University Press, 1999.

Hewitt, Kenneth. *Interpretations of Calamity: From the Viewpoint of Human Ecology.* Boston: Allen and Unwin, 1983.

Hoffer, Peter Charles. *Seven Fires: The Urban Infernos that Shaped America.* New York: Public Affairs, 2006.

Hoffman, Susanna M., and Anthony Oliver-Smith, eds. *Catastrophe and Culture: The Anthropology of Disaster.* Santa Fe: School of American Research Press, 2002.

Hogan, Charles. "Origins of U.S. Emergency Management." Anna Maria College Online Programs. http://online.annamaria.edu/mpa/resource/emergency-management -history. Accessed 23 Nov. 2018.

Holton, Woody. *Forced Founders: Indians, Debtors, Slaves, and the Making of the American Revolution in Virginia.* Chapel Hill: University of North Carolina Press, 1999.

Hoppit, Julian. "Financial Crises in Eighteenth-Century England." *Economic History Review,* 2nd ser., 39 (1968): 39–58.

Horn, James. *A Land as God Made It: Jamestown and the Birth of America.* New York: Basic Books, 2005.

Horowitz, Andy. "The Complete Story of the Galveston Horror: Trauma, History, and the Great Storm of 1900." *Historical Reflections* 41 (2015): 95–108.

———. "Hurricane Betsy and the Politics of Disaster in New Orleans' Lower Ninth Ward, 1965–1967." *Journal of Southern History* 80 (2014): 893–934.

Hunt, Lynn, ed. *The New Cultural History.* Berkeley: University of California Press, 1989.

Hunter, Louis C., and Beatrice Jones Hunter. *Steamboats on the Western Rivers: An Economic and Technological History.* 1949. Reprint, New York: Octagon Books, 1969.

Huntress, Keith Gibson. *Narratives of Shipwrecks and Disasters, 1586–1860.* Ames: Iowa State University Press, 1974.

Isenberg, Nancy, and Andrew Burstein, eds. *Mortal Remains: Death in Early America.* Philadelphia: University of Pennsylvania Press, 2003.

Jasanoff, Maya. *Liberty's Exiles: American Loyalists in a Revolutionary World.* New York: Knopf, 2011.

John, Richard R. *Network Nation: Inventing American Telecommunications.* Cambridge, Mass.: Harvard University Press, 2010.

———. *Spreading the News: The American Postal System from Franklin to Morse.* Cambridge, Mass.: Harvard University Press, 1995.

Johns, Alessa, ed. *Dreadful Visitations: Confronting Natural Catastrophe in the Age of Enlightenment.* New York: Routledge, 1999.

Johnson, Sherry. *Climate and Catastrophe in Cuba and the Atlantic World in the Age of Revolution.* Chapel Hill: University of North Carolina Press, 2011.

Johnson, Walter. *River of Dark Dreams: Slavery and Empire in the Cotton Kingdom.* Cambridge, Mass.: Harvard University Press, 2013.

Jones, Marian Moser. *The American Red Cross: From Clara Barton to the New Deal.* Baltimore: Johns Hopkins University Press, 2013.

Jones, William R. *A Critical Edition of the Poetical Works of William Falconer*. Lewiston, N.Y.: Edwin Mellen Press, 2003.

Joseph, M. K. "William Falconer." *Studies in Philology* 47 (1950): 72–101.

Kammen, Michael G. *A Rope of Sand: The Colonial Agents, British Politics, and the American Revolution*. Ithaca: Cornell University Press, 1968.

Kann, Mark E. *A Republic of Men: The American Founders, Gendered Politics, and Patriarchal Politics*. New York: New York University Press, 1998.

Kasson, John F. *Amusing the Million: Coney Island at the Turn of the Century*. New York: Hill and Wang, 1978.

Kendrick, T. D. *The Lisbon Earthquake*. Philadelphia: J. B. Lippincott, 1955.

Kent, Randolph, and John Ratcliffe. *Responding to Catastrophes: U.S. Innovation in a Vulnerable World*. Washington, D.C.: Center for Strategic and International Studies, 2008.

Kierner, Cynthia A. *The Contrast: Manners, Morals, and Authority in the Early American Republic*. New York: New York University Press, 2007.

Kinealy, Christine. *Charity and the Great Hunger in Ireland: The Kindness of Strangers*. London: Bloomsbury, 2013.

———. *The Great Irish Famine: Impact, Ideology, and Rebellion*. New York: Palgrave, 2002.

Kingston, Christopher. "Governance and Institutional Change in Marine Insurance, 1350–1850." *European Review of Economic History* 18 (2014): 1–18.

———. "Marine Insurance in Britain and America, 1720–1844: A Comparative Institutional Analysis." *Journal of Economic History* 67 (2007): 379–409.

Kirby, Andrew. *The Politics of Location: An Introduction*. London: Methuen, 1982.

Knott, Sarah. *Sensibility and the American Revolution*. Chapel Hill: University of North Carolina Press, 2009.

Knowles, Scott Gabriel. "Lessons in the Rubble: The World Trade Center and the History of Disaster Investigations in the United States." *History and Technology* 19 (2003): 9–28.

Kornfeld, Eve, "Crisis in the Capital: The Cultural Significance of Philadelphia's Great Yellow Fever Epidemic." *Pennsylvania History* 51 (1984): 189–205.

Kovacs, Claire L. "Pompeii and Its Material Reproductions: The Rise of a Tourist Site in the Nineteenth Century." *Journal of Tourism History* 5 (2013): 30–39.

Kozak, Jan T., and Vladimir Cermák. *The Illustrated History of Natural Disasters*. Dordrecht, Neth.: Springer, 2010.

Kozak, Jan T., and Charles D. James. "Historical Depictions of the 1755 Lisbon Earthquake." Earthquake Engineering Online Archive. NISEE e-Library https://nisee .berkeley.edu/elibrary/files/documents/lisbon/index.html. Accessed 23 Nov. 2018.

Kukla, Jon. *Patrick Henry: Champion of Liberty*. New York: Simon and Schuster, 2017.

Kunihara, Ken. "The Voice of God upon the Waters: Sermons on Steamboat Disasters in Antebellum America." *Coriolis: An Interdisciplinary Journal of Maritime Studies* 2 (2011). http://ijms.nmdl.org/article/view/9119.

Kupperman, Karen Ordahl. "Apathy and Death in Early Jamestown." *Journal of American History* 66 (1979): 24–40.

———. *The Jamestown Project*. Cambridge, Mass.: Harvard University Press, 2007.

———. "The Puzzle of the American Climate in the Early Colonial Period." *American Historical Review* 87 (1982): 1278–83.

Labaree, Benjamin W. *Patriots and Partisans: The Merchants of Newburyport, 1764–1815*. Cambridge, Mass.: Harvard University Press, 1962.

Lacqueur, Thomas W. *The Work of the Dead: A Cultural History of Mortal Remains.*
Princeton: Princeton University Press, 2015.

Landis, Michele L. "Let Me Next Time Be Tried by Fire: Disaster Relief and the Origins of the American Welfare State, 1789–1874." *Northwestern University Law Review* 92 (1998): 967–1034.

Landow, George P. *Images of Crisis: Literary Iconography, 1750 to the Present.* London: Routledge and Kegan Paul, 1982.

Larsen, Svend Erik. "The Lisbon Earthquake and the Scientific Turn in Kant's Philosophy." *European Review* 14 (2006): 359–67.

LeBeau, Bryan F. *Currier and Ives: America Imagined.* Washington, D.C.: Smithsonian Press, 2002.

Lefebvre, Henri. *Introduction to Modernity: Twelve Preludes, September 1959–May 1961.* Translated by John Moore. London: Verso, 1995.

Lehuu, Isabelle. *Carnival on the Page: Popular Print Media in Antebellum America.* Chapel Hill: University of North Carolina Press, 2000.

Levine, Lawrence W. *Highbrow, Lowbrow: The Emergence of Cultural Hierarchy in America.* Cambridge, Mass.: Harvard University Press, 1988.

Levy, Jonathan. *Freaks of Fortune: The Emerging World of Capitalism and Risk in America.* Cambridge, Mass.: Harvard University Press, 2012.

Lincoln, Margarette. "Shipwreck Narratives of the Eighteenth and Early Nineteenth Century: Indicators of Culture and Identity." *Journal for Eighteenth-Century Studies* 20 (1997): 155–72.

Lindberg, Paul. "From Private to Public Provision of Public Goods: English Lighthouses between the Seventeenth and Nineteenth Centuries." *Journal of Policy History* 25 (2013): 538–56.

Liscombe, Rhondri Windsor. *Altogether American: Robert Mills, Architect and Engineer, 1781–1855.* New York: Oxford University Press, 1994.

Louis-Charles, Hans M. "State Sovereignty and Natural Hazards: A Study on the Legacy of the United Kingdom's Imperial Practices and Disaster Management Activities of Their Island Possessions." PhD diss., University of Delaware, 2016.

Lovejoy, David S. "Satanizing the American Indian." *New England Quarterly* 67 (1994): 603–21.

Lübken, Uwe, and Christof Mauch. "Uncertain Environments: Natural Hazards, Risk, and Insurance in Historical Perspective." *Environment and History* 17 (2011): 1–12.

"Luna Park." Heart of Coney Island. http://www.heartofconeyisland.com/luna-park-coney-island.html. Accessed 12 Mar. 2019.

Macadam, Joyce. "English Weather: The Seventeenth-Century Diary of Ralph Josselin." *Journal of Interdisciplinary History* 43 (2012): 221–46.

Mackintosh, Will. "'Ticketed Through': The Commodification of Travel in the Nineteenth Century." *Journal of the Early Republic* 32 (2012): 61–89.

Maier, Pauline. *From Resistance to Revolution: Colonial Radicals and the Development of American Opposition to Britain, 1765–1776.* New York: Knopf, 1972.

Marshall, P. J. "Who Cared about the Thirteen Colonies? Some Evidence from Philanthropy." *Journal of Imperial and Commonwealth History* 27 (1999): 53–67.

Marx, Leo. *The Machine in the Garden: Technology and the Pastoral Ideal in America.* New York: Oxford University Press, 1964.

Mashaw, Jerry L. *Creating the Administrative Constitution: The Lost One Hundred Years of Administrative Law*. New Haven: Yale University Press, 2012.

Maxwell, Kenneth. *Pombal: Paradox of the Enlightenment*. New York: Cambridge University Press, 1995.

May, Peter J. *Recovering from Catastrophes: Federal Disaster Relief Policy and Politics*. Westport, Conn.: Praeger, 1985.

Mayer, Robert. "The Reception of a Journal of the Plague Year and the Nexus of Fiction and History in the Novel." *ELH* 57, no. 3 (1990): 529-55.

McCarthy, Kathleen D. *American Creed: Philanthropy and the Rise of Civil Society*. Chicago: University of Chicago Press, 2003.

McConville, Brendan. *The King's Three Faces: The Rise and Fall of Royal America, 1688-1776*. Chapel Hill: University of North Carolina Press, 2006.

McCormmach, Russell. *Weighing the World: The Reverend John Michell of Thornhill*. New York: Springer, 2011.

McCullough, David. *The Johnstown Flood: The Incredible Story behind One of the Most Devastating Disasters American History Has Ever Known*. New York: Simon and Schuster, 1968.

McIlvenna, Noeleen. *The Short Life of Free Georgia: Class and Slavery in the Colonial South*. Chapel Hill: University of North Carolina Press, 2015.

McMurtrie, Douglas C. *The First Printing in Virginia: The Abortive Attempt at Jamestown, the First Permanent Press at Williamsburg, the Early Gazettes, and the Work of Other Virginia Typographic Pioneers*. Vienna, Aus.: H. Reichner Verlag, 1935.

McNeill, J. R. *Mosquito Empires: Ecology and War in the Greater Caribbean, 1620-1914*. New York: Oxford University Press, 2010.

Mendes-Victor, Luis A., et al., eds. *The Lisbon Earthquake: Revisited*. New York: Springer, 2008.

Middlekauff, Robert. *The Mathers: Three Generations of Puritan Intellectuals*. New York: Oxford University Press, 1971.

Miller, Perry. "Errand into the Wilderness." *William and Mary Quarterly*, 3rd ser., 10 (1953): 3-32.

———. "The Religious Impulse in the Founding of Virginia: Religion and Society in the Early Literature." *William and Mary Quarterly*, 3rd ser., 5 (1948): 492-522.

Milleti, Dennis. *Disasters by Design: A Reassessment of Natural Hazards in the United States*. Washington, D.C.: Joseph Henry Press, 1999.

Miskolcze, Robin. *Women and Children First: Nineteenth-Century Sea Narratives and American Identity*. Lincoln: University of Nebraska Press, 2012.

Mitchell-Cook, Amy. *A Sea of Misadventures: Shipwreck and Survival in Early America*. Columbia: University of South Carolina Press, 2013.

Molesky, Mark. *This Gulf of Fire: The Destruction of Lisbon, or Apocalypse in the Age of Science and Reason*. New York: Knopf, 2015.

Moniz, Amanda B. *From Empire to Humanity: The American Revolution and the Origins of Humanitarianism*. New York: Oxford University Press, 2016.

———. "Saving the Lives of Strangers: Humane Societies and the Cosmopolitan Provision of Charitable Aid." *Journal of the Early Republic* 29 (2009): 607-40.

Montluzin, Emily Lorraine de. "'Every Body Apprehended an Earthquake': The *Gentleman's Magazine*'s Reporting of the 1755 Lisbon Earthquake and Its Aftermath." *Notes and Queries* 61 (2014): 409-17.

Mooney, M. J. "Tsunami: When the Sea Quakes." *Americas* 42 (July 1990): 24–29.

Moore, Peter. *The Weather Experiment: The Pioneers Who Sought to See the Future*. New York: Farrar, Straus and Giroux, 2015.

Morgan, Edmund S. *American Slavery, American Freedom: The Ordeal of Colonial Virginia*. New York: W. W. Norton, 1975.

Morgan, Edmund S., and Helen M. Morgan. *The Stamp Act Crisis: Prologue to Revolution*. Chapel Hill: University of North Carolina Press, 1953.

Morris, Christopher. *The Big Muddy: An Environmental History of the Mississippi and Its Peoples from Hernando de Soto to Hurricane Katrina*. New York: Oxford University Press, 2012.

Morrison, James V. *Shipwrecked: Disaster and Transformation in Homer, Shakespeare, Defoe, and the Modern World*. Ann Arbor: University of Michigan Press, 2014.

Moss, David A. *When All Else Fails: Government as the Ultimate Risk Manager*. Cambridge, Mass.: Harvard University Press, 2004.

Mulcahy, Matthew. "The 'Great Fire' of 1740 and the Politics of Disaster Relief in Colonial Charleston." *South Carolina Historical Magazine* 99 (1998): 135–57.

———. *Hubs of Empire: The Southeastern Lowcountry and British Caribbean*. Baltimore: Johns Hopkins University Press, 2014.

———. *Hurricanes and Society in the Greater British Caribbean, 1624–1783*. Baltimore: Johns Hopkins University Press, 2006.

———. "Making Sense of Disasters in Early America—and Today." *American Historian*, Feb. 2018, 37–42.

———. "The Port Royal Earthquake and the World of Wonders in Seventeenth-Century Jamaica." *Early American Studies* 6 (2008): 391–421.

Murphy, Kathleen. "Prodigies and Portents: Providentialism in the Eighteenth-Century Chesapeake." *Maryland Historical Magazine* 97 (2002): 397–421.

———. "Virginia's Great Fresh of 1771 and the Politics of Disaster Relief." *Virginia Magazine of History and Biography* 123 (2015): 298–323.

Murphy, Sharon Ann. *Investing in Life: Insurance in Antebellum America*. Baltimore: Johns Hopkins University Press, 2010.

Musson, R. M. W. "A History of British Seismology." *Bulletin of Earthquake Engineering* 11 (2013): 715–861.

Nash, Gary B. *First City: Philadelphia and the Forging of Historical Memory*. Philadelphia: University of Pennsylvania Press, 2001.

Nash, Roderick Frazier. *Wilderness and the American Mind*. 4th ed. New Haven: Yale University Press, 2001.

"Natural Disasters in 2017: Lower Mortality, Higher Cost." CRED CRUNCH, no. 50, Mar. 2018, https://cred.be/sites/default/files/CredCrunch50.pdf . Accessed 12 Mar. 2019.

Nelson, Megan Kate. *Ruin Nation: Destruction and the American Civil War*. Athens: University of Georgia Press, 2012.

Newman, Richard S. *Freedom's Prophet: Bishop Richard Allen, the AME Church, and the Black Founding Fathers*. New York: New York University Press, 2008.

Nord, David Paul. "Teleology and News: The Religious Roots of American Journalism, 1630–1730." *Journal of American History* 77 (1990): 9–38.

O'Brien, Susan. "A Transatlantic Community of Saints: The Great Awakening and the First Evangelical Network, 1735–1755." *American Historical Review* 91 (1986): 811–32.

Oleson, Alexandra, ed. *The Pursuit of Knowledge in the Early American Republic*. Baltimore: Johns Hopkins University Press, 1976.

O'Malley, Michael. "Local Relief during the Great Irish Famine, 1845–1850: The Case of Castlebar, County Mayo." *Eire/Ireland* 32 (1997): 109–20.

O'Neill, Karen M. "Broken Levees, Broken Lives, and a Broken Nation after Hurricane Katrina." *Southern Cultures* 14 (Summer 2008): 89–104.

Opal, Jason M. "The Labors of Liberality: Christian Benevolence and National Prejudice in the American Founding." *Journal of American History* 94 (2008): 1082–1107.

O'Shaughnessy, Andrew Jackson. *An Empire Divided: The American Revolution and the British Caribbean*. Philadelphia: University of Pennsylvania Press, 2000.

Outhwaite, R. B. *Dearth, Public Policy and Social Disturbance in England, 1550–1800*. Cambridge: Cambridge University Press, 1995.

Oviatt, F. C. "Historical Study of Fire Insurance in the United States." *Annals of the American Academy of Political and Social Science* 26 (1905): 335–58.

Oxford Dictionary of National Biography. Online edition.

Parker, Geoffrey. "Crisis and Catastrophe: The Global Crisis of the Seventeenth Century Reconsidered." *American Historical Review* 113 (2008): 1053–79.

———. *Global Crisis: War, Climate Change, and Catastrophe in the Seventeenth Century*. New Haven: Yale University Press, 2013.

Parkinson, Robert G. *The Common Cause: Creating Race and Nation in the American Revolution*. Chapel Hill: University of North Carolina Press, 2016.

Parrish, Susan Scott. *American Curiosity: Cultures of Natural History in the Colonial British Atlantic World*. Chapel Hill: University of North Carolina Press, 2006.

———. *The Flood Year 1927: A Cultural History*. Princeton: Princeton University Press, 2017.

Paskoff, Paul. *Troubled Waters: Steamboat Disasters, River Improvements, and American Public Policy, 1821–1860*. Baton Rouge: Louisiana State University Press, 2007.

Patterson, K. David. "Yellow Fever Epidemics and Mortality in the United States, 1693–1905." *Social Science and Medicine* 34 (1992): 855–65.

Pauly, Philip J. "Fighting the Hessian Fly: American and British Responses to Insect Invasion, 1776–1789." *Environmental History* 7 (2002): 485–507.

Perkins, Edwin J. *American Public Finance and Financial Services, 1700–1815*. Columbus: Ohio State University Press, 1994.

Pettegree, Andrew. *The Invention of News: How the World Came to Know about Itself*. New Haven: Yale University Press, 2015.

Philip, Cynthia Owen. *Robert Fulton: A Biography*. New York: Franklin Watts, 1985.

Piola, Erica, ed. *Philadelphia on Stone: Commercial Lithography in Philadelphia*. University Park: Pennsylvania State University Press, 2012.

Porter, Harry Culverwell. "Alexander Whitaker: Cambridge Apostle to Virginia." *William and Mary Quarterly*, 3rd ser., 14 (1957): 317–43.

Powell, J. H. *Bring Out Your Dead: The Great Plague of Yellow Fever in Philadelphia in 1793*. Philadelphia: University of Pennsylvania Press, 1949.

Prochaska, Frank. *Royal Bounty: The Making of a Welfare Monarchy*. New Haven: Yale University Press, 1995.

Purvis, Thomas L. *Colonial America to 1763*. New York: Facts on File, 1999.

Pyle, G. F. "The Diffusion of Cholera in the United States in the Nineteenth Century." *Geographic Analysis* 1 (1969): 59–75.

Quarantelli, E. L., ed. *What Is a Disaster?* London: Springer, 1998.

Quitt, Martin H. "Trade and Acculturation at Jamestown, 1607–1609: The Limits of Understanding." *William and Mary Quarterly*, 3rd ser., 52 (1995): 227–58.

Rappaport, Rhoda. "Hooke on Earthquakes: Lectures, Strategy and Audience." *British Journal for the History of Science* 19 (1986): 129–42.

Ratcliffe, John. "Bells, Barrels, and Bullion: Diving and Salvage in the Atlantic World, 1500 to 1800." *Nautical Research Journal* 56 (2011): 34–56.

"Remembering the Johnstown Flood." Johnstown Flood Museum. http://www.jaha.org /attractions/johnstown-flood-museum/flood-history/remembering-the-johnstown -flood/. Accessed 23 Nov. 2018.

Remes, Jacob A. C. *Disaster Citizenship: Survivors, Solidarity, and Power in the Progressive Era.* Urbana: University of Illinois Press, 2016.

Rigby, Catherine E. *Dancing with Disaster: Environmental Histories, Narratives, and Ethics for Perilous Times.* Charlottesville: University of Virginia Press, 2015.

Ritchie, Hannah, and Max Roser. "Natural Disasters." Our World in Data. https://our worldindata.org/natural-catastrophes. Accessed 23 Nov. 2018.

Robles, Whitney Barlow. "Atlantic Disaster: Boston Responds to the Cape Ann Earthquake of 1755." *New England Quarterly* 90 (2017): 7–35.

Rosen, Christine Meisner. *The Limits of Power: Great Fires and the Process of City Growth in America.* New York: Cambridge University Press, 1986.

Rosenberg, Charles E. *The Cholera Years: The United States in 1832, 1849, and 1866.* 2nd ed. Chicago: University of Chicago Press, 1987.

Rountree, Helen C. *Pocahontas, Powhatan, and Opechancanough: Three Indian Lives Changed by Jamestown.* Charlottesville: University of Virginia Press, 2005.

Rozario, Kevin. *The Culture of Calamity: Disaster and the Making of Modern America.* Chicago: University of Chicago Press, 2007.

Sandukas, Gregory P. "Gently Down the Stream: How Exploding Steamboat Boilers in the 19th Century Ignited Federal Public Welfare Regulation." 30 Apr. 2002. Digital Access to Scholarship at Harvard. https://dash.harvard.edu/bitstream/handle/1/10018995 /Sandukas_redacted.pdf?sequence=1. Accessed 12 Mar. 2019.

Sasson, Tehila, and James Vernon. "Practising the British Way of Famine: Technologies of Relief, 1770–1985." *European Review of History* 22 (2015): 860–72.

Sawislak, Karen. *Smoldering City: Chicagoans and the Great Fire, 1871–1874.* Chicago: University of Chicago Press, 1995.

Schulman, Vanessa Meikle. *Work Sights: The Visual Culture of Industry in Nineteenth-Century America.* Amherst: University of Massachusetts Press, 2015.

Schutz, John A. *Thomas Pownall, British Defender of American Liberty: A Study of Anglo-American Relations in the Eighteenth Century.* Glendale, Calif.: A. H. Clark, 1951.

Schwartz, Stuart B. *Sea of Storms: A History of Hurricanes in the Greater Caribbean from Columbus to Katrina.* Princeton: Princeton University Press, 2015.

Scott, Kenneth. "The Sandy Hook Lighthouse." *American Neptune* 25 (1965): 123–27.

Searchable Sea Literature. Williams Mystic. https://sites.williams.edu/searchablesealit/. Accessed 12 Mar. 2019.

Sears, John F. "Hawthorne's 'The Ambitious Guest' and the Significance of the Willey Disaster." *American Literature* 52 (1982): 354–67.

———. *Sacred Places: American Tourist Attractions in the Nineteenth Century.* New York: Oxford University Press, 1989.

Seeman, Erik R. *Pious Persuasions: Laity and Clergy in Eighteenth-Century New England.* Baltimore: Johns Hopkins University Press, 1999.

Shannon, Timothy M. *Indians and Colonists at the Crossroads of Empire: The Albany Congress of 1754.* Ithaca: Cornell University Press, 2000.

Shapiro, Barbara J. *A Culture of Fact: England, 1550–1720.* Ithaca: Cornell University Press, 2000.

Shepley, Genoa. "By Which Melancholy Occurrence: The Disaster Prints of Nathaniel Currier, 1835–1840." *Panorama* 1 (2015). http://journalpanorama.org/by-which -melancholy-occurrence-the-disaster-prints-of-nathaniel-currier-1835-1840/.

Shockley, Martin Staples. *The Richmond Stage, 1784–1812.* Charlottesville: University of Virginia Press, 1977.

Showalter, William J. "First Steamboat Explosion in the West." *Tallow Light* 47, no. 2 (2016): 41–43.

Shrady, Nicholas. *The Last Day: Wrath, Ruin, and Reason in the Great Lisbon Earthquake of 1755.* New York: Viking, 2008.

Sievers, Julie. "Drowned Pens and Shaking Hands: Sea Providence Narratives in Seventeenth-Century New England." *William and Mary Quarterly,* 3rd ser., 63 (2006): 743–76.

Simon, Bryant. *The Hamlet Fire: A Tragic Story of Cheap Food, Cheap Government, and Cheap Lives.* New York: New Press, 2017.

Simpson, A. W. Brian. *Cannibalism and the Common Law: The Story of the Last Tragic Voyage of the Mignonette and the Strange Legal Proceedings to Which It Gave Rise.* Chicago: University of Chicago Press, 1984.

Sirota, Brent S. *The Christian Monitors: The Church of England and the Age of Benevolence, 1680–1730.* New Haven: Yale University Press, 2014.

Slack, Paul. "Dearth and Social Policy in Early Modern England." *Social History of Medicine* 5 (1992): 1–17.

———. *The Impact of Plague in Tudor and Stuart England.* London: Routledge and Kegan Paul, 1985.

Smith, Hannah. *Georgian Monarchy: Politics and Culture, 1714–1760.* Cambridge: Cambridge University Press, 2006.

Smith, Mark M. *Stono: Documenting and Interpreting a Southern Slave Revolt.* Columbia: University of South Carolina Press, 2005.

Solnit, Rebecca. *A Paradise Built in Hell: The Extraordinary Communities That Arise in Disaster.* New York: Viking, 2009.

Spencer, David R. *The Yellow Journalism: The Press and America's Emergence as a World Power.* Evanston, Ill.: Northwestern University Press, 2007.

Steele, Ian K. *The English Atlantic, 1675–1740: An Exploration in Communication and Community.* New York: Oxford University Press, 1986.

Steinberg, Ted. *Acts of God: The Unnatural History of Natural Disaster in America.* New York: Oxford University Press, 2000.

Stevenson, D. Alan. *The World's Lighthouses before 1820.* London: Oxford University Press, 1959.

Stilgoe, John. *Lifeboat.* Charlottesville: University of Virginia Press, 2007.

Sutcliffe, Andrea. *Steam: The Untold Story of America's First Great Invention.* New York: Palgrave Macmillan, 2004.

Tate, Thad W., and David L. Ammerman, eds. *The Chesapeake in the Seventeenth Century: Essays on Anglo-American Society*. Chapel Hill: University of North Carolina Press, 1979.

Taylor, George R. *The Transportation Revolution, 1815–60*. New York: Rinehart, 1951.

Tebeau, Mark. *Eating Smoke: Fire in Urban America, 1800–1950*. Baltimore: Johns Hopkins University Press, 2003.

Thomas, Keith. *Man and the Natural World: Changing Attitudes in England, 1500–1800*. New York: Oxford University Press, 1996.

———. *Religion and the Decline of Magic*. New York: Scribner, 1971.

Thompson, Andrew C. *George II: King and Elector*. New Haven: Yale University Press, 2011.

Tierney, Kathleen. "Hurricane in New Orleans? Who Knew? Anticipating Katrina and Its Devastation." *Social Inquiry* 78 (2008): 179–83.

Tierney, Kathleen, et al. "Metaphors Matter: Disaster Myths, Media Frames, and Their Consequences in Hurricane Katrina." *Annals of the American Academy of Political and Social Science* 604 (Mar. 2006): 57–81.

Tilton, Eleanor M. "Lightning-Rods and the Earthquake of 1755." *New England Quarterly* 13 (1940): 85–97.

Todd, Janet. *Sensibility: An Introduction*. London: Methuen, 1986.

Todd, Margo. "Providence, Chance and the New Science in Early Stuart Cambridge." *Historical Journal* 29 (1986): 697–711.

Trotti, Michael Ayers. *The Body in the Reservoir: Murder and Sensationalism in the South*. Chapel Hill: University of North Carolina Press, 2008.

Turner, Elizabeth Hayes. *Women, Culture, and Community: Religion and Reform in Galveston, 1880–1920*. New York: Oxford University Press, 1997.

U.S. Census Bureau. "Population of 46 Urban Places: 1810." https://www.census.gov/population/www/documentation/twps0027/tab04.txt. Accessed 23 Nov. 2018.

———. "Population of the 100 Largest Urban Places: 1840." https://www.census.gov/population/www/documentation/twps0027/tab07.txt. Accessed 23 Nov. 2018.

———. "Population of the 33 Urban Places: 1800." http://www.census.gov/population/www/documentation/twps0027/tab03.txt. Accessed 23 Nov. 2018.

U.S. Department of Housing and Urban Development. "History of Federal Disaster Policy." https://www.huduser.gov/portal/periodicals/em/winter15/highlight1_sidebar.html. Accessed 23 Nov. 2018.

U.S. Department of Labor. "Factory Inspection Legislation." https://www.dol.gov/dol/aboutdol/history/mono-regsafepart02.htm. Accessed 23 Nov. 2018.

Valencius, Conevery Bolton. *The Lost History of the New Madrid Earthquakes*. Chicago: University of Chicago Press, 2013.

Vanek, Morgan. "The Uses of Travel: Science, Empire and Change in 18th-Century Travel Writing." *Literature Compass* 12 (2015): 555–64.

Vaughan, Alden T. *American Genesis: Captain John Smith and the Founding of Virginia*. Boston: Little, Brown, 1975.

———. "'Expulsion of the Salvages': English Policy and the Virginia Massacre of 1622." *William and Mary Quarterly*, 3rd ser., 35 (1978): 57–89.

Vickers, Daniel. *Young Men and the Sea: Yankee Seafarers in an Age of Sail*. New Haven: Yale University Press, 2005.

Vickers, Ilse. *Defoe and the New Sciences*. New York: Cambridge University Press, 1996.

Vogel, Charity. *The Angola Horror: The Train Wreck That Shocked the Nation and Transformed American Railroads*. Ithaca: Cornell University Press, 2013.

Waldstreicher, David. *In the Midst of Perpetual Fetes: The Making of American Nationalism, 1776–1820.* Chapel Hill: University of North Carolina Press, 1997.

Walker, Charles F. *Shaky Colonialism: The 1746 Earthquake-Tsunami in Lima, Peru, and Its Long Aftermath.* Durham: Duke University Press, 2008.

Walsham, Alexandra. *Providence in Early Modern England.* Oxford: Oxford University Press, 2001.

Ward, Harry M. *"Unite or Die": Intercolony Relations, 1690–1763.* Port Washington, N.Y.: Kennikat Press, 1971.

Waterman, Bryan. *Republic of Intellect: The Friendly Club of New York City and the Making of American Literature.* Baltimore: Johns Hopkins University Press, 2007.

Weaver, John C., and Peter de Lottinville. "The Conflagration and the City: Disaster and Progress in British North America during the Nineteenth Century." *Histoire Sociale—Social History* 13 (1980): 417–49.

Weinberg, Michael. "The Great New York City Fire of 1835." *TCC Bulletin.* https://www.transcollectorsclub.org/bulletin_previews/articles/10Autumn_Great_NY_City_Fire_feature.pdf. Accessed 23 Nov. 2018.

Wesley, Megan. "Early Lifesavers—the Cork Lifejacket." National Maritime Museum Cornwall. http://www.nmmc.co.uk/index.php?/collections/featured_objects/early_lifesavers_the_cork_lifejacket. Accessed 23 Nov. 2018.

Westergaard, Waldemar. *The Danish West Indies under Company Rule (1671–1754), with a Supplementary Chapter (1755–1917).* New York: Macmillan, 1917.

White, Sam. *A Cold Welcome: The Little Ice Age and Europe's Encounter with North America.* Cambridge, Mass.: Harvard University Press, 2017.

———. "Unpuzzling American Climate: New World Experience and the Foundations of a New Science." *Isis: Journal of the History of Science and Society* 106 (2015): 544–66.

Williams, Susan Millar, and Stephen G. Hoffius. *Upheaval in Charleston: Earthquake and Murder on the Eve of Jim Crow.* Athens: University of Georgia Press, 2011.

Winch, Julie. *Philadelphia's Black Elite: Activism, Accommodation, and the Struggle for Autonomy, 1787–1848.* Philadelphia: Temple University Press, 1988.

Winiarski, Douglas L. *Darkness Falls on the Land of Light: Experiencing Religious Awakenings in Eighteenth-Century New England.* Chapel Hill: University of North Carolina Press, 2017.

Witmore, Michael. *Culture of Accidents: Unexpected Knowledges in Early Modern England.* Stanford: Stanford University Press, 2001.

Yellott, John Bosley, Jr. "Jeremiah Yellott—Revolutionary War Privateersman and Baltimore Philanthropist." *Maryland Historical Magazine* 86 (1991): 176–89.

Young, Bryan J. *Patrician Families and the Making of Quebec: The Taschereaus and McCords.* Montreal: McGill-Queens University Press, 2014.

Zohn, Harry, and M. C. Davis. "Johann Christoph Wagenseil, Polymath." *Monatshefte* 46 (1954): 35–40.

INDEX

Page numbers in italics refer to illustrations or their captions.

Gibbon, James, 154
Gibbons, Major, 44–45
Gibbons, Thomas, 93–94
Gilman, Samuel, 161
Girardin, Louis Hue, 154
Glencoe, 196
Gloucester, Mass., 39
government: disaster prevention and, 1, 2, 29–30, 98, 164, 175, 199, 208; disaster relief and, xii–xiii, 5, 8–9, 10, 11, 30, 98, 118, 135–36, 164, 201, 206–8. *See also* Congress, U.S.; Federal Emergency Management Agency; regulation
governors: colonial, and disaster relief, 99, 102, 103, *106*, 107, 108–9, 111–13, 120, 127, 128–30; state, disaster relief and, 136, 206
Great Britain: aid to Portugal, 80, 91–95, 120; charitable associations in, 92, 99, 115, 118; earthquakes in, 70, 72, 74
Great Fresh, 100, 120, 122–26
Great Gale, 173, 181
Greene, Robert, 38
Greene, Thomas, 108
Grey, Zachary, 70

Haiti, 134, 135
Hakluyt, Richard, 41
Halifax, James, 85
Hamilton, Alexander, 127–28, 131, 138, 142
Hamilton, Eliza Schuyler, 138
Hamilton, James, 109
Hamlet, N.C., 211
handshakes, 140, 235n16
Hanover, Va., 81
Hanover, house of, 94, 96. *See also* George II; George III
Hanson, Alexander Contee, 238n53
Hanway, Jonas, 115–18, *116*, 119–20, 150, 211
Happy Deliverance, 53
Hare, Robert, 173
Harper's Weekly, 8, 203–4
Harrison, Benjamin, 207
Harvard College, 46, 85, 86, 179
Harvey, Hurricane, xii
Haven, Samuel, 96
Haverhill, Mass., 151
Hawthorne, Nathaniel, 197, 241n25

Hay, George, 153
Helen McGregor, 174
Hempstead, N.Y., 181
Henrico, Va., 27, 32
Henry, Patrick, 113, 122
Henry Clay, 197–98
Hervey, James, 81
Hessian fly, 141
Hewitt, Thomas B., 162
Heytesbury, Eng., 117
Hilliard, Chester, 179
Hillsborough, Lord (Wills Hill), 122, 125–26, 129
Home, 177
Homer, 40
Hone, Philip, 188, 190
Honiton, Eng., 117
hospitals, 115, 118, 119, 127, 130, 136–37, 140, 172
Howe, Thomas, 127
Howland, Southworth Allen, 186
Hudson River, 167, 168, 197
human agency: belief in, xiii, 39, 56–57, 62, 65–68, 102, 163–64, 167, 199, 211. *See also* benevolence; science
humane societies, 174, 197, 240n14
humanitarianism, 87, 91, 92, 99, 174, 206, 212. *See also* benevolence; sympathy
Hunt, Gilbert, *158*, 159
Hunter, Thomas, 80, 81
hurricanes, xi, 46, 55, 61, 173, 181, 192; Betsy, 212; as divine portents, 46–47, 56–57, 127–28; in England, 61; in Galveston, 8, 201, 203, 209, 212; Harvey, xii; Irma, xii; Katrina, xi, xiii, 3, 9, 17, 201, 211, 212, 213; Maria, xii, xiii, 9, 212; Sandy, *x*, xi, xii; shipwrecks and, 23, 24, 25, 39, 45, 49, 55; in West Indies, 10, 39, 55, 71, 100, 126–32, 142
hydraspis, *65*, 66

Illinois, 206
immigrants, 9, 58, 59, 143, 171, 188, 193, 203, 236n25
Inches, Captain, 88
India, 52, 110, 142
Indians. *See* Native Americans

Madagascar, 52
Madison, Wisc., 180
magazines, 52, 59, 66, 74, 85, 88–89, 122–23, 202, 203–4
malaria, 153, 211
Marblehead, Mass., 147
Maria, Dionysia Rose, 88, 97
Maria, Hurricane, xii, xiii, 9, 212
Marietta, Ohio, 170
mariners, 32, 39–40, 52–54, 60; cannibalism and, 48, 49, 50, 223n13; technical skills of, 55–56, 61, 62. *See also* ship captains
Marseilles: plague in, 61–62
Mary I (queen), 31
Maryland, 80
masculinity, 36, 53, 58, 130, 155, 157, 159, 187–88, 190–91
Massachusetts, 64, 69, 80, 107, 122, 152. *See also* Boston; New England
Mather, Cotton, 42, 44, 46–47, 48
Mather, Frederick Ellsworth, 198
Mather, Increase, 42, 44, 45–47, 46, 82
Mayhew, Jonathan, 84, 103, 107
McClary, Michael, 151
Mebane, Adam, 111–12
memorialization: of disaster victims, 53, 123, 153–54, 159, 164, 166, 185, 193
merchants, 49, 55, 62–63, 70, 95, 111, 122–25; disaster relief and, 4, 80, 91–92, 99, 107–8, 114–18, 120, 128, 131, 147, 149, 150; in Lisbon, 80, 88–92, 95; in London, 99, 101, 108, 109, 114–15, 122, 125, 128; in Montreal, 110, 111, 112; in New England, 107, 109, 147, 149, 150; in New York, 107, 144, 148; as sources of information, 4, 10, 62, 76, 88, 127–28
Merian, Matthaeus, 34, 35
Mexico, 181
Michell, John, 86
Michigan, Lake, 169
micro-history, xi, 9
Mifflin, Thomas, 136
military: post-disaster use of, 1, 206, 207, 208, 209
Mills, Robert, 173
Mississippi, 176
Mississippi River, 168, 207, 211

Missouri, 207
monarchy: benevolence and, 92–93, 94–97, 99, 114, 118–20, 147
Montreal: fire in, 110–19, 150, 211; merchants in, 110, 111, 112
Montserrat, 55
Monumental Church (Richmond, Va.), 159, 164
moral sense, 87
Morley, Joseph, 91
mortality: from earthquakes, 4, 69, 72, 74–75; from fires, 152, 153, 201, 211; from floods, 122, 201; from hurricanes, 100, 126, 132, 201, 211; at Jamestown, 14, 16, 30; at sea, 15–16, 39 40; from steamboat disasters, 170, 171, 174, 176, 179, 181, 191–93, 196–97, 241n20, 243n53; from yellow fever, 135, 140, 153
Moselle, 175, 176, 177, 178, 186
Moss, Charles, 85
mourning, public, 96–97, 140, 152, 153, 159, 161–62, 171
movies, 209
Mulcahy, Matthew, 10, 225n38
Murray, James, 111–13
music. *See* popular culture

Natchez, Miss., 167
National Flood Insurance Program, 208
national identity, 39, 41; American, 11, 133, 134, 139, 155, 159, 160, 165, 167, 191; British, 11, 37, 40, 41, 51, 68, 79, 80, 91–92, 95
Native Americans, 45, 51, 143, 168; in colonial Virginia, 17, 18, 20, 22, 27, 28, 29, 31–37; portrayed as savages, 27, 28, 31–37, 35, 49–50, 51, 90, 159
Nebraska, 207
Nelson, William, 123–26
Netherlands, the, 78
Nevis, 126
Newburyport, Mass., 149; fire in, 146, 160
New England, 26, 58, 108, 110, 147, 148; earthquakes in, 69, 72, 82–85, 123; maritime activities in, 39–40, 45; merchants in, 107, 109, 147, 149, 150; providential mission of colonists in, 45–48

Portland, Me., 149
Port Royal, Jamaica, 49; earthquake in, 71, 72, 73
Portsmouth, N.H.: fires in, *144*, 145–51, 153, 163, 165; relief committee in, 146, 148–51, 208
Portugal, 40–41, 70, 92. *See also* Lisbon
Pory, John, 28
Postal Service, U.S., 135
Powell, Nathaniel, 34, 36
Pownall, Thomas, 102, 103, *106*, 107, 108–9, 120, 124
Pratt, Henry C., 241n25
prayer, public days of, 80, 96, 123, 127, 153, 161, *162*
Price, Benjamin, 111–12, 113–14
Prince George, 59
print culture, xii, 9, 30, 51–52, 85, 91, 111, 154, 204; expansion of, 54, 62, 75, 98, 135, 146; images in, 12, *76*, 78, 98, 180, 181, 203–4
privateers, 54
Protestantism: English/British identity and, 18, 22–23, 26–29, 31, 37, 41 51, 80, 90, 115, 117
providence, divine: belief in, 20, 22–28, 53, 81–85; earthquakes and, 70, 71, 72; fires and, 102, 107, 159–60; hurricanes and, 46–47, 56–57, 127–28; human agency and, 56–57; Opechancanough's uprising and, 32–34, 37; shipwreck narratives and, 41–51, 52. *See also* religion
Providence, R.I., 108, 181
public health, 30, 141
Puerto Rico, xiii, 9, 212
Pulaski, 175, 176–77, 178, 187–88
Purchas, Samuel, 33
Puritans, 23, 26, 45, 160

Quakers, 49, 50, 51
quarantines, 10, 136, 137, 138, 142–43, 165
Quebec, 111, 112, 113
Quincy, Edmund, 147

race, 9, 10, 39, 140, 159, 188, 190, 203, 207, 212
radio, 219n6
railroads, 5, 179, 185, 190, 199, 201, 202, 206
Raleigh, N.C., 153–54

Raleigh, Walter, 15
Randolph, Edmund, 136
Randolph, Ryland, 122, *123*
Raritan Bay, 171
Ratcliffe, John, 17
Ray, David, 150
Reconstruction, 207
Red Cross, xii, 1, 3, 201, 206, 207, 208
Redfield, William C., 171, 173
Reformation, 49
refugees, 118
regulation, 12, 13, 30, 141, 165, 210; environmental, xiii, 210–11; fire, 101, 103, 155, 163, 211; public calls for, 172, 174, 175, 177–78, 194, 197–98
religion, 8, 11; benevolence and, 59, 103, 107, 115, 119, 139, 185, 211; European colonization and, 18, 25–28; science and, 46–47, 71–72, 74–75, 80, 82, 85–86; shipwreck narratives and, 41–52; as a source of comfort, 48, 59, 74, 153, 161–62, 185. *See also* clergy; providence, divine
religious revivals, 72, 82, 164
Richmond, Va., 124, 162, 204; churches and clergy in, 153, 161–62, 164; city council in, 152, 162; fire in, 12, 133, 152–64, *156*, *157*, 165, 178, 185, 201
Richmond Enquirer, 154, 157, 162, 163
Riley, Bennet, 143
risk, 5, 8, 62–63, 199, 209, 211
Ritchie, Thomas, 157, 162, 163–64, 238n53
Riverdale, N.Y., 197
Roanoke colony, 15
Robinsonades, 59–60
Roepstorff, Ulrich Wilhelm von, 130–31, 132
Rolfe, John, 31
Rotherhithe, Eng., 117
Royal Academy of Sciences (Paris), 66
Royal Navy, 63, 67, 68, 71, 115
Royal Society (London), 46, 68, 71, 85, 86
Royal Tar, 181, *187*
royal touch, 118
Rozario, Kevin, 5, 8
Ruggles, John, 195–96
Rush, Benjamin, 135, 136, 140
Russia, 76
Ryther, John, 42